Interpreting the Musical Past

"Old Paris," from the *Art Journal. The Paris Exhibition* 1900. London, 1901. Shelfmark 177 c.12. Courtesy of the Bodleian Library, University of Oxford.

Interpreting the Musical Past

Early Music in Nineteenth-Century France

KATHARINE ELLIS

OXFORD
UNIVERSITY PRESS
2005

OXFORD
UNIVERSITY PRESS

Oxford University Press, Inc., publishes works that further
Oxford University's objective of excellence
in research, scholarship, and education.

Oxford New York

Auckland   Cape Town   Dar es Salaam   Hong Kong   Karachi
Kuala Lumpur   Madrid   Melbourne   Mexico City   Nairobi
New Delhi   Shanghai   Taipei   Toronto

With offices in
Argentina   Austria   Brazil   Chile   Czech Republic   France   Greece
Guatemala   Hungary   Italy   Japan   Poland   Portugal   Singapore
South Korea   Switzerland   Thailand   Turkey   Ukraine   Vietnam

Copyright © 2005 by Oxford University Press, Inc.

Published by Oxford University Press, Inc.
198 Madison Avenue, New York, New York 10016

www.oup.com

Oxford is a registered trademark of Oxford University Press.

All rights reserved. No part of this publication may be reproduced,
stored in a retrieval system, or transmitted, in any form or by any means,
electronic, mechanical, photocopying, recording, or otherwise,
without prior permission of Oxford University Press.

Library of Congress Cataloging-in-Publication Data
Ellis, Katharine.
  Interpreting the musical past: early music in nineteenth-century France / Katharine Ellis.
      p. cm.
Includes bibliographical references.
ISBN-13 978-0-19-517682-7
ISBN 0-19-517682-0
   1. Music—France—19th century—History and criticism.   2. Music—Performance—History.
   3. National characteristics, French.   4. Nationalism in music.   I. Title.
ML270.4.E449 2005
780'.944'09034—dc22   2004021847

9 8 7 6 5 4 3 2 1

Printed in the United States of America
on acid-free paper

For Nigel

Acknowledgments

Authors of books such as this require time, support, and other people's money. Luckily, I received all three. First thanks must go to both the Music Department at Royal Holloway, University of London, and the Arts and Humanities Research Board of the UK. Their provision of research funding and leave (including a Research Leave Scheme award) allowed me total immersion in my subject for significant parts of the research and writing process. The Music Department Research Committee also helped fund illustrative materials and permissions. Conference papers in Toronto and Houston were supported with British Academy Overseas Conference Grants. In addition I profited immensely from the invitation by colleagues at New York University—Gage Averill, Edward Berenson, and Edward Roesner—to try out some of my ideas on their graduate students in the Fall semester of 2001.

Librarians and archivists in the UK and in France responded to requests for arcane material with promptness and equanimity and, in many cases, guided me towards still more interesting finds. In Paris, staff at the Tolbiac site of the Bibliothèque Nationale, at the Opéra, and in the Departments of Music and Manuscripts deserve particular thanks; I am also grateful to Nathalie Cousin at the Sorbonne and Jacqueline Razgonnikoff at the Comédie-Française. It was a particular pleasure to work in the French regions, where nothing was too much trouble for librarians and archivists at the Bibliothèque Municipale (Arras), the Bibliothèque Inguimbertine (Carpentras), the Archives

Municipales and the Bibliothèque Municipale (Dijon), the Bibliothèque et Médiathèque Municipale (Niort), and the Bibliothèque Villon (Rouen). In Britain, staff at the British Library (St Pancras and Colindale) and the Bodleian, Taylorian, and Music Faculty libraries in Oxford provided essential backup, often beyond the call.

Intellectual support has come from many directions. Annegret Fauser and Jann Pasler generously read an earlier (and even longer) version of the entire typescript and asked suitably tough questions. Elizabeth Bartlet, Carlo Caballero, Walter Corten, Lawrence Earp, Catrina Flint de Médicis, John Haines, Sarah Hibberd, Steven Huebner, Hervé Lacombe, Sophie Leterrier, Julian Rushton, Anne Stone, Gwendolyn Trietze, the Royal Holloway *Chopinistes* and my anonymous referees all shared their expertise. I owe the inspiration for the project itself to Donna Di Grazia. In addition, and during a gestation period dating back to around 1995, conference and seminar organizers helped me gain invaluable feedback. Timothy Baycroft, Edward Berenson, Hans Erich Bödeker, Susan Boynton, Rémy Campos, Annegret Fauser, Michel Fend, Matthew Head, Peter Holman, Steven Huebner, Barbara Kelly, Ståle Kleiberg, Alexandra Laederich, Miguel-Angel Marín, François de Médicis, Christian Meyer, Jean-Jacques Nattiez, David Nicholls, Michel Noiray, Manuela Schwartz, Philippe Vendrix, Michel Werner, and the late Eugene Wolf merit special mention in this regard. The same holds for current and former colleagues at Royal Holloway who made a particular impact on this book: David Charlton for encouraging me to pursue the project in the first place; Tim Carter, John Rink, and Andrew Wathey for unfailingly supportive leadership; and Jim Samson for wise and patient counsel at crucial moments. Those to whom certain ideas seem rather familiar will, I hope, forgive their silent absorption into my text. Those who are alarmed to see that I have tried to respond to their questions will perhaps take comfort in the knowledge that I regard wrong answers as mine alone.

My production team at Oxford University Press, Kim Robinson, Eve Bachrach, and Gwen Colvin have been unfailingly positive and helpful; their attention to detail is much appreciated, as is the deft copyediting of Susan Meigs. On a personal level, sincere thanks should go to the Paris team of Sonia Taylor, Orhan Memed, and the late Edith McMorran. Likewise, I am hugely indebted to my dedicatee, who has done more to hold this project together than I ever deserved. Our respective books will race each other through the presses. It doesn't matter whose wins.

Wootton, by Woodstock
August 2004

Contents

Abbreviations, xi

Introduction, xiii

PART I   Patterns of Revival

Chapter 1. 1800–1846, 3

Chapter 2. 1846–1878, 43

Chapter 3. 1878–1900, 81

PART II   Uses, Appropriations, Meanings

Chapter 4. *La musique française* at the Crossroads, 119

Chapter 5. Sources of Frenchness, 147

Chapter 6. Defining Palestrina, 179

Chapter 7. Baroque Choral Music:
            The Popular and the Profound, 209

Conclusion, 241

Personalia, 257

Bibliography, 263

Index, 285

Abbreviations

Bibliothèque Nationale de France   BNF
Archives Nationales, Paris   AN

Newspapers and Periodicals

L'art musical	AM
La chronique musicale	CM
La correspondance des amateurs musiciens	Corr
Le courrier musical	CouM
L'écho des orphéons	EO
La France chorale	FC
La France orphéonique	FO
La France musicale	FM
Le guide musical	GM
Le journal de musique	JM
Le journal de Rouen	JR
Le journal des débats	JD
Le journal des savants	JS
Musica sacra	MS
Le ménestrel	Mén
Le Mercure de France	MF
Le Mercure du dix-neuvième siècle	MD-NS
Le monde artiste	MA

Le monde musical	MM
La musique populaire	MPop
La nouvelle France chorale	NFC
L'orphéon	O
Le progrès artistique	PA
La réforme musicale	RéfM
Revue de la musique religieuse, populaire, classique	RMRPC
La revue de musique sacrée, ancienne et moderne	RMSAM
Revue de Paris	RP
La revue des deux mondes	RDM
La revue et gazette des théâtres	RGT
La revue et gazette musicale	RGM
La revue littéraire de l'Ouest	RLO
Revue musicale (Fétis)	RM
La semaine musicale	SM
La tribune de Saint-Gervais	TS-G
L'union musicale	UM
L'univers musical	UnivM

Introduction

"Old Paris": it was probably best seen from the steamboat that ferried visitors, throughout the summer of 1900, up and down the sites of the largest Exposition Universelle yet—a whole *quai* of the Right Bank built in scaled-down and half-timbered glory, evoking several centuries of Parisian architectural, artistic, and civic history. A tangled roof-line of turrets and gables sat atop multiple archways and balconies, the whole set off by a feint toward an ancient wharf—stilts, rickety landing stages, riverside huts and all (Frontispiece). In the afternoons, as *Le vieux Paris* drifted slowly by, passengers might have been startled by a strange, disembodied music wafting from the windows of Saint-Julien-des-Ménestriers, the little medieval church at its centre. Perhaps, having heard snatches of Lassus or Allegri from the river, they were tempted to alight and explore further, making their way through the miniature canyons created by buildings flanking the narrowest of cobbled streets. There, they would have been accosted by flower-sellers and orange girls in period costume; watched craftsmen at work in their studios; covered their ears as the town crier started up close by; perhaps stepped into the oasis of calm of the minstrels' church, peopled by Charles Bordes and his Chanteurs de Saint-Gervais, who gave their single mini-concert several times each day.

Among the 52 million tourists who came to the Exposition between April and November, the rich would probably not mind visiting *Le vieux Paris* on a Friday (the most expensive day), when the musical programmes at the church were to include large-scale works with orchestra; those with musical children might go mid-week, tempted by its "educational" programmes; the less affluent might decide to wait until Sunday (when the model village cost a mere 50c) and hear more "popular" music. It was best, however, to grab a seat early: the church regularly filled to capacity, with around 150 squeezed inside.[1] Whatever visitors decided, their diet was to be devotional or liturgical *musique ancienne*; the performances were, as an "insider" critic put it, to represent a kind of "sacred musical museum."[2] They were also, of course, propaganda for Paris's most radical school of music: the Schola Cantorum. For the estimated 100,000 people who attended over the course of six months, the Chanteurs, the Schola's most celebrated ambassadors, aimed to provide living proof that the heritage of Catholic church music could be vital, approachable, and infinitely preferable to liturgical music adapted from modern secular works.

Le vieux Paris was a historical theme park in an Exposition replete with historical reconstructions. The Swiss Village was just as olde-worlde as its Parisian rival (but—with its alps, lakes, and waterfalls—even more picturesque); the main German pavilion was designed to be redolent of Nuremberg; the British pavilion, of the Elizabethan period. Visitors were treated to displays of technological progress (the Palais de l'Éléctricité, the first Métro trains) side by side with elaborate and nostalgic tributes to the European past. In Philippe Julian's words, "museomania" ruled, and the celebration of progress was inextricably linked to the celebration of history.[3] Musically, the Exposition provided historicist experiences at every turn. In addition to the *Vieux Paris* performances, there was an international musicological conference held at the Bibliothèque de l'Opéra (23–31 July), with related *concerts historiques* involving Saint-Saëns (a lecture-recital on harpsichord music), Julien Tiersot, and Bordes.[4] Official concerts illustrated the history of French music from Adam de la Halle's *Jeu de Robin et de Marion* to the present and were written up in an extensive official "report" by the composer Alfred Bruneau.[5] Among musical applications rejected by the Exposition committee, an attempt by the conductor

---

1. Jean de Muris, *Tribune de Saint-Gervais* (henceforth TS-G), 6/4: April 1900, 93–95, at 94.
2. "musée musical sacré," TS-G 6/4: April 1900, 94.
3. Julian, *The Triumph of Art Nouveau*, 148–151. Julian's description of "Old Paris," which he views as more Gustave Doré than Viollet-le-Duc and as a model for parts of Disneyland, follows on pp. 152–55.
4. Bordes's program (28 July 1900) included Gregorian chant, extracts from the *Jeu de Robin et de Marion*, a Palestrina "Ave Maria," Lassus's "Quand mon mary vient de dehors," French popular chansons harmonized by Tiersot, Janequin's *Bataille de Marignan*, an extract (probably the final scene) from Carissimi's *Jephte*, and the closing sequence from Schütz's St Matthew Passion. The Belgian viola d'amore player Louis van Waelfeghem also played a sonata by Ariosti. See *Vincent d'Indy*, ed. Marie d'Indy, letter of 29 July 1900, 615.
5. Bruneau, *La musique française*, discussed in the conclusion to this book.

Eugène d'Harcourt to extend his run of *Messiah*, Bach's St Matthew Passion, and modern French oratorios as part of the official Exposition season, reveals the same impetus.

It is easy to be cynical about the role of early music at Expo 1900, and at Saint-Julien-des-Ménestriers in particular. Anyone who has grimaced at the sound of piped motets in French cathedrals or, on account of their soundtracks, eschewed those endlessly repeating educational videos at heritage sites, will scent theme-park muzak. Bordes and his singers were wise to that kind of charge—of prostituting sacred music as "local/historical colour" in a highly commercialized atmosphere. It was precisely for that reason that they did not perform in period costume, but in "town clothes, devoid of any fairground look."[6] Yet for musicologists it is also easy to be seduced by the propagandist genius of Vincent d'Indy and the Schola Cantorum faithful into believing that Bordes, the Chanteurs de Saint-Gervais, and the Schola more generally "rediscovered" Palestrinian polyphony, Lassus chansons, Bach cantatas, and then Rameau operas; and that through their numerous Parisian and regional concerts of the 1890s they almost single-handedly catalyzed the early music movement in France. Part of my purpose in this book is to show how misguided that perspective is, and to place early music in its French contexts from 1800 onward. More than that, however, I probe the reasons why early music mattered, as a distinct but fragmented musical category, to the French musical intelligentsia of the nineteenth century.

What interests me is teasing out the reasons why certain composers, repertories, and works stretching from Adam de la Halle to Handel (which is essentially what nineteenth-century musicians defined as *musique ancienne*) were revived in nineteenth-century France, through publication, performance, and polemic. The terms of that revival are also important, as is the question of why certain musics were disdained even though the means for their revival existed. These questions are particularly fruitful in respect to early musics because for much of the century they reflect the exception, rather than the rule, within musical life, and because in their variety they cause such disparate reactions.[7] Moreover, because in most cases a performing tradition has been broken, there is usually an active reason behind its attempted reinstatement. If revivalists are to influence people they cannot afford to let the object of their

---

6. "en habits de ville, sans apprêt funambulesque," G. de Boisjoslin, news report, *TS-G* 6/11: November 1900, 331. See also his comments in an earlier "Mois musical" column, *TS-G* 6/5: May 1900, 159.

7. Indeed, it is that disparity of reaction that has occasioned my adoption, where I particularly wish to guard against monolithic interpretations, of the plural "musics." Although *la musique ancienne* is singular in theory, it was nevertheless plural in both culture and practice.

crusade speak for itself. They must justify, attack, and defend, often in public. Early musics accordingly provide rich examples of the microhistorian's "normal exception," enabling—because of the unusual attention they attract—the analysis of cultural tensions that otherwise remain unspoken or veiled. The French early music revival offers us a vivid case study of how music's cultural meanings are fought over, distilled into a dominant vision, or reversed. Mapping those meanings leads us to the social and ideological premises behind their construction and their modification—not the "what" or "how" of musical meaning, but the "when," "for whom," and "why." And since particular understandings of music's meanings in turn affect attitudes and behaviour, the answers to such questions take us beneath the surface of public taste, antiquarianism, or cultural conservatism. The forces that underpin revivalist activity have much more to do with cultural politics: questions of national pride (or inferiority) and national identity, education and the democratization of musical experience, decadence and regeneration (whether religious or moral), and perceptions of musical style as embodying (value-laden) stereotypes of gender. They tell us much about French (and not just Parisian, or high-bourgeois Parisian) musical cultures. And some of them have proved extremely durable, helping us understand why we continue to conceptualize musical styles in the ways we do.

In the commercial arena the question of public taste is, of course, central; but much of the revivalist activity with which I am concerned here is undertaken by amateurs who are insulated from the vagaries of the market, or who use their own money to ensure the dissemination of the music in which they believe, almost without regard to questions of profit and loss. Examples of both cases span the century, from the publishing ventures of Pierre Porro and Alexandre-Etienne Choron during the Empire and the Restoration, to the vast sums invested by Charles Lamoureux on his Société de l'Harmonie Sacrée in the 1870s, to Eugène d'Harcourt's construction and running of his own concert hall in the 1890s. Those who were somewhat insulated from the market also include *maîtres de chapelle* across the country who spearheaded liturgical musical revival (though they were, of course, subject to the yo-yo effect of government decisions regarding the funding of church music), and the numerous aristocratic and high-bourgeois choral societies which sprang up from the July Monarchy onward, their finances guaranteed by annual subscriptions. In the most successful cases the profits from such concerts went to charity, thereby reinforcing the link, almost ubiquitous among such choral societies, between morally good music and morally good actions.

The fact that early music was not always financially viable in the open market, or that it was sometimes performed in elite or semi-private gatherings, does not mean that its impact on wider cultural life was negligible. Publications and concert series developed reputations extending far beyond their initial audience, not least because they generated journalistic debate in the daily newspapers and the working-class choral society press alike. In addition, the impact of small-scale operations could outweigh their immediate importance. The nineteen concerts of the prince de la Moskova's aristocratic Société des Concerts de Musique Vocale Religieuse et Classique (1843–46) for instance were regularly invoked later in the century by Palestrinians continuing the project to expunge the worldly from sacred music, and copies of the Society's published repertory were widely disseminated.

By definition, private societies which aim to improve public taste need access to the public. One of the by-products of such necessity is a close relationship with the press—one that sometimes can only be described as symbiotic. In an environment where founder members of societies regularly (and silently or anonymously) write up their own concerts in the journals with which they happen to have an existing relationship, separating puff from independent criticism—which may itself be biased—is a constant preoccupation for the historiographer. How are we to ascertain the significance of, or gauge reaction to, a particular event when confronted with little but insider reviews (Adolphe Adam for the Moskova society in *La France musicale*; Dieudonné Denne-Baron for the Société Académique de Musique Sacrée in *Le ménestrel*)? There are, of course, no simple solutions beyond interpreting material explicitly in terms of its insider character and seeking independent corroboration. But for all those instances where a direct connection can be detected there are others where the relationship may remain hidden because the society's archives are unavailable or because there is no evidence from other sources such as personal letters and papers, memoirs or obituaries. Journalistic interest is, quite simply, an occupational hazard.

In its concerns with musical life as much as with music itself, this book necessarily crosses disciplinary boundaries. No analysis of the use and signification of musics within a particular and potentially fragmented culture can ignore the effects of social, political, and religious questions on the beliefs and behaviour of artists and their publics. Looking outside the music is crucial; so, too, is embracing adaptations of "the music" as a valuable category of historical evidence. Fakes count for a lot. This history of early music in France is not primarily a history of aesthetics, or the chronicle of a teleological journey toward appreciation, but a history of use and appropriation for particular ends by particular constituencies. That is not to imply that "appropriation" is a dirty word, or that the proselytizers in this book are necessarily manipulative; it is simply to acknowledge that historical actors are no freer of cultural assumptions than am I, and to accept that they write and act according to beliefs that require explanation.

Aesthetics, then, have a distinctly ideological edge in this story. Once *la musique ancienne* became more than a novelty, taking concert space from living composers on a regular basis, its presence had to be justified actively. That justification—in which aesthetic judgments were frequently linked to notions of the regeneration, purification, or popularization of culture—necessarily brought with it the implication that certain modern traditions were decadent, elitist, and impure. And because so many of the early works that gained popularity in nineteenth-century France were sacred (irrespective of where they were performed and of whether they were Protestant or Catholic), questions of regeneration and moral health in music remained high on the agenda. The rise in France of specifically Catholic liturgical reformists of varying stripes, and Protestantism's increasing acceptability in government circles during the Third Republic, only served to heighten the importance of such questions. Moreover, the musical writings of the entire century are peppered with references to France's fragile musical reputation, both historically and in terms of her contemporary output. They peak, of course, around 1870, when feelings of musical inferiority, especially in relation to Germany, intensified in the wake of the Franco-Prussian War. It is arguable that nineteenth-century commentators sometimes exaggerated this sense of inferiority for rhetorical effect; and there are cases where from the outside (the pan-European success of French Grand Opera, is one such) it might even appear downright implausible. Nevertheless, inferiority is an inescapable fact of musical discourse about French compositions and French musical culture, and understanding it is essential if we are to appreciate just how astonishing a reversal of attitude underpinned, for instance, the country's neo-classical movement.

Questions of identity, chauvinism, patriotism, and nationalism are, accordingly, central to this study. However, the latter two terms, in particular, threaten to bring with them a certain amount of semantic chaos. The recent literature has illustrated the extent to which the forging of distinctions between them is fraught with difficulty even with respect to questions of direct political action, let alone those of cultural politics or historiography.[8] In writing French history the risks of anachronism are also high. As Carlo Caballero has recently noted, while the word "patriotisme" (love of homeland) is relatively old, the word "nationalisme" did not appear in any French dictionary before 1874, even though "nationalité," as a term almost synonymous with "race," had been in officially

---

8. See, for instance, the editorial introduction to Bar-Tal and Staub (Eds.), *Patriotism*, 2–10.

sanctioned use since 1835 (it appears in the *Dictionnaire de l'Académie*).⁹ And while the aggressively right-wing associations of "nationalité" that became predominant in France at the turn of the twentieth century bear little relation to those which governed questions of French national pride at the beginning of the nineteenth, the distinction between an expression or feeling of group loyalty defined either by race (Caballero's nationalism) or by a more general sense of belonging to a particular state or homeland (his patriotism) was by no means alien to French writing during the century: the ecumenical and civic "nation-contrat" of 1789, in which one chose to be French, lived alongside the blood-and-soil "nation-génie," with all its essentialist evocations of racial or tribal characteristics.¹⁰ The key difference in France, before 1871, is that the two were more easily (and frequently) conflated. Indeed, there are respects in which the stark separation of the end of the century is irrelevant to earlier periods. For in musical and more general cultural writings before 1870, the relation between race and state was as much a matter of pragmatic convention as of political philosophy. After all, the concepts of Italian and German style had, for centuries, operated independently of the existence of the nation-states that came into being in the late nineteenth century. And while such a description might seem to fit squarely into the race-centered definition of nationality espoused by historians and philosophers such as Ranke and Herder, who used narratives that emphasized the longevity of such affinities to proclaim a coherent (and superior) sense of the German nation *avant la lettre*,¹¹ it also left open the possibility that an artist could choose (or—more importantly for my purposes—be interpreted as having chosen) another nationality by displaying evidence of "belonging" to it. In the history of French music, the cases of Lully, Gluck, Sacchini, Spontini, and Cherubini as naturalized or adopted Frenchmen are instructive in this respect.

Nevertheless, even the path of ecumenical Frenchness could not avoid the question of identity. In order for consumers of national culture to wish to "belong," they must know, courtesy of family, friends, educators, historians, and other formers of cultural memory, to what they belong.¹² They must also value it. And it is here that the position of musical France in the nineteenth century

---

9. Caballero, "Patriotism or Nationalism?" 596.

10. Both Caballero ("Patriotism or Nationalism?" 595) and Fauser ("Gendering the Nations," 73–74) offer valuable discussions of these historical distinctions as they pertain to Third-Republic history, in which Ernest Renan's lecture "What Is a Nation?" (1882) is a key text on the ecumenical side of this debate, defining the nation as the agreed construct of its (self-selected) members.

11. For an excellent series of articles on this and related questions, see Applegate and Potter (Eds.), *Music & German National Identity*.

12. See also Flint de Médicis ("Nationalism and Early Music," 46), who stresses the "coterie" element of much "nationalist" musical activity in Paris at the end of the century and argues that the self-selection of the few led to the promotion of a vision of national identity that was deliberately unrepresentative of the French citizenry.

shows itself to be both "different" and interesting. As a nation-state which, following the Revolution, claimed to lead European civilization in the fields of rational thought, statecraft, human rights, and state guardianship of the arts, France began the century in Italy's musical shadow and spent much of the rest of it overshadowed by Germany. Musical nations that aspired to be nation-states dominated those—among them not only France but also Britain—that were. In addition to such harsh perceptions of the pecking order among living musicians and modern musical styles, the ecumenism of French attitudes to nationality early in the century brought self-inflicted wounds that were increasingly resented, especially from the 1860s: the French were squeezing "Frenchness" out of French music, yet the only genre in the nineteenth century that appeared to remain truly national—*opéra-comique*—was a secondary genre lacking in all-important aspects of heroic nobility.[13] In addition, the French intelligentsia of the early nineteenth century had to contend with the fact that they and their predecessors had, for aesthetic reasons now fatally tainted by Revolutionary politics, discredited their own Enlightenment culture. A large slice of French "collective memory," to use a famous phrase from Ernest Renan's "What Is a Nation?" lecture of 1882, was, at least temporarily, out of bounds. How, then, did Third-Republic musicians come to celebrate an overtly royal musical tradition that had been disparaged across two monarchies and two empires?

Much of the latter part of this book deals with the terms by which French writers and musicians rehabilitated portions of their own heritage as a model for a "French" music; how they decided what constituted it; and what motivated and sometimes divided them in their choices. Many of those choices were expressed in a competitive spirit, the main rivals being, inevitably, Italy and Germany. Increasingly, and particularly after the war, they were informed more by the race-inspired image of nationality than by the ecumenical one, even in avowed Republican hands such as those of Louis-Albert Bourgault-Ducoudray, Tiersot, or Jean-Baptiste Weckerlin. Authors also set great store by the question of national superiority—whether through the illustration of primacy (for instance, that the first opera was French) or ultimate sophistication (that the French capitalized on their capacity to benefit from others' mistakes). Such factors take cultural chauvinism or patriotism beyond the love of country and heritage in and of itself, and into the realm of what I shall term nationalism—in which one dignifies one's own culture at the expense of someone else's, and in which concepts of purity and purging of the Other are close neighbours.

---

13. See Fauser, "Gendering the Nations," 72 and 87, for examples of Third-Republic depression regarding the feminine nature of *opéra-comique*.

This book embraces a century of musical culture and half a millennium of music. Self-evidently, it is not comprehensive, whether in terms of the questions it asks or the works and musical events it discusses. Rather, it is an attempt to make sense of the more prominent patterns of use and neglect of music dating from the thirteenth to the mid-eighteenth centuries. Nevertheless, my own omissions warrant clarification. Although from a twenty-first century point of view Gluck's situation might appear to be analogous to that of Rameau (in the sense that special pleading was required to secure his acceptance as part of the living repertory), within nineteenth-century French historiography he fell into that part of the "classique" that postdated *la musique ancienne*.[14] Equally, I allow certain medieval repertories, virtually unheard in concert though sometimes much discussed, to remain outside my purview. Except as a thorn in the side of Palestrinian liturgical revivalists, Gregorian chant is one such; except as a foil for secular monody, early polyphony is another. Methodologically, too, this book is focused on the music's reception rather than its genesis or transmission. While identification of the works (including variants) that were known and performed has been an important part of my research, philology and editorial practice have not been a primary concern.

My approach to the relationship between coverage of Paris and coverage of the regions has been pragmatic. While most of the events in the book concern Paris, their intended significance frequently extends to the entire country (including, even after 1871, the regions of Alsace and Lorraine). However, we should not leave unquestioned the idea that the regions were docile in their acceptance of models from the capital, or that the capital was necessarily "ahead" of the regions. Indeed, extrapolating conclusions about "the French" from an analysis of Paris is a perilous exercise. Early music activists in some regions and towns (the Deux-Sèvres area, Strasbourg, Dijon, Toulouse, Montpellier, Carpentras, and Aix-en-Provence, Rouen and Lyon in particular) and in certain cathedrals (Autun, Moulins, Langres, Rouen) were often proud of their distinctiveness. As our understanding of musical life in the French regions deepens, taking into account liturgical as well as concert and theatrical life, my work as presented here will fast be superseded; I have, aided by some of the pioneers in this area, merely opened a few doors.[15]

The need to combine basic research findings with detailed analysis of the trends they reveal has prompted me to adopt a "double optic" in the two parts

---

14. On this distinction, see also Massip, "Berlioz and Early Music," 19–20.

15. François Lesure has laid the foundations for further comparative study in his indispensable *Dictionnaire musical des villes de province*. Excellent single-centre studies include Mussat, *Musique et société à Rennes*, and Geyer, *La vie musicale à Strasbourg*.

of this book, whose distribution and treatment of material are precariously balanced with an eye to the needs of both specialists and generalists, and the expectations of those who read whole books and those who use parts of them. The three chapters of part I map out the subject in progressively shorter (because denser) slices of the nineteenth century, articulated by the appearance or demise of various performing groups and repertories: 1800–1846, 1846–1878, and 1878–1900.[16] Although they take a broadly chronological journey through the various aspects of early music revival, these chapters are not designed to be a straightforward narrative. Instead, they offer a wide-angle view of the terrain, considering the main developments of each sub-period as they pertain to performance, aesthetics, education (in the broadest sense), and publishing. In their sketching out of interconnections between the main events and issues, they form an essential backcloth to part II, which zooms in to case studies of a few key repertories. Here I analyze perceptions of early French stage works at a time of crisis and transition (chapter 4); the search for the roots of musical "Frenchness" in monody and polyphony before 1600 (chapter 5); competing appropriations of Palestrina (chapter 6); and attempts at national monumentality through Baroque choral revival (chapter 7).

Taken as a set, these case studies reveal multiple interconnections. Historiographical myths of French primacy and superiority are as pervasive as expressions of national self-doubt, and all are intertwined with normative perceptions of morality, health, degeneracy, and gender traits as characteristics embedded in musical styles ripe for revival or neglect. We see multilayered processes of canonization at work: certain musics (such as Bach's instrumental works) eke their way into the public domain via reputation (history and criticism), publication (including teaching materials) and then, finally, a performance tradition; others (such as selected Janequin chansons) burst onto the performance scene from the outset, never to leave it. Central to all my stories, however, is the figure of the engaged musical amateur: the subscriber to a bourgeois musical society dedicated to the "old masters"; the *orphéon* singer singing Marcello at the Palais de l'Industrie; the local musician turned local historian or choir-trainer; the professional conductor turned "amateur," pouring personal funds into a potentially ruinous artistic enterprise. And it is the knowledge that this story involves some of the more ordinary people of history as participants and decision-makers (and not just as consumers) that renders it so important as an insight into the cultures—musical and otherwise—of nineteenth-century France, helping us to unlock the aspirations and beliefs that underpinned them.

---

16. The intensification of activity was such that around 60 percent of the early music activity in the performance listing on which this research is based dates from after 1870.

PART I

Patterns of Revival

I

1800–1846

The story of early music performance in nineteenth-century France has no clear beginning. Instead, it arises from eighteenth-century traditions that persisted despite changing ideologies brought by the Revolution, the Empire, the Restoration, and the July Monarchy. The new century saw a small number of works between 25 and 65 years old—by Pergolesi, Durante, Jommelli, Rousseau, and Rameau (the latter heavily diluted)—survive the turmoil of the 1790s and achieve a place in the repertories of Paris's leading musical institutions: the recently-opened Conservatoire, the *concerts spirituels*, and the Opéra. Most were sacred. Indeed, sacred music quickly emerges as central to the wider story, spotlighting the extent to which its nineteenth-century history has been neglected hitherto. Amid growing acceptance of the notion that music had a history worth preserving, certain repertories were revived while others remained either obscure or marginal. Some of reasons why are less than inspiring for the cultural historian. Inertia, convenience, lack of initiative, and habit all played their part in the preservation of a restricted early music repertory across the Revolutionary divide. We also see the beginnings of a vogue for "hit numbers" in which the effect of a single piece is so dazzling that it blinds people to the possibility that there might be similar, and potentially equally enjoyable, things around it.[1]

---

1. "Tubes," as coined for Bach by Fauquet and Hennion (*La grandeur de Bach*, 28).

But more active factors abound. The close relationship between repertory and function in *ancien-régime* music fundamentally affected later modes of reception for particular genres; and nationalist thinking, educational idealism, and perceptions of French musical inferiority influenced the progress and dissemination of early music in general. The evidence is to be found across the whole spectrum of musical activity, from the "sharp end" of performance, to teaching, publishing, historical writing, and invocation of the more nebulous idea of the museum spirit. This latter is not, however, a "blunt end" too far removed from performance to be relevant. Indeed, it is so central as to be the best place to start on a path that will lead, via consideration of publication, education, and aesthetic concerns, toward discussion of the activities of major players in early music during this period: in particular, Choron, François-Joseph Fétis, the prince de la Moskova, and Amédée Méreaux.

The Museum

In Paris, the idea of the musical museum came from Bernard Sarrette, first director of the Republican-inspired Conservatoire. Among his early plans was a library to contain "the works of masters of all ages and all nations."[2] Sarrette appears to have been particularly sensitive to the question of guardianship: the school was to have been called "Institution" until he objected, insisting on the title "Conservatoire."[3] From then on, Sarrette and his immediate colleagues in the French government shared a vision for a Conservatoire library that would provide a link between student musicians and their past. In later years, the spoils of the Napoleonic wars would allow students access to a pan-European musical heritage. Questions of national pride and competition were invoked explicitly at the laying of the library's foundation stone on 4 October 1801, when Jean Chaptal, scientist and Ministre de l'Intérieur, proclaimed: "It was left to France to erect a lasting monument to the glory of music, and necessary for its progress—a monument unknown to harmonious and fertile Italy."[4] As in the case of the Louvre, the French government wanted, at root, to create a

---

2. "les ouvrages des maîtres de tous les temps et de toutes les nations." Sarrette, inaugural speech, 22 October 1796, cited in Massip, "La bibliothèque du Conservatoire," 118.

3. Sarrette's demand for a "Conservatoire," and his equation of the new institution with other, great Republican museums, is quoted and discussed in Vanhulst, "La musique du passé," 51.

4. "Il était réservé à la France d'élever un monument durable à la gloire de la musique et nécessaire à ses progrès; monument inconnu à l'harmonieuse et fertile Italie." Given in Massip, "La bibliothèque du Conservatoire," 121.

monument to the history of art that would be "the envy of Europe."[5] And, as at the Louvre, a delicate balance between rupture and continuity was maintained in the gathering up of culture.

The library was not simply a collection of exemplary works. According to the Enlightenment spirit of celebrating human endeavor, it was an educational venture that illustrated both the good and the bad. Materials from the *ancien régime*, for instance, were kept, rather than being destroyed or sold off. Such attitudes were normal in official Republican circles, and illustrated in the art world by the work of Alexandre Lenoir, founder of the Republican Musée des Monumens Français (1795–1816), whose collection of French sculpture and tomb monuments represented the rescue of classes of art object that were otherwise often torn down or desecrated because their political or religious symbolism appeared to blind revolutionaries to their historical merits.[6] Lenoir did not ascribe all his objects high value. Some—especially those from the seventeenth century—were in the museum specifically as examples of the "degradation of the visual arts following the century of the renaissance."[7] Nevertheless, as lessons for future generations they earned their right to preservation. Lenoir's model thus compares usefully both with Conservatoire policy, which aimed at "completeness,"[8] and with the practice of François-Joseph Fétis, whose *concerts historiques* of the 1830s offered a musical "museum" of didactic material to underpin demonstrations of "good" and "bad" music (discussed below).

Important, too, in relation to Lenoir's museum model, is the spirit of secular reappropriation. Liturgical works, ripped from their context and performed in the concert-hall, were historical art exhibits, not ritual fabric. In France it was in the Conservatoire and at the *concert historique* that the musical museum as a repository of style history became a reality. Similarly, and not just in France, the museum concept inspired the first projects for the publication of corpuses of "monumental" music; and it lay behind the concept of the musical "classic." Finally, it brought practical benefits. Its political attractions were not lost on leaders of artistic concerns, who began to present themselves as guardians of cultural treasure, particularly when requesting government funding. It became almost a *sine qua non* to justify one's public utility via comparisons with the Louvre. Witness the committee of the Société des Concerts du Conservatoire in 1835, petitioning the Ministre des Beaux-Arts for public funding: "The Société des Concerts is, for artist-musicians, what the Louvre is for

---

5. McClellan, *Inventing the Louvre*, 1.
6. McClellan, *Inventing the Louvre*, 155–56.
7. McClellan, *Inventing the Louvre*, 190.
8. Massip, "La bibliothèque du Conservatoire," 117.

painters—the guardian of and the model for the best traditions, while helping and encouraging the [first] attempts of young composers."[9] The Society, though, became a victim of its own success in this regard: in 1892, when the Belgian critic Hugues Imbert looked back at the conducting career of Jules Garcin, he noted that one of the main prejudices he had to counter was the idea that the Society "must be, for music, what the Louvre is for painting."[10] Conservation had petrified into conservatism.

But in the 1820s and '30s the politics of the concept were often more complex, illustrating not only the close relationship between "sacred" and "classic," but also the secularizing power of museum terminology. Choron provides a telling case. His Parisian singing school, set up as a lowly Ecole Primaire de Chant in 1817 and supported financially by Louis-Philippe's nemesis, the duchesse de Berry,[11] metamorphosed several times in response to state clericalism and anticlericalism before its closure on Choron's death in 1834. Around 1818 Choron proposed a curriculum that emulated London's Academy of Ancient Music, whose goal was, he wrote, to "conserve the masterpieces of all ages."[12] When the school became a royal school of church music (from 1825), he used the opportunity to develop the very same "Ancient Music" repertory he had proposed earlier (*stile antico* repertory and Handel oratorio).[13] Then, almost overnight after the July Revolution, his Institution Royale de Musique Religieuse became the Institution Royale de Musique Classique.[14] His school's concert repertory remained stable, but of necessity its ostensible function changed. In a self-justifying pamphlet of the period he wrote that the school was, "to modern musical establishments, what the gallery of antiquities [in the Louvre] is to the Salon," and it was with increasing urgency that he resorted to museum terminology when, throughout the early 1830s, its very existence was threatened in a wave of anticlerical budget cuts that also saw the

---

9. "La Société des Concerts est pour les artistes-musiciens ce qu'est le Musée pour les peintres, le conservateur et l'exemple des bonnes traditions, tout en aidant et encourageant les essais des jeunes compositeurs." Archives Nationales, Paris (henceforth AN Paris) F^{21}4627, liasse 14.

10. "le Conservatoire [i.e., the concert society] doit être, pour la musique, ce qu'est le Louvre pour la peinture," *Revue d'art dramatique*, 7 (no. 157): 1 July 1892, 27–34, at 28.

11. According to Sophie Leo's anonymous *Erinnerung aus Paris*, of 1851. See [Leo], "Musical Life in Paris," 389.

12. "conserver les chefs-d'oeuvre de tous temps." Unpublished essay, "Considérations sur l'institution d'un Conservatoire particulier pour la musique d'église et de chambre," c.1818. Bibliothèque Nationale de France (henceforth BNF), Département des Manuscrits. Papiers Choron: n. a. fr. 265, ff. 53–56, at f. 54^r.

13. For more detail, see Vauthier, "Un chorège moderne"; Di Grazia, *Concert Societies*, 168–82; and my "Vocal Training."

14. The exiled duchesse de Berry's attempts to mount a Bourbon insurrection to overthrow Louis-Philippe began in November 1830 and ended only with her arrest and deportation from France two years later. See Fitzpatrick, *Catholic Royalism*, 111–20. It is unlikely that her close involvement with Choron's school before 1830 brought Choron anything but grief afterward, which may explain the precipitate rebranding.

death knell of the royal chapel.[15] As we shall see, this was not the last time that the museum spirit would be used to protect "classic" sacred music from anticlerical state hostility.[16]

As the above examples might suggest, in respect to performed music (as opposed to related phenomena such as publishing or libraries) the museum concept arguably came into its own only during the Restoration. Before that, more mundane considerations held sway, helping to explain the tenacity, in the concert and stage repertory, of survivors from the middle years of the eighteenth century.

Survival and Popularity

Concert- and theatre-going Parisians of 1800 knew a small number of early works, the vast majority of them Italian or Italianate; and, unless they played or sang them at home, they knew them essentially through performances by the Opéra and at the *concerts spirituels*.[17] Among concert and stage works (always more easily traced than domestic ones), three stand out as "repertory" works: Pergolesi's *Stabat mater*, Rousseau's *Le devin du village*, and Candeille's *Castor et Pollux*, which retained a modicum of Rameau's music. All three were in some sense understood as symbolic. Pergolesi's *Stabat* formed a bridge between Revolutionary and post-Revolutionary concert life, performed as it was at the last *concert spirituel* before the Terror (1792) and the first one under Napoléon (Opéra, 1800). The Opéra chose to revive the Candeille/Rameau *Castor* in December 1814, in celebration of the Bourbon Restoration. The *Devin* was an emblem for old chauvinistic debates about music and national identity.

Emphasis on Italianate music, to the detriment of French, increased steadily under Napoléon, with publications by Choron and Porro both directing and reflecting the early music side of dominant tastes among the musically literate.[18] In the first decade of the century, a handful of mid-eighteenth-century

---

15. "est aux établissemens modernes de musique, ce que la galerie des antiques est au Salon d'exposition." "Considérations sur l'Institution royale de musique classique," n.a. fr 265, ff. 58–70, at f. 67^r. See also Choron's final attempt (January 1834) to save his school, where the museum analogy is again used: Choron, *Considérations sur la situation actuelle*, 2–4, and 6.

16. See chapter 6, 199–200.

17. For a valuable overview of these concerts, see Ritterman, "Les concerts spirituels."

18. Napoléon imposed his mania for Italianate music wherever he could. For a discussion, see Mongrédien, *French Music*, 123–27. It was not for nothing that Napoléon charged Choron with the task of re-instating the Roman rite in French churches—a project halted by Waterloo but taken up with both zeal and success by Ultramontane Catholic reformers from the 1830s onward.

works appeared in print and on concert stages. Alongside Pergolesi's *Stabat*, the annual *concerts spirituels* took up the Durante *Litanies* in F minor and Jommelli's offertory "Confirma hoc, Deus" with some regularity from 1801[19]; in addition, Jommelli's *Requiem* in E flat of 1756 was performed at the Conservatoire almost from the moment Choron published it in 1805. More Jommelli (probably inauthentic), and a Leonardo Leo *Miserere*, would be taken from Choron's publications of c.1810 and included in the Conservatoire *exercices* before they were suspended in 1824, along with a single item each by Hasse and Handel.[20] Handel appeared at the Opéra, too, from 1803: "O Father, whose almighty pow'r" from *Judas Maccabaeus* formed part of the *pasticcio* oratorio *Saül*, a popular double-bill partner to the *Devin*. Handel was highly regarded in amateur circles: extracts from *Alexander's Feast* and probably *Acis and Galatea* were sung privately in the repertory of France's oldest music society, the Société Académique des Enfants d'Apollon, from around 1807.[21] Instrumental teaching pieces (whose performing history is more difficult to document) duly replicated the trend for Italianate music in the Napoleonic era and beyond: Pierre Baillot's Conservatoire students were nurtured on a diet including violin sonatas by Corelli, Tartini, and Locatelli, published by the Conservatoire as official music for the curriculum.[22] He also routinely taught them Geminiani, Pugnani, Bach, and Leclair.[23] Pianists following the Conservatoire's first piano method, that of Louis Adam (1805), would have learnt a more Germanic repertory: model pieces by C. P. E. Bach, Scarlatti, Handel (fugues from the Eight Keyboard Suites), and Bach (fugues from the *Well-Tempered Clavier*, which Simrock made available in a complete edition designated for Conservatoire use, from around 1801). Unsurprisingly, this repertory was only marginally "early" in 1800 (most was only 50 years old); but the absences—especially of indigenous sacred and stage music—are notable.

Gauging the relative popularity of such music is fraught because levels of contingency are high. Performance statistics, for example, are of limited value. They are a reflection of much more than public taste, and the limits of the possible vary according to the modes of use appropriate for each genre. Sacred

19. Mention of "the Jommelli offertorio" invariably refers to this particular piece, whose popularity was stressed on the title-page of an edition of 1811: *Offertoire . . . tiré du répertoire de la Chapelle Sixtine, exécuté par les Conservatoires d'Italie, de France, aux Concerts de l'Odéon, &c* (Paris: Pierre Porro, [1811]). Its rococo style renders it a "watershed" work by a composer whose *stile antico* works also remained in the repertory.

20. Undated handlist, AN Paris: AJ^{37} 84, liasse 8.

21. Information is limited. See the repertory lists for the society's monthly meetings in Decourcelle, *La Société académique des enfants d'Apollon*, 119–29.

22. Baillot was professor of violin from the Conservatoire's institution in 1795 to his death in 1842.

23. Letter of 21 December 1838 to Cherubini, given in Fauquet, *Les sociétés de musique de chambre*, 96.

music provides a good example. Between 1800 and 1830 Pergolesi's *Stabat* enjoyed around 10 percent of the performance exposure that Rousseau's *Devin* did (the latter garnered 180 performances between 1803 and 1829). Nevertheless it was arguably as popular. It was by many accounts both a classic work and a model of expressive sacred music and was a regular fixture in the repertory until around 1828.[24] Its popularity is best measured not by statistics but by the fact that there were so few appropriate occasions (Easter *concerts spirituels*) on which it was passed over in favor of something else (usually the Durante *Litanies*). Before the museum spirit took hold, performance opportunities for sacred works were dictated by the Church year, and critical responses to the *concerts spirituels* and other concerts reveal great sensitivity to the propriety of experiencing such music in an appropriate setting at an appropriate time. It was not until 1827, with the establishment of Choron's own *exercices*, that liturgical music was regularly presented as "abstract" concert music out of phase with liturgical tradition; nonetheless, Choron never programmed the Palestrina *Stabat*, the Allegri *Miserere*, the Palestrina *Improperia*, or other Sistine Chapel Holy Week repertory at any other time of year, and in any case he brought sacred works into his museum largely in order to increase their chances of being returned to their ritual environment.

The signal exception to this phenomenon before 1824—the Conservatoire *exercices*—may be explained by the fact that sacred repertory functioned as technical material. In 1804, an unsigned reviewer for the *Correspondance des amateurs musiciens*, a music-teachers' journal, encapsulated the worth of Durante's *Litanies*: "we should feel indebted to the Conservatoire for familiarizing its students with these all-too-neglected works by the creators of [musical] art. They will gain from it that precious purity of style which seems to be disdained nowadays; they will learn to sing a legato line, to sustain their sound, and to sing with good tone."[25] Repeatedly, the virtues of sacred music of the Italian Baroque, with or without *basso continuo*, were defined in terms of a kind of advanced *solfège* exercise which had the added benefit of offering morally unimpeachable texts and a regularity of harmonic practice that could itself be used as a model in composition training. The first vocal score of Pergolesi's *Stabat*

---

24. The phenomenon was not restricted to Paris, though information on the regions is scanty. However, Guy Gosselin documents a Maundy Thursday performance in Douai Cathedral in 1805 and a concert performance by the local Société des Amateurs two years later. See Gosselin, *L'âge d'or*, 84.

25. "on doit savoir le plus grand gré au Conservatoire de familiariser ses élèves avec les productions trop négligées des créateurs de l'art. Ils y puiseront cette précieuse pureté de style que l'on semble aujourd'hui dédaigner; ils y apprendront à lier les sons, à les soutenir et à assurer l'intonation." *Correspondance des amateurs musiciens* (henceforth *Corr.*) 2/22: 14 March 1804/23 ventôse an. 12, col. 174.

mater, published by Pleyel in 1803, met with precisely this kind of welcome, as did Porro's edition of Durante's *Litanies*, released in Paris two years later as part of an extensive *Collection de musique sacrée* spanning the first two decades of the century.[26]

Nevertheless, outside the Republican Conservatoire, the right context remained important. In 1811, the Théâtre de l'Odéon borrowed *concert spirituel* repertory by Durante and Jommelli for its own Easter concerts. Pierre-Louis Ginguené of the *Mercure de France* was scandalized:

> A few words will do: *non erat huis locus*; this was not their rightful place. Their place was at the *concert spirituel*, which was dedicated largely to music of this kind; the same holds true for the Conservatoire, where we listen to them with pleasure as study pieces for singers, as great and perfect models of composition in this austere style; but at the Odéon, *non erat huis locus*.[27]

Doubtless then, for audiences during the First Republic and the Empire, part of the attraction of the early music *concert spirituel* repertory was the anticipation of each performance as part of an annual ritual at a particular venue. Such love of familiarity was also convenient, especially for hard-pressed Opéra singers working on a single rehearsal and short of time to learn something new.

Several historical considerations demand resolution, therefore, before the "popularity" of a particular piece can be judged. In short, we need to know "why." Four overlapping concerns emerge during the first half of the century: stylistic value (the museum spirit), technical/educational value, ritual value, and familiarity. These forms of value influenced modes of listening (as with Ginguené), modes of signification among those who claimed to represent, while guiding, public taste, and modes of publication. The latter was more buoyant in the first decades of the century than we might have expected, and underpinned much revivalist activity while being emblematic of more.

---

26. See *Corr.* 1/16: 13 March 1803/21 ventôse an. 11, p. 4; and *Corr.* 3/18: 20 April 1805/30 germinal an. 13, col. 127.

27. "Un mot en dit la cause: *non erat huis locus*; ce n'est point-là leur place. C'était leur place au Concert Spirituel, consacré en grande partie à la musique de ce genre; ce l'est encore au Conservatoire impérial de musique, où l'on les entend avec plaisir comme morceaux d'étude pour le chant, comme grands et parfaits modèles de composition dans ce genre austère; mais à l'Odéon, *non erat huis locus*." G[inguené], *Mercure de France* (henceforth *MF*), 13 April 1811, 87.

Publishing and Education

Even when they proved to be business failures, new commercial editions (many destined for domestic consumption) indicated a high level of public interest in the music itself. Choron, for instance, was always in financial difficulty. Yet it would be misguided to interpret his seemingly perpetual insolvency as evidence of the public's apathy toward early music. Admittedly, it was because too few subscribers signed up that his project for a mammoth *Collection générale des ouvrages de musique classique,* to be published by subscription by Auguste Le Duc, ran to only a single volume (1810). Nevertheless, those subscribers numbered nearly four hundred. They received the first ever French editions of Leo's *Miserere,* a *Miserere* in G minor for five voices and *basso continuo* attributed to Jommelli, the latter's *Requiem, Stabat mater* settings by Josquin and Palestrina, and the latter's *Missa Ad fugam.* Choron's three-volume *Principes de composition des écoles d'Italie* (c.1808), a government-recognized method intended for French cathedral choir schools, attracted just over five hundred mostly individual subscriptions. In a specialist, luxury industry such as music publishing, these were high take-up rates. Moreover, they were subscription levels which French historical collections of the later nineteenth century—by which time a revivalist movement in early music had gathered considerable momentum—did not surpass.[28]

After Choron/Le Duc and Porro, the most significant publisher of early music was Marie-Pierre Launer (1787–1853), who took over part of the *fonds* of the publisher Carli some time after her marriage in 1825. After her husband's death in 1839 she began trading as "Veuve Launer," and changed the direction of the business to specialize in music from Dufay and Palestrina to Bach and Marcello. On her death in 1853 she had nearly tripled the value of her business to around 164,000F.[29] It was Launer who despite widespread disregard for the music published the first modern anthology of François Couperin's harpsichord works (J.-J.-B. Laurens's edition of 1841); Launer who produced the new and immensely popular complete vocal scores of Marcello's 50 psalm settings (supplanting Carli's edition of 1818); Launer with whom Adrien de Lafage worked to produce editions of Palestrina masses and motets that were so cheap that they were advertized in the *orphéon* press.

---

28. My interpretation here differs from that of Jean Mongrédien, who, possibly following Simms in his *Alexandre Choron* (p. 111), sees the failure of Choron's projects as an indication of a relative absence of interest in early music. See Mongrédien, *French Music,* 199.

29. See Devriès and Lesure, *Dictionnaire des éditeurs,* ii, 260.

By the time of the July Monarchy, then, there was considerable revivalist momentum in music publishing. It was enhanced by the manner in which the new periodical press became involved. Adolphe Ledhuy and Henri Bertini's *Encyclopédie pittoresque de la musique* (1833) contained music supplements featuring old French chansons and dances stretching back to the Chastelain de Couci; Bach, Rameau, and Couperin keyboard music; extracts from the *Ballet comique de la reine* and Rameau's *Dardanus* and *Le temple de la gloire*; and extracts from Palestrina's *Missa Ad fugam*, the G minor *Miserere* attributed to Jommelli, and Josquin's *Stabat mater*. The latter three were taken from Choron. Four years later, the organist Félix Danjou published a significant and wide-ranging collection of early music in the *Revue et gazette musicale* as "Archives curieuses de la musique." This collection of over 70 items marked the first published appearance in nineteenth-century France of works by Landini and Machaut (the latter courtesy of Bottée de Toulmon's transcriptions), as well as later, Franco-Flemish composers including Dufay; also new were Danjou's selections of harpsichord music by Frescobaldi, Louis Couperin, and Rameau, and a Palestrina "Adoramus te" that would soon become the master's best-loved choral piece.

Such works, and publishers' apparent enthusiasm for them as curiosities or as educational material, are evidence of the richness of nineteenth-century French responses to early music and signs of its increasing "normality." Arrangements are particularly important; so are examples of a change of use. That Handel oratorio excerpts, for instance, were being given new texts and turned into liturgical contrafacta as early as 1832 signals the extent of their popularity.[30] However, the element of cultural construction could extend further, beyond the rearrangement, reorchestration, and paraphrase of existing music to the celebration of known fakes as originals. A hugely popular sacred aria, "Pietà, Signore," was invariably sold as a Stradella "aria di chiesa," even though its authenticity was undermined from the 1840s and its existence (with a different text) cannot be traced further back than Fétis's *concert historique* of 24 March 1833. For the last two thirds of the century it had a Romantic cachet as the very aria whose beauty saved Stradella's life, dissuading hired assassins from carrying out their commission to avenge his lover's husband. It appeared in over 50 guises, adapted for a plethora of instrumental combinations and to at least three texts.[31] Here market forces held sway. Despite indications pointing to Louis Niedermeyer or Fétis as the author, for publishers to have put

---

30. See A. M. D. G., *Concerts spirituels ou Recueil de motets*, no. 90.
31. "Pietà, Signore" is still published, in a Schirmer print of 1914, under Stradella's name.

public education before myth would have been to deny themselves the profits of a potential best seller.³² As Weckerlin noted acidly in 1890, complicity was far more rational.³³

The Palestrina "Adoramus te" was also a fake, with an upper line by François Roussel and three resolutely homophonic lower voices all historical traces of which disappear beyond the first volume of Friedrich Rochlitz's *Sammlung vorzüglicher Gesang-Stücke* (preface 1835; published 1838), where it was listed as being by Palestrina.³⁴ It is probably the most important piece in the *Archives curieuses* from a historiographical point of view, because in common with many other fakes and reconstructed works its subsequent popularity tells us so much about the stylistic ideals that nineteenth-century musicians projected onto early musics. After all, there is little point in faking a piece of early music unless it successfully negotiates between the past and the present by corresponding to what people would like such a piece to be. That was the career path of other famous fakes: not only the Stradella "Pietà, Signore" but also the Arcadelt "Ave Maria" (1840s, elaborated by Louis Dietsch from one of the composer's polyphonic chansons), and, later, the Lassus chanson "Mon coeur se recommande à vous" (1860s, possibly by Weckerlin). All became "signature pieces" for the composer to whom they were attributed, helping to form an image of "early music" that was more creative than it was historical or educationally useful as an introduction to the heritage of compositional style.

Fakes aside, it is worth probing the question of "pedagogical value" further here. Although, like the museum mentality, it brought with it a secularizing power that would soon have serious implications for sacred music, it could also, in an era of progress and increasing professionalism, bestow on early

---

32. Biographical entries on Niedermeyer (Guy Ferchault/Jacqueline Gachet) and Stradella (Carolyn Gianturco) in *Grove Music Online* divide the spoils unevenly between Niedermeyer and Fétis, with Ferchault and Gachet opting for the former and Gianturco for the latter (though Gianturco also mentions Niedermeyer as a suspected author). *Grove Music Online*, ed. Laura Macy, http://www.grovemusic.com>. However, later nineteenth-century rumor favored Fétis, who claimed to own the original manuscript, had introduced the work to France with some ceremony, and whose behavior regarding this piece was consistently suspicious. It is of course not impossible that both were involved. The Stradella aria and other potentially Fétisian fakes are discussed in articles in preparation by Sarah Hibberd ("Murder in the Cathedral?") and Peter Holman. I am grateful to both for allowing me to benefit from their unpublished work.

33. Weckerlin, *Nouveau musiciana*, 68. Complicity came at the price of French probity as far as Weckerlin was concerned: the most serious risk was that in clinging to the Stradella attribution the prestigious Société des Concerts risked making France a laughing stock in Germany. Weckerlin made a particularly damning case for Fétis's authorship (67–69)—a hypocritical move if he was indeed, as I suspect, the author of the fake Lassus chanson "Mon coeur se recommande à vous" (see chapter 3).

34. Greer Garden notes that "this version was probably composed later than the 16th century" (*New Grove II*, xxi, 810). Given that a copy, correctly attributed to Roussel, was made by the Roman bibliophile Fortunato Santini as late as the 1820s, it is difficult not to attribute this "adaptation" and new attribution to Rochlitz himself. However, there is no evidence that anyone in France during the nineteenth century knew this particular piece was a fake.

musics a fatal whiff of amateurism. With certain genres, separation between early musics as part of a teaching canon (for composers or performers), and as part of a performing repertory, took place exceptionally quickly. The educational value of the Italian sacred music published by Porro and Choron was a double-edged sword that helped facilitate regular performance but simultaneously threatened to devalue each work as an artistic experience. By dwelling on the technical benefits brought by its study, critics kept it separate from higher things—the professional repertory dominated by operatic arias. The case of early instrumental music was even starker. At the Conservatoire the question of public performance simply did not arise. Instrumental chamber music was not featured in *exercices*, so Baillot's and Adam's teaching pieces remained firmly locked inside the curriculum. Moreover, early music was generally shunned as repertory suitable for the annual prize competitions. Cello music by C. P. E. Bach and Locatelli appears to have been featured *faute de mieux*,[35] but for pianists and violinists with a superabundance of newer repertory it was only at the turn of the twentieth century that Bach-playing, for instance (fugues for women pianists only, and solo sonata movements for violinists), was required of them.

Even during the "historicist" July Monarchy such public performance remained exceptional, its exceptionalism only highlighted by the positive evidence we can marshal of a growing "circle" inspired by the solo instrumental, keyboard (including organ) music and concertos of Corelli, Geminiani, Handel, and Bach.[36] Baillot's *concerts historiques* in 1833 and 1837 prove the point. Inspired doubtless by his participation in 1832 in Fétis's first *concert historique* (in which he played what was billed as a Cavalieri *Concerto passegiato* with cellist Auguste Franchomme and an arrangement (supposedly) of the *La romanesca* dance tune that was soon to become wildly popular), Baillot's first concert included *concerti grossi* by Corelli, Geminiani, and Handel, a Pergolesi concerto, an andante by Barbella, and piano music by Mozart and Beethoven played by members of his family. Yet this was not his first *concert historique*—in fact it built on the repertory of his concert of 14 February 1818, which included the Barbella, and (different) concerti by Corelli and Geminiani, together with a Handel trio sonata and two Tartini solo concertos. Like the concerts of 1833 and 1837, this one took place in Baillot's home. In 1818 that was not unusual; many of his

---

35. Ardouin, "La musique ancienne," 179. Ardouin's essay, however, is sketchy in the extreme, especially where dates are concerned.

36. François-Sappey, *Alexandre P. F. Boëly*, and Fauquet and Hennion, *La grandeur de Bach*, give particularly rich evocations of these circles, which included Mendelssohn, Hiller, the organist Boëly, violinists Baillot and Sauzay, and pianists Hélène de Montgéroult (briefly a Conservatoire professor) and Marie Bigot.

quartet concerts were given in private apartments, his own included. But in 1833 it was indeed unusual, since for his quartet concerts he was looking for larger accommodation in commercial venues and large hôtels.[37] His *concerts historiques* of the 1830s were thus "different": different from the overtly public events mounted by Fétis in theatres and concert halls, and different from his own chamber series. They were, effectively, concerts behind closed doors. And it is therefore difficult to see his concert of 1818 other than as an experiment he considered it unwise to repeat. Moreover, having begun performing his beloved Bach in 1833, for reasons that are unclear he stopped doing so, whether at concerts held at his house, or at subscription concerts, with two performances of accompanied sonatas (with Ferdinand Hiller) in 1835.[38] Neither did his concerts have any immediate legacy, beyond François-Antoine Habeneck's attempt to introduce the A minor concerto into the Société des Concerts repertory (1840).

The case of Chopin is even clearer cut: on several occasions in the 1840s he extolled the virtues of Bach's *Well-Tempered Clavier* as study material, both for himself and his pupils[39]; and close analysis of his music has revealed the extent to which he absorbed, and then transformed, Bach's practices of voicing and textural delineation.[40] But while he would play the Bach triple concerto BWV1063 in public in 1833, the solo keyboard music was not part of his concert repertory.[41] In fact, perhaps unintentionally, Chopin himself revealed where the boundary lay, telling his pupil Wilhelm von Lenz of how, instead of practicing his own pieces in preparation for a concert, he would play Bach for two weeks instead.[42] The arrival of Antoine Marmontel as a Conservatoire professor of piano in 1848 would radically change the public status of early keyboard music, and indeed early music more generally, since his pupils routinely took it into the concert hall; nevertheless, as later portions of this study will show, beyond hits such as the *Romanesca*, it took time for music typecast as educational to be accepted wholeheartedly in the professional realm.[43] And while from today's perspective we might well see the teaching and re-translation through composition of early music as equivalent, in terms of canoncity, to its

---

37. Fauquet, *La musique de chambre*, 48.
38. See Fauquet and Hennion, *La grandeur de Bach*, 65. On Hiller's importance as a conduit for Bach in France, see 59–60.
39. Fauquet and Hennion, *La grandeur de Bach*, 78.
40. See Eigeldinger, *L'univers musical de Chopin*, passim.
41. BWV1063, which Chopin played in public with Hiller and Liszt, is a different matter altogether and is discussed in chapter 2.
42. Given in Eigeldinger, *L'univers musical de Chopin*, 36.
43. Marmontel's piano pupils included several key figures in this study: Camille Bellaigue, Charles Bordes, Louis Diémer, Théodore Dubois, Vincent d'Indy, and the opera director Auguste-Emmanuel Vaucorbeil. He also taught Bizet.

use in performance, early nineteenth-century culture reveals a clearer sense of hierarchy.

The Problem of "French" Music

The almost complete absence of French music from the discussion so far is not coincidental, and the principal exception, mentioned earlier, only "proves" the rule: to celebrate the Bourbon restoration, on 28 December 1814 the Opéra began what would be a 22-performance run of the Candeille *Castor et Pollux*, keeping remnants of Rameau's score.[44] For all its symbolic significance, this revival went entirely against the grain of early nineteenth-century opinion on the merits of French music before around 1760 and did nothing to turn the tide of derision which characterized it. Once French opera of the late seventeenth and early eighteenth centuries had been overtaken by newer Italian styles toward the end of the eighteenth century, it was finally "eclipsed" at the beginning of the nineteenth. Its status dropped so low that the very appellation *la musique française* became a term of deprecation, indicating a grandiloquent and monotonous pre-Gluckian style consisting mainly of "heavy intoning."[45] The durability of this shift is amply illustrated by patterns in the conservation and revival of eighteenth-century repertory not only to 1814, but throughout the first half of the century. Burgeoning historicism did *la musique française* no favors; indeed it merely widened the divide between the perceived worth of the Italian and French traditions. In the first decades of the century, writers of different generations and persuasions regularly disparaged the music of the Louis XIV and Louis XV periods.

At the beginning of the century, the test case for such views on the Louis XV period specifically was Rousseau's *Le devin du village*, broadly perceived as a salvation from unremitting Frenchness. The unanimity of voice on Rousseau's contribution to French operatic history is telling. His was the first "modern" opera—the earliest French stage work whose style required no excuses because it symbolized the rejection of undiluted French values in musical composition.

---

44. The production of *Castor et Pollux* included some *airs de danse* and the choruses "Que tout gémisse" and "Brisons nos fers," but not "Dans ce doux asile," which Adolphe Adam would later make famous. The work had 22 performances, closing finally on 20 August 1817. For detail on the Rameau and Candeille versions, see De Lajarte, *Bibliothèque musicale du théâtre de l'Opéra*, i, 371–72. My dates for performances and reprises are taken not from De Lajarte, but from the more reliable manuscript "Journal de l'Opéra."

45. "lourdes psalmodies," Cannone, "L'éclipse de la musique baroque," 526. See also Weber, "*La musique ancienne*."

Here, for critics, was a work which had apparently saved the French from their own worst instincts, setting them on the path towards lyrical, Italian-influenced, opera. Jacques-Daniel Martine, a fellow Genevan, described it as "a masterpiece of naturalness and expression that will still be sung in a thousand years"; its author was the man who "made us realize just how ridiculous the old genre was, and who prepared the revolution that Gluck, Piccinni and Sacchini brought to our lyric tragedy."[46] In 1809 an unsigned reviewer for the *Mercure de France* wrote of the opera as though it offered a return to the Garden of Eden:

> It is rather like reading a simple but touching Eglogue after a Virgil epic: such is the pleasure of the lover of the countryside, who returns there, far from the bustle of the city, to rediscover tranquillity, pure air, simple traditions and gentle ways.[47]

As distant from modern music as it was from the "heavy and monotonous litany of old French opera,"[48] the *Devin* acted as a talisman against a return to the French style. Like the Pergolesi *Stabat mater*, it was, during the Empire at least, endowed with the status of a "classic." It had not aged, and indeed *could not* age, because of the unaffected manner in which Rousseau had portrayed real sentiment, as opposed to the posturings of the heroes in "French" *ancien-régime* operas.[49]

Those posturings provoked a lasting reaction. Choron's historical introduction to the *Dictionnaire historique des musiciens* of 1810 was both succinct and influential. In describing his shame at the seventeenth- and eighteenth-century decadence of his *patrimoine*, he began to turn a tradition of national disparagement into one of self-flagellation.[50] Three years later Martine followed suit, accusing the French of indulging in an ignorant, unthinking, and purely habitual liking for Lully and Rameau.[51] Younger colleagues did similarly: Ginguené (a former Piccinnist), Julien-Louis Geoffroy (a royalist, interestingly), Stendhal, Fétis, and, in the 1840s, Berlioz.[52] Nevertheless, there were

---

46. "un chef-d'oeuvre de naturel et d'expression, qu'on chantera encore dans mille ans"; "qui a fait sentir tout le ridicule de l'ancien genre, et qui a préparé la révolution effectuée dans notre tragédie lyrique par Gluck, Piccini et Sacchini." *MF* February 1814, 361; see also Martine's review in *MF* December 1814, 452–53.

47. "Il semble, après la lecture d'un chant épique de Virgile, lire un simple, mais touchant églogue: tel est le plaisir de l'ami des champs, qui y revient, loin du fracas de la ville, retrouver le calme, un air pur, des moeurs naïves, et de douces habitudes." *MF* 7 October 1809, 369.

48. "la lourde et monotone litanie du vieil opéra français." *MF* 7 October 1809, 369.

49. *MF* 7 October 1809, 369–70.

50. Choron and Fayolle, *Dictionnaire historique des musiciens*, vol. 1 (1810), lxxix-lxxx, given in Cannone "L'éclipse de la musique baroque," 532–33.

51. Martine, *De la musique dramatique*, 68–69.

52. For a recent analysis of the latter, see Massip, "Berlioz and Early Music," 25–28.

signs of an underlying fear that revival might be possible: in 1826, "M. R." of the *Mercure du dix-neuvième siècle* derided the royalist diehards who went to the Théâtre Feydeau for their Grétry, endless muttering "the terrible words *nationality* and *national genre*."[53] He wagered that for a revival of Rameau's operas to be a runaway success with an ignorant and gullible public one needed just two things: the ballets, and a flurry of press articles on nationality in music.[54]

When Saint-Saëns came to analyze the "problem" of French opera in 1879, he laid all the blame for anti-French sentiment on Stendhal's *Vies de Haydn, Mozart et Métastase* (1814).[55] By this stage Stendhal was, in his denigration of French "music" in general and Rameau in particular, merely following a trajectory that had already been outlined in the late eighteenth century. Nevertheless, he gave fresh impetus to an aesthetic code whose ramifications dogged the French musical intelligentsia for the rest of the century, first in relation to Italy and, soon, to Germany: a deep-seated sense of national backwardness, combined with bewilderment as to whether *any* feature of "French" music could legitimately be celebrated, especially if it was connected to the *ancien régime*. Two tenaciously held concepts resulted: the idea, present from Geoffroy's time, that France could claim the works of resident foreign composers as her own, because France had changed their authors' style and outlook[56]; and the ensuing theory of contemporary French opera as a *juste milieu* or golden mean between the Italian and the German, in which the problem of defining what was specifically "French" about the music of French opera was essentially left unaddressed. While such issues were as relevant to new composition as to the revival of early music, they played into the latter throughout the century in ways that were central to bringing the status of music into line with that of France's other arts. The necessity of holding on to the glories of French musical heritage, even if the artistic product was distasteful to nineteenth-century ears, was a central part of that process and had a significant impact on musicians' marking out of repertory either for active revival or for symbolic respect

---

53. "les terribles mots de *nationalité* et de *genre national*." *Le Mercure du dix-neuvième siècle* (henceforth *MD-NS*), 4th quarter, 1826, 71.

54. "Je tiens la gageure que si l'on remettait Rameau au jour avec accompagnement de ballets et d'articles de journaux sur la nationalité en musique, Rameau aurait un succès d'enthousiasme." *MD-NS*, 2nd quarter, 1826, 213. He could not have known how prophetic his words were in respect to the terms of post-1870 attempts to revive this music. Nevertheless, Rameau's music never quite died out in Paris; nor did he ever quite succeed as "M.R." predicted. See Pistone, "Rameau à Paris."

55. *Le Voltaire*, 30 July & 8 August 1879, 1st instalment. Saint-Saëns found Stendhal's treatment of Rameau particularly egregious: "[il] traite avec le dernier mépris l'immortel Rameau, le plus grand génie musical que la France ait produit; il déclare, du reste, que les Français n'ont jamais eu de la musique et n'en euront jamais: calomnie qui a fait son chemin" (ibid.).

56. For a brief history of this idea, see my "A Dilettante at the Opera," 58.

combined with practical oblivion. Respect for the historic nature of the music was, however, essential. Music that failed on this count (*ancien-régime* church music is an example) stood no chance of success. In any case, before 1848 the criteria by which all such choices were made were largely predictable: the Italianism of Napoléon's reign left *la musique française* crippled by perceptions of its deficiency as music.

To find a French music worthy of the name, musicians with historical sensitivity had to look further back than the eighteenth century—to a past during which the French had, alongside their Flemish cousins, been trend-setters in both musical composition and music theory. In their different ways, Choron and the Conservatoire's librarian Bottée de Toulmon each contributed to a line of thinking which placed the "golden age" of French music in what we would call the late Medieval and Renaissance periods, culminating, as they thought, in the role of Goudimel as Palestrina's Roman teacher. Choron's choir-school *exercices* of 1827 to 1832, which featured a variety of Italian-influenced music from Palestrina through Handel to Cherubini, included the works of just two noncontemporary French musicians. Neglecting the French Revolutionary repertory and the entire traditions of *grand motet* and French cantata, Choron went back to Josquin (the *Déploration sur la mort de Jehan Ockeghem*) and Clément Janequin (*La bataille de Marignan* and *Les cris de Paris*).[57] His reasons were overtly nationalistic, forming the counterweight to his deprecation of seventeenth-century composers. French and French-trained musicians had led European music all the way from Tinctoris to Goudimel; their international renown was indisputable (as Choron illustrated through copious quotation from the treatises of Italian scholars in particular); and they were "the stem from which came all of today's other European musical traditions."[58]

It was Choron's colleague François Fayolle who petitioned the Institut in 1812 to have Tinctoris's theoretical works translated at government expense.[59]

---

57. For detailed programme listings, see Boettcher, *Les exercices publics d'Alexandre Choron*, 121–35; Di Grazia gives a repertory listing in *Concert Societies*, 174–76.

58. "la tige d'où sont sorties toutes les autres écoles de musique aujourd'hui existans en Europe" ("De l'école française de musique et de son influence sur les autres écoles de ce même art en Europe." BNF Manuscrits: n.a. fr. 263, ff. 256–81, at f. 280). Two versions of this piece are bound together, one in note form. Without bothering too much about whether the composers he mentioned were French or Flemish, Choron focused primarily on demonstrating the lineage ("filiation") of French music, which he found wanting (too "aride" and "savante") only in the face of Palestrina's genius (ibid., f. 281).

59. See Simms, *Alexandre Choron*, 68. The manuscript, owned by Fayolle and later by Perne, contained all but one of Tinctoris's twelve treatises and was used by the lawyer and medieval music specialist Edmond de Coussemaker (1805–1876) to prepare the first French edition of Tinctoris's theoretical works, in 1875. Choron thought the manuscript contained the complete *oeuvre*. It is currently conserved as part of the Fétis collection at the Bibliothèque Royale Albert Ier, Brussels, Ms II 4147 (Fétis 5274).

As *membre correspondant* of the music section of the Classe des Beaux-Arts, Choron was in the advantageous position of being able to prepare an official report supporting a project with which he was intimately familiar and about which he was enthusiastic. Unsurprisingly, it received formal blessing. The minutes of the meeting of 5 December 1812, signed by Gossec, Grétry, Méhul, and Choron, presented Choron's report and the music section's verdict. Tinctoris's work was important for its method, rigor, precision, and clarity, and many of its precepts still held good. Most important of all:

> the class considers that it is useful and honorable for French literature, which is badly lacking in works of musical erudition, to have Tinctoris's . . . work translated and published. It will prove that for a long time France had the best and the only school of music in existence.[60]

The music section's reasoning is striking for its balancing of national pride against an admission of national inadequacy. It accords with that of Choron in his manuscript writings on early French music, and also with his rationale for preparing the *Dictionnaire historique des musiciens* with Fayolle. And while it is unlikely that Choron's report served as a model in the drawing up of future nationalist projects, the frequency with which similar ploys were used later in the century, especially after 1870, renders it an important historical precedent.

A second project to receive official recognition—this time from a subsection of the Ministère de l'Instruction Publique—also featured early Franco-Flemish music. In 1843 Bottée de Toulmon, librarian at the Conservatoire, presented a project to bring together all known masses based on "L'homme armé" and "De beata virgine" in a publication that would illustrate the continuity and superiority of French music of the period, while providing scholars, students, and amateurs with a corpus of monuments from which they could, for the first time in the modern era, make "objective" judgements about France's role in the history of music. By 1843, Bottée had gathered fifteen "L'homme armé" masses from Dufay to Carissimi [sic], and "De beata virgine" masses by Josquin, Brumel, Senfl, Morales, Palestrina, and Jacobus de Kerle. When he presented his report to the Comité Historique des Arts et Monumens he made

---

60. "la classe pense qu'il est utile et honorable pour la littérature française qui est très pauvre en érudition musicale que l'ouvrage de Tinctoris . . . soit traduit et imprimé. Il prouvera que la France a eu longtemps la meilleure et la seule école [de] musique qui existât." See Goudail, *Art, savoir et pouvoir*, i, 157–62, at 162.

no reference either to nationalist or religious sentiment. Rather, he appealed to the museum spirit, explaining that the effective comparison of styles was dependent on one's being presented with suitably related works.[61] Stacked thus, however, his cards were likely to lead to only one conclusion: that the Franco-Flemish school dominated composition of this kind and passed it to other nations. His report was enthusiastically received; however, like Choron's Tinctoris translation, the collection remained unfinished—a victim of De Toulmon's Casaubon-like approach to historical study.

Had it appeared, though, I doubt that it would have prompted a change in practice, since activity in reformist Catholic circles was making a performed revival of Franco-Flemish polyphony increasingly unlikely. Ultramontanism was already making waves in 1830s Paris (the Lamennais circle) and in the regions (Dom Guéranger's Benedictine revival at Solesmes). From the Bourbon Restoration, this new centralizing force from "across the Alps" had begun to threaten the liturgical independence and regional freedom of the old Gallican Church, which, formally instituted by Louis XIV as a way of preserving his power, demanded loyalty to King and country above all; still at its height in the mid-eighteenth century, it received its first death blow in 1789.[62] Ultramontanism, given new impetus in the 1830s because Catholics of varying persuasions banded together to resist Louis-Philippe's anticlerical reforms, never looked back.[63] But from the moment church reformers began looking to Rome, plainchant, and Palestrina for a musical liturgy worthy of France, Franco-Flemish sacred polyphony, as a recoverable national repertory, was doomed. For most of the century no one was predisposed to like the sacred music of this period, which had neither the allure of the truly medieval nor the mythologized purity of the Counter Reformation.[64] Historical and performing canons diverged wildly, as religious politics and musical taste overrode any sense of national pride. Indeed, in high-profile contexts such as Fétis's *concerts historiques* (1832–1835), Franco-Flemish sacred polyphony was as disparaged a repertory as *la musique française*. Culture shaped practice in a very particular way.

---

61. Bottée de Toulmon, *Rapport sur une publication de musique ancienne*, 6–7.
62. Latreille et al., *Histoire du catholicisme*, 13.
63. On the Ultramontane side, see Franklin, *Nineteenth-Century Churches*; for a summary of how Ultramontane ideas stimulated interest in medieval music manuscripts and their transcription, see Bergeron, *Decadent Enchantments*, 15–17.
64. See chapters 5 and 6.

The Cultural Influence of Fétis: The *concert historique*

No Francophone writer on music history could match Fétis as a setter of cultural agendas during this period. He pronounced: others either paraphrased or (belatedly) protested. Where he did not reconceptualize music history as it was then understood, he expanded on and consolidated the models of others (not least Choron), taking ownership of them in the process. From 1827 onward, when he set up the *Revue musicale*, his work became a gateway to history that few could afford to avoid. That what Fétis did in 1832 with his first *concert historique* was innovative and boldly symbolic has become a cliché in scholarship on 1830s musical Paris.[65] And the cliché is largely defensible. The first three concerts, which presented all the repertory Fétis had in hand, opened Parisian ears to unknown operatic and instrumental music and presented it in a wholly new way, not least in the occasional use of original instruments. However, Fétis's work is also ripe for reappraisal. This is not because of the irony that among the best-received works two were either probably (the *Romanesca*) or definitely (the Stradella aria) fake, though that is telling in itself; it is because a combination of scholarly deference to his celebrity and misunderstanding of his aims has caused his handful of *concerts historiques* to be regarded as more crucial in generating performing interest in early music than the evidence suggests. A paradox lies at the heart of the matter. Inspired by Choron (discussed below), Fétis aimed to teach via the institution of the public concert, while Choron had by contrast aimed to entertain via the demonstration of his pupils' progress. Therein lay the former's greater influence on culture (of which *concerts historiques* scattered through the century form a part) and the latter's greater influence on practice. The demands of chronology notwithstanding, I shall take culture first.

The alternation of historical lecture and musical exemplification characteristic of Fétis's *concert historique* format was not designed as either entertainment or artistic experience. More lecture-recital than concert, the format served to illustrate stylistic differences through comparison and to demonstrate teleology. And if his concerts inspired interest in early music generally

---

65. Fétis's concerts were as follows: 8 April 1832, Conservatoire (History of Opera); 16 December 1832, Conservatoire (Music of the Sixteenth Century); 24 March 1833, Salle Ventadour (Music of the Seventeenth Century); 2 April 1833, Salle Ventadour (near-repeat of History of Opera). A planned repeat of programme two, scheduled for 12 May 1833 and postponed twice, never took place. Two years later Fétis tried again, presenting a (disastrous) concert on 16 April 1835 at the Théâtre Italien (selections from previous concerts, entitled Progress in Melody and Harmony in the Sixteenth and Seventeenth Centuries). A second concert projected for 1835 did not take place. For a general introduction, see Robert Wangermée, "Les premiers concerts historiques."

(which is the reason they have been given historic importance), that was not his major concern. His was not so much an exercise in audience conversion to early music as a crash course in the art of separating the stylistic wheat (largely Italian and German music after 1600) from the chaff (largely French music, of any era). Recognizing the growing respect for the past in July Monarchy culture, Fétis argued that music should now become part of it:[66] King Louis-Philippe worked on his national museum of pictorial history at Versailles (1831–1837) and opened it to his citizens; Fétis put together his *concerts historiques*. He also provided his own documentary record. Self-serving reviews including summary lectures appeared in the *Revue musicale*, their subjectivity rendering them historiographically invaluable because of the breathtaking candor with which he evaluated each piece.

It was in his first, "Progress of Opera," concert (8 April 1832) that Fétis stressed France's backwardness most explicitly: the melodic content of the *Ballet comique de la reine*, was, he said, "not too good, as you will be able to see from the extracts that will be performed presently" (and which were offset, significantly, by extracts from Peri and Caccini's *Euridice*, Monteverdi's *Orfeo*, and Cavalli's *Xerse*).[67] Nevertheless, he added, the dance numbers were effective. Later in the lecture he turned to the question of Lully and Rameau in comparison with Pergolesi, Carissimi, Scarlatti, and Keiser. Presenting Lully as a willing clone of Carissimi who had been overrated by his French contemporaries because they knew no better and because they liked what they knew, Fétis pitted "Enfin il est en ma puissance" (*Armide*) and a chorus from *Persée* against an aria from Kaiser's *Basilius*, which, he said, demonstrated the German composer's superiority. The same went for an aria from Alessandro Scarlatti's *Laodicea e Berenice*: "such music," he said, "no longer belongs to the era of trial [and error]; it is the perfected art," embodying a level of expression which could not be surpassed.[68]

More sanguine when it came to Rameau, whom he viewed as having learnt much from the Italian tradition, he nevertheless found his works flawed by their bizarre (though effective) harmony and melodic contour. Yet where Pergolesi's *Serva padrona* was a model of perfection, Rameau's works would always be "monuments of one of the most remarkable periods of transition in

---

66. *Revue musicale* (henceforth *RM*) 6/12: 14 April 1832, 81. I have streamlined as much as possible the complex and inconsistent numbering systems used in this periodical.

67. "pas trop bonne, comme on pourra juger par les fragmens qui seront exécutés tout à l'heure." *RM* 6/12: 14 April 1832, 83.

68. "de semblable musique n'appartient plus à l'époque des essais; c'est de l'art perfectionné." *RM* 6/13: 28 April 1832, 98.

the history of the art."⁶⁹ Presenting French Baroque music as inferior to its Italian counterpart was old hat; what was new, and highly influential, was to conceptualize the problem in terms of imperfection, transition, and perfection. Where Choron had written subjectively of vitality and decadence in 1810, Fétis's appeals to teleology gave a similar judgement the air of scholarly legitimacy. Italian and Italian-inspired German opera was not better because it conformed more to Fétis's taste, but because he, as an historian of music, said it dated from a period of perfection.

We might perhaps expect Fétis, as a francophone Belgian who had in 1829 published a prize-winning, nationalist-inspired *mémoire* on the Franco-Flemish school, to celebrate the latter's achievements in his *concerts historiques*.⁷⁰ But he did not. Characteristically, when it came to the sacred music, his reasons had to do with style, not context. The Comtian element of his philosophy of music, which emphasized artistic "progress," situated harmonically "complete" music at around 1580 to 1600 and downgraded all that went before. In the lecture for his concert of sixteenth-century music (16 December 1832), Fétis stated that he had taken care to choose the finest and most beautiful available examples of each genre. Yet his audience was treated to the following introduction to the Kyrie from a Josquin "L'homme armé" Mass:

> This piece is by Josquin Desprez, the greatest artist of his century
> and the master of all the musicians who became distinguished later.
> You will not like this piece very much, because it consists almost entirely of mechanical working-out and because its harmonic practice is
> too remote from what you are used to hearing. Nevertheless, if you
> are minded to consider that it was composed nearly 350 years ago,
> you will admit that it is not devoid of merit. I thought I should offer it
> to you as a point of departure and comparison.⁷¹

---

69. "des monumens d'une des époques de transition les plus remarquables de l'histoire de l'art." *RM* 6/13: 28 April 1832, 99.

70. Fétis, *Quels ont été les mérites*. The *mémoire* was written in response to a competition question set by the Kingdom of the Netherlands' Institut des Sciences, de Littérature et des Beaux-Arts, on the Netherlandish contribution to music from 1300 to 1600. Raphael Georg Kiesewetter (1773–1850) won the gold medal; Fétis the silver. In a striking example of the slippage between Flemish and French that was to characterize discussion of these composers in France and Belgium throughout the century (see chapter 5), both essays discussed the composers whom Choron featured in his history of the French school. For a discussion of the tensions between the models of Auguste Comte and Victor Cousin in Fétis's philosophy of music history, see my *Music Criticism*, 33–45.

71. "Ce morceau est de Josquin Desprès, le plus grand artiste de son siècle et le maître de tous les musiciens qui se distinguaient par la suite. Vous aurez peu de penchant pour ce morceau, parce qu'il ne repose guère

Presenting the work of the greatest artist of his century is thus reduced to the historian's reluctant duty. For Fétis, the Josquin is not music (it is, rather, "pre-music" because its mechanistic construction precludes, in Fétis's terms, the tonal expressivity fundamental to music), but a primitive historical specimen that must be presented at this *concert historique* in order to illustrate the improvement that followed it. And although Fétis was considerably more generous toward secular music of a similar period, and toward late sixteenth-century Italian sacred music, all such repertory—even Palestrina—fell into the incomplete category of modal, *unitonique*, works.

Fétis did not, therefore, consider such pieces as a potential part of the living repertory, in whatever ritual context. And it is this attitude, together with its implications, that distinguishes him most strongly from Choron, with whom he otherwise had much in common. Both men were involved with influential biographical dictionaries of musicians; both were interested in music history; both taught at state-run music schools; both organized concerts dominated by early vocal and choral music. Choron seems to have ignored Fétis altogether in his papers and publications; Fetis, by contrast, heaped praise on Choron's performances but failed to acknowledge them as a precedent when he began his own *concerts historiques*. In addition, the timing of his venture—beginning when Choron was crippled by Louis-Philippe's budget cuts and unable to provide a full concert season—suggests opportunism. Given the impact of Choron's work, it is easy to see the temptation.

Choron: Democratization and the Living Museum

Narrow-minded but eclectic, divisive but engendering fierce loyalty, Choron was a man with a mission in Restoration Paris. Equally antipathetic to modern opera (which perhaps explains his lack of success as *régisseur* at the Opéra in 1815–17) and to instrumental music, he spent his life championing his own musical canon: essentially the sacred and vocal chamber works of the sixteenth-, seventeenth- and early eighteenth-century Italian schools, stretching

---

que sur un travail mécanique et parce que sa modulation est trop étrangère aux habitudes de votre oreille; toutefois, si vous voulez vous souvenir qu'il y a près de trois cent cinquante ans qu'il a été fait, vous avouerez qu'il n'est pas dépourvu de mérite. C'est comme un point de départ et de comparaison que j'ai cru devoir vous l'offrir." *RM* 22 December 1832, 374.

forward to Handel oratorio and extending outward to Janequin. With obsessive determination he sought to revolutionize music education, not just in Paris, but throughout France. His career flourished under Napoléon and the Bourbons; only with the advent of the July Monarchy did his previous affiliations mark him out for extinction.

During its years of greatest success, once it had its own concert hall (built in 1826), Choron's choir school presented an average of ten concerts per academic year from 1826/27 to 1830/31, climaxing at the 1829/30 season, which featured fourteen concerts.[72] Patronized by Bourbon royalty and nobility, by musicians (Cherubini and Rossini are known to have attended), and by Romantic poets and novelists including Hugo and Lamennais, they quickly became such a popular society event that on occasion Choron had to place benches in his school courtyard to accommodate the overflow.[73] Even in 1834, when Choron was nearly bankrupt and the school too small to do the really popular works such as *Messiah*, Joseph d'Ortigue reported that at one concert one hundred people who could not fit into the hall or the gallery ended up crowding onto the stage with the choir.[74] The legacy of Choron's 56 known performances included concert societies and schools; his reputation was kept alive through poems (doggerel and otherwise), encomia, and even a novel.[75]

Fueled by intense rivalry with a Conservatoire whose standard of singing teaching was at a particularly low ebb, Choron's concerts symbolized a different, and highly effective attitude towards musical training. But they also put the spotlight on a portion of the choral repertory unknown to Parisian concertgoers at the time: the Sistine chapel repertory of Palestrina and Allegri (the *Miserere* in a stripped-down version derived from Burney); the choral music of Handel (*Messiah*, *Alexander's Feast*, *Judas Maccabaeus*, *Athalia*, and *Samson*—often complete or in Parts, and sung in Latin or Italian translation); Marcello's *Salmi* and the vocal chamber music of Clari; and two secular chansons by Janequin. Choron did not altogether neglect more modern music, by Mozart, Haydn, Graun, Neukomm, Schneider, and Cherubini—his museum vision was driven by a desire to conserve classics of all ages. He was also open enough to modern music to commission a piece for mixed voices and organ from

---

72. Figures gleaned from the listings in Boettcher, *Les exercices publics d'Alexandre Choron*, 121–33. The year 1832 saw no concerts, possibly because of the Paris cholera outbreak, but doubtless also because Choron could not afford to pay the extra singers he had engaged in order to bring his choir for the 1830–31 season up to 1829–30 levels; concerts thereafter were sporadic.

73. *Figaro* 24 March 1827, cited in Boettcher, *Les exercices publics d'Alexandre Choron*, 31.

74. D'Ortigue, *La musique à l'église*, 104. The article was originally published in *La quotidienne* in May 1834.

75. See Albert de Calvimont's *Au mois de mai* (1835), in which Choron's concerts appear as an emblem of the sublime in the midst of cheap modern music (cited in Simms, *Alexandre Choron*, 157).

Berlioz.[76] Nevertheless, his focus, which in turn caught the imagination of his most influential reviewers, was the completely new genre of music that he programmed: the early music.[77]

His program planning was equally novel and, in its use of balance, symmetry, and pacing, entirely out of line with the traditional miscellanies music lovers heard elsewhere. In particular, he managed audience attention spans in ways uncommon until the 1890s, for instance by placing Janequin chansons between the Parts of a Handel oratorio, designating them *intermèdes* but nevertheless foregrounding them as the pivot of a programme based on contrast through symmetry. Such attention to presentational matters went unnoticed by reviewers but may have underpinned their largely warm reactions to the music itself. In Fétis and Porro at the *Revue musicale*, and Castil-Blaze at the *Journal des débats*, Choron found more general champions for his performances of Handel, Palestrina, and Allegri. Critics for *Le Figaro*, *La quotidienne* (the faithful D'Ortigue), and *La Pandore* also followed Choron's concerts closely. Here, Handel's music (with the exception of *Judas Maccabaeus*, which was regarded as monotonous) received an equally enthusiastic welcome; but it was also here that reviewers' demands for novelty reached their peak.[78] In contrast to the *concerts spirituels*, there was no ritual context in which the familiar might be eagerly anticipated; curiosity value thus militated against the element of repetition implicit in a concert series allied to a museum culture.

It is ironic, given that Choron's concerts inspired the creation of several musical societies specializing in *a cappella* Sistine Chapel repertory, that it was Handel, and not Palestrina, whose music dominated these *exercices*. More than that, it was a scaled-down Handel, with only a keyboard and bass accompaniment (the school had no orchestra). Perhaps it was therefore to capitalize on a popular repertory, while giving it back its full orchestral color, that the Opéra (in *concerts spirituels*) and the Conservatoire tried to emulate Choron by programming Handel extracts. Both, however, failed in the attempt. In 1827 the

---

76. The commission was apparently half finished by the end of 1828, but, if the piece was ever completed, it is now lost. Berlioz hoped it would be a passport to closer contact with the Saint-Germain elites who frequented Choron's concerts. See Hector Berlioz, *Correspondance générale*, vol. 1, ed. Pierre Citron (Paris: Flammarion, 1972), 220 (letter 106).

77. "genre de musique complètement neuf." Choron's early music repertory, as described by one of his more trustworthy biographers (Gautier, *Eloge d'Alexandre Choron*, 60). The oxymoron of the novelty of early musics—especially those dating from before c.1580—was a commonplace of 1830s and '40s criticism.

78. Boettcher astutely observes that Choron was under constant critical pressure to provide variety, and that at least one critic (for *La Pandore*) never reviewed the same piece twice (Boettcher, *Les exercices publics d'Alexandre Choron*, 106 and 87). In general, critical responses to Choron's *exercices* indicate that his concerts were regarded not as student demonstrations, but as events which one attended for pleasure.

Opéra announced that it would present those works that had made the most impact at Choron's school[79]; the following year it advertized selections from *Messiah* but had to abandon them, and its replacement—a performance of Marcello's psalm setting "I cieli immensi narrano" in an arrangement with trumpets and cymbals—received nothing but condemnation from none other than Fétis.[80] When François Habeneck's Société des Concerts du Conservatoire programmed its first ever piece of early music (29 March 1829), the result was a disastrous rendition of the Hallelujah chorus that was to remain a touchstone of the Conservatoire's choral incompetence for the rest of Choron's life. At every available opportunity he wrote gleefully of Habeneck's singers staggering in heterophonic disarray towards the closing double bar. Fétis, hearing the same movement in England later the same year, said the Conservatoire had disfigured it.[81] Doubtless chastened, Habeneck touched no Handel for a decade.

Others took up the challenge. In 1837 Philippe Musard, the conductor and composer of fashionable *galops* and *contredanses*, did something unprecedented. He tried, via Handel, to effect a change in the musical taste of his promenading audience of shop attendants, clerks, and upper-class refugees from high-class concerts.[82] A programme consisting of excerpts from *Alexander's Feast* and *Messiah*, together with Palestrina's madrigal "Alla riva del Tebro" (a Choron favorite) awaited those who went to his *concert spirituel*, which was previewed in the press as a popularizing event organized for Musard's "profane crowd" in emulation of the great festivals of London, York, and Manchester. It was to feature a massive 150 singers.[83] According to François Benoist, the Conservatoire's professor of organ-playing, the experiment was not an instant success. Nevertheless, in characterizing the music as "simple, but strongly rhythmic," he touched on the central stylistic aspect that was to inspire musicians of the late 1860s and early 1870s to advocate the composer's works as vehicles for massed community singing.[84] Handel revivalism in the July Monarchy, however, remained a limited and resolutely elite affair. The initiatives of Edouard Rodrigues, who published the first versions and anthologies of Handel oratorio in French in the late 1830s and 1840s, were mostly private,

---

79. *RM* (no. 8) April 1827, 206.
80. *RM* April 1828, 251–53.
81. *RM* [June] 1829, 461.
82. Musard's audience is thus characterized in Weber's *Music and the Middle Class*, 109–10.
83. "vulgaire profane." *Revue et gazette musicale* (henceforth *RGM*) 4/12: 19 March 1837, 99 (unsigned news item). The nature of choral festivals in England and Germany, and Handel's central place in them, would have been well known to readers of the major music journals, whose news columns routinely covered them.
84. "simple, bien que fortement rhythmique." *RGM* 4/13: 26 March 1837, 105.

with performances taking place at his Paris residence.⁸⁵ And while the Société des Concerts under Habeneck eventually revisited this repertory, it was mostly to perform individual numbers only, among which the triumphal march from *Judas Maccabaeus*, translated as "Chantons victoire," became ubiquitous.

The question of "non-elites," however, was an important one which Choron had himself raised. His "museum" repertory was, in fact, a model, living, repertory that he wished to see adopted nationwide for the good of the French citizenry. Nothing less than the national revitalization of singing, both in and outside church, would do. Democracy began at home: although his audience appears to have included much of *le tout Paris*, his one-hundred-strong choir consisted not just of his boarding students (a maximum of 24), but also of the pupils from Paris's poor schools whom he taught alongside them. Instinct told Fétis that persons of low social standing would be unable to understand music that was not of their time; in 1833 he was to lament their infiltration into the otherwise initiated audiences of his *concerts historiques*.⁸⁶ He was genuinely surprised by Choron's results.

> The success M. Choron has achieved with his teaching system should attract government attention all the more because this learned musician has brought it about with children taken indiscriminately from among a population that is poor and, unfortunately, ill-suited to music and to the arts in general. . . . Just think, à propos of this, what might happen if this teaching system were applied to high-class pupils.⁸⁷

Much as Choron must have been grateful for Fétis's continued support, the terms of that support would have been alien to him. For he was, in modern terms, "class-blind," and his celebrated tours of regional France in search of singing voices ripe for training resulted—not always successfully—in the presence of former farm laborers among the singers of the Opéra chorus.⁸⁸ It was

---

85. We know, however, of one series of public concerts: three charity performances of Handel's *Judas Maccabaeus* and Mendelssohn's *St Paul* at the Salle Herz in March and April 1847.

86. See his remarks about [raucous] undesirables at the Salle Ventadour concert of 2 April 1833 (*RM* 6 April 1833, 80). Fétis had been forbidden to use the Conservatoire hall, where he was confident no such kinds of person would have turned up.

87. "Le succès obtenu par M. Choron dans son système d'enseignement doit autant plus fixer l'attention du gouvernement que le savant musicien à opérer sur les enfans pris sans choix dans une population pauvre et, malheureusement, mal disposée pour la musique et pour les arts en général. . . . Qu'on juge d'après cela de ce qui pourrait arriver si le système d'enseignement dont il s'agit était appliqué à des sujets d'élite." *RM* 3 November 1832, 319.

88. So long as they could be taught by rote, Choron's peasant tenors from the Midi proved a spectacular success with both Spontini and Persuis at the Opéra, not least because they could reach a "*ré* de poitrine." By

thus logical for contemporaries to compare Choron's teaching methods not only with those practised at the Conservatoire, but also with those of the great popular educators of Louis-Philippe's France: Bocquillon Wilhem, the founder of the French working men's *orphéon* movement, and Joseph Mainzer, the German educationalist who passed through France before settling in Britain. For Berlioz, whose frequent references to the value of Choron's work kept his name alive long after his death, and whose project of 1836 for the Gymnase-Musical included a singing school explicitly modeled on the same principles, hope for the continuation of Choron's work lay with these two men. But after a promising concert by Mainzer's Association Polytechnique in 1836, a ragged performance of mostly operatic music in 1838 dashed his hopes: "farewell, great Gluck choruses; farewell Lesueur Masses, Marcello psalms, Handel oratorios, Palestrina madrigals .... Last Sunday's concert offered cruel proof of the vanity of this entire, long-cherished, hope."[89]

A later attempt to introduce *orphéon* singers to such music exposed different problems that were to become a major obstacle to the reception of Palestrina specifically: in 1843 a choir of seven hundred gathered in Notre-Dame to sing a Christmas Mass adapted to music by Palestrina, Marcello, and others. While the Marcello "Offertory" was sung effectively, the Palestrina "O salutaris" was not, and the *Revue et Gazette*'s critic Maurice Bourges explained why. Music of this time and style, he wrote, should not be put into the hands of *orphéon* singers because it

> invariably goes against the grain of their experience and their mode of hearing. Besides, the performance of this kind of music is bearable only when it is sung by fine voices, by consummate musicians, and above all to an audience of interested lovers of the antique. It will do nothing for the musical civilization of the masses.[90]

Bourges was prophetic. After Choron's death nobody was able to continue his work in the class-blind manner in which he had pursued it. If Handel became

---

contrast, his basses (from Picardie) learnt quickly, but lacked musical talent. See Fétis's descriptions in *RM* October 1829, 266–68.

89. "adieu, les grands choeurs de Gluck; adieu, les messes de Lesueur, les psaumes de Marcello, les oratorios de Handel, les madrigaux de Palestrina .... Le concert de dimanche dernier a démontré d'une façon vraiment cruelle la vanité de tout cet espoir longtemps caressé." *RGM* 5/18: 6 May 1838, 186.

90. "contrarient sans cesse en eux les habitudes et les penchants de l'oreille. L'exécution de ce genre de style n'est d'ailleurs supportable que lorsqu'elle est confiée à de fort belles voix, à des musiciens consommés, et surtout devant un auditoire de curieux antiquaires. La civilisation musicale des masses n'en peut tirer aucun profit." *RGM* 10/1: 1 January 1843, 6.

the preserve of elites (the Société des Enfants d'Apollon and the private meetings *chez* Edouard Rodrigues), the music of Palestrina became even more solidly typecast as a music of the high aristocracy. Indeed, it was through a regular attender of Choron's concerts, the son of Napoléon's Maréchal Ney, and self-styled "prince de la Moskova," that the music of Palestrina regularly appeared on the concert stage once more—this time at the Salle Herz.

La Société des Concerts de Musique Vocale Religieuse et Classique (1843–46)

In his recent monograph on the prince de la Moskova's choral society, Rémy Campos writes that one of his aims is to recover some of the strangeness of the society's activities in relation to the "norms" of musical life that surrounded it.[91] In 1843 it must indeed have been strange to witness a choir of around 80 aristocrats, most of them women (aristocratic men were harder to recruit) singing music by Palestrina, Haydn, Handel, Lassus, Clari, Marcello, and Victoria in a hall where these high-born performers habitually attended virtuoso and chamber music concerts.

Anyone coming across documents relating to the foundation of the society for the first time will be struck by the glittering array of aristocratic "dames patronesses"—Legitimist or Orléanist members of the faubourg Saint-Germain community—who at once gave the society its public glamor and acted as genteel doorkeepers. They either vetted or personally recommended every one of the society's members.[92] Yet from its director's point of view the Society was not just about class: it was emblematic of an Ultramontane philosophy of liturgical regeneration. Along with Louis Niedermeyer and Henri [Heinrich] Panofka, the prince was a member of the St Cecilia Society of Rome and in 1843 attempted (not very successfully) to co-opt the most prominent members of his aristocratic membership to the cause of "regenerating" Catholic church music. Across Europe the recipe was now becoming standard: rejection of contemporary musical traditions (which included a great deal of opera-based music) in favor of a return to Palestrina and the *stile antico*.[93] Altogether, Moskova negotiated a careful and subtly calculated path. He presented his society to

---

91. Campos, *La Renaissance introuvable?*, 21. For detail on Moskova, see also Di Grazia, *Concert Societies*, 184–201.

92. Campos, *La Renaissance introuvable?*, 62–63 and 87.

93. Campos, *La Renaissance introuvable?*, 33. On the St Cecilia Society of Rome, headed by Giuseppe Baini during this period, see Giazotto, "La congrégation de Sainte-Cécile," 9–13.

potential members as a secular organization dedicated to the artistic renewal of "la musique classique" (the word "religieuse" did not appear as part of the society's title on the prospectus cover), claiming Choron's school as his natural antecedent. But, at least at the outset, he also tried to integrate the Society within a network of Catholic musical societies under the aegis of the Roman Cecilian movement. The concerts themselves provided a graphic illustration of the society's split personality. Moskova set aside audience seats in the Salle Herz for interested clergy ripe for conversion to the Ultramontane musical cause. The abbé Stéphen Morelot even wrote of "a kind of privilege of entry" in this respect.[94]

Although the success of the Moskova society was largely dependent on its founder's charisma and fortune, the conducting prince was not a one-man show in the manner of Choron. He delegated responsibilities: to Bottée de Toulmon (for historical matters), to Louis Dietsch (his chorusmaster), and to Niedermeyer and then Jean-Baptiste Weckerlin (his deputies). Support from outside was widespread: the abbé Morelot, the pianist and harpsichordist Amédée Méreaux, De Lafage (a disciple of Baini and Choron), the antiquarian Laurens, and the painter Etienne Delécluze (a biographer of Palestrina), all championed his work.[95] A set of programmes for the society's concerts is to be found among the papers of the young Weckerlin, the future founder of a revived Société Sainte-Cécile in 1865 and Librarian at the Conservatoire; Paul Scudo (another Choron student) followed the concerts assiduously; and Danjou, an Ultramontane of a more extreme (and populist) hue than Moskova, watched his progress with guarded optimism. Most important of all, the society had a faithful insider critic, Adolphe Adam, who wrote long and enthusiastic reviews in Léon and Marie Escudier's *La France musicale*—a journal not known for its sympathy toward early music, but dedicated to that of Italy.

Moskova's sung repertory bore strong resemblances to that of Choron. There is no documentary evidence to confirm that he shared Choron's dim view of the French *grand motet* tradition; but he behaved as though he did, ignoring it in favor of Italianate sacred music of the sixteenth to eighteenth centuries. He performed mostly secular Franco-Flemish music, including Lassus, Arcadelt, and Janequin (whose music was arguably the best loved in the society's entire repertory),[96] and adaptations of Machaut and Adam de la

---

94. "une sorte de privilége d'admission." "S. M." [abbé Stéphen Morelot], in Félix Danjou's *Revue de la musique religieuse, populaire, classique* (henceforth *RMRPC*), 1 (1845), 161.

95. Campos, *La Renaissance introuvable?*, 42.

96. *La France* musicale (henceforth *FM*) 8/17: 27 April 1845, 131. In *FM* 9/15: 12 April 1846, Adam noted that the audience listened inattentively to a Palestrina Sanctus because everyone was waiting for the Janequin *Chant des oiseaux* (114).

Halle.⁹⁷ On the rare occasions that Lully was sung, it was performed by a guest soloist who brought it in the manner of a "suitcase aria"; the society's performance of Rameau's "Dans ce doux asile" from *Castor et Pollux* was also exceptional, and probably a concession to its arranger for full choir—the faithful Adam.

In this Ultramontane environment, then, early French music thrived, but according to familiar ideological patterns. Moskova was no nationalist; but it had been almost impossible to perform Janequin's *La bataille* since its introduction by Choron without mention of its nationalist connotations. Accordingly, when Moskova programmed battle pieces by Andrea Gabrieli and Janequin together, Adam moved into nationalist mode, counting Gabrieli as Italian (historians of the period tended rather to count him as "honorary Franco-Flemish") and accusing him of plagiarizing his French predecessor.⁹⁸ Moreover, although Adam did not mention it, the fact that the *Bataille*, and indeed all the French music performed at the society's thirteenth concert (23 April 1845) was secular, was key to its success. Sacred music of the same vintage was unacceptable. In March 1845 he suggested the inverse experiment: that the society might sing some pre-Palestrinian sacred music—even the most extravagant examples—in order "to heighten Palestrina's glory and to illustrate just how complete his reform was."⁹⁹ This was a rather Fétisian idea, and in a later review Adam even used the Fétisian word "spécimen" to denote the scientific value of such pieces. But in May he mused that perhaps there had been noble dissent at the idea of singing such ungrateful music. Even the finest results from "cruel" rehearsal of "one of those mad works" which mixed ribald secular song and plainsong would be "hardly flattering" to the choir's members (he mentioned, indirectly, the ladies).¹⁰⁰ By contrast, Arcadelt's "Il bianco e dolce cigno" and the pavane "Belle qui tiens ma vie" showed him how vital music was when there was no counterpoint to stifle its dance rhythms:

---

97. Moskova could, for instance, have transcribed any number of Lalande motets from the 18-volume set published by Boivin in 1729, or the "quelques vieux motets" (the disparagement comes from Nicolas Roze, librarian from 1807 to 1819) contained within the royal collections that were deposited triumphantly at the Conservatoire Library in 1812. See Massip, "La bibliothèque du Conservatoire," 124.

98. *FM* 8/23: 8 June 1845, 179, given in Campos, *La Renaissance introuvable?*, 94.

99. "on pourra choisir les plus raisonnables; mais il serait peut-être bon de ne pas entièrement repousser l'exhibition des plus extravagantes, ne fût-ce pour rehausser la gloire de Palestrina, nous montrer combien fut complète la réforme qu'il opéra. . . ." *FM* 8/10: 9 March 1845, 74.

100. "Il est cruel, en effet de travailler avec un soin et une persévérance inouïs des parties hérissées de difficultés, pour arriver à un résultat assez peu flatteur"; "une de ces folles compositions où une chanson populaire se promenait avec des allures bourgeoises et même ses paroles souvent plus qu'égrillardes, à travers le grave plain-chant de l'Eglise." *FM* 8/20: 18 May 1845, 153, given in Campos, *La Renaissance introuvable?*, 117.

I would willingly assign the pavane "Belle qui tiens ma vie" a very ancient origin, from well before the period when the contrapuntal and figured style came to prevail. In effect, from the moment when composers gave themselves themes to treat in imitation . . . , there necessarily resulted from such organization a rather ungainly character . . . whose influence on rhythm, the essential element of all popular music, was extremely destructive.[101]

Prophetically, as we shall see, Adam highlighted merits in the early French chanson and dance traditions which he and others (notably Fétis) found sadly lacking in the historically glorious corpus of Franco-Flemish sacred music of the same era. The nature of those merits had been outlined by Fétis in his *concert historique* lecture of 16 December 1832, where he opined that, in its emphasis on melodic line, chamber music of the same period seemed "to have had no other goal than to relax the mind from the fatigues of counterpoint through its free production of melody."[102] Using a much-quoted phrase, he declared the French "more songwriters than musicians," lauding the "gracious melody" of a French *villanelle* and the "vivacious, almost mocking" tone of an unidentified Janequin chanson.[103] The effects of such opinions were far-reaching, and not restricted to early music. A suspicion of counterpoint as antiexpressive, scholastic, and (pejoratively) virtuosic characterizes much French critical writing throughout the century and dates back to Rousseau's *Lettre sur la musique française* of 1753; it numbered composers as diverse as Josquin, Bach, Mozart, Cherubini, Mendelssohn, Saint-Saëns, and Brahms among its victims. The fulminations of Berlioz (including the *Damnation of Faust* funeral "Amen") have received scholarly attention; beyond that, the historiography of such suspicion has yet to be written.[104]

What was the legacy, as opposed to the immediate impact, of Moskova's short-lived society? Like that of Choron's *exercices*, it was fundamentally

---

101. "Nous assignerions volontiers à la pavane *Belle qui tiens ma vie* une origine fort ancienne et de beaucoup antérieure à l'époque où le style du contre-point et de la figure vinrent à prévaloir. En effet, du moment où les compositeurs se proposèrent des thèmes à traiter en imitation . . . , il devait résulter de cet agencement un caractère un peu boiteux . . . dont l'influence sur le rhythme, élément essentiel de toute musique populaire, fut éminemment destructive." *FM* 8/17: 27 April 1845, 131, given in Campos, *La Renaissance introuvable?*, 189–90. Campos misses the wider significance of this comment, interpreting it as simply an example of dry antiquarianism on Adam's part.

102. "la musique de chambre composée dans le même temps semble n'avoir eu pour but que de délasser l'esprit des fatigues du contre-point par une facile production de la cantilène." *RM* 6/48: 29 December 1832, 377.

103. "On a dit que les Français ont toujours été plus chansonniers que musiciens"; "élégance gracieuse" (villanelle); "l'esprit sémillant et presque goguenard" (Janequin). *RM* 6/48: 29 December 1832, 378.

104. On Berlioz, see Hirschberg, "Berlioz and the Fugue."

Palestrinian, a factor reflected in later concert reviews and in the invocation of Moskova's name as a byword for regenerative liturgical influence in the literature of its successor societies. For although in the 1830s enthusiasts such as D'Ortigue had noted with pleasure that Danjou and Dietsch regularly performed Counter-Reformation music at Saint-Eustache, where they were organist and *maître de chapelle* respectively,[105] the amount of such activity in Paris overall was paltry, and church services were not (yet) good shop windows for the repertory. Similarly, the published collection of editions which Moskova prepared (probably with Niedermeyer and Dietsch's help), and which was used regularly by the society's members, reached well beyond the confines of Paris in the form of individual fascicules used by at least two musical constituencies: choral and philharmonic societies (Niort, Rouen) and conservatoires (Geneva).[106] In Paris itself, Moskova's society became a model. Where, in 1843, it was unheard of for a group of leisured amateurs to sing regularly in public, let alone to hire a concert hall and put on a full season of concerts, in the second half of the century such societies became commonplace, contributing significantly to the variety of Parisian concert life. And while they did not all specialize in early music, several strands of the repertories established by Choron, Fétis, and Moskova persisted for the rest of the century.

By the 1840s, the staples of the *concert spirituel* had been eclipsed by a new, and predominantly older, Italianate sacred repertory presented throughout the concert season in secular surroundings: Allegri's *Miserere*; Victoria's responsory "O vos omnes," and the dubious "O Jesu dulcis"; Ingegneri's Holy Week responsories (thought to be Palestrina, and therefore prized all the more); Palestrina's *Missa Ad fugam* and the Pope Marcellus Mass, the *Requiem* and the *Stabat mater*; Janequin's *Bataille*; a small selection of Lassus chansons, especially "Fuyons tous d'amour le jeu" and "Margot, labourez les vignes" (both known as "Les vendanges"), and extracts from the *Penitential Psalms*; Volckmar Leisring's Easter hymn "O filii, o filiae" (a Société des Concerts staple); the anonymous "Alla beata Trinita" (which Fétis had harmonized for his *concerts historiques*, and which he was none too pleased to see turn up without his permission on the Société des Concerts' programmes); Handel's "Chantons victoire"

---

105. D'Ortigue, *La musique à l'église*, 128. The original article was published in *La quotidienne*, June 1838.

106. Campos mentions the Geneva and Niort examples in *La Renaissance introuvable?*, 107–108. Extracts from Moskova's collection are also among the nineteenth-century materials at the Bibliothèque Musicale de Rouen, which include the library of the Société Académique de Musique Sacrée (1861–72), directed in Paris by Charles Vervoitte before his return to Rouen around 1872, and used thereafter by the local Société Philharmonique. The 11-volume collection was entitled *Collection de musique vocale religieuse et classique*. For a summary contents list, see Campos, *La Renaissance introuvable?*, 246–53; for a more detailed listing of the Palestrinian repertory, and a comparison of the editions of Choron and Moskova, see my "Palestrina et la musique dite "palestrinienne", 184–85.

["See, see, the conqu'ring hero comes"] and the Hallelujah chorus; Marcello's *Salmi*, especially a truncated no. 18 "I cieli immensi narrano"; the opening of J. S. Bach's "Jesu meine Freude" adapted as a "Tantum ergo"; finally, the spectacularly successful "Pietà, Signore." These were the works on which a repertory of early vocal and choral music was built in the second half of the century in Paris.

Regional Perspectives

Tempting as it is to see Moskova's society as a model not only for Paris but also for the whole of France, it would be wrong to do so. The regions did not always take their cue from the capital; sometimes they rebelled, or provided precedents.[107] Alsace, fully incorporated into France in 1798, pursued musical traditions more akin to those across the Rhine; the Midi was in many ways another country, proud of its own composers irrespective of the dictates of Parisian musical fashion; the musical culture of the Protestant belt in the mid-west was different again. Nevertheless, perceptions of regional ignorance abounded, sometimes fueled from within.

The memoirs of the Béziers composer Alexandre Guibal du Rivage are undated but describe regional music of the pre-1830 period. Their tale is of a France whose regions are hopelessly backward, parochial, and dominated by musical incompetents who prefer to write for the church than the theatre because they are thereby insulated from public expressions of hostility towards their efforts.[108] An entertaining polemic with, no doubt, a large grain of truth, the document is revealing for what it tells us about traditionalism in this part of regional France. Guibal du Rivage's central complaints are that provincial musicians are uncomprehending of the progress represented by the Paris Conservatoire and actively resist its innovations by clinging to outdated and local repertories. The "new school" of composition, which he never defines, is unknown to them: hapless local composers who have reached only as far as Campra and Mondonville nevertheless "believe they are [a new] Marcello or Pergolesi."[109] This

---

107. Beethoven's "Pastoral" was, for instance, heard in Douai in 1823, six years before its Paris premiere under Habeneck (see Gosselin, *L'âge d'or*, 83).

108. For the memoir, entitled "La musique en province ou recherches philologiques touchant les défauts et les ridicules de la musique et des musiciens de la province," see Bèges and Bèges (Eds.), *Alexandre Guibal du Rivage*, 29ff. Translated extracts, with commentary, are given in Mongrédien, *French Music*, 195, 254, 257. Internal evidence indicates that the memoir dates from 1820 at the earliest.

109. "Ils se croient des Marcello ou des Pergolèse." Bèges and Bèges (Eds.), *Alexandre Guibal du Rivage*, 56.

is a revealing gold standard for someone who otherwise flaunts his "modern" principles, because here we have yet another proponent of the pro-Italian and anti-French philosophy that dominated debate in Paris. For Guibal, "backward" is not defined chronologically but stylistically; and it helps reiterate the sense of the limited but tenacious survival of pre-1760 Italian music into the nineteenth century.

Nevertheless, in his own general area of the Midi he would indeed have found (and doubtless been depressed by) evidence of the survival of French eighteenth-century traditions long abandoned in Paris. Lalande's sacred music is a case in point. Castil-Blaze was, as far as I can tell, the only Paris writer of the period who actively defended the music of Lalande, printing a biography in the *Journal des débats* and recommending that Choron investigate his music (Choron ignored him).[110] His history of the royal chapel, published just two years after the institution was disbanded by Louis-Philippe, contained a version of that defence, in which Castil-Blaze had referred to Lalande as "the only master of our old school who can legitimately be compared to foreign composers of the same period"[111] and pointed to the "Dixit Dominus" and the "Te Deum" as the only current survivors among his church works. They were still sung liturgically in the provinces but were threatened with obsolescence as the amateurs who sang them became too aged to continue.[112] How widely his music was performed, whether liturgically or in secular contexts, in the provinces in the first half of the century, has yet to be clarified.

However, Lalande's music formed the centrepiece of the annual patronal festival at the Cathedral of Saint-Siffrein in Carpentras. The festival, preceded by a fair, took place on 26/27 November each year, and drew crowds from as far as Avignon, Aix, and even Marseille. The traditional choral Vespers service of 27 November, which opened with Lalande's "Dixit Dominus" of 1729, was suspended during and after the Revolution, but reinstated around 1803 to 1804;[113] it continued until 1838, although the Lalande itself was dropped some time after 1824.[114] The Carpentras Vespers service, described by the local antiquarian Laurens as a kind of *son et lumière* event replete with ritual significance, began as the late November sunset illuminated the cathedral at the start of

---

110. *Journal des débats* (henceforth *JD*) 1 June and 25 July 1827, n.p.

111. "le seul maître de notre ancienne école qui puisse entrer en comparaison avec les musiciens étrangers de la même époque." *JD* 1 June 1827, n.p.

112. *JD* 25 July 1827, n.p. Cf. his *Chapelle-musique*, 126–27.

113. See Dubled, "Le fonds musical," 2.

114. See Caillet, *Les vêpres de Saint-Siffrein*, who gives 1825 as the approximate date when the Lalande was dropped (49); J.-J.-B. Laurens gives 1831, *Almanach du Comtat* (1882), 27.

the Lalande (darkening to dusk by its close) and climaxed with the installation of a pyramidal candelabra of one thousand candles suspended from the ceiling above the nave.[115] Writing against the grain of received opinion (but consonant with the views of the Avignonnais Castil-Blaze), Laurens compared the majestic nature of Lalande's "Dixit" to that of Handel's greatest oratorios: *Messiah, Judas,* and *Israel*. His view was promptly countered by his editor Danjou, who in a footnote sided with the Fétisian view and accused Laurens of nostalgic misjudgement: "Lalande and Couperin," he wrote, "were undoubtedly great masters; but they are not, for all that, comparable to the artists who illuminated the German and Italian schools."[116] Yet despite his unfashionable love of music of the French Baroque (Danjou mentions Couperin because it was Laurens who anonymously edited the Launer Couperin edition of 1841), Laurens was no nationalistic monomaniac. He and Fétis shared an early enthusiasm for J. S. Bach, whose music Laurens even planned to edit in its entirety until he realized how complicated the source work would be; and his library was eclectic in the extreme, even including Purcell and the English madrigalists and a sizeable amount of instrumental chamber music, from viol consorts to *concerti grossi*. Nevertheless, he and the regional tradition he tried so hard to uphold fitted precisely into the Guibal du Rivage category of "backward" Francophile culture in what we would now term *la France profonde*. And while his activity was later to be hailed as a prophetic example of decentralization,[117] in the 1820s and 1830s it could only be perceived as regressive.

Fragmented though it is, much of the information about regional performances of early music that reached press sources concerns the liturgical music used for major religious festivals. This may be because so little survived from the operatic repertory (a predictable exception is a run of Rousseau's *Devin du village* in Marseille, in 1818) and because the regional concert life of burgeoning Sociétés Philharmoniques, contrary to Guibal du Rivage's view, tended to feature newer music, including that brought by guest artists. But press sources reveal that a chorus from *Messiah* ("The glory of the Lord," sung in French)

---

115. *RMRPC* 3 (1847), 49–72. The discussion of Lalande is on pp. 56–58. For a good example of Laurens's emotional reminiscence of the Saint-Siffrein festival, his appropriation of Lalande as a regional icon, and his views on the regeneration of church music in France, see his open letter given in Henry Devillario, "Carpentras," *Conciliateur de Vaucluse*, 13 (no. 716): 13 December 1862, n.p.

116. "Lalande et Couperin . . . étaient assurément de grands maîtres; mais on ne saurait pour cela les comparer aux artistes qui ont illustré les écoles allemandes et italiennes." Danjou footnote in *RMRPC* 3 (1847), 58. Danjou was absolutely right about Laurens's nostalgia, which pervades his writings on musical life in Carpentras in the first decades of the century.

117. See E. Durand-Gréville's obituary, *L'artiste*, 61/1: January 1891, 47–68. Durand-Gréville was a close friend.

featured in a Société Philharmonique concert at Tours in 1840; in 1843 the Batta brothers visited Bordeaux and brought an arrangement of *La romanesca*, already celebrated in Paris through Baillot's chamber concerts; otherwise, little early music has come to the surface. Strasbourg, though, enjoyed a particularly rich and historically varied musical life. Handel's *Jephtha* was featured at town choral festivals during the 1830s; more important, because of its Cecilian connotations, Holy Week music at the Cathedral in 1841 included performances of a Tommaso Baj *Miserere* (probably the famous nine-part setting of 1713) on both Maundy Thursday and Good Friday.

From the 1840s, Rouen, too, proved to be a major centre for early music, and it would continue to be so at least until the late 1870s. Since the mid 1830s it had been home to the pianist Amédée Méreaux, who doubled as the town's most prominent music critic and wrote for the *Journal de Rouen* for several decades. Méreaux's background was crucial to his single most memorable contribution to Rouen's musical life. His father and grandfather were composers; his love of the French *clavecinistes*, whose works he would later edit, derived from his exploration of the family music collections. It was Méreaux who, in 1842 organized a series of *concerts historiques* in which he presented a chronological survey of vocal and instrumental music dating from the fifteenth century to the nineteenth. The first two concerts (6 and 13 March 1842), which took place at his home on the rue Fontenelle, reached as far as Haydn. Exceptionally well attended, they were enthusiastically written up in the *Journal de Rouen* by an anonymous author (probably not Méreaux);[118] the news also reached Paris via the *Revue et gazette musicale*. Whatever the difficulties of disentangling the network of journalistic nterest, the excitement generated by Méreaux's concerts cannot be denied. The concert of 6 March had to be repeated by popular demand, and was acclaimed by an even larger audience than had attended the first. Drawing on instrumental and vocal forces from Rouen's theatre, Méreaux's programme included items familiar to Parisians from Choron and Fétis's concerts. Janequin's *Les cris de Paris* and Palestrina's madrigal "Alla riva del Tebro," an extract from Marcello's "I cieli immensi narrano," an air from Lully's *Armide*, another from Handel's *Alexander's Feast*, and an extract from Pergolesi's *Stabat mater* were included, as were less familiar items such as Josquin's *Stabat mater*, which Choron had published but never performed, and vocal pieces by Lambert, Guedron, Mouton, and Goudimel. In addition,

---

118. On 6 March 1842, the day of the first concert, the *Journal de Rouen* printed extracts from an essay written by Méreaux to accompany his *concert historique*; the critic noted that time constraints had prevented the publication of the whole document, which had arrived only that morning.

Méreaux included two string pieces: *La romanesca* and Corelli's *La follia* variations (in an arrangement for violin and cello).

However, from the point of view of the history of historical concerts, most unusual of all was the high proportion of keyboard music, all played by Méreaux himself. In this respect his model may have been Ignaz Moscheles, whose London historical concerts had been reviewed by Fétis in the *Revue et gazette musicale* in 1840. Like Moscheles, Méreaux also appears to have played a harpsichord. The *Journal de Rouen*'s reviewer uses the word "clavecin" constantly; there is no mention of a piano either in Méreaux's programmes or in press sources. In this first concert, his choice was eclectic: Couperin and Rameau (individual *pièces*), Bach (a prelude and fugues) and Handel (a concerto and an *air varié*—probably the "Harmonious Blacksmith"). For the second programme, he played Scarlatti and C.P.E. Bach. This was the first significant body of harpsichord music, whether played on harpsichord or piano, known to have been presented to French audiences in the nineteenth century, and it was soon to bear fruit, not least through the work of Méreaux's star pupil—whom he referred to as holding "an honorable place as an interpreter of the clavecin repertory"—Charlotte de Malleville.[119]

In fact, the following years saw several pianists present Baroque keyboard repertory to Paris audiences. Charles-Valentin Alkan's early recitals of 1844 included works by Bach and Scarlatti; Sophie Bohrer astounded audiences the following year by playing Bach fugues from memory; Méreaux himself presented some of the music from his first Rouen *concert historique* at a charity concert at the Paris Conservatoire in May 1844; and in January and February 1848 Thérèse Wartel gave two performances (on the piano) of parts of Bach's harpsichord concerto BWV 1052 in D minor, the second of them by public demand, at concerts of the Société de Musique Classique directed by the violinist-conductor Théophile Tilmant at the Salle Herz.

Méreaux's *concerts historiques* were path-breaking in their propagation of Baroque keyboard music—a repertory that Méreaux promoted throughout his career. Similarly, they are important for their openness to other French musical traditions. For whereas parts of Méreaux's historical introductions bore a close resemblance to texts that might have been written by Choron or Fétis, other parts welcomed French music in a manner hitherto unknown in French writing on music. His introduction to the Josquin *Stabat mater*, which he described as a "composition touchante," bears comparison with Fétis's introduction to the same composer's music a decade earlier:

---

119. "une honorable place comme interprète de la musique clavecique." Bibliothèque Municipale de Rouen, Dossier 92N "Amédée Méreaux," notes on his *curriculum vitae*.

> Josquin Desprez ... was one of the greatest musicians of the end of the fifteenth century, and the one whose reputation shone most brilliantly. He was a pupil of Ockeghem, the famous Flemish composer. Despite the arid use of counterpoint in his works, which was imposed on him by the tastes of his time, we can see regular harmonic progression and elegant interlacing of parts in his style, and a freedom of melodic usage .... If one takes oneself back to the time when he was writing, and if one thinks of the limited resources at his disposal, one cannot but admire the nature of this great genius.[120]

But it was not just Josquin whom Méreaux recovered from the clutches of the detractors of *la musique française*: he did the same for Michel Lambert, who had "contributed to the re-establishment of sacred music," and Lully, whose air "Plus j'observe ces lieux" he described as "admirable in its melody, its coloration and its noble simplicity," with a delicious accompaniment—a passage that Gluck respected when he came to rewrite the scene in his own *Armide*.[121] Méreaux did not argue that there was no decline in French music at the end of the sixteenth century; he simply presented the most supportive case possible. Similarly, although he mentioned "faults" in Rameau's harmonic system, he then concentrated on his originality, his dramatic gifts, and his power of the picturesque in opera and harpsichord music. More significantly, he introduced the Couperins as a French dynasty equivalent to that of the Scarlattis in Italy and the Bachs in Germany, with François the purveyor of avant-garde music of "finesse and delicacy ..., infinite good taste and spirit."[122] Such enthusiasm for French Baroque music, especially that of a genre so unfashionable that it had been neglected altogether in other musical *milieux* (including Fétis's *concerts historiques*), was indeed unprecedented, and it would be built upon in the coming years.

---

120. "Josquin Després ... fut un des plus grands musiciens de la fin du XVe siècle, et celui dont la réputation eut le plus d'éclat. Il était élève d'Ochenheim, fameux compositeur flamand. Malgré les combinaisons arides qu'il emploi dans ses ouvrages, et qui lui sont imposées par le goût de son siècle, on remarque dans son style une harmonie régulière, une élégance dans l'enchaînement des parties, une liberté dans la mélodie .... On ne peut qu'admirer la nature de ce grand génie, quand on se reporte au tems où il écrivait, et quand on songe au peu de ressources qu'il avait à sa disposition." *Journal de Rouen* (henceforth *JR*), 6 March 1842, n.p.

121. "contribua à rétablir la musique religieuse" (Lambert); "admirable de mélodie, de couleur et de noble simplicité" (Lully). *JR* 6 March 1842, n.p.

122. "fin et délicat ..., infiniment de goût et d'esprit." *JR* 6 March 1842, n.p.

2

1846–1878

When a novelty threatens to alter the balance of cultural power by becoming mainstream, voices are likely to be raised in protest. So it was with early music in mid-nineteenth-century Paris. As I have argued elsewhere, some objections were practical: that the music of living, and particularly French, composers, was being squeezed out of programs as the average age of the works being performed increased.[1] And there were also cynics such as Léon Escudier, whose well-aimed sarcasm had the capacity to touch raw nerves. He hardly missed an opportunity, in his journal *L'art musical*, to take aim at the "résurrectionnistes": "It seems that we do not have enough musical institutions dedicated to the dead.... Frankly, we no longer know where people will stop with this mania for presenting so-called 'classic works," he quipped in 1863.[2] He demanded a definition: must one have been dead 50 years, perhaps? Must the music simply be boring? Must it appeal to certain social classes (doubtless a jibe at wealthy amateurs)? The answers to such rhetorical questions were irrelevant: he viewed the whole movement as a "reactionary path."[3] Escudier's immediate problem was, of course, the "museum" being built around Haydn, Mozart, and Beethoven. But early music appeared as its

   1. See my *Music Criticism*, 66.
   2. "il paraît que nous n'avons pas suffisamment d'institutions musicales, dédiées aux morts. ... En vérité, nous ne savons plus où l'on s'arrêtera avec cette manie d'exhibition d'oeuvres qu'on nomme classique." *AM* 3/20: 16 April 1863, 158.
   3. "voie anti-progressiste." *AM* 3/20: 16 April 1863, 158.

extreme (and extremist) aspect; hence the term "résurrectionnistes." However, misgivings also came from more surprising quarters. Even certain music historians advised against putting history into practice, arguing effectively that their writings were intended to aid understanding, not to encourage performance. Perverse though it might seem, this was one logical extension of the museum culture underpinning the *concert historique*: so long as early music was known about and available in printed editions there was ample opportunity to compare schools and styles. Performance of the works themselves was unnecessary.

Such arguments, which were regularly aired in the 1850s and 60s, were a response to the accelerating integration of selected early musics into concert life. Such integration is most clearly observed in the transformation of the piano repertory during a period when concerts built around a single pianist (but which nevertheless featured a mixture of ensembles and soloists) gave way increasingly to solo piano recitals featuring a variety of musical styles extending from Bach, Handel, and Scarlatti to Chopin, Rubinstein, and, eventually, Brahms.[4] But it was also easily detectable in the setting up, in the 1860s and '70s, of several concert societies featuring "classic" and "historical" music of various kinds. The statutes of the Société des Concerts de Chant Classique (Fondation Beaulieu, founded 1860) expressly outlawed the performance of music by a living composer.[5] Weckerlin, former assistant to Moskova, chorusmaster for the first Société Sainte-Cécile (under François Seghers and Auguste Barbereau, 1850–55), and founder of the second Société Sainte-Cécile in 1865, regularly divided his programs into a first half entitled "Partie Historique" and a second half dedicated to "Compositeurs Vivants."[6] The Société Académique de Musique Sacrée (1861–72) and the Société Bourgault-Ducoudray (1869–74) both promoted early sacred polyphony and (to differing extents) Baroque oratorio.[7] Charles Lamoureux's Société de l'Harmonie Sacrée (founded 1873–74) was set up in emulation of its London namesake, the Sacred Harmonic Society,

---

4. For an analysis of the general development of the piano recital in the nineteenth century, see Jim Samson, "The Practice of Early-Nineteenth-Century Pianism." Its role as a medium emblematic of middle-class attempts to stabilize cultural forms through investment in the work-concept is further discussed in his *Virtuosity and the Musical Work*, 23–28.

5. "Art. 1 . . . La Société n'exécutera que des morceaux de chant dont les auteurs auront cessé d'exister." *Statuts de la Société des concerts de chant classique*, 1.

6. The society had nothing to do with Cecilianism; it was an entirely secular concert society in both its incarnations. See Di Grazia, *Concert Societies*, 198; also 223–40, including a repertory list (235–36) that amply reveals Weckerlin's love of old French chansons, discussed in chapter 5.

7. See Di Grazia, *Concert Societies*, 297–314 (Société Académique, including repertory list); and 328–41 (Bourgault-Ducoudray, also including repertory list).

with a repertory to match.⁸ Neither were Parisian stages immune to the phenomenon of early music, although here the small number of performances helped preserve the element of novelty or curiosity throughout the period. Important revivals took place: 1852, 1853, and 1858 saw the Opéra and the Comédie-Française team up to present Lully's *Le bourgeois gentilhomme*; 1862 and 1863 yielded two separate revivals of Pergolesi's *La serva padrona*, in French at the Opéra-Comique and in Italian at the Théâtre-Italien; the Comédie-Française mounted Charpentier's *Le malade imaginaire* in 1860 and Lully's *Psyché* two years later. The trend intensified in the 1870s with an immensely successful series of Sunday *matinée* performances of stage works with incidental music by Lully and Charpentier at the Gaîté theatre in 1875 and 1876.⁹ Finally, the latter part of the Second Empire and the beginning of the Third Republic saw concerted attempts to naturalize the choral music of Handel and Bach into French culture.¹⁰ The Second-Empire resurgence of French music should make us wary of investing too much in theories of post-1870 nationalist fervor catalyzing a sudden return to heritage in France; indeed, such wariness underpins my avoidance of 1870 as a historical caesura. But the situation was unexpectedly complex, and more frequent performances of French music, even after 1870, did not necessarily signify a markedly increased appreciation of or sensitivity to musical heritage. The shape of the market for early music in published form provides a better test; for it is here, within an ever-expanding industry catering to the amateur at home, that publishers' commercial decisions in respect to early music—French and foreign—reveal its increased place in French musical life.

Anthologies, Adaptations, Monuments

Important as Veuve Launer was in the dissemination of early music during the 14 years of her business (1839–53), she was not alone. Most mid-century publishing houses included a proportion of such music in their catalogues, whether directly or as supplements to music journals. Over a dozen houses, including Canaux, Durand & Schoenewerk, Maho, Gérard, Mackar and Legouix, produced sheet music and vocal scores that would have found their way onto domestic music stands. In addition, Launer's successors, Antoine-Edouard

---

8. Di Grazia, *Concert Societies*, 341–55, including repertory list.
9. Discussed in detail in chapter 4.
10. Discussed in detail in chapter 7.

Meissonnier and Simon Richault, already had a track record for publishing early music. They reissued her Couperin harpsichord edition in 1856, and thereafter expanded her list considerably. Their catalogue of sheet music was extensive—often taking the form of arrangements of the increasing number of popular "hits" in the early music repertory—but they also published major didactic collections such as Ernest Deldevez's anthology of seventeenth- and eighteenth-century violin music (1857–69).[11]

Periodical supplements became increasingly important. Heugel's *Le ménestrel* published *La maîtrise* (1857/8–1860/61), with its monthly supplements of organ and *a cappella* sacred music; the Repos publishing house acted similarly for the *Revue de musique sacrée, ancienne et moderne* (1860–70), which printed much of the repertory of the Société Académique de Musique Sacrée. Presenting this repertory in such concentrated form within a journal was unusual, and reflects not only the specialist readership of the titles concerned but also a measure of confidence in the move away from the music supplement's traditional role as a fashionable diversion. Arthur Heulhard's journal *La chronique musicale* (1873–76) concentrated on early French stage music—dances and airs—arranged for solo piano; in 1877, Armand Gouzien, the Wagnerian editor of the *Journal de musique*, published a series of piano arrangements from *Messiah* as a complement to the pro-Handel articles he printed in the main portion of the journal.

Other evidence also points to a thriving industry. The manner in which early music was packaged reflected practices used for operatic *morceaux détachés*, whose title-pages invariably mentioned the names of singers closely associated with particular roles. In 1863–64 the pianist Wilhelmine Szarvády marketed three collections of her best-known early repertory in this manner.[12] In 1872 Eugène Delaborde dedicated his cadenza to the finale of Bach's D minor keyboard concerto (BWV 1052) to Szarvády and published it independently of the concerto itself, *chez* Hartmann and with his name emblazoned on the cover.

Transcriptions and fantasias also tell us a great deal about the marketability of particular pieces. Almost as popular as the "Pietà, Signore" was Marcello's "I cieli immensi narrano," which appeared in its original form in three editions during the century, but in adapted form in many more. The first chorus

---

11. Ernest Deldevez, *Pièces diverses choisies dans les oeuvres des célèbres violonistes-compositeurs*. The work was adopted by the Conservatoire and approved by the Institut de France.

12. The total of nine pieces was made up entirely of Baroque music: Scarlatti, Rameau, Pergolesi (a vocal transcription), Chambonnières, Balbastre, Couperin, and Benedetto Marcello. See the three volumes of Szarvády (Ed.), *Trois morceaux de piano*.

and its associated alto solo were all that was usually performed. The work became a staple at the Société des Concerts, the music of its opening chorus featured alongside Stradella's aria (arranged as an "O salutaris") and the aria and chorus "Ye men of Gaza" from Handel's *Samson* in the official series of piano reductions of the Société's repertory, published by Schoenenberger in the 1850s. A second piano version is noteworthy: also billed as connected with the Société des Concerts, it saw Camille Stamaty apply the principles of operatic paraphrase to Marcello's music.[13] Toward the end of the century Théodore Dubois would adapt the opening chorus of "I cieli immensi" for liturgical use as two Easter motets: "Christus resurrexit" and "Illuxit dies tertia." The pieces, published in 1878 and *c*.1899, respectively, were effectively identical: in both, Dubois lengthened the introduction, interpolating organ ritornelli and adding a unison Alleluia to close. He was not the first to make such significant changes to Marcello's work. Orchestral parts at the Bibliothèque Nationale, Paris, include a multisectional "Marcello" psalm put together by Rodrigues in 1840. It contained edited highlights of the composer's psalms 18 and 21, short-circuiting from the opening Grave and Adagio of psalm 21 to the celebrated chorus of psalm 18, the grandeur of whose ending was emphasized with string tremolos and the obligatory dramatic *rallentando*.[14] Such music was, then, raw material in both form and function, as the continued popularity of early music contrafacta crossing from secular to sacred usage also attests. Handel's "Lascia mio pianga" (*Rinaldo*) became a sacred-music favorite,[15] Gounod's *Méditation* on Bach even more so.

Marketing strategies suitable for cheap sheet music were less sustainable for multivolume projects, many of which continued to depend on old-fashioned subscriptions. Nevertheless, three key collections illustrate the increasing ambition that came with enhanced commercial backing: François and Rosine Delsarte's *Archives du chant* (3 vols., 1855–64, privately published), Aristide and Louise Farrenc's *Le trésor des pianistes* (14 vols., 1861–74, published by Aristide Farrenc's own firm), and Amédée Méreaux's *Les clavecinistes de 1637 à 1790* (2 vols., 1864–67, published by Heugel). The first two sold internationally, but with much smaller subscriber numbers than those for Choron's proposed collection of sacred music of 1810; Méreaux's collection was simply

---

13. Camille Stamaty, *Concerts du Conservatoire. 18ᵉ psaume de Marcello* (1856).

14. Manuscript copies in BNF Musique: L. 18817.

15. It is to be found, with other contrafacta and alongside genuine and fake works, in one of the key sacred anthologies of the period: *Echos du monde religieux*, 7 vols. (Paris, Flaxland etc, 1857–1901). "Lascia ch'io pianga" also appeared, with its original text, in Flaxland's companion volume, *Echos d'Italie*, 6 vols. (Paris: Flaxland etc, 1851–74).

placed on the open market. In the *Archives du chant* the Delsartes presented an eclectic mix of French, Italian, and German music ranging from harmonized plainchant and old French chansons to sacred music by Palestrina, Lassus, Jommelli, Couperin, and Haydn, and operatic music by Lully, Monsigny, Rameau, and Mozart. Subscribers numbered only 133 but included a mixture of European royalty, the music trade (Broadwood, Schott), and prominent singers, including both Pauline Viardot (who was to publish her own collection of "classic" vocal music in 1861) and her father, Manuel Garcia. Equally significant were the churchmen who subscribed to the sacred music only (and the fact that the Delsartes thought to cater to them)—the Cardinal Bishops of Bordeaux, Reims, and Tours, the Archbishop of Paris, and the Bishops of Soissons and Beauvais. Their subscriptions represented high-level interest in and probably enthusiasm for the movement to replace the operatic pastiches and improvized *fauxbourdon* of French liturgical music with repertory based around Counter-Reformation and *stile antico* traditions.[16]

The Farrencs' subscription lists of 1863 (118 names, 121 copies) and 1864 (166 names, 179 copies) tell a similar story and involve some of the same characters. Their successes reached as far as Moscow and Calcutta but centered on Paris (54 percent of sales), the French regions (22 percent), England (8 percent) and Belgium (6 percent). By contrast, German cities hardly featured (Leipzig and Berlin each yielded a single subscription). Common to the Delsarte and Farrenc lists were members of the Rothschild family, the Norwegian pianist and early music enthusiast Thomas Tellefsen, Pauline Viardot, Broadwood and Schott. The most important difference (and marking a distinct contrast with, for instance, the fate of Choron's subscription editions) was the involvement of the French state with the *Trésor*, both indirectly, through three official Conservatoire subscriptions, and directly, through no fewer than ten subscriptions from the Ministre de la Maison de l'Empereur et des Beaux-Arts, which would find their way to regional conservatoire libraries.[17]

The *Trésor*, which Louise Farrenc completed after Aristide's death in 1865, was a monument to the history of keyboard music from the English virginalists to Chopin; but it was also intended to be a series of attractive and varied *moments*

---

16. Though the Delsartes were unprecedented in including two sacred pieces by Couperin, an "Ave maris stella" (inauthentic?) and an "Ave regina."

17. For an example, see Charles Poisot's request of 16 March 1870 to the Ministre des Beaux-Arts for volumes 9 to 15 of the *Trésor*, to complement the earlier volumes which his Dijon Conservatoire library had already received. Such munificence was not automatic: Poisot was reduced to the ploy of asking for the gift to be made in honor of Napoléon III's birthday. AN Paris: F^{21} 1318 Dossier "Correspondance générale." The 501 subscribers to Choron's *Principes de composition* of c.1808 included 18 individuals from the Conservatoire, but there were no institutional subscriptions beyond the purchase of a copy for the Conservatoire Library.

musicaux. Hence the Farrencs' publishing inspiration: to release each *livraison* in the form of a mixed selection with a flimsy paper binding, seemingly incoherent page numbering, and a provisional table of contents. It was only when the collection was complete that its owners could, at their leisure, use the final, cumulative table of contents to have the pieces bound in chronological order by composer and school—at which point those "incoherent" page numbers would suddenly make perfect canonical sense. Even more than Moskova's *Collection de musique religieuse*, then, the "monumental" look of the complete edition belies its original use as music to perform, rather than music to refer to. The advertizing methods used by the Delsarte and Farrenc camps reinforce this idea. Both mounted concerts—effectively *concerts historiques* for demonstration purposes— featuring the music their anthologies contained. Delsarte, a child pupil of Choron's who had failed as a singer in adulthood at the Conservatoire, sang the repertory he and Rosine edited; the Farrenc collection was represented by the pianist Marie Mongin, Louise Farrenc's star pupil, who was soon to be perceived as a specialist in early music because of the high proportion of *clavecin* repertory she integrated into her programs.[18]

Despite the continuing appearance of volumes in the *Trésor* collection, the publisher Heugel must have judged that the market for large-scale publishing projects was not saturated. In 1867 he published—and exhibited at the Exposition Universelle—Amédée Méreaux's *Les clavecinistes de 1837 à 1790*, a two-volume set comprising a monograph on harpsichord music, its composers, and its performance style, and new editions of the music. The volume was the natural extension of Méreaux's *concert historique* activities in Rouen, but it was also indicative of his wish to rehabilitate the music with which he had grown up. The "gap" in the market, however, had not so much to do with repertory (duplications abound) as with the more commercially refined criterion of editorial approach. Where the Farrencs' editing prized the presentation of the music as a quasi-*Urtext*, Méreaux's was a prescriptive text including fingering and dynamics and with even the simplest ornament written out fully. For that reason he viewed his publication as a pioneering venture in the popularization of early keyboard music; his preface contained a barely disguised attack on the Farrencs' publication and also, tellingly, referred to early music's new integration in

---

18. The Farrencs organized an "Audition du *Trésor des pianistes*" on 8 April 1861 at the Salons Erard to coincide with the release of the first *livraison*. The only work that did not come from the *Trésor* was Louise Farrenc's Piano Trio no. 2; thereafter Mongin played short pieces by Byrd, Gibbons, Bull, Frescobaldi, Chambonnières, Purcell, F. Couperin, Handel, Rameau, J. S. Bach, Porpora, Padre Martini, C.P.E. Bach, Kirnberger, Wernicke, Lindemann, Hummel, and Scarlatti. Delsarte had presented three *Archives du chant* concerts at the Salle Herz in the early summer of 1856, soon after the collection's launch.

musical life: "A few years ago," he wrote, "this musical literature remained at the level of a *curiosity*; today it has reached that of a *utility*, an indispensable element of education."[19] With the exception of Edouard Rodrigues, who defined his editions of Handel oratorio against those of Choron (Choron's were in Latin or Italian; in an explicitly patriotic gesture Rodrigues used French), Méreaux presents the earliest example of one French editor of early music competing against another. That competition is itself suggestive of increased momentum in the practice of early music. But the nature of Méreaux's argument—that the presentation of an unfamiliar musical style in a manner intelligible to its new audience was a necessary condition for its popularization—is more important because it indicates a new level of sophistication and maturity in the publishing market for early music and in the ways its practitioners thought about it.

Bachians, Pianists, and Virtuosity

The emphasis on piano, or piano and voice, in the *Archives du chant*, the *Trésor*, and the *Clavecinistes*, reflected two new strands in French performance traditions: a significant increase in the use of early music by concert pianists; and the growing popularity of a limited number of excerpts from French Baroque opera, usually performed by Delsarte, the baritone Adolphe Alizard, or by soloists at the Société des Concerts. I shall return to that repertory in a moment. However, it was the sudden appearance of pianists playing Handel, Scarlatti, French *clavecinistes*, and—particularly—J. S. Bach that raised the more immediately difficult questions about the place and significance of early musics in a modern concert repertory. For all Méreaux's eclecticism and patriotism, J. S. Bach stood at the center of his musical universe. The frontispieces of *Les clavecinistes* are traditional in their use of a Classical "portal" effect where the names of the featured composers are listed down the supporting pillars, with the collection's title in the center. But the pillars on the first frontispiece of Méreaux's collection do not feature Bach's name: instead, the names of the four great Bachs are to be found clustered in the middle of the portal opening, just above the representation of a harpsichord keyboard (Fig. 2.1). The second frontispiece is more explicit: a Classical pedestal features the title of the collection and "pillars" listing its composers, Bach included. But the pedestal is there to support the main image, in which, against a backdrop of organ pipes and

---

19. "Cette littérature musicale était encore, il y a quelques années, à l'état de *curiosité*; elle est, de nos jours, devenue une *utilité*, un élément indispensable d'éducation." Méreaux, *Les clavecinistes de 1637 à 1790*, i, 1.

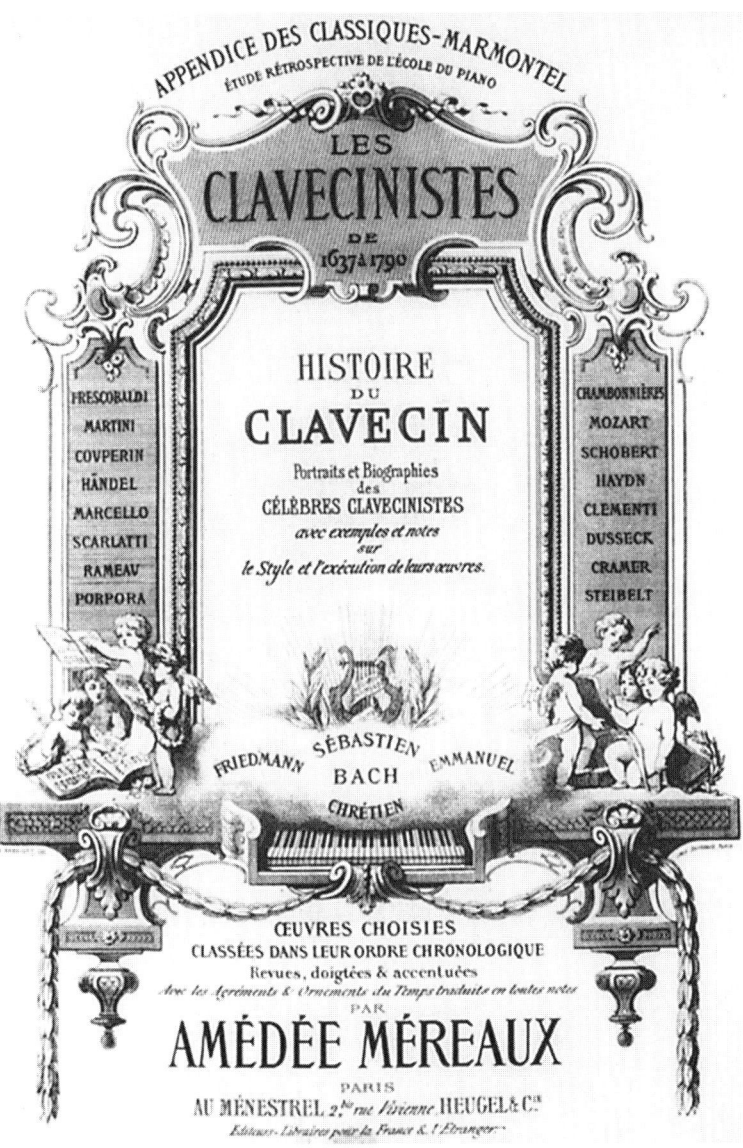

FIGURE 2.1. Amédée Méreaux, *Les clavecinistes de 1637 à 1790*. Paris, 1864–67. Frontispiece 1. Courtesy of the Bibliothèque Nationale de France, Paris.

clouds, a toga-clad maiden lovingly places laurel leaves on a medallion portraying Bach, who stares at us from the center of the picture. To complete the symmetry of adulation, a cherub playing a lyre gazes upwards to watch the maiden's act of homage (Fig. 2.2).

Bach was indeed at the center of the integration of early music into pianists'

FIGURE 2.2. Amédée Méreaux, *Les clavecinistes de 1637 à 1790*. Paris, 1864–67. Frontispiece 2. Courtesy of the Bibliothèque Nationale de France, Paris.

concert repertories. It is perhaps not surprising: the first Baroque keyboard music to appear in a nineteenth-century French edition (by Imbault) contained the fugues from the *Well-Tempered Clavier* (c.1801) and was soon followed by Simrock's complete edition. In the years up to 1846 there were relatively few public performances of Bach's music in Paris and (with the likely exception of

Alsace) probably throughout France as a whole. I have found nothing antedating the July Monarchy. But in 1833 an unprecedented thing happened: on 15 December, Chopin, Liszt, and Ferdinand Hiller played the opening Allegro from the Triple Concerto (BWV 1063) in the Conservatoire hall under Habeneck.[20] Two years later the same trio repeated the performance, this time at the Salons Pape. It seems as though these performances had little immediate impact; there was certainly no rush of copycat performances. But there was indeed a delayed reaction that made this work one of the Bach "hit numbers" of mid-nineteenth-century Paris.

For it was in the later 1840s and the 1850s that Bach's keyboard music became a regular feature of Paris concerts. The Triple Concerto was at its height in the 1850s, played by various pianists, mostly involving permutations of Alkan, Hiller, Tellefsen, Wolff, the young Saint-Saëns, Méreaux, and De Malleville. Less spectacular than BWV 1063 but more often played was the Concerto in D minor BWV 1052, which for the most part drew different pianists, including Thérèse Wartel (1848), Alkan (1849), Louise Mattmann (1856), Aglaé Massart (1857), and Marie Mongin (1862), in a largely female tradition that seems to have stretched all the way to the princesse de Polignac (1899, when she also played the "Triple"). A third important category included the fugues for harpsichord and organ and isolated dance movements. The larger-scale harpsichord works were virtually unknown in performance: the "Goldberg" Variations had been in print in France since 1804 but were, as far as I can establish, never played; during this period a performance of the Chromatic Fantasia and Fugue BWV 903, such as that given by Wilhelmine Szarvády on 20 February 1858, was exceptional. The "Italian" Concerto broke into the regular repertory earlier (its first known performance was by Henri Ketten in April 1860), through its being taken up thereafter by Saint-Saëns in the mid-1860s and played frequently at Société Saint-Cécile concerts. It would, in the 1890s, be a favorite of both Louis Diémer and Raoul Pugno. Other categories of keyboard music regularly played in concerts—toccatas, preludes, dance movements, and fugues—were presented either on a standard piano or a pedal-piano, the latter being used in particular by Alkan and Lemmens in the 1850s.

If the above survey suggests that the entry of Bach's keyboard music into concert life was steady and unproblematic, closer analysis reveals the opposite. I have argued elsewhere that early keyboard music in general was viewed in mid-nineteenth century France with some ambivalence, as of subprofessional

---

20. An earlier performance, projected for March 1833, seems not to have taken place.

difficulty.²¹ In a milieu where pianistic virtuosity was highly prized, the choosing of pieces that lacked the modern technical innovations of wide stretches, double octaves, or fast arpeggio or scalic figures, aroused contempt. The fact that in the 1850s and 1860s a disproportionate amount of such music was being played in public by women pianists only made matters worse, suggesting to those who subscribed to stereotypes of womanhood that this music was facile, shallow, and undemanding. Given the prevalence of these attitudes, for women to play "teaching pieces" from the *Well-Tempered Clavier* in public recitals smacked of deceit. Were they not using music respected for its compositional skill as an excuse for foisting their immature performing talents on a gullible audience? Pianists such as Szarvády found their way out of this conundrum by mixing early music with much more technically demanding fare. (As the first pianist to play Brahms's First Piano Concerto in Paris, Szarvády herself was hardly vulnerable to the charge of amateurism.) But specialists, such as Mongin, could not escape. In addition, as I have already discussed, Bach's reputation suffered from an antipathy to fugue. Berlioz had dismissed the Bach Triple Concerto of Chopin, Hiller, and Liszt as a "stupid and ridiculous psalmody," unworthy of its performers.²² By contrast, Edouard Fétis had been unreservedly enthusiastic about their performance and the self-abnegation of the virtuoso that it represented. But twice in the same review he characterized Bach's music as "delicate." It would appeal, he wrote, to those "music-lovers blessed with a certain delicacy of sensibility"; it also demanded, and received, a performance showing "perfect understanding of its character, and perfect delicacy."²³

Two decades later, self-abnegation and delicacy were more problematic. The playing of harpsichord and even fortepiano music was taken as an indication of a pianist's artistic limitation unless there was direct evidence to the contrary. Yet the opposite—intense expressivity, or explicit virtuosity—was also suspect. Henri Blanchard censured Alfred Jaëll in 1855 for whipping up audience excitement by accelerating at the end of an unidentified Bach fugue in C major;²⁴ Adolphe Botte complained that Clara Schumann over-pedaled fugal passages with deep bass lines.²⁵

---

21. In my "Female Pianists," 363–66.
22. "cette sotte et ridicule psalmodie," *Le rénovateur*, 29 December 1833, given in Fauquet and Hennion, *La grandeur de Bach*, 70.
23. "les amateurs doués d'une certaine délicatesse dans sa manière de sentir"; "avec une intelligence de son caractère et une délicatesse parfaites". Edouard Fétis (signed), *RM* December 1833, 399 and 400.
24. *RGM* 22/11: 18 March 1855, 84, given in my *Music Criticism*, 71.
25. *RGM* 39/12: 23 March 1862, 96.

The perilous line to be negotiated is indicated in reviews of the organist-pianist Jaak Nikolaas Lemmens, a pioneer of Bach performance in Belgium and France, and, most famously, the organ teacher of Alexandre Guilmant and Eugène Gigout. Reviewing a piano recital at the Salle Erard on 11 February 1856, Paul Scudo found Lemmens's performance of Beethoven's Sonata in C# minor self-satisfied and contented (which, he indicated, spoke volumes about the performer's emotional limitations), and concluded that his Bach, a G minor fugue from the *Well-Tempered Clavier*, was his finest performance because the piece was "very well suited to M. Lemmens's vigorous, but rather dry, talent."[26] Complaints about cold, brittle, and arid tone-quality multiplied in reviews of performances of early keyboard music (Saint-Saëns and De Malleville were frequent targets), and yet the combination of rhythmic precision and tip-of-the-finger brilliance continued to be lauded as the ideal manner of its interpretation.[27]

There were two ways for male Bachians to try to escape such contradictory difficulties. The first involved monumentalism and safety in numbers—teaming up to perform the spectacular that was Bach's concertos for multiple keyboards.[28] The second was less common and more radical: to avoid the solo harpsichord repertory and the conventional piano and to play the organ works on a pedal piano. On 23 April 1853 the new pedal piano designed by Erard was inaugurated by Alkan, the organist Lefébure-Wély, and the pianist Camille Stamaty, teacher of Saint-Saëns. Blanchard saw it as a means of salvation from dry-as-dust early music "fanatics," the precision of whose interpretations was "arid and bare." This updated instrument would, he wrote, "restore to classic music the inspiration, the warmth and the pomp that presided over its creation."[29] This was faulty reasoning of an interesting kind. For what the advent of Erard's pedal piano did was not to encourage the presentation of familiar pianistic repertory via a different medium, but to allow pianists to access a new repertory: organ music. Free of associations of subprofessional status or excessive delicacy, and despite its fugues (which had their rightful place in church),

---

26. "convient surtout au talent vigoureux, mais un peu sec, de M. Lemmens." Scudo, article of 15 July 1856, included in his *Critique et littérature musicales*, 110.

27. See, for instance, an unsigned review of Emma de Staudach's Scarlatti, which she played "avec cette précision de rhythme et ce toucher léger qui sont les conditions indispensables de l'exécution des oeuvres de l'ancienne école." *RGM* 24/11: 15 March 1857, 86.

28. Massart and De Malleville appear to be the only women who played such works in the professional realm during this period, the latter mostly alongside her teacher. However, at the Conservatoire prizegiving concert in 1856 the young Louis Diémer played BWV1063 with two prizewinners in the women's piano class: Mlle Marchand and Mlle Danvier.

29. "sèche et nue"; "[The pedal piano] offre la ressource de rendre à la musique classique l'inspiration, la chaleur et la pompe qui ont présidé à sa création." *RGM* 20/18: 1 May 1853, 160–61.

Bach's organ music enjoyed considerable respect, not least for the virtuosity required to master its pedal parts. It was also, for all that there were women organists (Conservatoire-trained, and even *titulaires*), a male-dominated music.[30] For Alkan and Lemmens the organ music on a pedal-piano was thus ideal: Bach without the stigma, as it were. And it was on this modest scale that they introduced Paris audiences to two works which, from 1878 onwards, were to be the Bach warhorses of the virtuoso organ repertory, holding audiences of up to seven thousand people enthralled: the Toccata in F (BWV 540) and the Fugue in G minor (BWV 542).

Trends in Baroque Instrumental Music

Of course, Baroque keyboard music did not mean Bach alone. The music of Handel, Couperin, Rameau, and Scarlatti regularly reached the concert stage, even more commonly via female hands. Before the advent of the *Trésor des pianistes*, De Malleville had already done much to promote the work of the French *clavecinistes* so beloved of Méreaux; Szarvády regularly played Scarlatti sonatas and Rameau *pièces*; Louise Farrenc, too, though less regularly; and in the 1860s, Mongin, De Malleville, Caroline Remaury, and Saint-Saëns all continued championing this repertory. Their work would be continued with new vigor by the most famous name in the revival of Baroque keyboard music before Wanda Landowska—Louis Diémer. Handel's "Harmonious Blacksmith" variations and the passacaglia closing the Suite in G minor were the most popular choices (for De Malleville especially); among French *clavecin* pieces, Rameau's "Le rappel des oiseaux," "Les tendres plaintes," and "Les niais de Sologne," and Couperin's "Soeur Monique" and "Les tours de passe-passe" topped the billing. Critical responses were mixed, alternately lauding and condemning the French repertory for its picturesque and decorative character. Both were markers of a rococo prettiness and, concomitantly, a lack of gravity.

---

30. See Sykes, *Female Piety and the Organ*, 221–38, and François-Sappey, *Alexandre P. F. Boëly*, 136. However, I am unconvinced by Sykes's contention that Bach organ music was feminized (by analogy with his harpsichord music) (ibid., 232). Pauline Viardot famously played her own Cavaillé-Coll, but for the first reports of women playing Bach's organ works as concert repertory we must wait for the pupils of Franck (from 1872) (ibid., 233) and the concerts of Eugène Gigout's organ school, from 1885. For the pedal piano, I know of only one example of a woman playing Bach (a prelude and fugue) in a public concert before 1878: Annette Falk, as part of a concert given by the Maurin-Chevillard quartet on 10 February 1859. For an illustration of the bifurcated reception of Bach keyboard musics, see Scudo's review of Lemmens (cited above, n. 26), where the "piano" music is dry but its composer is "le grand créateur de la musique d'orgue." Scudo, *Critique et littérature musicales*, 110.

Reviewing Couperin's "Le reveil-matin" at a *concert historique* of 1856 organized by Félix Le Couppey and his pupils, the publisher and critic Marie Escudier had to insulate Couperin's work from the taint of the "picturesque" in order to promote it: "Without being imitative music, this piece makes one dream of all the little things that happen as part of country life on a bustling morning."[31] Blanchard swung both ways. In Couperin's "Le moucheron," played in "virtuoso" fashion by De Malleville in 1855, he applauded the music's "delicious effect," which encouraged reverie and evoked the industrious bee balancing on lilac blossom in a gentle evening breeze: "it is like a far-off echo of the art of olden times, lulling one with sweet memories of the past."[32] But after suffering an evening dominated by early music from the *Trésor*, played by Louise Farrenc's pupils, he rebelled. This was, he wrote, boring and tiresome, the music itself over-decorative and fussy "with its gruppetti, its mordents, its style stuffed full of *imitations*."[33] Learnedness, then, was problematic, but so was the picturesque and the detailed. But if the music could induce nostalgic reverie such problems appeared to vanish. In their critiques of the effects of Couperin's music on the imagination, Escudier and Blanchard expressed sentiments that were over forty years ahead of their time, for it was in precisely these terms that French harpsichord music, together with dance music of the same period, would eventually gain acceptance.

Though less well represented in concert life, string music proved more acceptable, perhaps because string-playing, being an almost entirely male activity, lacked the disruptive element of overtly gendered associations. The first violinists to champion Baroque repertory were Baillot (Corelli, Tartini, Handel, Geminiani, Bach) and Alard (Corelli, Bach). Thereafter the concert repertory narrowed, effectively, to variation sets: Corelli's *La follia*, variations on *La romanesca*, and, in due course, the Bach chaconne. The Bach concertos made no real impact on the concert repertory until the 1890s. With the exception of the chaconne, the same holds for the solo works. Sonatas by Gaviniès and Leclair, though available in modern editions, remained unplayed at a professional level. Alard's introductions to pieces in his *Les maîtres classiques du violon* (published from 1861) suggest one of the reasons why: they were too pervasively ornamental.

Although Alard almost certainly viewed Corelli's adagios as written out

---

31. "Sans être de la musique imitative, ce morceau nous fait rêver à tous les accidents qui se produisent dans les bruyantes matinées de la vie champêtre." *FM* 20/20: 18 May 1856, 158.

32. "prestidigieuse"; "effet délicieux"; "c'est comme un écho lointain de l'art rétrospectif qui vous berce des suaves souvenirs du passé." *RGM* 22/9: 4 March 1855, 67.

33. "avec ses gruppetti, ses mordents, son style continuellement serré d'*imitations*." *RGM* 24/49: 6 December 1857, 394.

in incomplete form, he nevertheless demanded that they be played unadorned. There was no hint of encouragement to ornament the opening movement of Op. 5/1 or its adagio, which he said "requires great stylistic simplicity."[34] He also chose his Leclair sonatas (Book 4 no. 3 in D, 1743; and Book 3 no. 6 "Le tombeau" in C minor, 1734) for their grandeur of style; and, in the case of the 1743 sonata, he emphasized the "noble simplicity" of its (very Corellian) slow sarabande.[35] What Alard prized in Leclair was, therefore, its closeness to the Italianate. Yet detailed ornamentation was to be avoided, even when historical precedent suggested it might be used, and even though it might contribute to the element of virtuosity inherent in the work. In a move typical of an age that was beginning to see a musical canon as residing in the text rather than the performed work, ambivalence towards florid ornamentation meant that a defining feature of Italian style was stripped out; but suspicion of local decoration also meant that one of the defining features of the eighteenth-century French sonata style became devalued.[36] It was an echo of the ambivalence surrounding French keyboard music of the same period and the continuing, though now more muted, antipathy towards most music of the French Baroque.

Virtuosity was nonetheless key in violin music and was the principal reason why extracts from Bach's unaccompanied works were usually enthusiastically received. The sheer physicality of multiple-stopped, contrapuntal, and arpeggio passages attracted comment, causing critics to reflect on the supreme demands Bach made of both instrument and player. Far from arousing disparagement, Bach's violin music appeared prodigious, the chaconne becoming a virtuoso test-piece. Was this really, mused Adolphe Botte in 1858, "the great organist, the doctor of music . . . living amongst all those scholastic formulae; courting only the muse of learned counterpoint"? Or was it pastiche—the work of a modern able to overlay the old rules with capricious fantasy and "the most creative imagination of today"?[37] That such questions were even asked put Bach's solo violin music in a league of its own from the moment it began to be played in public. But it simultaneously reinforced the expectation that Bach

---

34. "demande une grande simplicité de style." Alard (Ed.), *Les maîtres classiques du violon*, n.p. The collection is replete with Italians, including Corelli, Tartini, and Nardini; but Alard also includes Bach and Leclair. For Nardini's music he was more relaxed than for Corelli's, recommending a middle way between no ornamentation and the "overloaded" graces of the 1760 Venice edition (which he printed).

35. "style noble et simple." Alard called the first movement of the 1743 sonata "large et majestueux," and the opening of "Le tombeau" "majestueux et dramatique." Alard (Ed.), *Les maîtres classiques du violon*, n.p.

36. On concerns about ornamentation see my "Berlioz, the Sublime, and the *Broderie* Problem."

37. "le grand organiste, le docteur en musique . . . vivant au milieu de toutes les formules scolastiques; ne courtisant que la muse des savantes combinaisons"; "l'imagination la plus créatrice d'aujourd'hui." *RGM* 25/50: 12 December 1858, 410–11. The violinist in question here was Henri Vieuxtemps.

usually provided his listeners with learned formulae aplenty. The exception merely reinforced the image of the norm.

The Popularization of Early Choral Music

Audiences who heard these piano and violin repertories came overwhelmingly from the leisured classes. Blanchard even wrote of De Malleville as having her own "rich and aristocratic clientèle"—those who frequented the more select Paris concert halls.[38] And, while the publication of anthologies was a useful form of musical dissemination for professionals and wealthy amateurs, the outlay was beyond the pockets of the vast majority. Even sheet music covering this repertory was expensive. Szarvády's editions of harpsichord pieces retailed at 9F per volume—typically two days' wages for the artisans who helped build the pianos on which she played. With the exception of effusive language to welcome the pedal-piano, rhetorics of regeneration and public education are absent from reviews of instrumental repertories performed during the period. The same is true of larger-scale works presented to the audience at the Société des Concerts, whose first taste of a Handel "concerto grosso" was in any case an orchestration by Auber of the composer's keyboard music.[39] It was not in such closed arenas that the debate about regeneration through the democratization of "classic" music happened, but among the conductors of larger-scale ventures: choral and orchestral societies. Admittedly, some societies were primarily interested in their own "regeneration"; but others showed more enthusiasm for the dissemination of the music they valued most. The result was that the Second Empire, which saw a spectacular rise in the number of *orphéon* choirs and brass bands intended to help civilize (and control) the peasant, laborer, and artisan classes, also witnessed considerable debate and experiment in respect to their musical education and experience.

Pride of place as a popularizer went to the indefatigable Jules Pasdeloup, whose affordable version of the Société des Concerts, the Concerts Populaires, attracted crowds of around four thousand to the Cirque Napoléon (Cirque d'Hiver) on Sunday afternoons from 1861. From the outset, Paseloup included small doses of early music in programs otherwise based around the Viennese classics and, before long, Wagner. Unsurprisingly, he included the established

---

38. "riche et aristocratique clientèle." *RGM* 24/9: 1 March 1857, 68.

39. The piece was billed as "Theme, Variations and Fugue" and was first presented at the concert of 3 February 1858. See Elwart, *Histoire de la Société des concerts*, 299.

hits: a third supplementary concert of the 1861–62 season (Good Friday, 18 April 1862) featured not only the famous "Stradella" aria (a common choice), but also a certain prelude for choir and orchestra based by Gounod on Bach, with the solo line taken by all the first violins. Yet Pasdeloup also extended the concert repertory—sometimes despite derision—to extracts from Bach's orchestral suites and to new numbers from Handel's oratorios. A concert of 19 April 1863 was particularly important in this latter respect, since he followed Beethoven's Ninth Symphony with a set of Handel "selections" (the word, in emulation of the English tradition, is his). Here, the exigencies of paying a chorus militated against his popularizing instinct: he had to double the ticket prices to cover his costs, and some seats remained empty.[40] Nevertheless, a large audience enjoyed the Hallelujah chorus and the victory chorus from *Judas* and demanded encores of the "nightingale" chorus from *Solomon* and an aria from *Alcina* sung by Pauline Viardot.[41] Over the next few years, Pasdeloup and others (notably Weckerlin and Bourgault-Ducoudray) tried to restore Germanic choral music of the late Baroque to the place it had enjoyed in Choron's time.[42] This was the new age of Handel and Bach.

Their choral music was not revived in France with equal speed, consistency, or enthusiasm. Bach in particular posed multiple problems. He was perceived as steeped in Protestant tradition, evinced especially in his chorale-based works; the tradition of the *testus* appeared alien; his contrapuntal writing raised age-old critical hackles about the triumph of calculation over inspiration; and, crucially, his vocal writing, sometimes described as "instrumental," was too taxing. And while Handel too fell foul of some of these critical strictures, he was never viewed as "difficult"—indeed, in the 1860s the straightforwardness of his choral music became its cardinal virtue. Even when his music showed generic relationships with Bach's more cerebral and Protestant style, there were enough countervailing factors for Handel to be forgiven. Nevertheless, the reasons why the *Brockes-Passion* never became a repertory piece and why the French in general preferred *Judas Maccabaeus* to *Messiah* are not difficult to find: narrative declamation of the Word was anathema, and critics who made a point of complaining about the presence of so much recitative in oratorio and

---

40. See Gustave Chouquet in *AM* 3/21: 23 April 1863, 165.

41. Almost certainly "Verdi prati." According to the historian Gustave Chouquet, who was typically disparaging about one chorus from *Solomon* (it was music to read silently, not to inflict on an audience), Viardot embellished the aria with questionable taste. *AM* 3/21: 23 April 1863, 165.

42. Pasdeloup had known certain Handel oratorios from his youth: in 1839 and 1845 he had prepared the piano accompaniments to Edouard Rodrigues's anthologies, *Choeurs de Haendel*, and *Choeurs de "Judas Maccabée,"* published by Martinet and Richault respectively.

Passion music usually pointed to monotony, dryness, or interruption of the dramatic flow.[43] Similarly, although Handel's use of fugue occasionally drew criticism, nothing could overshadow the power, excitement, and raw energy he seemed able to convey, especially in choral movements.

While old staples of Italian choral music by Leo, Durante, and Jommelli gradually disappeared from concert programs, and even that of Marcello faded somewhat, editions and performances of Handel increased beyond measure. In 1864–65 the publishers E. Gérard et Cie released a series of vocal scores of Handel's oratorios in a new French translation by Sylvain Saint-Etienne at between 2F and 3F50 each. Gérard also published some of the arias and choral numbers as *morceaux détachés*. As Saint-Etienne explained in a puff article placed in *L'union musicale*, their format, musical text, and intended readership were identical to that of Novello's cheap octavo edition: "the popular edition I have announced will come in timely fashion to offer a means of studying [Handel's oratorios] more easily, and of popularizing them completely."[44] Félix Baudillon of the *Revue et gazette des théâtres* agreed, recommending these editions to all those who preferred serious music to that which was "frivolous and ephemeral." Tellingly, he claimed that *orphéon* societies would find numerous suitable pieces therein.[45]

Saint-Etienne's translations were intended to be sung by the new Société du Grand-Concert set up with Félicien David, a project which had been loudly trumpeted by Charles Soullier, editor of *L'union musicale*, as offering the works of the old masters alongside modern works *"in exceptional conditions: fine performances at budget prices."*[46] Concerts were to take place on the site of the old "Colonnes d'Hercule" bedding shop on the rue Richer, which was accordingly to be remodeled as a concert space seating three thousand people. Despite an announcement in August 1864 that mentioned auditions, and despite numerous subscription

---

43. Sextius Durand found the St Matthew Passion recitatives unattractive (*FM* 32/20: 17 May 1868, 150); Mathieu de Monter described the tenor role in Handel's *Brockes-Passion* as a "a burdensome task" (*RGM* 36/14: 4 April 1869, 115); even the Bachian Ernest Reyer complained of monotony in the recitatives of the St Matthew Passion (*JD* 21 April 1874); Henry Cohen found them a ridiculous interpolation (*CM* 4, no. 20: 15 April 1874, 81) and stated his preference for *Judas Maccabaeus* above *Messiah* and *Alexander's Feast* specifically because of their absence (*CM* 6, no. 35: 1 Dec 1874, 224); Hugues Imbert preferred the B minor Mass to other "oratorios" because its lack of recitatives helped it escape the monotony that plagued such pieces (*GM* 1891, given in *MS* 13/9: April 1891, 66).

44. "L'édition populaire que nous annonçons vient à point pour donner le moyen de les étudier plus facilement et de les populariser tout à fait." *L'union musicale* (henceforth *UM*) 3/15: 15 and 16 October 1864, 238.

45. "productions frivoles et éphémères." *Revue et gazette des théâtres* (henceforth *RGT*) 36 (no. 1456): 3 September 1865, 2.

46. "dans des conditions exceptionnelles de bonne éxecution et de bon marché." "C. S." [Charles Soullier], *UM* 3/11 and 12: August 1864, 185.

pledges, the Société du Grand-Concert, which was dependent on prospective *sociétaires* being able to afford to take up a total of 1200 shares at 500F each, never materialized. The attempt, however, was historically important for its organizers' dual focus on Handel and the less-affluent sectors of the Paris public. It also followed a model that was becoming increasingly common in Second-Empire Paris: the mixed, amateur choral society, usually dedicated to early music and the "classics," sometimes undertaking charity events but only occasionally supporting new music.

In this respect, however, Paris lagged well behind certain of the French regions. The Société des Concerts de Chant Classique (Fondation Beaulieu, 1860–1912), named after its founder Désiré Martin-Beaulieu, was one of the first such societies to be set up in Paris. But it was a recreation for the capital of his Association Musicale de l'Ouest, which brought together mixed choral societies from the Protestant belt around Niort and the surrounding area (initially Poitiers, Limoges, Angoulême, and La Rochelle). They would meet for an annual two- or three-day noncompetitive festival at one of the five home towns. Beaulieu's intention, as revealed in an anonymous essay of 1836–37, was to set up a society "along the lines of those which exist in Germany."[47] Its repertory would be varied, he wrote, but "if one kind of music had to be overlooked, it would not be . . . that of early music, nor that which dates from just before our era": since theatres put on new compositions all the time, Beaulieu argued, musical associations would be fulfilling a valuable function by "reviving" the masterpieces of the great composers of the past.[48] Sacred music, in particular, would be featured. He cited as key the oratorios of Bach, Handel, and Haydn, and the *a cappella* music of the late sixteenth century.

Beaulieu's festival concerts were indeed eclectic, but they never reflected the full scope of the project outlined in 1836–37. From 1835 to the early 1840s, no early music was featured. The Niort festival of 1843 seems to have brought the first early repertory—Allegri's *Miserere*. Thereafter, Beaulieu's Association, while it rarely fulfilled his initial aims of performing of complete, early works, nevertheless presented extracts from Bach and Handel long before they were heard in Paris. It was also Beaulieu's Association Musicale which, after its founder's death, presented one of the few known performances of a large-scale choral work by Handel in regional France (and outside Alsace) before the 1870s: *Alexander's Feast* in Niort on 7 June 1864.

---

47. "à l'instar de celles qui existent en Allemagne." *La revue littéraire de l'Ouest* (henceforth *RLO*) (1836/7), 47–59, at 47. The pamphlet was also published independently.

48. "si quelque genre pouvait être négligé, ce ne serait pas, à mon avis, la Musique ancienne, ni celle peu antérieure à notre époque"; "faisant revivre." *RLO* (1836/7), 51.

Alsace, too, was a thriving centre for Baroque choral music, especially from the 1860s. Protestant music dominated. Isolated Handel oratorios had been known since the 1830s; but Strasbourg added to them a Bach revival that began with performances of Cantatas BWV6 and 104 in 1866 and 1867 and which continued to outstrip Parisian activity, accelerating significantly after 1871, the year the city's Société de Chant Sacré was founded and France lost the region to Germany.[49] Pasdeloup's celebrated St Matthew Passion of May 1868 at the Panthéon (followed by the *Ode for St Cecilia's Day* as light relief) was indeed an unprecedented event for Paris, but it would have seemed like a natural outgrowth of tradition had it been premiered on France's eastern border. Nevertheless, few Parisians would have known much about Alsatian musical traditions. Indeed, the relative absence of Alsace from the regional pages of Parisian music journals, other than during the Rhineland festivals, attests to the sense of its "otherness" except in the wake of 1870–71. The same was true of Niort: indeed, one wonders at what point Beaulieu's activity would have come to Parisian notice had he himself not placed articles in the capital's music journals.[50]

In short, if regional societies such as these are, for the historian, potential precursors to Parisian amateur societies singing early sacred music, they were not an acknowledged model among the Parisians themselves. Among Catholic societies, that distinction went to the prince de la Moskova, himself a successor to Choron. It was he whose blessing was sought and obtained in 1861–62 by the founders of the Société Académique de Musique Sacrée, set up by Georges Schmitt (organist at Saint-Sulpice) and then led by Charles Vervoitte (former *maître de chapelle* at Rouen Cathedral). The society, invariably presented as Vervoitte's brainchild, was a gathering of aristocrats, Ultramontane clergy, artists, and the high bourgeoisie that gave charity concerts intended to kindle a revitalization of "true" church music.[51] Its secretary was none other than Saint-Etienne; its resident organist, Saint-Saëns.

The choir was renowned for singing Sistine Chapel repertory (even after 1866, when its repertory changed somewhat) and for singing largely to its own kind: aristocrats and church dignitaries from the Papal nuncio, Mgr Chigi,

---

49. Geyer, *La vie musicale à Strasbourg*, 223–24. Significantly, Parisian performances of Handel's choral music in the early 1870s were often given in aid of a fund to reclaim Alsace.

50. Frustration is detectable in an article by "A.B.," secretary to the Société Philharmonique de Niort, sent to Théodore Nisard's *Revue de musique ancienne et moderne* in December 1856. He protests at an article in the *Revue et gazette musicale* in which Léon Kreutzer lamented the total absence of mixed choral societies (for oratorio especially) in France. While sympathizing in general, the author reminds Kreutzer that Niort had boasted such a society for 20 years (773–75).

51. D'Aldin and Roger, *Société académique de musique sacrée*, 5–7.

downwards.⁵² Among those who accepted this remit, the Société Académique attracted little but praise. It was only those who saw the potential for wider social action who were disappointed, not least because it seemed to give too few public performances to make an impact. This was the aristocracy at play. As the left-wing Auguste de Gasperini put it, its members were working for a charitable cause, "for their pleasure and their glory," and for nothing else.⁵³ And, as early as 1865, a reviewer signing himself "N" cast doubt on the effectiveness, as a popularizing force, of a society that had performed only six times in the four years since its foundation.⁵⁴ Ironically, the most far-reaching (and problematic) result of the Société Académique's work was to cement the perceived connection between *a cappella* polyphony and elitism, a connection that dated from the activities of Vervoitte's inspiration, the prince de la Moskova. For even though the Société Académique's repertory stretched well beyond sixteenth-century polyphony, and even though it mounted concerts for cotton workers, its character as a revival of Moskova's initiative only reinforced the notion that Palestrinian repertory was itself, in the widest sense, aristocratic and therefore inaccessible to those who did not belong to social or artistic elites.

After the dissolution of the society in 1872, Vervoitte continued to present the same selection of early choral music in Rouen with the newly reconstituted Société Philharmonique. His performances of Palestrina, Lassus, Handel, and Rameau found ready support from both local audiences and Amédée Méreaux, who was still writing for the *Journal de Rouen*. But the whiff of exclusivity persisted. In January 1872, Méreaux reported that the former orchestral society had invited the local *orphéon* choir (the Société Boieldieu) to act as its chorus. Méreaux noted that expanding the choir to include women seemed desirable, since it would enable the society to mount the much-neglected oratorio repertory.⁵⁵ But within a couple of months the *orphéon* singers had been edged out. The society's chorus, now to be conducted by its president Charles Vervoitte, would instead be made up of "gracious and skilled lady-musicians ... [who] have been more than willing to unite their voices with those of the amateur male singers of our salons."⁵⁶ Although the Société Boieldieu's conductor,

---

52. The Papal nuncio attended the society's concert of 20 May 1868 in Saint-Roch. Such interest from a high-ranking Vatican official was to bear fruit: Vervoitte was awarded the Ordre Pontifical de Saint-Grégoire-le-Grand in 1873. See Loth, *Notice sur M. Charles Vervoitte*, 21. For more detail on this society, and that of Bourgault-Ducoudray, see my "A Tale of Two Societies."

53. "pour leur plaisir et leur gloire." *Mén* 33/15: 11 March 1866, 17.

54. *AM* 5/19: 6 April 1865, 149.

55. *JR* 28 January 1872, n.p.

56. "gracieuses et habiles musiciennes ... Ces dames ont bien voulu unir leurs voix à celles des dilettantes-chanteurs de nos salons." *JR* 27 March 1872, n.p.

Henri Martin, rehearsed the new choir, his men did not sing in it. The refounding of the Rouen Société Philharmonique under Vervoitte thus provides an enlightening footnote to the issue of amateur choral performance and social class, also suggesting that although Vervoitte's Parisian activities contributed to the perception of Palestrinian music, specifically, as elite music, that perception may simply have been a by-product of his own tendency to avoid working with the lower classes.

I stress the social tensions in the popularization of early music because throughout the 1860s and 70s the lower classes' musical enfranchisement was the subject of heated debate. A handful of mixed *orphéon* societies, such as that at Le Havre (founded *c*.1858), sang the choral repertory of Haydn, Mozart, and Handel[57]; and because the Orphéon de Paris included children, it could, from 1854 to 1858 at least, boast performances of popular favorites by Palestrina (the fake "Adoramus te"), Leisring, Lully, Handel, and Rameau.[58] But the vast majority of *orphéons* were all-male, singing dedicated repertory dominated by simple three- or four-part unaccompanied pieces, many of them composed by specialists such as Camille de Vos and Laurent de Rillé, who knew their market and did not strive to challenge expectations. On the whole, *orphéon* singers' musical experience was resolutely contemporary. Nevertheless, it was during this very period that the amount of early and "classic" music known to *orphéon* choirs expanded significantly, to include short pieces (often specially arranged) by Rameau, Lassus, Marcello, Handel, and even the "elite" Palestrina. The choice represented the core of the most celebrated though usually the most straightforward examples of the early choral music that had been known in Paris since Choron's day: the Hallelujah chorus and the victory chorus from *Judas*; trios and choruses from Rameau's *Dardanus* and *Hippolyte*; the opening of Marcello's "I cieli immensi narrano"; the "Adoramus te" attributed to Palestrina; and, though rarely, Janequin's *La bataille de Marignan* and Lassus's chanson "Fuyons tous d'amour le jeu." These pieces never seem to have appeared as compulsory test repertory at *orphéon* competitions, and they represent a drop in the ocean of *orphéon* activity of the period. Nevertheless, most were published in editions directed at the *orphéon* market, and concert reviews reveal that they were indeed occasionally performed.

Two events in Paris are of particular importance: a meeting of six thousand singers for three concerts in March 1859 at the Palais de l'Industrie; and a partial

---

57. As reported (unsigned) in *La France chorale* (henceforth *FC*) 2 (no. 41): 10 December 1862, 2.
58. Di Grazia, *Concert Societies*, 132; in 1859, they would add the opening chorus from Marcello's "I cieli immensi narrano" (152) and, between 1862 and 1873, Arcadelt (the Dietsch arrangement of an "Ave Maria"), Lassus, and Lotti (157).

performance, by around five hundred singers, of Palestrina's *Stabat mater* at Saint-Roch on 18 April 1868. Both were organized by Eugène Delaporte, formerly organist of Sens Cathedral and in 1868 president of the Comité de l'Association des Sociétés Chorales de Paris.[59] The Palais de l'Industrie concerts, advertized as the first "Réunion des orphéonistes de France," involved 22 Parisian societies and 41 from French départements. They included *orphéon* music by De Rillé and Louis Lacombe, but also the septet from *Les Huguenots*, the priests' chorus from *Die Zauberflöte*, and the opening of Marcello's evergreen "I cieli immensi narrano," with new Latin words by De Lafage. To at least one of the participating societies this was a familiar work: the Société Chorale d'Agen omitted it from the charity concert they gave as a dry run for the Paris event, because it was too well known to need rehearsal.[60] The piece's more widespread familiarity at this time is also signaled by its inclusion in the program for the combined festival of French and English *orphéons* held in London in the summer of 1860.

Though it involved fewer singers, Delaporte's undertaking of 1868 was more ambitious. According to Méreaux, writing for *Le ménestrel*, it attracted crowds so numerous that even the vast space of Saint-Roch could not accommodate everyone. For Méreaux the concert held two attractions: Palestrina himself, and the fact that this work, which had not been sung in public since Moskova's time, was to be performed by "the newest disciples of the art of music in the nineteenth century."[61] Méreaux was gracious: accompanied loudly by the choir organ to help with pitching and intonation, the choirs produced a performance that was, he said, technically secure, even if it left something to be desired aesthetically. Emile Mathieu de Monter, a staunch supporter of the popularization of early sacred music, was sterner. With its Latin sung in strong Parisian accents, the piece sounded like "a much weakened and nearly disfigured echo of the Sistine chapel"; worse, with all the "hesitations, gaps, passages missed out [. . .] one had some difficulty in recognizing this great and touching music."[62] De Monter concluded that the enterprise had been foolhardy. The piece was simply too difficult.

---

59. For detail on Delaporte, see Di Grazia, *Concert Societies*, 124–28.

60. Undated report from the *Abeille agenaise* reprinted in *L'orphéon* (henceforth *O*) 5 (no. 84): 15 February 1859, n.p. The same was true of the septet from *Les Huguenots*.

61. "les plus jeunes adeptes de l'art musical au XIXe siècle." *Mén* 35/21: 19 April 1868, 164. Delaporte was not among the choir's conductors; he was, however, the organizing force behind the event.

62. "un écho bien amoindri et presque défiguré de la Sixtine. . . . Dans les hésitations, les ignorances, les lacunes d'exécution . . . , l'on avait quelque peine à reconnaître cette musique grande et touchante." *RGM* 35/16: 19 April 1868, 124.

[T]here are certain masterpieces [. . .] which cannot be tackled with impunity and without special preparation; it is undoubtedly a good thing to initiate *orphéonists* into the majesty of sacred music; . . . but, from the easy and well-trodden paths of their customary repertoire, to aspire to enable them to reach the sublime heights of Palestrina, this was too ambitious an enterprise to succeed.[63]

Most severe of all was the abbé Goumard, who as *maître de chapelle* of a major Paris church (he does not say which), had recently given up trying to perform the *Stabat mater* with a group of skilled, musically literate singers, because the music was beyond them. Scandalized in any case by the thought of this work being sung other than on its appointed day of the Church year (the concert was on Easter Saturday), he was no less shocked by what he heard: "because the choir was having terrible problems in maintaining the pitch, despite the organ's help . . . the performance had to be stopped short after a few verses. From that point, noise, uproar, scandal, not to mention disillusionment!"[64] For all the wrong reasons, Delaporte's attempt to bring Palestrina to Paris *orphéon* societies became a landmark event in the history of the composer's fortunes in France; it seemed to prove that, since the experiment of 1843 with a multiauthor parody Mass at Notre-Dame, nothing had improved the capacity of *orphéon* singers to perform his music. Unsurprisingly, Vervoitte, *maître de chapelle* of the host church, was nowhere to be seen.

Four years later, a more successful attempt to involve *orphéon* societies in the performance of early music was launched with the participation of the Société Chorale Le Louvre and Les Enfants de Lutèce in Bourgault-Ducoudray's performances of Handel's *Acis and Galatea* and *Alexander's Feast*. He also—with his *orphéon* singers—continued to program earlier polyphonic music such as Janequin's *Bataille* and the sixteenth-century sacred music that was supposedly beyond their capacities. In soliciting their co-operation, Bourgault-Ducoudray made a radical attempt to bolster a choir of wealthy amateurs with one comprising artisans and laborers.[65] By the early 1870s his society had already made a considerable impact as a regenerative force of potentially national significance, and

---

63. "il y a de certains chefs-d'oeuvre . . . auxquels il ne faut pas toucher impunément et sans préparation spéciale; sans aucun doute, il est bon d'initier les Orphéonistes à la majesté de la musique sacrée; . . . mais, des sentiers faciles et battus de leur répertoire habituel, vouloir leur faire atteindre aux sublimes hauteurs de Palestrina, l'entreprise était trop hardie pour réussir." *RGM* 35/16: 19 April 1868, 124.

64. "le choeur ayant mille peines à garder la tonalité en dépit du concours de l'orgue . . . on a dû s'arrêter court après quelques strophes. De là bruit, tapage, scandale, sans compter les déceptions!" *Revue de musique sacrée, ancienne et moderne* (henceforth *RMSAM*) 9/5: May 1868, 38.

65. For detail, see my "A Tale of Two Societies."

it became clear that alongside Weckerlin and Pasdeloup he was at the centre of a new push to rehabilitate choral music, Baroque oratorio particularly. With the Société Sainte-Cécile and the Société des Oratorios respectively, Weckerlin and Pasdeloup had done much to promote this repertory. Weckerlin had featured Handel's *Ode for St Cecilia's Day* in 1866 as part of his eclectic selection of pre-1800 music which took up fully half of each of his programs; Pasdeloup was narrower and, for that, more focused. Having performed the *Ode* in 1867 with the Société de l'Athénée, he then founded the short-lived Société des Oratorios—a dedicated choir to add to his orchestra. His two performances of just over half of Bach's St Matthew Passion and Handel's *Ode for St Cecilia's Day* at the Panthéon in May 1868 helped galvanize critical opinion on the necessity of spreading such music nationwide. His credentials for such a task were impeccable: not only was he the founder of the Concerts Populaires; he also had strong *orphéon* connections, having directed half of the Paris *orphéon* (the *rive droite*) in the early 1860s.

The immediate inheritor of this legacy was Charles Lamoureux. As early as 17 September 1872 he had, as the new deputy conductor of the Société des Concerts du Conservatoire, petitioned the committee to institute annual Easter performances of sacred choral music by Bach and Handel, presenting the idea as one of "patriotic" significance.[66] After postponing a decision, the committee, largely on the advice of Lamoureux's chief conductor Ernest Deldevez, finally refused him the following June. Undaunted, Lamoureux returned on 1 July 1873 with a more specific proposal: to mount the St Matthew Passion on Easter Saturday 1874 as a concert supplementary to the society's series. In meticulous detail, he described how many extra singers he would need, where the orchestra would be placed, how he would organize rehearsals, and how he would go about obtaining a translation. More objections—mostly concerning finances—ensued. The project was rejected by six votes to two.[67] It was this second rejection that caused Lamoureux to fund the project himself, obtaining authorization from the Société des Concerts committee to employ its orchestral players at each performance. On 19 December 1873 his society, shortly to be named the Société de l'Harmonie Sacrée, presented the first of six performances of most of *Messiah* to audiences of around four thousand in another circus arena: the Cirque des Champs-Elysées. The St Matthew Passion (rather more than half of it) followed in March and April 1874, with multiple

---

66. Archives of the Société des Concerts. Procès-verbaux [BNF Musique: D. 17345 (8), 90]. Together with Deldevez's reminiscences of his litany of objections to the idea, Lamoureux's proposal, discussed again on 3 June 1873, is reproduced in Ernest Deldevez, *La Société des concerts*, 270–73.

67. Archives of the Société des Concerts. Procès-verbaux [BNF Musique: D. 17345 (8), 178–80], given in Deldevez, *La Société des concerts*, 274–75.

performances of *Judas Maccabaeus*, and another *Messiah* series, the following season. Critics were, with few exceptions, bowled over by the prospect of a French choral tradition in the making. Deldevez never forgave the insolence of his deputy, and doubtless bridled at the barbed comments journalists aimed at the Société des Concerts for failing to undertake such a project itself.[68] However, Lamoureux's attempt came at considerable personal cost. Estimates placed the outlay for his 1874 St Matthew Passion alone at one hundred thousand francs (fully a third of his outlay for *Lohengrin* in 1887).[69] While he made economies of scale by using a circus arena that could take an audience of four thousand, by his own account he lost money. Pasdeloup, too, found it almost impossible to break even if a professional concert involved a paid choir.

It is hardly surprising, then, to find most performances of Baroque choral repertory in amateur hands. Several took place in the French regions, with the Dijonnais providing a shining example—and, seemingly, one of very few—of the kind of popular singing of Handelian oratorio advocated and implemented by Bourgault-Ducoudray and implicit in Lamoureux's appeal to the music's "patriotic" relevance. Two characters were central: Arthur Deroye, who set up the Société Chorale de Dijon from the fusion, in 1870, of two *orphéons*; and Charles Poisot, founder of the Société des Dames. Hot on Lamoureux's heels, between January 1874 and January 1876 they mounted four performances of Handel's works (*Messiah* twice, though not complete, *Alexander's Feast*, and *Acis*), usually with Poisot at the piano and Deroye conducting. It was only for the 1876 performance of *Acis* that Deroye succeeded in realizing a long-cherished ambition—to perform such repertory with orchestra. Reporters were almost uniformly ecstatic, proudly telling their readers that the citizens of Dijon were the first non-Parisians to hear *Acis* with orchestra.[70] What reporters did not emphasize was that the orchestration was Handel's, not Mozart's, as was more customarily heard in Paris. For the score and parts had been lent by the only conductor in Paris who insisted on using the original Handel: Bourgault-Ducoudray.[71] The links here went deeper, in the social constitution of the combined forces. The local press listed "ladies, music-lovers, the entire Choral Society [the *orphéon*, and] children from the *maîtrise* of Saint-Bénigne

---

68. See, for instance, Gaston Escudier's review of the first performance of *Messiah* (*AM* 12/52: 25 December 1873, 412).

69. For figures from "Caliban" on Charles Lamoureux, see *Le Figaro* 27 April 1887, n.p.

70. See reviews in *La Côte d'Or* 14 January 1876, n.p., and the *Progrès de la Côte d'Or* 15 January 1876, n.p. The same point is stressed in E. Belin (Ed.), *La Société chorale de Dijon*, 12–13. Among the local papers, only Dijon's *Le bien public* did not share the general enthusiasm (*Bien public* 13 January 1876, n.p.).

71. On the loan, see *La Côte d'Or* 14 January 1876, n.p. (unsigned). The use of Handel's original orchestration is confirmed in *Le progrès de la Côte d'Or* 15 January 1876, n.p.

[Dijon Cathedral]."⁷² Teaching staff at the Dijon Conservatoire were also involved. While there is no evidence that the social mix included the aristocracy, it nevertheless ranged widely across Dijon's population. The same was true of the earlier Handel performances, which combined the Société Chorale and the Société des Dames. As such, these were remarkable events in a society where rules governing the social mixing of the sexes, in particular among the petit bourgeoisie and lower classes, seemed intractably strict.⁷³

Emulation of Parisian choral activity also reached Aix-en-Provence, where two performances of *Judas Maccabaeus* in 1877 and 1879 were reported in the local press as barometers of the town's musical vitality. Here, too, the beginnings were modest, with the first performance accompanied by piano only, and the second by a string octet. An outgrowth of the activity of the *maîtrise*, these performances formed part of a plan to present a series of pieces of "classic" music in the town. Marbot, the *maîtrise*'s director, gave a progress report at the annual prize-giving of August 1876. Liturgical music, he said, had been in decline since Pergolesi's *Stabat mater*. However, Choron, De Lafage, and others had shown that regeneration was possible, and although some churches in the Aix area had taken up "dubious" repertory, others had kept hold of their Carissimi, their Campra (a local boy, of course), and their Haydn. But he saw the possibility of annexing oratorio, presented in concert, to the repertory of liturgical music.⁷⁴ It was in this context, and in full recognition of how far France lagged behind Germany and England, that Marbot perceived the utility of his concerts of *musique classique*. They generated the same levels of enthusiasm in Aix as had the Handel performances at Dijon, although they lacked the element of social integration. Indeed, it was a matter of pride to the correspondent for Toulouse's *Musica sacra* that the *maîtrise* performed alone. The 1877 concert, in the Archbishop's residence, was such a draw that audience members—who applauded each difficult passage and especially the two closing fugues—traveled from as far away as Marseille to hear it. Congratulating the people of Aix on the concert, the reporter noted that "The English would have been envious," concluding with a call to arms for *maîtrises* round the country: "Let's get all our

---

72. "dames, amateurs, Société chorale toute entière, enfants de la Maîtrise de Saint Bénigne." *La Côte d'Or*, 14 January 1876, n.p.

73. Whether Poisot and Deroye would have been able to fuse their societies of women and men is, of course, another matter. As I discuss in chapter 7, precedent suggested that it would have been supremely difficult to turn an exceptional event of this kind into a regular occurrence.

74. "douteux." Speech reported in *La Provence* 20 August 1876, given in *Musica sacra* (Toulouse; henceforth *MS*), 2/10: 6 September 1876, 112–14.

maîtrises working like this, and they will again become what they once were—one of the glories of the Church and of French art."[75]

Music and the Liturgy

Alongside Choron and De Lafage, the revivalists whom Marbot invoked in his prize-giving speech of 1876 were Niedermeyer and D'Ortigue. It was Niedermeyer who, from 1853 to his death in 1861, had directed the successor to Choron's school, where Saint-Saëns famously taught Fauré: the Ecole de Musique Religieuse (Ecole Niedermeyer).[76] It was D'Ortigue, a passionate Ultramontane and defender of the rights of plainchant, who acted as chief editor of the journal they founded together, which promoted the ideals (centring on plainchant, Palestrinian polyphony, and Bach's organ music) of the school itself: *La maîtrise*. The Comité de Surveillance des Etudes contained familiar names, including the prince de la Moskova, Dietsch (*maître de chapelle* at the Madeleine), and Georges Schmitt. Both Dietsch and Niedermeyer had, of course, been associated with Moskova's society in the 1840s: this was a meeting of like minds. Unlike Choron's school, the Ecole Niedermeyer was an all-male establishment for the training of *maîtres de chapelle* and organists; similarly, however, it was vulnerable to government policy changes, fulfilling its original function only until 1884, when anticlerical government directives forced it to become a more general, ostensibly secular, conservatoire.

Established as a state institution on a much more formal basis than Choron's school, and initially answerable to the Ministère de l'Instruction Publique et des Cultes, the Ecole Niedermeyer was one sign of Napoléon III's building of bridges with the Catholic church, whose various arms flourished during his reign. On both sides of the Gallican/Ultramontane divide, the clergy were largely welcoming of his regime.[77] Enhanced funding from central

---

75. "Les Anglais en eussent été jaloux! . . . Faisons partout ainsi travailler nos maîtrises, et elles reviendront ce qu'elles ont été jadis, l'une des gloires de l'Eglise et de l'art français." *MS* 3/5: 6 April 1877, 59.

76. See Galerne, *L'Ecole Niedermeyer*; Di Grazia, *Concert Societies*, 201–13; and Sako, *The Importance of Louis Niedermeyer*. Sako's work on the career paths of students at the school is particularly important for the future study of music in the French regions.

77. Latreille et al., *Histoire du catholicisme en France*, 308–12. On the liturgical conflicts of this period, see Gough, *Paris and Rome*. Gough's section on liturgical music is, however, too general to offer much insight. His slavish linking of Ultramontanism with calls for a return to Gregorian chant alone (at the expense of Palestrinian polyphony) is wide of the mark (163–67); moreover, he neglects to define or discuss eighteenth-century Gallican musical traditions at all.

government supported the expansion of the country's *maîtrises*, many of which participated in an overhaul of liturgical music in which Palestrina began to take pride of place. This was the path taken by most of the self-consciously "regenerative" cathedrals. Langres, Autun, and Moulins headed a Second-Empire revival of Palestrinian music. Yet despite the historical links between Cecilianism and Ultramontanism, the relationships between such activity and card-carrying Ultramontanism were not straightforward. A sense of Catholic heritage more generally appears to have been just as important. At Rouen, for instance, early Italian sacred music was encouraged by Archbishop Blanquart de Bailleul (1795–1868), himself a staunch Gallican. A prize-giving concert under Vervoitte at the Archbishop's palace on 6 August 1855, which took the form of a *concert historique* "similar to those of previous years," included Palestrina's "Sicut cervus," a three-voice "Pleni sunt coeli" and a four-part Gloria; a Carissimi "Gaudeamus"; three extracts from Marcello, including "Coeli enarrant" (i.e., the famous "I cieli immensi" in Latin), the "Libera me" from Jommelli's *Requiem*, and works by Haydn, Romberg, Janequin (*La bataille*), Handel (a chorus from *Samson*), Mendelssohn (a chorus from *Elijah*), and Vervoitte.[78] Although there is no corroborating evidence, it is difficult not to conclude that this repertory includes that which was sung liturgically. It is, incidentally, closely related to that of the Société Académique, and taken almost entirely from the repertories of Choron and, especially, Moskova.

Stronger evidence for a full-scale Palestrinian revival comes from that cluster of cathedrals in the east of the country: at Autun, Langres, and Moulins. The first to adopt this repertory appears to have been Langres. Its *maîtrise*, newly instituted in 1852, was run by members of the Couturier family. Two were particularly prominent: the organist Nicolas-Mammès (*b*.1840) and his uncle Claude (*b*.1816), one of no fewer than three uncles resident as teachers at the *maîtrise*. Claude, an acquaintance of both Danjou and Morelot, was the driving force behind the introduction of the music of Palestrina, Victoria, Bach, and Handel at the cathedral. But both men probably supervised the in-house production of choir-books containing a selection of their own *a cappella* music alongside generous helpings of Palestrina. By 1852 the cathedral had adopted the Roman rite under the guidance of the Ultramontane Bishop of Langres, Mgr Parisis (served 1835–51). This was an environment in which the myth of Palestrina's saving of church music through the Pope Marcellus Mass was preached as gospel, and where his teacher Goudimel's Protestantism could not

---

78. "semblable à ceux des années précédents." *Chronique de Rouen*, 9 August 1855, n.p.

be acknowledged. Monteverdi, the starting-point for modern music in Fétisian historiography, sat at the head of a romantic theatricality in church music that sent the Couturiers scuttling back to the safety of Tridentine precepts.[79] The Pergolesi *Stabat mater* was too operatic for liturgical use: as models for "true" church music for voices and organ respectively, only Palestrina and Bach (significantly, the models of the Niedermeyer school) would do.

The histories of two other revivalist cathedrals—Moulins and Autun— are closely linked. It was through their experience of practice at Autun that the directors of the *maîtrise* at Moulins adopted a Palestrinian repertory. June 1865 was a turning point: the *maîtrise* directors, the abbés Lacour and Melin, and the *maître de chapelle* Charles Duvois, traveled the 70 kilometres or so to the monastery at Paray-le-Monial, where they heard the Autun choir sing sixteenth-century polyphony. Lacour recommended that Duvois emulate them.[80] By 1868, they had, like Langres, brought together their own corpus of pre-1600 motets (a large proportion taken from Proske's *Musica divina*), of which fully half was devoted to Palestrina and Victoria.[81] From that point, the *maîtrise* rapidly developed an enviable reputation for its sacred polyphony. Vervoitte, who inspected regularly from 1872 to 1880 as part of the government's monitoring of public subsidy, regarded it as a model[82]; later inspections by Théodore Dubois confirmed its musical richness, though amid a more general educational poverty.[83] Gounod stopped by in 1877 just to hear the traditional Good Friday liturgy of Palestrina, Victoria, and Allegri under their new (since 1874) *maître de chapelle*, the abbé Chérion. Until Chérion's departure for the Madeleine at the end of 1896, the *maîtrise* of Moulins was undisputedly the finest and most versatile in France. A draft inspection report of 20 June 1889 described it as the pride of the town and the Département and commented on the large crowds its singing attracted. Remarkable for its early music, which was the object of "special observance," it was more than a choir raising historical interest, since it also sang a great deal of more modern music.[84] For under Chérion it was not as ideologically rigid as Langres,

---

79. Noël and Roussel, *M. l'abbé Nicolas Couturier*, 102. Their "history of church music" skips straight from Palestrina to Bach.

80. Rannaud, *La maîtrise de la cathédrale de Moulins*, 11.

81. The collection was entitled *Liber motetorum ad usum ecclesiae cathedralis molinensis*. Rannaud, *La maîtrise de la cathédrale de Moulins*, 11.

82. Rannaud, *La maîtrise de la cathédrale de Moulins*, 15–16.

83. AN Paris: F²¹ 1327 Moulins Cathedral *maîtrise* inspection reports, 1883–1901.

84. "un culte spécial." AN Paris: F²¹ 1327 Moulins Cathedral *maîtrise* inspection reports, 1883–1901. The repertory that Dubois recommended to Chérion c.1882–85 to "complete" his music list contained much

instead mixing Gounod and Bach choral music with its Palestrina and Victoria.

Missing at both Langres and Moulins, however (and probably elsewhere, most of the time), was the music of early French traditions. That might be expected at Langres, but perhaps less so at the more eclectic Moulins. Yet it is a measure of the strength of Ultramontanism in music that "liturgical reformism" in France almost inevitably meant "Cecilianism": either adherence to plainchant, or to *a cappella* polyphony, or both. We know little about the longevity or revival of the French *grand motet* or of the music of the French Baroque organists in liturgical contexts. There must, however, have been outposts of a kind of musical Gallicanism. Carpentras, in a limited way, was one such. As Marbot indicated in 1876, Aix was another. Containing a core of Palestrina (De Lafage's 1840s edition of the motets and a few other pieces) and Tommaso Baj's *Miserere*, but little else in the way of Sistine chapel repertory, the cathedral library is by contrast replete with copies of the motets of Lalande (55 items) and three locals—Campra (14 items), Gilles (15 items), and Pellegrin (21 items)—scores that did not lie idle during the nineteenth century. There is scant reference to Aix in the pages of Aloys Kunc's Toulouse journal *Musica sacra*, which otherwise covered regional church news assiduously. But since *Musica sacra* was an avowedly Ultramontane publication we should perhaps not expect detailed coverage of cathedrals that retained seventeenth- and eighteenth-century French music in their liturgies. There was, however, also a hint of such activity in Paris, at the very church to which the abbé Chérion was to move in 1896: La Madeleine. Dietsch's repertory, as indicated in his anthology of liturgical music published between 1854 and 1857, shows an unusually strong Gallican streak, with the music of Lalande and Campra particularly well represented.[85] The nearby church of Saint-Philippe-du-Roule followed suit: in 1869 its *maître de chapelle* Emile Bourdeau published six pieces from the choir's repertory under the title *Renaissance du chant religieux*. Of those six pieces, two were by Lalande ("O dulcis amor" and "Tota pulchra es") and two by Campra ("Cantate domino" and "Genitori"). Given the history of *ancien-régime* repertory in the historiography of church music from Choron onwards, to give the title "renaissance" to such a collection was a provocative act. Yet it was also indicative of a larger-scale phenomenon: movement toward rehabilitation of the once-detested *musique française*.

Renaissance or Baroque music (including his own version of Marcello's Psalm no. 18 as "Christus resurrexit") but also listed works up to and including his own liturgical compositions. (AN Paris: F²¹ 4610 Liasse 8. Unsigned list in Dubois's characteristic handwriting and purple ink.)

85. Dietsch (Ed.), *Répertoire de musique religieuse de l'Eglise de la Madeleine* (1854–57).

La musique française Reconsidered

Nothing here could compare with the efforts of the Ultramontanes in respect to Italianate sacred music; this was not a concerted attempt, by a closely knit group, to change musical practice. Rather, the sense of a challenge to prevalent cultural attitudes arose from the density of largely unrelated events preceding the Franco-Prussian War. Three anthologies dating from before 1870 led the way to greater familiarity with the half-forgotten repertories of *tragédie en musique*, early *opéra-comique* and *opéra-ballet*. In 1850, Charles Dufort published eleven extracts from Lully's stage music (*Amadis, Persée, Acis et Galatée, Armide, Roland,* and *Phaëton*). Presented for domestic consumption in vocal score, they were published at the editor's expense and represented a relatively modest challenge to prevailing critical tastes and the general disparagement of such French music. More ambitious, but still privately published, was the Delsartes' *Archives du chant*, which made an extensive corpus of such music available (44 extracts from Lully; 27 from Rameau).[86] Finally, in 1869 Ernest Deldevez published a commercial edition of orchestrated arrangements stretching from Beaujoyeulx to Gluck.[87]

Deldevez's approach was not universally welcomed, for his arrangements were, where he thought it necessary, edited highlights that cut, pasted, and generally reshaped the originals. His "Trio des Parques" from Rameau's *Hippolyte et Aricie*, a version of which he presented at the Société des Concerts, was one such. It interleaved the Trios of Act III scene 5 and Act II scene 4, starting with the orchestral introduction to the Act III Trio, moving back to the Act II Trio "Du destin le vouloir suprême," and re-entering the Act III Trio a tone low (to preserve continuity of F major and F minor for the entire sequence) at Pluto's address to the Fates. In the process he was able to dispense with 56 bars of conversation between Pluto and Mercury, and a short air, while compressing

---

86. Together with Pauline Viardot, who sang in his *Archives du chant* concerts, François Delsarte was able to extend the concert tradition of Lully's music beyond the party piece that was Caron's Hell scene (*Alceste*), made famous in the 1830s and 40s not only by Adolphe Alizard, but also by Gustave-Hippolyte Roger (ironically, at Moskova's concerts) and Hermann Léon, and in the following decade by Louis-Henri Obin. In addition, he brought the music of Rameau—represented even less well than that of Lully once *reprises* of Candeille's *Castor* ceased on 20 August 1817—to the fore. In 1856 alone, he presented extracts from *Thésée, Proserpine, Atys,* and *Acis* alongside music from *Hippolyte et Aricie, Castor et Pollux,* and Collasse's *Les saisons*.

87. Deldevez (Ed.), *Pièces diverses choisies dans les oeuvres des célèbres compositeurs*. This collection is also important for its inclusion of excerpts from the dramatic music of Monteverdi, Caccini, Peri, Cavalieri, and Cavalli—much of it for the first time in France. Before him, only Castil-Blaze had broached this repertory, in his self-published collection *Théâtres lyriques de Paris* (1855).

the two Trios into one relatively short piece and thereby maximizing the emphasis on the choral passages.[88] Deldevez thus provided a practical demonstration of the prevalent antipathy toward seventeenth- and eighteenth-century French styles of declamation, which, though increasingly lauded in theory, suffered in practice in comparison with choruses, airs, and dance movements. Editors of postwar publications either followed, or actively tried to neutralize, this trend.[89]

While from 1852 Lully had the lion's share of performances of early stage music during the period, Rameau had devotees. Two champions—Adolphe Adam and Charles Poisot—stand out. Adam's choral arrangement of the *air* "Dans ce doux asile" from *Castor et Pollux*, prepared at some time in the 1840s, became Rameau's most popular choral extract, largely through its frequent presentation at the Société des Concerts.[90] Adam was also the first, in 1852, to write a dedicated Ramiste apologia. Yet that apologia is as important for its sense of compromise as for its passages of eulogy. Encapsulating the anxiety of the supporter of old French music in the middle of the century, Adam's biography stressed those parts of Rameau's output that displayed "grandeur," "noblesse," and originality, and skated (explicitly) over the smaller, late works. In addition, Adam's journey ended not with a peroration and a demand for wider recognition, but with equivocation and a depressed plea for the readers whose patience he fears he has sorely tried to show more tolerance of a composer whose faults were not his own, but of his environment: "I am keenly aware of just how little I have succeeded in getting others to share my admiration for the beautiful things which Rameau's operas contain, and to make them realize the deficiencies relating to his education and his era."[91] The contrast between Adam's tail-between-legs ending and the confident enthusiasm of, for instance, Victor Schoelcher's *The Life of Handel* (which appeared just five years later) could hardly be greater. But Adam was explicit: the state of French music in the eighteenth century meant that he could not, and would not, try to equate Rameau with his most famous Italian and German contemporaries.[92] If

---

88. Deldevez (Ed.), *Pièces diverses choisies dans les oeuvres des célèbres compositeurs*, 60–72.

89. See chapter 4.

90. Adam had originally made a concert piece from a combination of the chorus "Brisons nos fers" and his choral arrangement of "Dans ce doux asile," but only the latter was taken up by Narcisse Girard, then conductor of the Société des Concerts. Adam recounts the story as part of his Rameau biography of 1852 (included in Adam, *Derniers souvenirs*, 63–67).

91. "dont j'ai, sans doute, fatigué la patience"; "je sens combien peu je suis parvenu à faire partager mon admiration pour les belles choses que renferment les opéras de Rameau, et à faire comprendre les défauts qui tenaient à son éducation et à son époque." Adam, *Derniers souvenirs*, 71.

92. Adam, *Derniers souvenirs*, 69.

Rameau deserved an apologia, then, it was strictly in the context of the second-division musicianship that was *ancien-régime* France.

Poisot's revivalism was more far-reaching than Adam's, encompassing editing, performance, and fundraising. Alongside his activity as a Handelian, he championed Rameau tirelessly both in Paris and in his (and Rameau's) native Dijon. One of the prime movers behind the commemorative Rameau festival held in Dijon in the summer of 1876, Poisot had proselytized on the composer's behalf since the mid-1860s and was to edit all but two of the Rameau volumes in Michaëlis's monumental *Chefs-d'oeuvre classiques de l'Opéra français* of 1877–84. His collection of piano music, the *Bibliothèque classique des pianistes*, contained an entire volume of Rameau: the first and second suites for harpsichord (also available in the *Trésor des pianistes*, but, as he pointed out, only at considerable expense, since one had to subscribe to the complete collection); an extract from *Les Indes galantes*; and two unpublished pieces taken from manuscripts at the Paris Conservatoire. In introducing his material to buyers, Poisot uttered thoughts that were to become leitmotifs of pro-Rameau writing in the next decade:

> I should like to express a wish in ending this (already over-long) preface; it is that the French government should do for the works of Rameau that which George III of England has done for those of Handel; that which a committee of German artists is now doing, in Leipzig, for the works of the immortal J. S. Bach.[93]

The sense that France was slow in celebrating her own composers, and that since the late eighteenth century she had too consistently preferred imports from abroad, intensified from the mid-1860s to the end of the century, with new impetus after the Franco-Prussian War. French music journals had always published reports of musical activities in neighboring countries; yet during this period those reports ceased to have the neutral tone of reportage. Instead, they began to reveal evidence of a combination of envy, depression, and lack of confidence. There were, increasingly, new reasons to re-evaluate historical French music, and to attempt to quash lingering doubts about the inherent quality of *la musique française*.

---

93. "Qu'on me laisse exprimer un voeu en terminant cette notice, déjà trop longue; c'est que le gouvernement français fasse pour les oeuvres de Rameau, ce que le roi George III d'Angleterre a fait pour les oeuvres de Händel, ce qu'un comité d'artistes allemands fait aujourd'hui, à Leipzig, pour les ouvrages de l'immortel Jean-Sébastien Bach." Preface to vol. 25 (*Oeuvres choisies de Rameau*) of Charles Poisot's series "Bibliothèque classique des pianistes," n.p.

But those doubts were real indeed—so real that the concert programs for the first Dijon Rameau festival, held in the summer of 1866, contained no Rameau at all. It was simply too risky. Twelve years later, at the festival which saw the unveiling, after 16 years of fundraising, of the maquette of the composer's statue, the organizing committee scheduled one all-Rameau concert, followed two days later by a further half-program of his music. Quite by accident, the timing was opportune for those who wished to make grand statements about competing cultures: the festival began just days before the opening of the first Bayreuth Festival. Anti-Wagnerian Parisian journalists grasped the nationalist baton and ran with it, pitting a French national hero against an arrogant German invader; in Dijon, however, such national symbolism had no purchase whatever. The response of the local press was largely adverse; and after the first dose of the composer's music, the public voted with its feet when offered the second.[94]

The *clavecin* music fared slightly better, but was quite capable of evincing expressions of derision or boredom if it failed to pique the imagination. Sometimes it attracted no comment at all; at others the perils of playing it were all too clearly confirmed by a frosty reception from audience and press alike. Reviewing the harpsichord pieces played at one of Delsarte's concerts in the spring of 1860, the critic Adolphe Botte did nothing to encourage the idea that the audience had misjudged the quality of the works it heard. They remained unnamed, as did the hapless pianist:

> Nothing should be taken to extremes, not even the most salutary of musical reactions, and I think that *retrogradist* pianists are wrong in their wish to make harpsichord music heard at any price. Of course, there are some very beautiful pieces; but they are not all beautiful, and as with works of all eras, there are some very mediocre ones. Does the fault lie with the performance or the composition? I don't know. Nevertheless, it is a fact that the Couperin and Rameau pieces were received with a frostiness whose irreverence merits note.[95]

---

94. I discuss this event, and its significance, in detail in my "Rameau in Late Nineteenth-Century Dijon."

95. "Il ne faut rien exagérer, pas même les réactions musicales les plus salutaires, et nous croyons que les pianistes rétrogradistes ont tort de vouloir faire entendre à toute force des pièces de clavecin. Certes, il y en a de fort belles; mais toutes ne le sont pas, et, comme dans les ouvrages de tous les temps, il y en a de très-médiocres. Est-ce la faute de l'exécution ou celle de la composition? Nous ne savons [pas]. Toutefois est-il que les pages de Couperin et de Rameau ont été accueillies avec une froideur dont l'irrévérence mérite d'être signalée." *RGM* 27/15: 8 April 1860, 127.

Despite the efforts of a clutch of pianists who took small corners of this repertory to their hearts, it rarely pleased audiences until the 1890s. By contrast, there were already signs in the 1870s that French Baroque music was more palatable when suitably repackaged. Deldevez's modernizations and Adam's arrangements were one option; the evocation of old French dances through pastiche was another. Henry Cohen remarked in the *Chronique musicale* of 1874 that new interest in writing orchestral suites marked a renewal of eighteenth-century ideas.[96] But such interest had been detectable since the 1850s, when the foundations were laid for a reverential neo-classicism that developed in the final quarter of the century. Among other composers, Gounod (*Le médecin malgré lui*, 1858), Saint-Saëns (*Suite pour orchestre*, 1863), Massenet (orchestral suites, 1864–81), Fauré (gavotte from the F major Symphony), and Bizet (incidental music to *L'Arlésienne*, 1872) made notable contributions. The enfolding of one style into another caused an otherwise skeptical reviewer of Gounod's "Molière opera" to point out how quintessentially French was the simple elegance of the composer's overture.[97] It also enabled Gounod to pass off an earlier version of that overture (1851) as part of Lully's incidental music to *Le bourgeois gentilhomme* (Comédie-Française, 1852).[98]

However, when Botte wrote so testily of *retrogradist* obsession, France was still 35 years away from a project to produce Poisot's much-desired collected edition of Rameau's music. And while publication projects and increased concert performances had significantly raised the profile of *la musique française*, the period to 1878 saw no sudden transformation in its fortunes. However, that very year proved that such a transformation was indeed possible, given the right circumstances and the right repertory. It offered a spectacular example of how a single individual who seized an opportunity could change entrenched perceptions, attract a brand new audience, and render the supposedly scholastic the object of frenetic enthusiasm—all within a few years. That individual was the organist Alexandre Guilmant; the venue, the new Trocadéro Salle des Fêtes with its Cavaillé-Coll organ; the composers, Bach and Handel.

---

96. *Chronique musicale* (henceforth *CM*), 3 (no. 16): 15 February 1874, 177. For a detailed examination of this phenomenon in precisely these terms, see Morris, *The Wellsprings of Neo-Classicism in Music*.

97. "La partition . . . est une tentative de retour vers les formes surannées. On n'imite pas mieux les anciens maîtres. . . . Si M. Gounod a voulu être simple, clair, élégant, il a réussi." Escudier, *FM* 22/3 (17 January 1858), 17.

98. Sources conflict as to whether Gounod or Auber arranged the 1852 score. Weckerlin [MS annotations to BNF (Musique): Rés. 1841] and Yon (*Jacques Offenbach*, 107) give Auber; Huebner (*New Grove II*, "Gounod", Gounod. Since the score (Comédie-Française, 6-Pi-41) contains the interpolated music for the "Air des Garçons Tailleurs" that Gounod later adapted for use in the Overture and Act II finale of his "Lullian" score *Le médecin malgré lui* (1858), he seems by far the more plausible contender. I am grateful to Steven Huebner for help in clarifying Gounod's role here.

3
1878–1900

Few could have predicted the impact of the six organ recitals that Alexandre Guilmant organized for the Exposition Universelle of 1878. Free of charge, and each featuring a different organist, they attracted near-capacity audiences to the vast Salle des Fêtes at the Trocadéro, where a new 60-stop Cavaillé-Coll organ had been installed. Here, in the only Paris concert hall with an organ permanently *in situ*, Guilmant began what was to be a twenty-year exploration of the organ repertory of Handel, Bach, Buxtehude, Frescobaldi, Clérambault, and modern composers (including himself).[1] His activity was a continuation, within instrumental music, of Lamoureux's attempts to popularize the Baroque oratorio repertory in Paris, yet Guilmant was infinitely more successful in drawing a mass public and then keeping its interest. He was central to many of the stories of early music in the late nineteenth century in France: to the seemingly inexorable rise of organ music old and new, liturgical and in concert, in Paris and all over France; to the broadening of taste for instrumental music of the Baroque period; to a new enthusiasm for Bach cantatas in the 1890s (with Bordes and the Chanteurs de Saint-Gervais); and to the setting up of the Schola Cantorum, both as a society for the propagation of church music across France, and, from the autumn of 1896,

---

1. His solo concerts ran uninterrupted from 1879 to 1898, and then from 1901 to 1906. For a general survey, see Smith, "The Organ of the Trocadéro and Its Players."

as the last in the chain of church-music schools descended from those of Choron and Niedermeyer.

Guilmant was central to a further change in emphasis in the history of early music: the emergence of the virtuoso soloist as active propagandist for particular early repertories. Despite increasing interest among instrumentalists, the early and middle years of the century had seen revivals of early music centre mostly around choral repertories: its propagandists therefore tended to be conductors and teachers who founded their own musical societies. While new choral societies on this model still appeared in the last decades of the century (Concordia, the Chanteurs de Saint-Gervais, the Société des Grandes Auditions de France, and the Société L'Euterpe are the most conspicuous examples), the number of international soloists who promoted early music increased significantly. The pianists Louis Diémer and Raoul Pugno, the flautist Paul Taffanel and the oboist Georges Gillet, the viola player Louis van Waefelghem, cellist Jules Delsart and several violinists, including Sarasate, Paul Viardot, and Ysaÿe, were at the forefront of such activity. Among organists, Eugène Gigout's reputation in the 1870s rivaled that of Guilmant, while in succeeding decades Charles-Marie Widor (like Guilmant, a pupil of Lemmens) and Louis Vierne followed their example.

The increase in instrumental activity did not mean that choral endeavors were relegated to second place. The period contained its fair share of choral milestones: specifically, the first complete Parisian performances of Bach's St Matthew Passion (Concordia, 1888) and B minor Mass (Société des Concerts du Conservatoire, 1891), and of Handel's *Israel in Egypt* (Société des Grandes Auditions de France, also 1891). But the Second-Empire phenomenon of concert societies largely dedicated to early music was replaced by a preference for a much more broad-ranging repertory on the model of Lamoureux, whose Handel and Bach choral performances of the early 1870s had given way, by 1875, to an oratorio repertory focused on living French composers: Massenet, Gounod, and Franck in particular. In Paris, the exception to this new eclecticism in choral society programming was Bordes and his Chanteurs de Saint-Gervais, who focused almost exclusively on music before 1750. Their bringing of a host of Bach cantatas to Parisian attention in the 1890s was of paramount historical importance. Yet the works with which Bordes and his choir made the most impact in concert were the chansons of Lassus, closely followed by early Baroque novelties of composers—Schütz and Carissimi—hardly heard since Fétis.[2] And while the

---

2. Extracts from Carissimi's *Jephte* had been part of the Société Chorale d'Amateurs' repertory (1865–1914?; founded Antonin Guillot de Sainbris) since at least 1875, but otherwise his music was virtually unknown. See Di Grazia, *Concert Societies*, 324.

mainstream concert repertory of early music featured a few key composers at whose pinnacle stood Bach (and, for figured liturgical music, Palestrina), Bordes resolutely expanded the repertory to take in composers and genres hitherto ignored, notably the operatic repertory of late sixteenth- and early seventeenth-century Italy.

Amid an exponential increase in early music activity in the last two decades of the nineteenth century, the winnowing out of certain repertories, already detectable during the 1860s and '70s, continued apace. With the exception of Palestrinian music and Bordes's championing of the early Italian Baroque, a general trend may be observed: Italian music gave way to that of Germany and, to a limited extent, France. Handel and then Bach completely displaced Marcello for early choral music and dominated early instrumental music. Palestrina remained a model, but interest in Lassus and other Franco-Flemish or Spanish sacred polyphonists increased dramatically. There were renewed attempts to rehabilitate French stage music of the seventeenth and eighteenth centuries, at least in print. The music became widely available in the series *Chefs-d'oeuvre classiques de l'Opéra français* (1877–1884); in addition, work on Rameau's collected edition was begun in 1894 and a large portion of his *Dardanus* given a private concert performance by Bordes and the Chanteurs de Saint-Gervais at the princesse de Polignac's rue Cortambert *atelier* the following year.[3] Other French repertories gained even more ground: the polyphonic chanson and the instrumental (often dance-based) miniature of the seventeenth or the eighteenth century. Each revival brought with it considerable intellectual and cultural baggage, some of it appropriated publicly by reformers, some of it remaining just under the surface of the rhetorics used by contemporary writers.

The religious history of the period is fraught. Moves toward founding a French branch of the Cecilian movement took place, belatedly, in 1887, just a few years after a wave of anticlerical government measures had forced the Ecole Niedermeyer and *maîtrises* all over the country to secularize their curricula in order to retain their rights to state funding. And while the First Vatican Council vote of 1869/70 in support of Papal Infallibility had instituted Ultramontanism to an even greater degree than previously in French churches, there was still fierce dissent within a beleaguered Catholic church. Nevertheless, as local histories attest, it was precisely during this period— and up to the formal separation of Church and State in 1905—that a limited

---

3. 23 April 1895. This was the first performance of substantial parts of the opera since 1784. Act II was performed complete alongside excerpts from all other acts. See Kahan, *Music's Modern Muse*, 373.

number of *maîtrises* spread across the country enjoyed their richest musical years. The Schola Cantorum (founded 1894) placed itself at the centre of that activity.

The Virtuoso as Propagandist: Alexandre Guilmant and Louis Diémer

From Guilmant's point of view, the Trocadéro concerts did not arise from nothing. Since the early 1860s he had participated in an activity unique to organists and indicative, in its increasing frequency, of the extent to which the Church flourished in the Second Empire and even during the Third Republic: the public inauguration of new and restored organs in major French churches. It was commonplace at such events for the *titulaire* to play the first piece, then to hand over the performance to the guest organist, who had devised a program to display the instrument's quality and range. Such displays were not just religious celebrations; they were crucial publicity exercises for the market leaders in organ-building, Cavaillé-Coll and, later, Merklin. In his role as "demonstrator" of the new instrument, the organist had necessarily to be a virtuoso who could reveal its range fully, through changes in registration, through pedal technique, and in displays of speed and power. Guilmant was one such, Gigout another.

The repertory for these occasions was necessarily wide, routinely including an improvisation and a couple of pieces by the featured organist. But the other common thread was Bach, through whose music the quality of an instrument's pedal board could be shown fully. It was probably for that reason that certain pieces soon became regular inauguration fodder: the Toccata in F BWV540 (without its fugue); the Fugue in G minor (BWV542 often without its fantasia—this was the "great" G minor fugue arranged by Liszt in 1868–69); the "Wedge" fugue BWV548; the Toccata and Fugue in D minor BWV565 and the Passacaglia with fugue in C minor BWV582. Guilmant took part in the inauguration of the restored Saint-Sulpice organ in 1862 and then gave a solo recital on it on 2 May. He began with a Handel concerto which Antoine Elwart considered too slight to show off the instrument fully. An improvisation, a *Pastorale* by Kullak, and a *Cantilène* of his own followed. Then came the centrepiece: Bach's Toccata and Fugue in D minor. Elwart went into raptures:

> What style! what fullness! unalloyed genius! The audience was transported. A. Guilmant, who has a feel for the masters, did not play this

fine composition too fast. He understood that, in a vast building, chords need time to develop fully; and the bass passagework he played on the pedal-board was rendered with perfect clarity.[4]

The Salle des Fêtes of the Trocadéro was also a "grand vaisseau"—a secular cathedral, in fact. Seating five thousand, it had a booming acoustic that was apparently unflattering to almost all instruments except its very own Cavaillé-Coll organ. It was here, rather than on the inferior organ of the Trinité (where recitals would in any case have been frowned upon), that Guilmant conducted his project to convert the Parisian public to Bach and, in the first instance, Handel. From 1879 he was followed at the Trocadéro by Gigout, organist at Saint-Augustin, who usually gave two annual recitals, starting immediately after Guilmant's had finished.

Guilmant opened the 1878 series of Exposition organ concerts with a varied program that, according to the *Ménestrel*'s anonymous reporter, was intended to provide a gentle introduction to an unfamiliar repertory. The public warmly applauded works by Lemmens, by Martini, and by his predecessor at the Trinité, Charles-Alexis Chauvet. By contrast, a Handel concerto and the Bach Toccata in D minor "had the sad fate of making the public restless," he wrote. "Too bad for the public. Let us console ourselves with the thought that its musical education will gradually improve."[5] Similar reactions awaited both Guilmant and Gigout when they programmed Bach the following year. Gigout himself noted that when Guilmant played a Bach Prelude and Fugue in A minor the occupants of the hall's cheapest seats did not take to it,[6] but Gigout himself suffered a worse fate only a few weeks later. It was partly his own fault for making Bach's Fantasia and Fugue in G minor the closing item of his second program. Following the time-honored custom of leaving concerts before

---

4. "Quel style! quelle ampleur! que de génie! L'auditoire était transporté. A. Guilman [sic], qui a le sentiment des maîtres, n'a pas exécuté cette belle composition dans un mouvement trop précipité. Il a compris que, dans un grand vaisseau, il faut donner aux accords le temps de se développer dans toute leur plénitude; aussi les traits de basse exécutés par lui sur le pédalier ont-ils été rendus avec une netteté irréprochable." *L'univers musical* 10/19: 8 May 1862, 148. With some prescience, Elwart predicted that Guilmant, who had burst onto the Paris scene the previous year, would soon return as a *titulaire*. By 1871 he had replaced Charles-Alexis Chauvet at the Eglise de la Trinité.

5. "ils ont eu le triste sort d'emener des distractions dans le public. Tant pis pour le public. Consolons-nous en pensant que son éducation musicale se fera peu à peu." "X . . . ," in *Mén* 44/37: 11 August 1878, 295. This reporter was one of many to comment on the hall's acoustic problems.

6. Defined as "la partie la plus populaire de l'assistance." "E. G.," in *Mén* 45/30: 22 June 1879, 238. Gigout's name appeared on the journal's masthead from 28 March 1880; I infer his authorship of the article from the fact that articles signed "E. G." were almost exclusively reviews of Guilmant's organ recitals, which he followed closely.

the end, three-quarters of his audience got up as he began the work.[7] Yet despite their recognition that Bach was not (yet) what their audiences had come to hear, Guilmant and Gigout persisted in programming his grandest organ works, even fueling the idea of virtuoso competition when Gigout began his 1879 concerts with the work Guilmant had played last: Bach's Toccata in F "with pedal solos," as the program billed it. Neither was public coolness toward Bach consistent. The response to his Prelude and Fugue in D major BWV532, played by Guilmant on 22 July 1879, was "extremely enthusiastic," approaching the ovation given to violinist Sighicelli, whose rendition of a Handel sonata brought him several curtain calls.[8]

Both organists' concerts attracted crowds of thousands, with hundreds regularly turned away. The pricing structure accounts for much: Guilmant's concerts were not charitable events; they were billed as "Concerts Populaires du Trocadéro" and had prices to match. His top ticket price was 3F; his lowest a mere 50c. Moreover, to provide variety both he and Gigout included instrumental and vocal solos in their programs. In 1879, Saint-Saëns and Taffanel played, the latter with his favorite Bach piece, the Flute Sonata in B minor. Paul Viardot played for both organists, often bringing Corelli's *La follia* variations. Their singers, who included the former Opéra baritone Numa Auguez, mixed extracts from Handel's oratorios with modern operatic numbers. The recipe proved irresistible: in 1879, Guilmant's recitals were so successful that he programmed two supplementary ones, to follow Gigout's pair of concerts. And it should be noted that the very concert at which Gigout had seen most of his audience disappear during his final piece had attracted a phenomenal seven thousand people, some of them clustered around and on the stage, filling the stairs between rows of seats, and pressing in from the corridors.

It is hardly surprising, then, to see Guilmant expand his project in 1880, when he sent press releases to Paris musical journals advertising a series of concerts, with orchestra this time, based around the Handel organ concertos. In terms of public taste, it was shrewd to favor Handel rather than Bach in 1880, and Guilmant's reasoning followed current logic in seeing Handel as the more "popular" of the two composers because of his clear simplicity:

---

7. *RGM* 46/28: 13 July 1879, 230 (unsigned; probably Charles Bannelier). The perils of working with the press are well illustrated by the discrepancies in the coverage of this concert: *Le ménestrel* printed a review, signed "GOYON," which claimed that this audience "remained impressed and attentive right to the end" [sont restées jusqu'à la fin impressionnées et attentives]. *Mén* 45/33: 13 July 1879, 263. I am more inclined to believe the *Revue et gazette musicale* critic (probably Charles Bannelier, a Bach fan and translator of the St Matthew Passion for Lamoureux), whose "regret" at having to report the exodus has a ring of truth.

8. Guilmant drew "les applaudissements les plus enthousiastes." *RGM* 46/30: 27 July 1879, 247 (unsigned; probably Charles Bannelier).

Two men have been musical giants: Bach and Handel. Bach is characterized by his complex writing, dominated by great thoughts, without concern for outward effect or for audience opinion. Handel is characterized by clarity of thought; he is greatness in simplicity. Both had, therefore, a highly-developed sense of beauty; but this feeling revealed itself within them in entirely different ways.[9]

Because of the increased expense of hiring an orchestra, it was probably at this point that Guilmant set up his Association Artistique des Grands Concerts d'Orgue du Trocadéro, for which he had, by 1882, secured 290 "membres fondateurs." They included a light sprinkling of the aristocracy, all the major French organ manufacturers, numerous organists (three of whom were female) and other musicians (Colonne, Diémer, Gounod, Bourgault-Ducoudray, Guillot de Sainbris, Eugène d'Harcourt, Massenet, Dubois, Teresa Milanollo), one Symbolist poet (Mallarmé), a publisher (Théodore Michaëlis), and a Republican icon and Handel biographer (Victor Schoelcher).[10] His prices increased (tickets were 5F, 3F, 2F, and 1F), but the crowds did not diminish, and Guilmant's concerts gained the status of an institution. He frequently programmed two Handel concertos in a single performance and made the sinfonias from Bach's cantatas 35 and 49 a regular feature. Gradually increasing the importance of Bach's music within eclectic selections of works, in the early 1880s he emblazoned his programs with legends such as "Audition d'oeuvres de BACH et de HAENDEL pour Orgue et Orchestre." Irrespective of the composition of his programs, Guilmant therefore persisted in telling his audience that they were (or ought to be) attending in order to listen to the works of the two "giants" of music. All else, even his Frescobaldi and Clérambault, was secondary.

During the nearly twenty years that Guilmant spent playing Baroque organ music to packed houses at the Trocadéro, pianists continued to include the

---

9. "Deux hommes ont été les géants de la musique: Bach et Haendel; Bach se distingue par ses combinaisons complexes, dominées par de grandes pensées, sans souci de l'effet extérieur et de l'opinion d'une assemblée, Haendel se distingue par la netteté de sa pensée, il est grand par sa simplicité. Tous deux ont donc un vif sentiment du beau, mais ce sentiment se manifeste chez eux dans un ordre d'idées absolument différent." *Mén* 46/24: 16 May 1880, 191. Later in the press release Guilmant stressed that Handel had written his organ concertos to "satisfy public taste" [pour satisfaire le goût du public], thereby suggesting that Parisian public taste might also require such satisfaction.

10. Lists for 1882 (190 names), 1888 (643 names), and 1896 (635 names) are in the BNF (Musique): Fonds Montpensier.

solo music of Handel, Scarlatti, and Bach in their programs, and the Bach double and triple keyboard concertos never left the repertory. There was no question, however, that such music could hold seven thousand people enthralled; nor that the same pieces could be repeated year after year to public acclaim. In respect to Bach, the Trocadéro concerts of Guilmant and Gigout served to demonstrate the implications of a trend already detectable in the use of the pedal piano by Alkan, Lemmens, and other male pianists and organists in the middle of the century.[11] Bach's organ music was immune from the taint of feminization and inferiority that had dogged his most familiar harpsichord music, because, like his solo violin music, it could be seen to pose real virtuoso challenges. Biographical accounts reaching back into late eighteenth-century Germany (Gerber) and England (Burney), of course, helped sustain that image. Proof comes from the derision reserved for organists who played parts of the *Well-Tempered Clavier* in public, since it was an admission of professional inadequacy to resort to such "fuguettes."[12] Technology also played its part in the masculine ethos of organ playing, at the Trocadéro and in the tradition of organ inauguration itself. Both were rooted in the demonstration of technological excellence in an industry in which French manufacturers were rapidly gaining ascendancy, as their piano-making forebears had done for several decades until the shock of their defeat by Steinway of New York at the Exposition Universelle of 1867. For most of his concert career, Guilmant played both Baroque and modern repertories on brand new or recently restored organs designed for large spaces: the most powerful, technically advanced, and richly colored instruments in existence. French industrial supremacy produced turbocharged Bach.

Yet during the same period much of the animus against pianists and Baroque harpsichord repertory also evaporated, to be replaced by either benign acceptance or a more sharply focused brand of criticism, often aimed at performance style. Diémer's performing career spanned, and went well beyond, the transition. He was an uncommon virtuoso whose levels of facility, control, flexibility, and precision induced mock despair in his reviewers.[13] Rare dissenters

---

11. Women and pedal pianos still did not seem to mix: in 1889 Camille Bellaigue complained about the unfeminine indignity of a woman negotiating the pedal board (see his *L'année musicale*, 136).

12. See Gustave Dorieux's scathing report on a *titulaire* competition at Notre-Dame, Nice, where two contestants did just this. *MS* 5/5: May 1879, 55.

13. "Cabalette," of the *Semaine artistique et musicale*, showered him with exclamation marks in 1889: "What impeccably accurate playing! What delicacy of fingerwork! What technical prowess! Diémer was acclaimed!" [Quel jeu correct et impeccable! Quelle délicatesse de doigté! Quelles ressources de mécanisme! M. Diémer a été acclamé!] *Semaine artistique et musicale* 1/17: 6 April 1889, 4. Henry Eymieu of the *Monde musical* noted his "marvellous precision" [précision merveilleuse] in Bach's Brandenburg Concerto No. 5 *Monde musical* (henceforth *MM*), 2 (no. 44): 28 February 1891, 5; Amédée Boutarel wrote of his Brandenburg No. 5: "The pianist

excepted, his fingerwork was lionized, not feminized. His repertory during the nineteenth century stretched from Loeillet and Daquin to Liszt, Brahms and his own works; and although he never abandoned the piano for *clavecin* music he was unusual in his championing of the harpsichord. Most famously, in conjunction with musicians who were to become long-standing chamber partners, he gave two concerts at the "centenary" Paris Exposition Universelle of 1889—a display of French achievement for which the piano manufacturers Pleyel, Erard, and Tomasini all presented new harpsichords.[14] At the Exposition concerts Diémer played a Taskin instrument of 1769, now in the Russell Collection, Edinburgh; he also demonstrated a new, six-pedal Pleyel harpsichord designed by Gustave Lyon, a model of which he "adopted" and played regularly thereafter.[15]

Diémer was a darling of the salon circuit (and presided over his own), for which gatherings he often played entirely modern programs, including his own music. He was also beloved of chamber musicians, with whom he played much of his early music repertory. Successively, he acted as pianist for the Alard-Franchomme Quartet (for 12 years from 1861) and for Taffanel's Société des Instruments à Vent (from 1878/9 until 1893) and as harpsichordist with Van Waefelghem's Société des Instruments Anciens (from 1895 until the death of Jules Delsart, the group's gamba player, broke up the group in 1900).[16] His early music repertory was selective and unusual. By the late 1870s it was becoming commonplace for pianists to include a short item by Handel, Bach, or Scarlatti (or, more usually, two of the three) in solo recital programs. Diémer acted differently. He neglected Scarlatti's harpsichord music entirely, and avoided Handel (apart from the passacaglia in G minor from the 7th keyboard

---

won over the entire audience with his easy playing, which has no hint of stiffness, and the despair-inducing perfection with which he can, *ad infinitum*, repeat the same passages, which find themselves always identical under his fingers, the 10th time just like the first." [Le pianiste a ravi la salle entière par son jeu plein d'aisance, sans ombre de raideur et la perfection désespérante avec laquelle il sait réitérer, un nombre illimité de fois, les mêmes passages qui se retrouvent sous ses doigts, la dixième fois comme la première, toujours identiques.] *Mén* 61/3: 20 January 1895, 20.

14. Jules Delsart played viola da gamba; Paul Taffanel flute; Georges Gillet oboe d'amore, Guillaume Remy and Armand Parent violin, and Louis van Waefelghem viola d'amore. On these concerts, see Fauser, *Musical Encounters*, chapter 1.

15. Becker-Derex, *Louis Diémer*, i, 249–50. The Pleyel harpsichord gave him considerable control over timbre and dynamics. See Arthur Dandelot's admiring review in *MM* 6/24: 30 April 1895, 476. The instrument was modeled on other examples of Taskin's late harpsichords, which were fitted with knee pedals that allowed for extensive dynamic flexibility.

16. Because of Diémer's virtuoso status it is traditional to view the Société as "his" society; contemporary evidence, however, suggests that the driving force behind its founding was the viola d'amore player Louis van Waefelghem, who was also responsible for much of the program planning. It was Van Waefelghem who organized a trial soirée on 8 March 1893 at Diémer's house, complete with an historical lecture from Mme Duvernoy-Viardot. See the unsigned review in *MM* 4/21: 15 March 1893, 364.

suite). In other Handel works he invariably acted as accompanist—to Gillet's oboe, Taffanel's flute, or Nadaud's violin. Similarly, his approach to Bach was oblique. Though he played a great deal of it, especially with Taffanel's society and for the conductors Colonne, D'Harcourt, and Lamoureux in the 1890s, very little was the solo harpsichord music (isolated dance movements and the "Italian" Concerto only), and he never participated in the vogue for organ fugues on pedal piano. Indeed, it seems that he simply did not play fugues. His core Bach repertory consisted of chamber pieces in which he acted as joint soloist or accompanist: the string and wind sonatas, the Triple Concerto and, with Taffanel's group, Brandenburg Concertos 4 and 5, for which he and his colleagues became the first consistent champions. Why, given his superlative pianism, Diémer did not tackle the harpsichord toccatas, the Goldbergs, and the Chromatic Fantasia and Fugue, is unknown, although his tendency to present Bach as a composer of chamber music, coupled with his avoidance of the organ fugue repertory, may be enough to suggest that he did not wish to use Bach as he used many other composers—as a solo virtuoso vehicle.[17]

The repertory for which he is most celebrated and which appeared in his programs from his début concerts of 1864 onward was the music of the French *clavecinistes*. It was Diémer who turned Couperin and Daquin into household names, while regularly playing some of Rameau's more familiar works. And while he never wrote tracts defending *clavecin* music, like Méreaux and Farrenc before him he edited new and unusual selections of the repertory, publishing over 80 pieces in his *Les clavecinistes français du XVIIIe siècle* (1887–1912). As a performer, in the last decades of the century he had a virtual monopoly on this music. Saint-Saëns occasionally performed the Rameau *Pièces en concert*; but once Mongin and Tardieu de Malleville had stopped playing regularly, there was no pianist except Szarvády (whose concert appearances were by then very rare) who had any real sympathy for the repertory. Moreover, foreign pianists tended to limit themselves to the trinity of Bach, Handel, and Scarlatti; the equivalent French repertory lay stubbornly outside the international canon. Yet Diémer changed that perspective completely within France. And he did it by breaking apart the "feminine = slight and unworthy" paradigm that had dogged it so consistently.

---

17. The "Goldberg" Variations would have been beyond the attention span of all but the most fanatical of Bach audiences. To my knowledge they remained unplayed in public in France during the century, although variations XII and XXIV feature in the teaching material used by Diémer's Conservatoire teacher, Antoine Marmontel, and were copied out by his students. See the album entitled "Classe Marmontel, 1855–56," BNF (Musique) W. 36, which contains much Bach (from the *Well-Tempered Clavier*, the two-part inventions and the Partita in C minor), and music from suites by Handel (the famous G minor passacaglia) and Couperin.

The odds were against Diémer's tactic working. His approach trapped *clavecin* music in the stereotypically feminized mould of the exquisite miniature and arguably militated against any larger cause, patriotic or otherwise. Moreover, he played a fraction of the *clavecin* music he edited, and avoided the big pieces. Not for him the grandeur and low basses of a "La Raphaèle" or "La Ténébreuse," or even the virtuosity of "Les Cyclopes": birds, bells, and nature scenes at the top of the keyboard were his speciality. Some of these became "signature pieces" that he used as encores or crowd pleasers, often grouping them (perhaps as mini sonatas) in sets of three: in the 1890s Couperin's "Le reveil-matin," Daquin's "Le coucou," and Rameau's "Le rappel des oiseaux" were ubiquitous; Dandrieu's "Le ramage des oiseaux" and Couperin's "Les papillons" and "Le carillon de Cythère" scarcely less so.[18] His public clamored for these pieces, routinely demanding encores, especially Daquin's "Le coucou."[19] Critics, too, were unanimous in their admiration for Diémer's refined accounts and duly reported the audience's rapture: in 1894 Léon Schlesinger described Diémer as "knowing how to give [Couperin and Daquin's pieces] the popularity they enjoyed 150 years ago!"[20] Diémer's ability, too, to switch instantly from the modern to the Baroque, proved irresistible. After a thrilling performance of a Liszt Hungarian Rhapsody at a "festival populaire" conducted by Lamoureux in 1895, he sat back down and gave a "marvellous" performance of the famous rigaudon from *Dardanus*. As Arthur Pougin reported: "renewed curtain calls and renewed cries of *bis*."[21]

Like his predecessors, Diémer never, in the period up to 1900, gave his audience the sense that the French Baroque repertory was anything more than a disparate collection of three-minute character pieces. Just as he played only single dance movements from Bach's suites, so he never played anything approaching a complete Couperin *ordre*; neither, as an editor, did he take the *ordre* as a meaningful unit in his *Les clavecinistes français*. The concert

---

18. His predilections were well understood: in 1892 E. Mangeot noted that the Couperin "Reveil-matin," the Daquin, and a certain Bach Gavotte were his "three favorite pieces" [ses trois pièces favorites]. *MM* 3 (no. 69): 15 March 1892, 11.

19. See, for instance, an unsigned report of a Van Waefelghem/Taffanel/Diémer concert of 28 February 1893 (*MM* 4/21: 15 March 1893, 364), where Diémer is introduced thus: "M. Diémer is the master of the harpsichord; the 'Cuckoo' is always encored" [M. Diémer est la maître du clavecin, le *Coucou* est toujours bissé]. Diémer and "Le coucou" are mentioned in the same breath, as though the one defines the other.

20. "auxquelles [the Couperin and Daquin] il a su rendre la popularité dont elles jouissaient il y a cent cinquante ans!" *Mén* 60/1: 7 January 1894, 7. Diémer had played as part of a historical concert given by Bordes and the Chanteurs de Saint-Gervais at the Salle d'Harcourt on 27 December 1893.

21. "Nouveaux rappels et nouveaux *bis*." *Mén* 61/2: 13 January 1895, 12. For this concert (8 January) Lamoureux had reduced ticket prices in order to attract a wider public. In addition to the Liszt, Diémer played a Saint-Saëns concerto.

programs he devised with Van Waefelghem (viola d'amore), Grillet (hurdy-gurdy), and Jules Delsart (viola da gamba), in their guise as the Société des Instruments Anciens, further enshrined the trend. A concert of 2 May 1895, from the first full season, contained seventeen pieces grouped by instrumental combination into eight items; an orchestral concert (conducted by Taffanel) organized by Van Waefelghem in March 1893 as part of the group's testing of the ground, contained eighteen pieces divided into nine items. These figures were typical. Moreover, although Delsart regularly played extracts from Bach's cello suites, he, too, never played one complete. The proportion of French music in all the group's concerts was extremely high, but the parcels were small and the attention span demanded of the audience concomitantly low.

To suggest that Diémer might have performed a whole *ordre* is not anachronistic: French musicians knew, not least from modern compositions, what a French dance suite was. Moreover, there was elsewhere a distinct move towards "completeness" as an indicator of seriousness within concert programming. Lamoureux programmed large Wagnerian tableaux, if not complete acts; Colonne and Pasdeloup were causing a sensation with the *Damnation of Faust*, again complete, and filling an entire afternoon's concert. The first complete performances of the B minor Mass and the St Matthew Passion were trumpeted as such; Ysaÿe, Pugno, Taffanel, and Guilmant illustrated how single movements of Baroque sonatas and concertos were giving way to sonata/concerto cycles; courtesy of Bordes, arias from Bach cantatas were being replaced by series of complete performances. Pugno and Ysaÿe gave their recitals in the same high-society hall used by the Société des Instruments Anciens: the Salle Pleyel. Their concerts of the late 1890s generally contained four items at most, principally complete sonatas. In 1896 they gave a historical survey of the genre, taking in three sonatas per recital (the first, on 8 May, included Bach's E major sonata). A similar series the following year began on 30 April with the Sonata in B minor. In 1899 they became more daring, with a series featuring one composer per concert. The first (27 January 1899) was devoted to Bach, the second to Beethoven, and the third to Grieg. Apart from the Chaconne in D minor, which Ysaÿe played without its preceding dances, Bach was presented complete: the violin sonatas in C minor and A major, and the "Italian" Concerto.

While such extreme thematic programming was unprecedented in chamber-music circles,[22] it was the natural extension of the pair's approach

---

22. Hugues Imbert called it "audacious" [un coup d'audace] but admitted that in the event, and despite the uniformity and scholasticism of Bach's style, "the attention of the dilettante audience never wavered" [l'attention des *dilettanti* n'a pas affaibli]. *Le guide musical* (henceforth *GM*) 45/6: 5 February 1899, 127.

towards Handel and Bach at Colonne's Sunday series at the Châtelet theatre and his smaller-scale Thursday series at the Nouveau-Théâtre. Here, in the last years of the century, they dominated the solo items, sometimes even playing two concertos each in a single performance. Here too, Baroque dance movements were occasionally integrated into their parent works (Ysaÿe and Bach's Partita in D minor BWV 1004, 11 April 1897; Pugno and an unidentified Handel keyboard suite, 12 January 1899), while concertos were invariably presented complete. The same was axiomatic for Charles Bordes when he began his concerts of Bach cantatas at the Salle d'Harcourt in autumn 1893. The need for completeness was also one of the main sources of frustration for those, such as Arthur Pougin, who hoped for a revival of French Baroque stage music: for him, short excerpts gave no hint of the power and drama of the whole and seemed only to undersell the composer concerned. Yet arguably that "underselling" was precisely what drew audiences to Diémer.

Of course, there were still early "lollipops" galore, Handel's Largo from *Xerxes*, arranged for *cor anglais* and up to twenty harps being one of the more colorful crazes of the 1890s.[23] But these pieces remained lollipops, whereas Diémer's repertory provided something more like a slice of history packaged as entertainment. This, then, was more likely to be the attraction of the Société des Instruments Anciens, in response to whose publicity people "literally trampled over each other in the salle Pleyel."[24] As with the Trocadéro organ concerts, the novelty value of the sound world was undeniable. Van Waefelghem and Delsart played adapted seventeenth-century instruments; the violinist Remy possessed a quinton of around the same period.[25] Diémer's harpsichords, with their potential for grading sonority were, as far as Diémer himself was concerned, a prerequisite for success.[26] To supportive critics such as F. Emery-Desbrousses, the sounds he produced appeared nostalgic: "the slightly veiled sonority, the slightly shrill and mélancholic timbre makes one think of the reedy and quavering voices of long-departed ancestors"; the Society

---

23. The work has a faintly comic history of Wagnerian plushness at the D'Harcourt concerts. It began in 1895 with a simple arrangement, played by the oboist Louis Bleuzet, to which were added four harps in January 1898. Rapidly increasing popularity then led D'Harcourt to place it at the end of a concert (possibly in an attempt to keep the audience captive). By March 1898 the number of harps had increased to six; by the end of May, to "twenty Lyon-system chromatic harps" [vingt harpes chromatiques du système Lyon]. *Mén* 64/23: 5 June 1898, 183, unsigned.

24. "On se foulait littéralement dans la salle Pleyel." Pougin, *Mén* 61/14: 7 April 1895, 109.

25. Described in affectionate detail in *MM* 4/21: 15 March 1893, 364, unsigned.

26. See his letter to Gustave Lyon of 15 June 1908, in which he mentions the centrality of what he calls the "added" pedal system to his capacity to revive the music of Rameau, Couperin, and Daquin. See Anon. (Ed.), *Mélanges Couperin*, 113. Diémer played at least one other reproduction instrument, with two foot and two knee pedals, by Erard. *MM* 4/21: 15 March 1893, 364, unsigned.

played "quaint pieces which were nevertheless charming."[27] Arthur Pougin's vocabulary was as revealing. The second concert of 1895 was, he wrote, "absolutely exquisite"; a Couperin work was "delicious in effect," Diémer's playing was "full of grace, finesse and elegance."[28] It was as though the Société had, temporarily, transported its audience back to the *ancien-régime* world of grace, discretion, and elegant *salonnières*. In 1902, two years after the society's dissolution, Van Waelfeghem's programs still captured its ambience perfectly, with images of period instruments elegantly framing the performers' names, in rose-coloured print (Fig. 3.1). His concert of 24 March 1902 was open to the public, but he also invited guests by means of a personally topped and tailed letter printed to match the program and folded into it. It is difficult not to conclude that the Society's concerts had the same feel of a semi-private entertainment.

The Van Waefelghem and Diémer concerts were certainly very like soirées in the Society's retention of the multi-item structure of the musical evening, so distant from the increasing seriousness of the large-scale public concert. Significantly, after some aggressive nationalism in reports of their concerts at the Exposition Universelle of 1889, reviews revealed not a hint of reverence for the music, or even pride in the fact of its being French.[29] *Belle époque* hedonism now reigned supreme; resistance to the picturesque as artificial or as childish had seemingly evaporated. Important historically as precursors of the original instrument movement, the Société's concerts were not appreciated in anything so arid as a musicological light, or as a history lesson, an attempt at regeneration, or a celebration of musical *patrimoine*. This was idealist, escapist entertainment of a kind enshrined in the *Vieux Paris* medievalism of the 1900 Paris Exposition. Was it "serious" in the manner of German music? No, but in the 1890s that, at last, did not matter. It was nostalgic, refined, and evocative of French civilization. In fact, in its replication of old salon culture, it offered a precious taste of that civilization. The rococo could be embraced once more. Sporadically, the Opéra did the same for courtly dance, which increasingly drew the same compliments as Diémer's instrumental repertory. Gustave Robert's reaction to a "concert historique" of 8 December 1895 at the Opéra is emblematic. He was—and I detect no disparagement in the diminutive—enchanted by the "animated

---

27. "la sonorité un peu voilée, le timbre aigrelet et mélancolique fait penser aux voix fluettes et tremblottantes d'aïeules depuis longtemps disparues . . . des pièces vieillottes, mais charmantes quand même." F. Emery-Desbrousses in a profile of Diémer, *MM* 7/5: 15 July 1895, 87.

28. "absolument exquise"; "l'effet est délicieux"; "plein de grâce, de finesse et d'élégance." Pougin, *Mén* 61/14: 7 April 1895, 109.

29. On the nationalist tone of 1889 adopted by Adolphe Jullien and Charles Darcours, among others, see Fauser, *Musical Encounters*, chapter 1.

FIGURE 3.1. Program for a Louis van Waefelghem concert of 24 March 1902. Courtesy of the Bibliothèque Nationale de France, Paris.

little pictures" that were danced to music by Rameau and Lacoste. They reminded him of Watteau's *fêtes galantes* paintings.[30] Perhaps in the most profound way, then, Diémer's concerts were indeed vehicles for nationalist

---

30. "tableautins animés." Robert, review of 15 December 1895, *La musique à Paris, 1895–96*, 103–104. On the allure of the *fête galante* at the turn of the century, see Suschitzky, "Debussy's Rameau," esp. 405–408.

sentiment, but now expressed as practice, not culture, and offering the opportunity for a small but influential slice of the population to act out its ideal of Frenchness.[31] The mentality itself was not new:

> Finesse, grace, elegance, purity—he possesses all the requisite qualities to captivate an audience . . . . Nourished with the beauties of the old French school, he knows how to recount them with a ravishing discretion and sureness of touch—just a few notes, imprinted with exquisite delicacy, and penetrating color, are enough to transport you mentally to an era in which the rigaudon, the gavotte and the passecaille flourished. M. Moreau galvanized his audience thus, through his quite archaic interpretation of a delicious minuet from Lully's *Le bourgeois gentilhomme*. Strange miracle! If you like spiritism, go and hear our striking virtuoso. You will feel yourself transported to the past.[32]

Thus did an unsigned reviewer from the *Guide musical* (ironically, a Belgian journal) characterize the aural tourism of violinist Henri Moreau's performance of a minuet from Lully's *Bourgeois gentilhomme* in 1879. Nevertheless, it took until the 1890s for such attitudes to become common in musical discourse and to be celebrated in the concert arena. Only then could enthusiasm for large-scale Bach and the French dance miniature coexist.

Choral Activists and the Rise of Bach

While Guilmant brought audiences to their feet at the Trocadéro—hailed as the organist who had brought Handel to the populace—others looked on enviously. One such was Clément Loret, organ teacher at the Ecole Niedermeyer, who was at pains to point out that his own edition of 12 Handel organ concer-

---

31. See Flint de Médicis, "Nationalism and Early Music," esp. 47, where she discusses the *snobisme* associated with Diémer and Van Waefelghem's concerts.
32. "Finesse, grâce, élégance, pureté, il possède toutes les qualités voulues pour captiver un auditoire . . . Nourri des beautés de la vieille école française, il sait les détailler avec une discretion et une sûreté de touche ravissantes, quelques notes seulement, empreintes d'une délicatesse exquise, et d'un coloris pénétrant, suffisent pour vous transporter dans l'idée à l'époque où florissaient le rigaudon, la gavotte, la passecaille. M. Moreau a galvanisé ainsi son public, par l'interprétation, toute archaïche, d'un délicieux menuet du *Bourgeois gentilhomme* de Lulli. Etrange miracle! Si vous aimez le spiritisme, allez entendre notre étonnant virtuose. Vous vous sentirez transporté en plein passé." *GM* 25/22 & 23: 29 May and 5 June 1879, n.p., unsigned.

tos, transcribed for organ alone, had been in print since well before Guilmant's concerts and was regularly used by students there.[33] Bach, too, was staple fare for organists at the Ecole: at competition time Guilmant's signature pieces were routinely chosen as required test repertory. Why, then, did the Ecole Niedermeyer's activities not feature in the voluminous discussions of the Guilmant phenomenon? The answer may be summed up briefly: anticlericalism. Under Gustave Lefèvre's direction the Ecole lost propaganda battles at almost every turn during the 1870s and early 1880s. It put on concerts that went unreported in the press unless the school submitted puff reviews (which it did only infrequently), and it attracted significant press attention only twice a year: at the summer competitions and prize-givings, and at the annual Easter Monday concerts at Sainte-Chapelle, which were actually too popular for their own good, thereby attracting close attention from anticlerical Republicans.[34] Lefèvre set up his Société des Concerts in 1872, on the school's return from wartime exile in Switzerland, explicitly modeling it on that of Moskova. Annual series of twelve fortnightly concerts took place between April 1872 and 1884[35]; in addition, the society choir sang several concerts in the Salle des Conférences of the Trocadéro during the Exposition Universelle of 1878, including music by Allegri, Janequin, Waelraut, Carissimi, Lotti, Frescobaldi, Le Maistre, Guédron, Clari, Nanino, Pergolesi, and Durante.[36] Given the extent of the competition at the Exposition Universelle, these concerts were never going to reach the front pages of the musical press. But it was symptomatic of a general forgetfulness regarding the school's activities in the early years of the Republic that its concerts were reported only sporadically and in small print. Within Paris, it was the invisibility of the Société that made Bordes's institution of the Chanteurs de Saint-Gervais shine so brightly as a Palestrinian revival born, seemingly, out of nothing. Yet Lefèvre's society is historically important because it was the only one to keep sixteenth-century polyphony alive in Paris concert life between the mid 1870s and the mid 1880s—a period otherwise dominated, in early music terms, by high Baroque repertory.

33. Reported in *RGM* 47/28: 30 May 1880, 223.
34. Yet even the Sainte-Chapelle Easter concert of 1880 was reviewed in *Le ménestrel* by an insider signed "E. G."—the school's former pupil, Eugène Gigout. Nevertheless, the Sainte-Chapelle concerts always brought capacity audiences, and the school's regular concerts appear to have attracted a loyal following, doubtless headed by the numerous aristocrats whose names were listed among the patrons of the society (including the comtesse de Paris, the duchesse de Chartres, the comtesses de Chambrun, d'Haussonville, d'Hautpoul, née princesse de Wagram, and Mme Drouin de Lhuys). The Archbishop of Paris and the Bishops of Autun and Dijon were also patrons. See Galerne, *L'Ecole Niedermeyer*, 55.
35. Galerne, *L'Ecole Niedermeyer*, 56.
36. Galerne, *L'Ecole Niedermeyer*, 57.

The school accepted only boys and men, but its Société des Concerts choir included adult singers of both sexes from "the highest classes of society"[37] and featured soloists from the Opéra singing alongside talented amateurs.[38] One such amateur was the soprano Henriette Fuchs, whose performances of Bach and Handel arias were a highlight of both the Ecole Niedermeyer concerts and those of the Fondation Beaulieu, at which she was also a regular soloist.[39] Despite the involvement of society figures, Lefèvre's concerts, however, remained essentially *exercices* in which students presented a variety of short instrumental and vocal/choral items. There is no evidence that the society ever put on a complete, large-scale work in the manner of Choron, Bourgault-Ducoudray, or Lamoureux. That task was taken on by Fuchs herself, who with her husband, Edmond, set up the choral society Concordia in 1879. Like so many elite amateur societies of the nineteenth century in Paris, Concordia was dedicated to the public performance of choral "masterpieces" in aid of charity, its membership founded on a close (claustrophobic, even) network of wealthy families.[40] Under the guidance of its founders, Gounod (Président d'honneur in the mid-1880s) and Widor (its regular conductor), Concordia championed Handel, promoted Rameau, and showed particular reverence for Bach. A bicentenary concert was held at the Conservatoire (21 April 1885) followed by an expensive (indeed, financially disastrous) venture in 1888: a complete St Matthew Passion that was intended to rekindle the enthusiasm that had surrounded Lamoureux's performances of the work in 1874.[41] From around 1884 the society gave performances of Bach's cantatas "Gottes Zeit" and "Ein feste Burg." They also gave the Paris premiere of the Magnificat at their 1885 bicentenary concert. Their performances were both expensive and exclusive. The best seats for the Bach bicentenary and the St Matthew Passion cost 20F; the cheapest, 5F

---

37. "les plus hautes classes de la Société." Galerne, *L'Ecole Niedermeyer*, 56.

38. Instrumental soloists were rare, unless they came from the school itself; but a recurring name is that of Charlotte Tardieu de Malleville, who played Scarlatti and the French harpsichord repertory, sometimes on a harpsichord, at concerts of the 1870s.

39. For a typical report of her singing, see *AM* 17/16: 18 April 1878, 125, where her contribution to the Ecole Niedermeyer's annual Sainte-Chapelle concert is lauded by A. Landély-Hettich.

40. The statutes for 1880–1881 reveal several countesses among the associate (nonperforming) members, with the comtesse de Chambrun, a famous *salonnière*, among the performing members. Honorary members included several early music revivalists and sympathizers: Bourgault-Ducoudray, Diémer, Dubois, Fauré, Gounod, Reyer, Saint-Saëns, Vaucorbeil (director of the Opéra), Johannes Weber (critic for *Le temps*), and Weckerlin (Anon., *Concordia. Société chorale*). Although the statutes allowed prospective members to be put forward by any two members of the society, a list from 1887 reveals that almost all the performing members since 1879 had been recommended by one or other of the Fuchses (Anon., *Concordia. Assemblée générale*).

41. Lamoureux did not follow his St Matthew Passion of 1874 with other complete performances of large-scale Bach choral works but increasingly limited himself to two early choral pieces: the cantata "Phoebus and Pan," first performed on 2 December 1883, and the Christmas Oratorio (often excerpted).

and 3F, respectively. Nevertheless, they presaged a widespread Parisian revival of Bach's choral music in the following decade.

Two institutions were closely involved: the Société des Concerts and the Chanteurs de Saint-Gervais, working in collaboration with D'Harcourt. Other amateur societies, such as L'Euterpe and the Société des Grandes Auditions, contributed, and a private society grouped around the former politician the comte de Chambrun (b.1821) also put on important, though isolated, performances in the Hôtel de Condé, where his late wife had presided over a brilliant Wagnerian salon. The Société des Concerts' record vis à vis Bach's choral music was, until the early 1890s, lamentable, with technical deficiencies marring their every performance. Between its inception and 1885, the society had presented just three works: the antiphonal and homophonic sections of the motet "Ich lasse dich nicht" (BWV Anh III 159, now attributed to Johann Christoph Bach), set to the text "Qui propter me crucem"[42]; from 1875, the homophonic sections of "Motet no. 4," "Komm, Jesu, Komm," sung in French as "Viens, viens ô Jesus"; and, also from 1875, selections from the Credo of the B minor Mass. Whether the innovations of 1875 were Deldevez's reponse to Lamoureux's separatism of 1872 is not known, but they failed miserably. The "Credo," "Incarnatus est," and "Crucifixus" were so botched on their first performance (January 1875) as to be unrecognizable. Deldevez presented these extracts once more, at Easter the following year, and then gave them up until 1881. Interestingly, he neglected to include them in his listing of the Société des Concerts' repertory from 1828 to 1885.[43] Nearly a decade later, the choir, now conducted by Jules Garcin and trained by Joseph Heyberger, was still severely challenged by this music. A complete Mass in B minor was scheduled for the *concerts spirituels* of 1890 but had to be abandoned because the choir was under prepared. First postponed to a supplementary concert on 27 April, this concert, too, was cancelled because of "the lack of time for choir rehearsals."[44] The first of three closely spaced performances was eventually given, amid widespread press excitement, the following

---

42. Divested of its contrapuntal section, the piece was so easy that it was featured in the *Nouveau répertoire de l'orphéon*, published by Gérard in 1859. It was a favorite at the Conservatoire, performed 19 times between its introduction and 1885, a figure exceeded, for this kind of choral item, only by Leisring's Easter hymn "O filii, o filiae" (23 performances) (Deldevez, La Société des concerts, ed. Streletski, 257). Alongside a setting of the "Tantum ergo" to the opening section of "Jesu meine Freude," this "Qui propter" was the only Bach to be performed in Latin; all other known performances of Bach's music were sung in French.

43. They ought to appear alongside Bach's motets in Deldevez's *La Société des concerts*.

44. "l'insuffisance de temps pour les études du chant." Committee minutes of 8 April 1890, 12, BNF (Musique): D. 17345 (12) Société des Concerts. Procès-verbaux du Comité.

season, on 22 February 1891. Thereafter, the work was repeated in 1893, 1895, and 1899.

For further, significant expansion of the Bach choral repertory during this period we must look both to Concordia and, particularly, to Bordes and the Chanteurs de Saint-Gervais, whose Bach cantata cycles of 1893/4 and 1895 (at least a dozen cantatas, to full halls), together with their liturgical performances and other concert performances of Bach's cantatas and motets, made a substantial amount of the composer's sacred choral music available to a wide public throughout the last decade of the century and into the next. While Bordes never put on the large-scale works, he achieved critical mass with the smaller ones.[45] Performing in a variety of venues, including their home church of Saint-Gervais, the Salle Erard and the infinitely more "popular" Trocadéro and Salle d'Harcourt, the Chanteurs also contributed to the Concerts Colonne at the Nouveau-Théâtre, the Société Nationale, the princesse de Polignac's concerts, and the Concerts Guilmant. The entire concert scene, in other words. This flexible group of between 10 and 80 singers enjoyed wide public acclaim and professional respect, undertaking a schedule of concerts that no amateur choir could match. Where Concordia might manage three concerts in a year, the Chanteurs gave around twenty in Paris alone, sometimes giving completely different programs on successive days. In addition, they undertook regional tours that were extensive and equally crowded. Between 1894 and 1900 Bordes's choir visited 75 towns, sometimes singing in two on a single day.[46] Even Choron's busiest season, with fourteen concerts, looks slack by comparison.

The story of the provinces is patchier. Despite the visits of organists such as Guilmant and Gigout to organ inaugurations across the country, and their participation as soloists at local concerts, the average town-dweller's experience of Bach was meagre in comparison with that of Parisians. Nevertheless, several towns had regular concert series at which early music was featured, if only occasionally: Concerts Populaires (e.g. Angers, Rennes), Concerts Classiques

---

45. The princesse de Polignac's plan of 1895/6 for him to conduct the St John Passion never came off. See Kahan, *Music's Modern Muse*, 95. Bordes's known Bach repertory from 1892 to 1900 comprises several of the motets (including the misattributed BWV Anh 159), the Funeral Ode, and many cantatas, including: "Bleib bei uns" BWV6 [Reste avec nous]; "Gottes Zeit" BWV106 (Actus tragicus) [Tout selon la volonté de Dieu seul]; "Wachet auf" BWV140 [Tous debout, le veilleur chante]; "Also hat Gott die Welt geliebt" BWV68 (with the celebrated "Pentecost" cantata, "L'amour ardent du Créateur"); "Ach Gott vom Himmel" BWV2 [Grand Dieu du haut du ciel]; Cantata "per ogni tempo" "Ich hatte viel Bekümmeris" BWV21 [J'avais de l'ombre plein le coeur]; "Jesu der du meine Seele BWV78 [Jésus pour nos pauvres âmes]; "Aus tiefer Not" BWV38 [Vers toi Seigneur montent nos cris]; "Aus der Tiefen" BWV131 [De l'abîme] and "Ihr werdet weinen und heulen" BWV103 [Vous pleurez, vous gémirez].

46. See Bordachar, *Charles Bordes*, 20. More details, along with a map outlining the Chanteurs' tours, is given in René de Castéra's insider's history, *Dix années d'action musicale religieuse*, 29–35.

(e.g. Le Havre, Marseille), or amateur orchestral societies such as in Bordeaux, which had both a Cercle and a Société Philharmonique. Here, the secular music of Handel and Bach was featured to the exclusion of almost all other pre-1760 composers, and was largely limited to instrumental items—especially, in the case of Bach, the numerous "meditations" on his keyboard preludes that sprang up in the wake of Gounod's original. Other centres emerged more strongly, Lyon in particular. By the late 1870s Lyon's *maîtrise* had begun to put on complete Handel and Mendelssohn oratorios; Bach's "Actus Tragicus" had also been featured in its programs.[47] In 1879 it presented Janequin's *Bataille de Marignan* and excerpts from a Scarlatti oratorio at its annual concert. Participation in civic music-making was particularly rich in early and sacred music during the Third Republic, with various choirs forming, one of which, La Saint-Cécile, included *Messiah*, the St Matthew Passion, and Palestrina's Pope Marcellus Mass in its post-1884 repertory.[48] The city was even home, from 1892, to a society, La J.-S. Bach, which was dedicated to the performance of the composer's organ works on pedal piano.[49]

Further study of the French regions will doubtless uncover more of this kind of activity. But nothing is likely to reveal a density of Bachian activity comparable to that of the very area of France that was no longer French: Alsace. Strasbourg had cultivated Germanic traditions in respect to Baroque choral music since the foundation of the Protestant Société de Chant Sacré in 1852 and had seen its first concerts of Bach cantatas in the 1860s. Those traditions strengthened after 1871. French Alsatian residents having been forced in 1872 to adopt German citizenship or move elsewhere, those who remained lived amidst a growing influx of new German citizens whose presence accelerated the process of assimilation into the new Reich. Protestant and Catholic traditions coexisted: Franz Stockhausen (1839–1926), *maître de chapelle* of Strasbourg Cathedral and a future Cecilian, instituted the singing of sixteenth-century polyphony there shortly after his arrival in 1868.[50] But he also, as director of the municipal choir and the Conservatoire chorus, mounted annual performances of Bach passions and the B minor Mass. The St John Passion appeared astonishingly early, in 1886, thereby preceding by some years the French premiere of 1903.[51] As such, Stockhausen contributed, along with fellow conductors

---

47. Reuchsel, *La musique à Lyon*, 38.
48. Reuchsel, *La musique à Lyon*, 77.
49. Reuchsel, *La musique à Lyon*, 84.
50. Honegger, "Le Conservatoire de Strasbourg et ses liens avec le Théâtre et l'Orchestre municipal (1855–1918)," 683.
51. For general information on musical life in nineteenth-century Strasbourg, see Honegger, *Le Conservatoire et l'Orchestre philharmonique de Strasbourg*, and Geyer, *La vie musicale à Strasbourg*.

Louis Saar and Ernest Munch, to a veritable Bach mania in Strasbourg, where from 1885 no fewer than three choirs put on major performances of his choral works, clustered around Christmas and Eastertide.

In Paris, critical responses to Bach were mixed; but all were tinged with the recognition that a cult was in the making. Witness the diatribe to which Camille Bellaigue treated readers of the *Revue des deux mondes* on 28 April 1888, just in time for Concordia's St Matthew Passion of 16 May at the Conservatoire. In "L'ennui dans la musique" (Tedium in Music), Bellaigue divided selected musicians into three categories: third-rate bores; second-rate bores; and first-rate bores (Bach and Wagner headed this latter category). For Bellaigue, whose provocative text caused several critics to express moral outrage (surely the reaction he wanted), Bach worship had taken over Bach appreciation. Hyperbole seemed the best antidote:

> Of all the great musicians, the greatest, perhaps, that is to say he without whom music itself would not exist, the founder, the patriarch, the father, the Abraham, the Noah, the Adam of music, Johann Sebastian Bach, is the most tedious. Handel comes only afterwards.... Read through one of his concertos, especially the Concerto for Three Pianos (horrible Trinity!), read (I shudder at my blasphemy!) the St Matthew Passion! For ten minutes one is astonished; after fifteen, enraged.... How many times, in the midst of one of these gigantic oratorios, these single or double choruses with orchestra and organ, how many times, crushed under these four-square, merciless rhythms, lost amid this algebra of sound, this living geometry, smothered by the answers of these interminable fugues, one wants to close one's ears to this prodigious counterpoint, to listen to a soft, lyrical performance of the Andante from Mozart's Clarinet Quintet, or the Allegretto from [Beethoven's] Symphony in A.[52]

Alongside the laying bare of his personal tastes, Bellaigue tapped into longstanding though nearly outdated complaints about Bach's dry learnedness and a

---

52. "De tous les grands musiciens, le plus grand peut-être, c'est-à-dire sans lequel la musique n'existerait pas, le fondateur, le patriarche, le père, l'Abraham, le Noé, l'Adam de la musique, Jean-Sébastien Bach, est le plus ennuyeux. Haendel ne vient qu'après lui.... Lisez un de ses concertos, surtout le concerto pour trois pianos (horrible trinité!), lisez (je frémis de mon blasphème!) *La Passion selon Saint Mathieu!* Pendant dix minutes, on est étonné; au bout de quinze, enragé. Que de fois au sein d'un de ces oratorios gigantesques, de ces chœurs ou doubles chœurs avec orchestre et orgues, que de fois, écrasé sous ces rhythmes carrés, impitoyables, perdu dans cette algèbre sonore, dans cette géométrie vivante, étouffé par les replis de ces fugues interminables, on voudrait

widespread antipathy to the algebra of fugue and to Germanic complexity (for which read also a reference to Wagnerian obfuscation). The support he received in the lighter musical press showed that his four-page tirade against the music of Bach did not leave him looking entirely foolish; Concordia's reception suffered accordingly. Julien Torchet, an anti-Franckiste writing in *Le monde artiste*, cited Bellaigue's essay at length as a pretext to review the 16 May concert while simultaneously ignoring it (he did, however, admire the soloists' resignation to the "severe discipline" of performing this "great and tedious masterpiece").[53] Bellaigue, he observed, had been abominable: "He had the audacity to say aloud what most of us think to ourselves. Since the sun has dark spots, he wrote that the sun has dark spots."[54] Less sarcastic but equally damning, Auguste Mercadier of *Le progrès artistique* accused Concordia of "pushing the cult [of Bach] to the point of idolatry."[55] Bellaigue had pricked the bubble of pomposity he detected in attitudes towards a composer who had—in the period since Pasdeloup's and Lamoureux's initiatives—become widely revered as a touchstone of musical genius. The tradition continued: "Rameau," who had already reviewed the Conservatoire's B minor Mass for the *Monde artiste* in 1891, ostentatiously avoided doing the same in 1892. He recommended a reading of Bellaigue's latest work on Bach (a comparison of the B minor Mass and the *Missa solemnis*) and declined to list the "unfortunate soloists who contributed to the performance of the famous Bach Mass."[56] The previous year, he had gleefully spread the rumor that on hearing that the Bach was to be programmed, 25 percent of the Société des Concerts' subscribers rushed to sell their usually jealously guarded tickets "through aversion or fear" to Bach lovers. The result: "people were bored stiff, but they applauded loudly."[57]

---

fermer l'oreille à ces combinaisons prodigieuses, pour entendre chanter tout bas l'*andante* du quintette avec clarinette, de Mozart, ou l'*allegretto* de la symphonie en *la*." Given in Bellaigue, *L'année musicale*, 116–19.

53. "discipline sévère"; "grand et ennuyeux chef-d'oeuvre." *Le monde artiste* (henceforth *MA*), 28/21: 27 May 1888, 393.

54. "La faute de M. Bellaigue est, je l'avoue, abominable. Il a eu la hardiesse de dire tout haut ce que la plupart entre nous pensent tout bas. Le soleil ayant des taches, il a écrit le soleil a des taches." *MA* 28/21: 27 May 1888, 394.

55. "elle pousse le culte jusqu'à l'idolatrie." *Le progrès artistique* (henceforth *PA*), no. 523 (vol. 11): 26 May 1888, n.p. Concordia's literature oozes with reverence. Its publicity leaflets made much of the society's work "to the great glory of the master" [à la plus grande gloire du maître] (Leaflet for St Matthew Passion, 1888); Edmond Fuchs's speech of 3 December 1887 to the society quoted the honorary president, Charles Gounod: Bach was simply "the greatest genius that ever existed" [le plus grand génie musical qui ait jamais existé] (Anon., *Concordia. Assemblée générale*, 6).

56. "malheureux solistes qui ont concouru à l'exécution de la fameuse Messe de Bach." *MA* 32/8: 21 February 1892, 174.

57. "par aversion ou crainte"; "on s'est ennuyé ferme, mais on a fort applaudi." *MA* 31/11: 15 March 1891, 169.

Notwithstanding the wit and tenacity of its exponents, Bach-bashing was a minority sport in 1880s and '90s Paris. And it was itself, like Wagner-bashing, an indication of the strength of Bach fervor. It did little to dim enthusiasm for a wide range of Bachian events, from Guilmant's concerts to Colonne's Thursday Nouveau-Théâtre series,[58] from the Chanteurs' series of Bach cantatas to the Pugno/Ysaÿe all-Bach concert of 27 January 1899. How is it to be explained? Was it partly youthful *snobisme*, as Gustave Robert of *La revue illustrée* suggested in 1894? Possibly, not least because of the shared passion for both Bach and Wagner among music-lovers (which Robert also noted, and to which Bellaigue had referred indirectly by yoking them together).[59] Wagner and *snobisme* were already recognized as bedfellows. But the Wagner connection went deeper, reaching to links that were routinely being made between Bach's polyphony and Wagner's orchestral writing, and the latter's debt to the former. There was also the question—given the complementary Bach/Wagner pairing, of whether Bach really was just dry abstraction.

Some Bach performers, instrumentalists especially, thought not. Hence Robert's disapproval when faced with the interpretations of Bach's slow movements by Pugno and Ysaÿe. At a Colonne concert, the latter clearly milked the central ritornello movement of the E major concerto for all it was worth. Robert's preferred tempo (per eighth-note pulse) would have been around 69; Ysaÿe's was around 40–42:

> For the audience it was much more seductive. The bass rhythm expansively sobbed by the cellos; the harmonies of the upper parts softened as much as possible; all contributed to make of this Adagio (now transformed into a Lento in 3/2) something mysterious in the manner of a Romantic nocturne.[60]

In a later review, Robert intimated that the program note described this same movement, played at the Châtelet by Ysaÿe on Good Friday, 1900 (13 April), as a "novel poignant in its sadness."[61] An unsigned *Ménestrel* critic wrote of the same performance that the expressivity of the Adagio was "so heart-rending it

---

58. This was Arthur Dandelot's observation. *MM* 9/16: 30 December 1897, 307. Colonne targeted his Thursday concerts at a less "popular" audience than his Sunday series.

59. Gustave Robert, *La musique à Paris, 1894–95*, 127–29. The latter was not a claim restricted to the elite press. See, for instance, Hippolyte de Vos on Wagner's own Bach cult in *NFC* 23/2: 16 January 1891, n.p.

60. "Pour l'auditoire c'était bien plus séduisant. Le rhythme des basses largement pleuré par les violoncelles, les harmonies des parties hautes adoucies autant que faire se pouvait: tout contribuait à faire de cet Adagio (ainsi transformé en un Lento à 3/2) quelque chose de mystérieux comme un nocturne romantique." Robert, *La musique à Paris, 1898–1900*, 111–12.

61. "*roman* poignant de tristesse." Robert, *La musique à Paris, 1898–1900*, 306.

brought tears to the eyes."⁶² By the 1890s, then, Bach was a composer of deep emotion, and in Paris to stay. Only one question remained. Was he Wagner's antidote (where Wagner was "the death knell for good music as cayenne pepper was the death knell for good food"⁶³)? Or was he, as D'Indy had it, Wagner's ideal complement?⁶⁴ Either way, Bach won out.

From Chanteurs to Schola

Almost unknown as a musical figure in Paris before Holy Week 1892, Charles Bordes, former pupil of Franck and Marmontel, was appointed *maître de chapelle* at Saint-Gervais, just east of the Hôtel-de-Ville, in March 1890. He began by following a slightly unusual path that included the liturgical use of Schubert's masses. But he soon changed direction, inspired by the abbé Perruchot, *maître de chapelle* at the nearby Notre-Dame des Blancs-Manteaux, who introduced him to Palestrina.⁶⁵ The ensuing history is well known: on Maundy Thursday 1891 (26 March) Bordes, with Julien Tiersot as his second conductor, programmed the Palestrina *Stabat mater* and Allegri's *Miserere* liturgically, using a choir of men, boys, and women. The following year, and with Vincent d'Indy's help (150 rehearsals shared between them),⁶⁶ he instituted a full Holy Week liturgy of Bach, Josquin, Palestrina, Lassus, Victoria, Lotti, and Allegri, after which two dozen of his adult singers agreed to form the Chanteurs de Saint-Gervais, whose mission was the propagation of Palestrinian liturgical music. Thereafter, Bordes and his *maîtrise*, sometimes aided by the Chanteurs, presented sung services of often unknown Palestrinian music at Saint-Gervais for each major feast day.⁶⁷ A hybrid of

---

62. "tellement déchirante qu'elle provoquait les larmes." *Mén* 65/3: 15 January 1899, 20.

63. Hippolyte Barbedette's rhetorical question reads: "Quand donc en aura-t-on fini avec ce système de la complication à l'outrance, qui est vraiment la mort de l'art musical, comme le poivre de Cayenne est la mort de la saine cuisine?" *Mén* 65/3: 15 January 1899, 20.

64. In a letter of 9 April 1908 to the singer Claire Croiza, D'Indy outlined a program being considered by the committee of the Concerts Lamoureux. The first half contained three extracts from Bach's Christmas and Easter oratorios and the cantata "Schlage doch" (attrib.); the second consisted of Act 3 scene 1 of *Siegfried* (Erda/Wotan), Siegfried's Funeral March, and Act 3 scene 1 of *Parsifal* (Gurnemanz/Parsifal). D'Indy commented, "C'est un beau programme—et symbolique!" BNF (Musique): l.a. vol. 55a, 93 (D'Indy).

65. Bordachar, *Charles Bordes*, 11.

66. See De Castera (Ed.), *La Schola cantorum*, 5.

67. From 1894, and possibly earlier, Bordes was joined by the abbé Perruchot; in 1896 the *maîtrise* of Saint-Jacques du Haut-Pas, under Blondel, sang Allegri's *Miserere* and was welcomed by G. de Boisjoslin into the fold of "Palestrinian" churches (*Tribune de Saint-Gervais* 2/2: February 1896, 32). The two Marais churches of Saint-Gervais and Notre-Dame des Blancs-Manteaux were, for the rest of the century, the central proponents of Palestrinian liturgical music in Paris, sometimes combining forces. Toward the end of 1894, for instance, Notre-Dame des Blancs-Marteaux programmed the following: Palestrina Pope Marcellus Mass (All Saints); Victoria

concert and liturgy, they were advertized in advance through posters and leaflets which gave complete music lists. The 1891 services with sermon cost 1F and 2F; funding for 1892 came from subscriptions of 50F and 30F and on-the-door tickets costing between 50c and 2F. For the 1892 series, free front-page publicity in *Le Figaro*, courtesy of the director Francis Magnard (father of the composer Albéric) ensured that the high society of Paris turned up in force. The services sold out, attracting wide and enthusiastic press coverage, which helped create a loyal critical following for Bordes's later initiatives.[68]

It was in the wake of his success at Saint-Gervais in 1892 that Bordes expanded his horizons, scheduling regular concert appearances for his choir. Bach was a focal composer; however, Bordes's historical curiosity produced programs whose eclectic appeal outstripped that of any other performing group. It was he who introduced Parisian and, from 1894, regional audiences, to Carissimi's *Jephte*, and to selections from Schütz's *Symphoniae sacrae*. Just as Guilmant had expanded the organ repertory backwards to the early Baroque, championing Buxtehude, Frescobaldi, and Clérambault once he had established secure places for Bach and Handel, so Bordes did the same for choral music. He used Schütz, for instance, as the "interlude" composer in all three of his Bach cantata concerts of 1895, rather in the manner of Choron's use of Janequin. And following Guilmant, who had devised a *concert historique* for the 1889 exposition (and who later published its repertory), Bordes and Dukas revived that tradition at the Salle d'Harcourt from 1893, presenting a roughly chronological survey of church, court, and operatic music from Josquin to Purcell.[69] The first two concerts—both in 1893—were unusual: the first (13 December) in its inclusion of excerpts from Caccini's *Euridice*, Monteverdi's *Orfeo* (Orfeo's "Possente spirito," sung by Mazalbert) and Gagliano's *La Dafne*; the second (27 December) for Schütz's "O quam tu pulchra es" and "Veni de Libano," both from the *Symphoniae sacrae*; and for the almost unprecedented attention given to English music. The program ended with excerpts from Purcell's *King Arthur*, then unknown in France (it was hardly

---

Mass "O quam gloriosum" (Immaculate Conception); Palestrina *Missa brevis*, a Magnificat, motet "Dies significatus," and a Handl motet "Ecce concipies" (Christmas). See the TS-G 1/1: January 1895, 12. From 1896, the churches of La Madeleine and Saint-Sulpice also presented Palestrinian repertory.

68. Paul Dukas in *La revue hebdomadaire* was one such; so, too, were Camille Bellaigue of the *Revue des deux mondes* (henceforth *RDM*), himself restoring the pro-Palestrinian tradition of Paul Scudo, and Hugues Imbert of the Brussels-based *Guide musical*. Félicien de Menil, writing for the *Progrès artistique*, and Arthur Dandelot, critic for the *Monde musical* and a confessed "fervent admirateur de l'art palestrinien" (MM 9/14: 30 November 1897, 265), were also staunch supporters.

69. The series of 12 concerts was a collaborative effort with Paul Dukas and the conductor Gustave Doret at the Salle d'Harcourt. For an affectionate portrait of D'Harcourt, and his generosity toward Bordes, see Paul Dukas, "Charles Bordes," in *La revue musicale* 5/10: 1 August 1924, 97–103, at 98.

known in England), and included the only English piece to have broken into the regular "early" repertory: Orlando Gibbons's "The Silver Swan" in its chivalric French guise of "Le croisé captif."[70] Both concerts included organ and harpsichord music, played by Gigout and Diémer respectively. In addition to sacred music by Palestrina, Victoria, Aichinger, Nanino, and Lotti, they also included familiar extracts from the stage works of Lully and Beaujoyeulx, and, finally, pieces that were arguably to become the Chanteurs' most popular repertory: the polyphonic chansons of Lassus and Janequin. The programs devised by Bordes and Dukas for these two concerts of early music are historically important: they contain every musical category and genre for which the Schola Cantorum, as an educational establishment, would become famous at the beginning of the twentieth century (D'Indy's edition and premiere of Monteverdi's *Orfeo* in 1904/5 are simply the best known of many examples). Moreover, they reveal the extent of Vincent d'Indy's debt to Bordes and Dukas in carving out the musical values of a school which has since—not least because of the influence of his *Cours de composition musicale*—become so closely associated with D'Indy's own musical philosophy that its musical values have appeared attributable to him alone.

The excitement generated by Bordes's Holy Week experiment of 1892 indicated his talent for public relations. It was a talent that led to his being central to the formation, on 6 June 1894, of the Schola Cantorum as a society dedicated to the promotion of "true" church music throughout France.[71] Despite being listed alongside G. de Boisjoslin as a lowly secretary, Bordes was its leading light, responsible for setting up the monthly *Tribune de Saint-Gervais* and the music publishing venture that underpinned the society's efforts. Its first presidents were Guilmant, the prince de Polignac, and Bourgault-Ducoudray. D'Indy acted as treasurer. Given its relatively narrow Catholic and liturgical aims, the Schola and its supporters represented a wide spectrum of musical and political opinion. The *Tribune's* contributors included the Republicans Bourgault-Ducoudray and Julien Tiersot, and the Benedictines of Solesmes, Dom Pothier and Dom Mocquereau; the anti-Bachian/anti-Wagnerian Bellaigue and the Bachian/Wagnerian Camille Benoît (in addition to the Wagnerian Georges Servières and the Bachian André Pirro). Other writers included

---

70. This madrigal had been known to the French as "Le croisé captif" since the early 1840s, when Moskova's society sang it (it was published in the Moskova anthology and also in Weckerlin's *Echos du temps passé*). Its original text appears to have remained unknown until Henriette Fuchs published her translation— "Le cygne d'argent"—for the Société Haendel (Paris: Mustel, 1911).

71. For a detailed history of the Schola Cantorum and early music, see Catrina Flint de Médicis, *The Schola Cantorum*.

Henri Expert and Michel Brenet (pseud. for Marie Bobillier—France's first female musicologist), André Hallays, Adolphe Jullien, and D'Indy. Alongside De Boisjoslin, who managed the all-important news column, they each, in their different ways, contributed to the propagation of a moderate Ultramontane musical ideology in which Gregorian chant as taught at Solesmes and Palestrinian polyphony (whether original or pastiche) were paramount.[72]

In practice, the "action palestrinienne" that formed one of the two planks of the Schola Cantorum's mission centred on three types of activity: concerts, church conferences, and the setting up of regional Schola branches. This latter form of dissemination, with which the Schola achieved considerable success, brings the nineteenth-century historical cycle back to the beginning: it was precisely this kind of relationship between centre and periphery that Choron had envisaged as the ideal means of improving liturgical music, and indeed all kinds of sung music-making, nationwide. It was, of course, also the model which the Paris Conservatoire had been operating since 1826, when the first official branches were created out of municipal conservatoires in Lille and Toulouse.

"Insider" histories of Bordes, particularly those of the abbé Bordachar and the Schola-trained composer René de Castéra (1873–1955), are undoubtedly trustworthy in their portrayal of an intrepid 25-strong mixed choir engaged in a punishing schedule of concerts, services, and gala events, "beating the bounds" of France by rail or mail coach and putting up, heroically, with budget accommodation. Equally trustworthy, and significant, are their accounts of times, such as at Bordeaux and Avignon (the 1899 conference), when Schola delegates received a hostile reception. But their silences speak louder. Even in De Castéra's relatively detailed account of the Chanteurs' tours to 1900, there was no mention of visits to those cathedrals that had the longest-standing Palestrinian traditions: Autun, Langres, and Moulins. Neither was there any real acknowledgement of the Cecilian work of the Toulousain Aloys Kunc (1832–1895), or his successor, as editors of *Musica sacra* (1874–84, 1887–1901). Neither, finally, was there a hint that at some of the Chanteurs' other venues, such as Périgueux, Nevers, Dijon, and Lyon, cathedral musicians had already embraced sixteenth-century polyphony, if not chant.[73] By contrast, De Castéra

---

72. On the basis of the raw figures, the propaganda exercise was a success: on first publication the *Tribune* had a mere 200 subscribers; in a letter of 15 February 1900 to Marnold, describing his vision of the Schola (his "idées de mégalomane," as he called them), he mentioned that the *Tribune*'s subscription list numbered 800. BNF (Musique): l.a. vol. 12, 137–39 (Bordes).

73. See the government inspection reports of *maîtrises* (1883 onward) in AN Paris: F^{21} 1328, box 1. Other than at Moulins, Palestrina is the only sixteenth-century composer named; the only other "early" composers used in the liturgy are the Italians popular in concert repertories in the earlier part of the century. Marcello and Pergolesi.

dwelt on the contribution of card-carrying people and institutions, such as the Société Sainte-Cécile in Toul and the *maître de chapelle* at the church of Saint-André in Niort. The propaganda element is clear: Bordes, the Chanteurs, and the Schola itself were to be presented as pioneers, even when aspects of their work had been pre-empted, and even if it meant that revivalist activity went underreported because certain beacons of the "action palestrinienne" had not officially joined the Schola's cause. Michel Brenet betrayed some discomfort on this score in an encomium of 1909 to Bordes. The repetitious nature of the Société des Concerts' programs, she wrote, had done nothing to educate the people about this music. Neither had the student concerts of the Ecole Niedermeyer, so that "few of them had heard that in regional churches, at Langres, at Moulins, perhaps elsewhere too without anyone knowing about it, a glimmer shone, intermittently, of what had once lit up the entire horizon of musical Catholicism."[74] Bordes's secret, then, was not primacy so much as a talent for external relations work and the organizational energy to see his projects to fruition.

The *Tribune* presented a slightly less selective history of the regeneration of Catholic church music in France, and there was no aggressive sectarianism in the propaganda which De Boisjoslin provided. Although the Schola's relationship to other branches of French Cecilianism is unclear, the journal followed certain rival manifestations of regeneration with some enthusiasm: prize-givings at the former Ecole Niedermeyer (where Bach's organ music was still championed) were covered positively, and De Boisjoslin acclaimed Georges Marty's work with the choral class at the Conservatoire in the journal's very first number.[75] Moreover, the abbé Chérion's arrival in 1896 at the Madeleine (he had been in charge of the *maîtrise* at Moulins Cathedral) was enthusiastically reported.[76]

We have relatively little information on the reactions of congregations to the many performances of *a cappella* polyphony, which Schola-affiliated and Schola-sympathetic choirs gave, and which were dutifully recorded in the *Tribune*. What

---

74. "bien peu d'entre eux seulement avaient entendu dire qu'en des églises de province, à Langres, à Moulins, peut-être ailleurs encore, sans que l'on en sût rien, une lueur brillait, par intervalles, de ce qui avait autrefois éclairé tout l'horizon musical catholique." Michel Brenet in *TS-G* 15 (special number: *Charles Bordes 1863–1909. In memoriam*), 13–14.

75. See *TS-G* 1/1: January 1895, 12, where the class's performance of Lotti's *Crucifixus* and a *Sanctus* a3, and Palestrina's "Rex virtutis," is praised. Marty regularly presented Palestrinian and French sixteenth-century repertory at examination time. It has become traditional to view the Schola Cantorum, especially in its guise as an educational establishment (from October 1896), as offering a curriculum that was entirely in conflict with that of the secular, Republican Conservatoire. In respect to Marty's work with the choral class, this was not the case. It is also worth noting that Théodore Dubois, the Conservatoire's director from 1896, wrote sacred music in the Palestrinian style, dedicating one mass *alla Palestrina* to none other than the abbé Chérion.

76. *TS-G* 2/5: May 1896, 78–79.

the *Tribune* provides, instead, is a chronicle of successful promotion gathering momentum throughout the period up to and beyond 1900. That dissemination was particularly important as a way of demolishing myths about the repertory's difficulty. When the Chanteurs included the Jacobus de Kerle mass "Regina coeli" for men's voices in their Pentecost services of 1895, De Boisjoslin welcomed the piece because it was "very easy to sing" and recommended it particularly to working men's choral societies.[77] The Chorale d'Amiens took up the challenge, presenting their St Cecilia's Day celebrations "palestriniquement," as the *Tribune* put it.[78] Such a puff review (as it undoubtedly was) benefited the Amiens society and the Schola equally on the "democratization" question: no wonder, then, that alongside the Viadana "O sacrum convivium," it was described in De Boisjoslin's column as among those "magnificent works" "that ought to be in the repertory of every Choral Society wishing to renew and elevate its repertory," and that the choral society members were reported as being "captivated by the character, at once severe and brilliant, of this kind of music."[79]

Accessibility was a byword in the *Tribune*. Directly, in performance, and indirectly through De Boisjoslin's column, Bordes, the Chanteurs, and the Schola attempted to cut through the myth of technical challenge, whether for performers or listeners, that still clung to the polyphonic music they wished to promote. Writing to Guy Ropartz to organize a forthcoming Chanteurs tour, Bordes assured him that the Bach cantata "Bleib bei uns" was "very accessible"[80]; De Boisjoslin used similar language in respect to *stile antico* repertory. In February 1896 he wrote emphatically of the "very easy nature" of Allegri's *Miserere* (doubtless the stripped-down version), recently taken up by the *maîtrise* of Saint-Jacques du Haut-Pas.[81] All "Palestrinian" repertory, he wrote, shared that same characteristic. As though to prove the point, on the same page he printed news of M. André, organist at Saint-Maurice, Besançon and director of the Orphéon Bisontin, who had recently performed one of the Schola's recommended works—Andrea Gabrieli's motet "Angeli archangeli"—and who now planned to do more such repertory.[82]

---

77. "d'une exécution très-abordable." TS-G 1/5: May 1895, 16.

78. The report was probably sent in by the choir's director, M. Bertiau. TS-G 1/11: November 1895, 15.

79. "magnifiques oeuvres . . . qui devraient être du répertoire de toute Société chorale désireuse de renouveler et d'élever son répertoire," "captivés par le caractère sévère et brillant à la fois de ce genre de musique." TS-G 1/11: November 1895, 15.

80. "très accessible." He suggested a program which also included Janequin's *Bataille* and some unidentified chansons. BNF (Musique): l.a. vol. 12, 171 (Bordes). Undated.

81. "l'absolue facilité." TS-G 2/2: February 1896, 32.

82. TS-G 2/2: February 1896, 32. The Gabrieli motet had appeared as a music supplement to the April 1895 edition. On accessibility, see also De Boisjoslin's more muted comments in TS-G 1/11: November 1895, 15.

The Schola's presentation of "musique palestrinienne" as easy to sing offered a challenge to two important constituencies: the extreme Ultramontane lobby for the restoration of Gregorian chant *tout court*; and the lobby of *maîtres de chapelle* who wished to continue to use modern (i.e. more-or-less operatic) music in the liturgy. Its presentation of Bach's choral music in the same vein, together with its almost total neglect, in the 1890s, of Handel, cut across other critical divides. Of course, Guilmant never ceased to promote Handel's organ concertos; but in terms of sacred music the Schola famously and consistently neglected Handel in favor of Bach.[83] Doing so went against the grain of received wisdom about the two composers' relative accessibility, according to which it might be expected that the Schola would embrace Handel's works alongside those of Carissimi, Buxtehude, Schütz, and Bach. But instead Handel was brushed aside. This is especially counterintuitive given that Guilmant was a Schola founder and Bourgault-Ducoudray a president. Personal taste may have played its part. D'Indy was known to dislike the oratorios intensely—which, for Fauré, made it all the funnier to find him forced into playing the organ by the comtesse de Greffulhe for her Société des Grandes Auditions performances of *Israel in Egypt* in June 1891.[84] Bordes's view is less easily gauged, though the almost complete absence of Handel in the Chanteurs' repertory of the 1890s may indicate a dislike equal to that of D'Indy. In addition, Handel's odes and oratorios had, well before the time of the Schola's formation, acquired two reputations which sat uneasily with its allegiances: in the very process of being presented as "popular," they had been rendered Republican and non-Christian. By contrast, from appearing excessively Protestant in the 1860s, Bach's sacred music was now widely accepted as both superior and, rather than Protestant, universally Christian.[85] In fact, the Handel question serves only to highlight the element of propaganda in the use of the term "accessible" in the *Tribune*. Far from being a neutral statement, it was a defensive move against opposition ready, on more objective, stylistic, grounds, to appeal to technical difficulty as a sufficient reason for nonparticipation in the Schola's preferred liturgical repertory. That first Palestrinian Holy Week at Saint-Gervais had, after all, required 150 rehearsals.

---

83. The sole example of the performance of Handel's music occurs as half of a Bach/Handel *concert historique* in the D'Harcourt/Chanteurs series (17 January 1894). Catrina Flint-de Médicis has identified a Handelian "bulge" in the Schola's activities from 1900 to 1902, but Handel's position relative to Bach remained unaltered from that of the 1890s. Flint de Médicis, "The Schola Cantorum, Early Music, and French Cultural Politics."

84. On D'Indy's discomfiture and Fauré's glee, see Fauré's letter of 6 June 1891 to Paul Poujaud, in Nectoux (Ed.), *Gabriel Fauré*, 173: "Poor d'Indy at his great organ, it must have put years on his life." Contrary to Nectoux's note (173, n. 2), by the second performance (10 June) D'Indy had found reason to escape to the Midi. Guilmant had to replace him. *MM* 3 (no. 51): 15 June 1891, 6.

85. Discussed in chapter 7, 236.

112   PATTERNS OF REVIVAL

Regions, Nationalism, and *la musique française*

The Schola's active dedication to regional promotion, in the 1890s and after 1900, was timely, even if the thrust of the Schola's mission was essentially a centralizing, Ultramontane one. The Third Republic's emphasis on centralization and unification (especially in respect to educational practice and language) encouraged protest, and led to the intensification, particularly in regions which already considered themselves "different," of a sense of specifically regional identity. This was the period of the nineteenth century when interest in local musical history accelerated most sharply, as witnessed by the number of papers—many of them presenting new archival findings on "local" composers—presented to local Académies des Beaux-Arts and published in their *Bulletins*.[86] Folk-song studies in the French regions became a contested space for this very reason: was one collecting to preserve regional variation, or to provide a fund of songs that could be designated, irrespective of precise provenance, as "French"?[87] A key event in 1896 illustrates how the relationships between local and national history, regionalism and nationalism, had to be negotiated with increasing care. The town of Arras planned a commemorative festival to celebrate the more than six hundred years of the *Jeu de Robin et de Marion*, traditionally regarded as the first *opéra-comique* and the work of one of its most glorious children. It was to include a staged performance with performers from the Comédie-Française and the Opéra-Comique. The score, fully orchestrated, was prepared by Julien Tiersot, the text updated by Emile Blémont, and the festival organized by two committees, one in Paris, the other in Arras. They agreed that the public dress rehearsal would take place in Paris, at the Opéra-Comique, but with a press embargo on discussion of the music, so as not to "deflower, through premature analysis, the novel interest that the work offered to Adam de la Halle's compatriotes."[88] The premiere was reserved for Arras. Such consideration for regional

---

86. One gains an insight into this acceleration from studying the exhaustive bibliographical work carried out by Jean Peyrot shortly before World War I. Peyrot's subject was a history of early music in nineteenth-century France, with particular emphasis on composers' biographies. His card index of references, arranged by composer, repeatedly shows the same pattern of increasing local attention, especially for composers of the Franco-Flemish school. The Fichier Peyrot is conserved at the BNF (Musique).

87. On the contrast between Republican and regionalist approaches to the dissemination of folk song (including those of D'Indy and the Schola), see Pasler, "The *chanson populaire*," 203–9. Fulcher has shown that the *chanson populaire* had, for different reasons, been something of a political pawn since the 1830s. See her "The Popular Chanson."

88. "déflorer par une analyse préventive l'intérêt de nouveauté que la pièce offrait aux compatriotes d'Adam de la Halle." Ch. Vaillant, *L'avenir d'Arras et du Pas-de-Calais* 26/149: 23 June 1896, n.p., quoting Francisque Sarcey

sensibilities was unprecedented in 1896, though it would become stronger, not least at the hands of Bordes, D'Indy, and the Schola.

For, like the promoters of Adam's play, the Schola's leaders, too, trod a careful line in respect to the relationship between regionalism and nationalism, to both of which Bordes and D'Indy were, in different ways, sympathetic. Ultramontane sympathies clashed with the regional and national separatism that had always characterized Gallicanism; yet in matters secular (especially folk song and opera), both Bordes and D'Indy prized the vibrancy of regional traditions, in particular the distinctiveness of the Midi and its associated "génie latin." That "génie latin" was very much alive in liturgical practice in the Midi during the first decades of the Third Republic. The Cathedral of Saint-Sauveur at Aix-en-Provence held an early-morning Good Friday sermon in Provençal during the 1870s and 80s[89] and regularly featured the liturgical music of its most distinguished local composer, Campra (a motet "Domine me secundum"), alongside that of Dumont (a *Messe royale*, harmonized), Carissimi (the *Miserere*), Pergolesi (extracts from the *Stabat mater*), and Bach (set as a "Tantum ergo") during Holy Week services of the 1870s. But where the Schola was prepared to publish Provençal folk songs in the original language, it could not yet condone the sacred music of a composer such as Campra. Nothing was said in print or, it seems, in surviving correspondence; but, along with Lully, Rameau, and Charpentier, these composers were doubtless too overtly Gallican to form part of the approved Schola repertory.[90] There were, admittedly, only two Rameau sacred works in print in France before their rehabilitation in the complete edition in 1897; nevertheless, there was considerably more Lalande and Campra available, either in eighteenth-century printings (Lalande's complete motets took up 18 volumes in the 1729 Boivin edition) or, as we have seen, the occasional nineteenth-century publication.

The argument against "Gallican" music gains in potency if we consider the extent to which the Schola embraced French secular music of the same period: consistently, Bordes and his singers championed not only Lully and Rameau, but also Charpentier and, later, Gustave Moreau, whose music for Racine's *Athalie*

---

in *Le temps*, 22 June 1896, n.p. The word "déflorer" is doubtless a pun on the plot, which involves the attempted rape of Marion.

89. The practice was, however, contested. In 1890 an unsigned writer for the *Semaine religieuse de l'Archidiocèse d'Aix* wrote approvingly of the reintroduction of French: "the riposte of French elegance against the armed assault of Provençal" [la riposte de l'éloquence française à l'assaut d'armes du provençal]. *Semaine religieuse*, 12 (no. 544): 13 April 1890, 157–58.

90. Dumont, who had reputedly insisted on retaining plainchant roots in his masses, was a different matter; and the only known *Messe royale*, in its various modernizations, was consistently applauded by Ultramontanes.

and *Esther* was presumably acceptable because, written for the pupils of Mme de Maintenon's school at Saint-Cyr, it was sacred music theatre, not liturgical music.[91] Among those connected with the Rameau complete edition, begun in 1894, Schola affiliates were well represented (D'Indy and Dukas both edited operatic volumes). But neither edited the motets. That task fell to Saint-Saëns, who took advantage of autographs and eighteenth-century copies in the Bibliothèque Nationale to edit the composer's five extant examples, of which only two—the fugal "Laboravi" and "Quam dilecta" in vocal score—had appeared in print in either the eighteenth or the nineteenth century.[92] France's seventeenth- and eighteenth-century church music thus found no national outlet for secular performance, and therefore for familiarization among a wide public, for almost the entire century. Vilified by Choron and decisively excluded from his publications, concerts, and curriculum, it was ignored by the Ecole Niedermeyer and again sidelined by the Schola Cantorum at the end of the century.[93] Except for occasional performances in its composers' native towns, the *grand motet* and other genres of church music of the *grand siècle* and the eighteenth century remained virtually forgotten until well after 1900.

For the same reasons in reverse, some "regional" composers of early music fared better at the Schola. Elzéar Genet, le Carpentrassien, was one such. Laurens became interested in him in the 1840s, writing an impassioned article on his music for Danjou's *Revue de la musique religieuse, populaire, classique*, in which he clashed swords with Fétis (who had compared Genet's *Lamentations* unfavorably with those of Palestrina).[94] Laurens had heard the Genet *Magnificat sexti toni* in 1840, sung by Thibaut's choral society in Heidelberg. He studied more of Genet's music from 1879, when the Conservatoire acquired a copy of five of his Masses, and determined to bring the composer's music back to life in Carpentras. He received no support, moral or otherwise, but finally succeeded in 1886, when, on 27 November (the patronal festival of Saint-Siffrein), the work was integrated into the festival tradition.[95] Laurens died in July 1890.

---

91. In the introduction to his edition of Moreau's *Esther* (1902), Charles Bordes described its choral music as having "the essential characteristics of Christian song" [les traits essentielles de la lyrique chrétienne] (6). The Schola first produced *Esther* at the Théâtre de l'Odéon, Paris, on 18 December 1902.

92. The Ramiste Charles Poisot edited both editions, which are undated (but before 1867) and c.1876 respectively. The nineteenth-century edition of "Laboravi" was erroneously attributed to Charles Vervoitte (whose Ultramontane sympathies would in any case have made him an unlikely enthusiast) by Charles Malherbe in his preface to Saint-Saëns's edition of the Rameau motets (J.-P. Rameau, *Oeuvres complètes*, v, viii).

93. The sole exception, as far as I can tell, is the Société des Concerts, which took up Rameau's "Quam dilecta" in 1898. The Conservatoire presented it again as part of a student *exercice* (Marty's choral class) the following year.

94. J.-B. Laurens, "Carpentras," in *RMRPC* 3 (1847), 49–72. The passage on Genet's music is at 49–54.

95. Laurens's innovations were long-lived, lasting "almost to our own time." Lesure, *Dictionnaire musical des villes de province*, 126.

Had he lived a few years longer, he would have found support for this side of his revivalist work. For whereas Bordes and the Schola left the sacred music of Lalande and other French motet composers well alone, that of Genet was acceptable; and much noise was made in the *Tribune* about the Chanteurs de Saint-Gervais's performance, on All Saints' Day 1899, of one of the masses in the Schola's collection: "A l'ombre dung buissonnet." Bordes's selection of Genet is not in itself important; neither—except as an example of the belated acceptance of *chanson*-based masses—is his selection of this particular piece. But Genet's music was stylistically acceptable for liturgical performance and for dissemination throughout the network of Schola-affiliated institutions specifically because it was *a cappella* polyphony.

That was one of the reasons why Bordes and the Schola could also, belatedly, act as champions of the sacred music of Josquin, Pierre de La Rue, Goudimel, and Lassus, thereby creating a Franco-Flemish canon of sacred music which would be enlivened with Spanish elements chiefly from Victoria and Morales. An overarching sense of national pride fueled the belief that, despite all their weaknesses in writing "inappropriate" sacred music, members of the Franco-Flemish school deserved to be revived. New work on folk song also helped. Tiersot's influential history drew on older visions of the rootedness of the *chanson populaire* but applied them to once disparaged sacred works. They acquired new value not as sacred music per se, or indeed as a national style to be emulated in the manner of *ancien-régime* dance, but as repositories of French musical authenticity. Instead of the secular and sacred genres existing in conflict, the two genres thus became complementary in a familiar, secularizing, way: the sacred framework was the museum that conserved the secular jewel.[96]

Characteristically, then, the evocation of an idea of ancient "Frenchness" of style was reserved for secular music. In concert, the chanson triumphed in the hands of Lassus especially. His lightness of touch, freshness, and vitality—all perceptible despite the contrapuntal texture—delighted reviewers and audiences alike. The critical tropes that welcomed his chansons were at least twenty years old when Bordes began conducting them; such tropes themselves were mostly adapted from the traditional reception of Janequin's *Bataille de Marignan*. A review of January 1870 of a Bourgault-Ducoudray concert that featured "Mon coeur" illustrates their longevity:

---

96. Tiersot's *Histoire de la chanson populaire* was written in 1885 for the Prix Bordin and published in expanded form in time for the Exposition Universelle of 1889. For a fuller discussion, see chapter 5.

"Mon coeur se recommande à vous," a sweet and charming madrigal by Roland de Lassus, opened the concert. It is a slight, unpretentious work, simple and delicate, with a certain aura of artlessness, but full of exquisite grace. The melodic line undulates and glides like a harmonious sigh.[97]

Léon Schlesinger, too, wrote in 1893 of this "very graceful and touching" Lassus chanson.[98] Here, it seemed, was the ideal French sixteenth-century chanson. And "ideal" it was. For, as in the cases of the Palestrina "Adoramus te" and the Stradella "Pietà Signore," one of the most famous pieces turns out to be that height of mythification, a fake, possibly prepared by Weckerlin in the early 1860s.[99]

Nevertheless, it is no coincidence that with the exception of his comment on the chanson's undulating melodic line, Lucien Augé's description could be mistaken for a commentary on most of the French Baroque repertory of Louis Diémer and the Société des Instruments Anciens. For the qualities of delicacy and grace, unpretentiousness, and artless charm, were fast becoming accepted as quintessential, and—what is more—valued, traits of "Frenchness." And while several conductors, including Choron, Moskova, Vervoitte, and Bourgault-Ducoudray, had included a limited number of French chansons in their repertories, none before Bordes had been able to do so in a climate in which the secular output of French Baroque composers was popular enough to attract positive comment along the same lines. The idea of a historically defined, and distinct, French "musical character" had been problematic since the displacement of *la musique française* by the Italian operatic tradition in the late eighteenth century; the end of the century saw the critical rhetorics for two historical traditions come together to allow the affectionate and, above all, nostalgic redrawing of the portrait of French secular music from the sixteenth to the early eighteenth centuries: the aesthetic and ideological backdrop for a French neo-classical movement that was already in the making.[100] It is to the detailed twists and turns of that journey that I shall now turn.

---

97. "*Mon coeur se recommande à vous*, doux et charmant madrigal de Roland de Lassus, ouvre la séance. C'est une petite oeuvre sans prétention, simple, délicate, avec un certain parfum de naïveté, mais pleine d'une grâce exquise. La phrase mélodique ondule et glisse comme un soupir harmonieux." Lucien Augé in *FM* 34/5: 30 January 1870, 34.

98. "très gracieux et touchant." *Mén* 59/51: 17 December 1893, 405.

99. See Melamed, "Who Wrote Lassus's Most Famous Piece?" Melamed identifies the piece as a fake, but cannot trace its authorship further back than the late 1890s. However, it first turns up 30 years earlier in Weckerlin's programs of the 1860s for the Société Sainte-Cécile.

100. The best survey of the music is still Messing's *Neoclassicism in Music*, at pp. 24–43.

PART II

Uses, Appropriations, Meanings

4

La musique française at the Crossroads

Not since the Terror had there been a period more humiliating than the bloody internal strife of the Paris Commune; not until 1940 would there be anything to compare with the ignominy of defeat at Prussian hands in a mere six weeks in the summer of 1870. The fallout from both was considerable. The perception that Germany had a braver and better-prepared (and therefore implicitly, more masculine) army than the French drained the confidence of a nation whose pride in being a significant military force had hitherto been bolstered by memory of victorious campaigns under Napoléon I. Culture, too, came under scrutiny as a potential source of national weakness. Those who had protested French decadence in the late 1860s could justifiably shout louder, their calls for regeneration strengthened by the efforts of new converts. The pained re-evaluation of central aspects of French life thus extended widely, from the nature of masculinity and the need for better military training to the value of education and culture, and, in Republican minds at least, the welding of the French people into a cohesive nation sharing a single language and celebrating a common sense of heritage inculcated in young citizens from their earliest school days. From the musician's perspective, education had indeed fared badly during the Second Empire: music had become an optional subject at primary level in 1867, just two years after it had been made compulsory. Jules Ferry's educational reforms belatedly reversed that decision, making music a compulsory subject in primary education from the spring of 1882 onward.[1]

Nevertheless, French music had little symbolic part to play in popular education. There was no patriotic musical cult in Third-Republic schools that could compare, for instance, with educationalists' veneration of the literary classics, Molière in particular. Neither would there be anything to compare with 1870s evangelizing for Handel oratorio as a cultural, educational, and morally strengthening activity for the adult population.[2] Rather, it was among the intelligentsia and arguably *for* the intelligentsia that the cultural activity of elevating national heroes past and present served to "prove" France's artistic greatness, offering an opportunity for journalists, editors, and musicians to help heal their battered psyche and to present a cure for that of the nation.[3] The predictability of such activity has provoked sarcasm. In his 1960 biography of Rameau, Jean Malignon saw the composer as just so much cultural ammunition, flung—belatedly—into the face of the Germans, in an attempt "to bolster one's courage and one's faith in the national destiny of France."[4] Nevertheless, in respect to the heroes of France's musical past, appeals to what Ernest Renan was to call "collective memory" are more complex than Malignon's disparagement might suggest.

Publications relating to *ancien-régime* stage music after the Franco-Prussian War reveal a significant acceleration of interest in the repertory, conceived in expressly nationalist terms. But culture is not the same as practice, and heightened symbolic value does not necessarily make a repertory acceptable for professional or other public use. Certainly, that was the case with French stage music of the "golden age" and the eighteenth century. Indeed, the wildly successful educational "matinées classiques" of 1875–76 at the Théâtre de la Gaîté, with music by Lully and Charpentier, actually demonstrate the failure in practice of the nationalist enterprise suggested by the publication history of French Baroque stage music. They also, together with other evidence, illustrate the process by which laudable elements of *la musique française* became progressively winnowed down to its dance music, thereby proving the longevity of Fétis's opinion of 1832 (*à propos* of the same repertory): "For a long time, graceful dance and tasteless singing were the lot of the French."[5] But

---

1. For a typically feisty account of France's music-education woes, see Weber, *La situation musicale*. On masculinity after 1870, see Berenson, *The Trial of Madame Caillaux*, esp. 114–17; and Nye, *Masculinity and Male Codes of Honor*, esp. 148–71.

2. See chapter 7.

3. On the centrality of "greatness," see Gildea, *The Past in French History*, chapter 3.

4. Malignon, *Rameau*, 117–19, as paraphrased in Paul, "Rameau, D'Indy and French Nationalism," 46.

5. "Danser avec grâce et chanter sans goût fut long-temps dans la destinée des Français." *RM* 6/12: 14 April 1832, 83.

another irony of culture versus practice militated, until the 1890s, against wholehearted acceptance of the implications of Fétis's viewpoint: for while the musical preferences of the intelligentsia unfailingly tended toward comedy, the Watteau-like miniature and dance, the aspects of Frenchness that they most wished to applaud in the abstract comprised the dramatic realism of French declamation and the masculine *gravitas* of large-scale tragedy. Reconciling the two, especially in the aftermath of a lost war, was fraught with difficulty.

Comparisons with contemporary attitudes towards historical stage plays are necessary here. For, increasingly, the standard comparator for those wishing to appeal to the museum spirit was not the Louvre, but the Comédie-Française, which had, since its reconstitution in 1799, consistently mounted the works of Corneille, Molière, and (to a lesser extent) Racine, alongside new plays. Despite the Revolution and all that it signified to Republicans, they agreed with monarchists that the drama of the *grand siècle* of Louis XIV represented the essence of French literary culture.[6] Corneille, a symbol of French imperial grandeur since Napoléon I, remained emblematic of France's literary greatness during the Third Republic.[7] Molière, the model bourgeois moralist, could heal the nation through laughter.[8] The Paris Opéra did not, and could not, compete on the same level. Indeed, frequent calls, after 1870, for the Société des Concerts to act as a "museum" for French Baroque stage music were predicated on the realization that the Opéra could not do so itself.[9] Finally, in 1879, its *cahier des charges* included the new demand that it act as a "museum" of opera; the following year its director, Auguste-Emmanuel Vaucorbeil, began his series of *concerts historiques* of operatic and ballet music.[10] But fully staged productions were out of the question, even for a man who had, in 1874, argued precisely the opposite case in the Assemblée Nationale:

---

6. See Albanese Jr., *Molière à l'école républicaine*; "Molière républicain"; and "The Molière Myth in Nineteenth-Century France." See also his "Corneille à l'école républicaine." The "tendre" Racine fared less well as a national icon. See Eustis, *Racine devant la critique française*. On the musical side I cannot agree with Charles B. Paul's thesis that in historical writing about Rameau, Rousseau, and the *Guerre des bouffons* from 1876 (Arthur Pougin's *Rameau*) onward, there is an ideological split between left-wing writers who sided with Rousseau and the idea of a "populist" Revolution, and right-wing Ramistes who saw the Revolution as a plot hatched by a small, mainly foreign, circle (Paul, "Music and Ideology," 396–98). Pougin, for instance, whom Paul presents as on the anti-Rousseau side (400–401), was no right-winger, but a radical Republican; Republican too were other Ramistes, including Johannes Weber and Julien Tiersot.

7. Albanese, "Corneille à l'école républicaine," 146–47.

8. Paul Janet, "La philosophie des comédies de Molière," *Revue politique et littéraire*, 17 (1872), 387–92, given in Albanese, *Molière à l'école républicaine*, 103.

9. Between 1873 and 1894, Arthur Pougin, Maurice Cristal, Michel Harold, Paul Dukas, and Auguste-Emmanuel Vaucorbeil all called for a "museum" for French opera, preferably at the Société des Concerts.

10. Unfortunately, Vaucorbeil's *concerts historiques* did not expand the repertory of extracts beyond that which was already familiar to Conservatoire audiences (as Ernest Reyer complained in *JD* 30 May 1880).

> Today the *classics* of dramatic music are nothing more than a memory, and we are never given an opportunity to hear them. While Corneille and Molière, Racine and Regnard have remained the glory and the honor of the literary stage, where they are always shown, the great composers of yesteryear are banished from the lyric stage.... It is genuinely sad that the present generation is condemned to ignorance of a single work by Lully, Campra, Rameau, or Destouches, these fathers of the French lyric stage.[11]

Had French musicians felt confident in the achievements of their own modern operatic school, such neglect of tradition might not have mattered. But in the late 1860s, in the wake of Meyerbeer's death, a universally acclaimed successor had not been revealed. Self-confidence in grand opera, France's most prominent and exportable musical commodity, was low; and a worrying question would not go away: how French was modern French opera? For Henri Blaze de Bury, reflecting on French music in 1872, there was far too much German influence—Bach and Mendelssohn—in Gounod and Thomas.[12] Gustave Bertrand concurred and went further: France lacked (and, by implication, needed) a "militant" French opera. He warned that Paris, through being too cosmopolitan, "will forget to be national."[13] Wagner's ascendancy, combined with the infamous contempt of *Eine Kapitulation*, was the final straw. There was every reason, then, for postwar musicians to call for the elevation of French operatic models dating from a period when German opera did not appear to threaten all around it.[14] What was needed was a canon of national heroes who symbolized patriotic summits of achievement—"Fathers of the Third Republic..., forming a continuous ridge along which one moves from genius

---

11. "Les *classiques* de la musique dramatique ne sont plus aujourd'hui qu'un souvenir, et jamais l'occasion ne nous est offerte de les entendre. Tandis que Corneille et Molière, Racine et Regnard sont restés la gloire et l'honneur de la scène littéraire, où ils sont toujours représentés, les grands compositeurs d'autrefois sont bannis de la scène musicale.... Il est vraiment triste que la génération présente soit condamnée à ne pas connaître un seul des ouvrages de Lully, de Campra, de Rameau, de Destouches, ces pères de la scène lyrique française." Vaucorbeil, *Mémoire présentée à l'Assemblée Nationale*, 6.

12. De Lagenevais [Blaze de Bury], *RDM* 1 February 1872, 846.

13. "obliera d'être national." Bertrand, *Les nationalités musicales*, 4.

14. Some of the central figures discussed below, including Arthur Pougin and Arthur Heulhard, were anti-Wagnerians; others, such as D'Indy and Adolphe Jullien, were not. Paul Lacome was ambivalent; nevertheless, both he and D'Indy defended the value of early French opera explicitly by reference to Wagnerian models, and we find both Lacome and Jullien writing for Heulhard's fiercely anti-Wagnerian journal, in the service of a higher nationalist ideal.

to genius."[15] Literary projects such as Hachette's series of critical editions, "Les Grands Ecrivains de la France" (launched in 1862), showed the way for musicians, although it was not until the first volume of the Michaëlis collected edition of French opera (1877), that they were able to respond fully.

La chronique musicale and the "Founders" of French Opera

As an attempt to set up historical idols, Arthur Heulhard's *La chronique musicale* provided a stepping stone. In an *Art musical* article of March 1872, provocatively entitled "L'invasion allemande en musique," he had prepared the ideological ground, comparing the benign operatic invasions of Lully, Gluck, and others with Wagner's malignant power.[16] Officially, his journal was to concentrate on new music; in fact, it became a major repository for research on the history of French music (especially music for the stage). Free of the commercial pressures experienced by music publishers whose journals had to promote house composers, Heulhard, who was independently wealthy, could indulge his own tastes and serve "his" public: the leisured intelligentsia. This was no tabloid journal printed in cramped type on low-grade paper. A book-like octavo format complemented the thick vellum, large type, and generous white space—of all of which he was proud.[17] Subscribers paid 130F for the entire "collection" of eleven volumes, which also boasted abundant engravings and music supplements.

Heulhard argued that a new refinement in French taste demanded a journal that would be both beautiful and useful. The *Chronique*'s music supplements were also educational—intended for the study of one's *patrimoine* at the family piano.

> We shall . . . resuscitate the inspirations of our old French masters piece by piece, and you will see how many unknown geniuses, how many neglected talents we shall bring forth from the darkness which hides even their names. And I do not need to point out that these pages of music will be chosen with discernment, that they will remain adorned in all the artless grace of their original virginity, in their original versions. I should add that the repertory of our forgotten

---

15. Compagnon, "Proust's *Remembrance of Things Past*," 217.
16. *AM* 11/10–11: 7–14 March 1872.
17. See *CM* 1 (no. 1): 1 July 1873, 9.

ones, our disparaged ones, is teeming with masterpieces (the word is not too strong), and that our national melodies can still hold their own against their Italian and German rivals, to whom the capricious taste of the Gallic race has too harshly sacrificed them.[18]

He kept his promise. The journal published the first versions of several key studies of French opera of the postwar decade: Paul Lacome's *Les fondateurs de l'Opéra français* (1873); then, all in 1874, Théodore de Lajarte's *Les airs à danser de Lulli à Méhul*; Charles Barthélemy on Voltaire and Rameau's *Samson* and on Perrin and Cambert's *Pomone*; De Lajarte on operatic pastiche and self-borrowing in eighteenth century France; Pougin on Lully; and part of Jules Bonnassies's *La musique à la Comédie-Française*. The result, in combination with Gustave Chouquet's monumental history of French opera, was that the years 1873–74 saw an unprecedented surge of interest in, and support for, *ancien-régime* stage music. It was, seemingly, the music of the moment.

Outwardly neutral (mostly) in their historical content, the articles in Heulhard's journal were nevertheless nationalist by virtue of their being printed together at this particular time in this particular place. The uneven spread of subject-matter confirms this view. Of nearly 180 historical and discursive items, 66 percent dealt with (overwhelmingly French) theatrical/musical history between 1650 and 1789, 23 percent with current affairs and post-1870 repertory, and a mere 11 percent with subjects relating to the period 1801 to 1870.[19] The decadence of the Second Empire was effectively ignored, except insofar as its repertory was covered in reviews; German music, too, was under-represented. But even within this *ancien-régime* historical agenda there was another at work. Readers who began a subscription in 1873 unaware of the existence of the Couperins' organ and *clavecin* music, the *grand motet* tradition, or Leclair's instrumental music would have found nothing in the journal to cure their ignorance. Everything other than stage

---

18. "Nous ressusciterons ainsi, par fragments, les inspirations de nos vieux maîtres français, et l'on verra combien de génies méconnus, de talents ignorés nous tirerons de l'ombre qui nous dérobe jusqu'à leurs noms. Nous n'avons pas besoin de dire que ces pages seront choisies avec discernement, qu'elles resteront parées de toutes les grâces naïves de leur virginité première, dans leur version originale. Ajouterai-je que le répertoire de nos oubliés, de nos dédaignés, surabonde en chefs-d'oeuvre (le mot n'est pas trop fort), et que nos mélodies nationales font encore belle mine auprès de leurs rivales d'Italie et d'Allemagne, auxquelles le goût versatile de la gent gauloise les a trop dûrement sacrifiées?" *CM* 1 (no. 1): 1 July 1873, 9.

19. These figures are based on a count of subject-coverage per installment.

music was sidelined, as though opera and ballet alone constituted France's musical heritage.

A journal's opening article usually has something of the manifesto about it, and Heulhard's was no exception. Lacome's "Les fondateurs," which will be my main focus here, served as a microcosmic presentation of the *Chronique musicale* project. It attempted to do three things that would become routine in writings advocating rehabilitation, here and elsewhere: to undermine Rousseau's condemnation of French *ancien-régime* music as oxymoronic, as primitive, as graceless, and as unmelodic; to redefine musical Frenchness in positive terms; and to trace a glorious historical lineage. It is of course a measure of the deep-seated nature of Rousseau's influence that Lacome should feel the need, 120 years after the fact, to respond so vehemently to the *Lettre sur la musique française* of 1753:

> A study of this kind will, I hope, convince everyone that by Rousseau's time (and he was in no doubt about it), an entirely French *music*, which had produced masterpieces having no relation to reigning schools and prevailing taste, had already existed for half a century; moreover, that the shadowy genres sown by these works in barren ground unfailingly prepared the coming of our own modern school, confirmed since by a series of dazzling works and which, I am sure, is far from having spoken its last word.[20]

Yet for all the blasts at Rousseau, Lacome's approach was hesitant. The French school, *he is sure*, is far from having spoken its last word. Writing nearly a decade after Meyerbeer's death, he seemed to doubt the bright future of French opera; and as part of a process familiar to historians of cultural nationalism, his search for origins as a means of bolstering faith in contemporary culture simultaneously revealed his own unease about it.

The essence of Lacome's 1873 project was to argue that French opera had not stagnated after Lully's death and to reclaim the "foundations" of French

---

20. "Il résultera, je l'espère, d'une étude ainsi conduite, la conviction pour chacun que déjà, du temps de Rousseau, sans qu'il s'en doutât, il existait depuis un demi-siècle une *musique* bien française, qui avait produit des chefs-d'oeuvre sans nul rapport avec les écoles régnantes et le goût du jour; en outre, que les genres obscurs semés en terre ingrate par ces ouvrages préparaient infailliblement l'avénement de notre moderne école, affirmée depuis par une série d'oeuvres éclatantes, et qui, j'en ai la conviction, est loin d'avoir dit son dernier mot." *CM* 1 (no. 1): 1 July 1873, 40.

opera for France.²¹ Campra, Collasse, and Destouches—a forgotten, and truly French, generation—had developed opera from declamation towards dramatic expressivity. Melody and dramatic sensitivity were key, and Act I of *Callirhoé* was, on both counts, "a masterpiece ... absolutely revolutionary for its time."²² In Campra and Destouches, Lacome found a free-flowing yet un-Italianate melodic practice underpinned by pictorial styles of orchestration that moved beyond mere accompaniment. To prove it he argued two kinds of stylistic distance: remoteness from the Italian Lully, his fall guy (and a composer of "tiring monotony"),²³ and closeness to the moderns. Accordingly, he likened the melodic outline of Campra's "Ah! que mon coeur va payer chèrement" (*Hésione*) to Donna Anna's "Non mi dir." More strikingly, to rehabilitate "dry" French declamation and present it as modern he did the same with Destouches's "poétique et chantante" recitative, comparing it with that of both Wagner (*Lohengrin*) and Gounod (*Roméo*), and thereby becoming one of the first to claim a French ancestry for Wagnerian speech-melody.²⁴ But more important in the rebuttal of Rousseau specifically was the establishing of positive, but recognizably French, qualities in the music—the "exquisite sensitivity" of Collasse, and the "gracefulness of poetic feeling and sensitivity" in Destouches's melodic writing.²⁵ These categories were not Lacome's invention; they were in use in musical criticism as far back as the late 1850s. It was their applicability to *la musique française* that was disputed. Yet, and despite the presence of complete *airs* in the *Chronique musicale*'s music supplements, Lacome never gave detailed exemplification of his claims about style, preferring to remain on the level of assertion—effusion, even—rather than demonstration.

Perhaps that fact hints at why he could not maintain his enthusiasm in the medium term. The book version of "Les fondateurs" (1878) dampened down the effusiveness of the original. Passages referring to modernity were cut or trimmed, and Campra and Destouches became merely the shadowy "foundations" of a gothic cathedral whose spire and rose windows still prompted admiration. Lacome modified his earlier judgments, and played back into Rousseau's hands:

---

21. The idea of stagnation was received wisdom re-animated by Gustave Chouquet's *Histoire de la musique dramatique* of 1873 (see esp. 122–23); the idea of de-centring Lully was pushed further back, chronologically, with Pougin's *Les vrais créateurs* of 1881 on Perrin and Cambert.
22. "un chef-d'oeuvre... absolument révolutionnaire dans son temps." *CM* 1 (no. 5): 1 September 1873, 227.
23. "fatigante monotonie." *CM* 1 (no. 1): 1 July 1873, 40.
24. *CM* 1 (no. 5): 1 September 1873, 225 and 229.
25. "exquise sensibilité"; "la grâce du sentiment poétique et de la sensibilité." *CM* 1 (no. 5): 1 September 1873, 229.

> The qualities that I am highlighting, and which shine through here and there in the form of an *air*, a *duo*, or a *chorus*—real prototypes aimed towards the future and for refined tastes—are too often drowned in interminable and tiring passages that bear the stamp of their time and of the Lullian school.[26]

We do not know whether Lacome changed his mind or overstated his beliefs in the first place; but the 1878 version suggests that Lacome's rhetoric of 1873 may have been more reflective of a heightened need to promote (or defend) the *patrimoine* than indicative of support for the repertory per se, so it would be unwise to accept its premises blindly. At the very least, Lacome's aesthetic retreat reveals an underlying fragility of support for French opera of the period. Evidence from elsewhere reinforces that impression. Even those, such as H. Lavoix *fils*, who supported publication projects, believed the music impossible to revive.[27] Johannes Weber, hearing Obin sing Caron's *air* from Lully's *Alceste* at the Société des Concerts in 1875, opined that even if it were superbly performed the work would fail.[28] And while the *Chronique musicale*'s Henry Cohen and the *Journal de musique*'s Michel Harold complained about the performance of nothing but excerpts, they were outnumbered by doubters.[29]

A Monument to French Opera: The *Chefs-d'oeuvre classiques de l'Opéra français*

Yet there was no doubting the symbolic value of French operatic heritage and the importance of being able to see it in physical, monumental form. That was the goal of the publisher Théodore Michaëlis, who published Lully's *Thésée*, edited by De Lajarte, as the inaugural volume of the *Chefs-d'oeuvre classiques de l'Opéra français* (1877–84). Like the projects of Heulhard and Lacome, that of Michaëlis was surrounded by explicitly nationalist rhetoric. It was also a brave move for a fledgling publishing house (just one year old) which, as an agent

---

26. "Les qualités que je signale, et qui éclatent par-ci par-là sous la forme d'un *air*, d'un *duo*, d'un *choeur*, véritables ballons d'essai sur l'avenir et le goût des raffinés, sont trop souvent noyées dans d'interminables et fatigantes pages, marquées au coin de la mode du jour et de l'école de Lulli." Lacome, *Les fondateurs de l'Opéra français*, iii.

27. RGM 45/44: 3 November 1878, 355.

28. *Temps*, 9 February 1875.

29. See Cohen in *CM* 3 (no. 13): 1 January 1874, 34, and Harold in *JM* 4 (no. 203): 17 April 1880, 2. Despite a strong allegiance to early music (many music supplements contained keyboard music by Handel and by the French *clavecinistes*), Armand Gouzien counteracted his own contributor's views the following month by claiming that the naive structure of the early French stage works presented at the Opéra's *concert historique* of 1880 had understandably forced Vaucorbeil to select short excerpts only. *JM* 4 (no. 209): 29 May 1880, 1.

for French novelists' interests abroad, and a specialist in chansons and vocal scores for operetta, revealed no other pretensions to publish monumental works. The *Chefs-d'oeuvre*, edited by historians, librarians, and musicians, including several of Michaëlis's own operetta composers, was the first attempt at a collected edition of French stage music for the royal court and the Opéra—*tragédies en musique, opéras-ballets,* and operas, the "continuous ridge" stretching from the *Ballet comique de la reine* to the work of Sacchini, Méhul, and Cherubini. Here, foreigners offered no threat to the nationalist cause. By adapting their style to French taste, they had proved the pre-eminence of the French as an operatic nation. That, at least, was how the argument had run since Julien-Louis Geoffroy's pronouncements to the effect that "These works belong to us because we inspired them."[30]

Michaëlis's project started modestly, with only six volumes appearing in the first two years. However, around the summer of 1880 he decided to expand to 60 volumes, launching an advertizing campaign the like of which French music publishing had never seen. Its blatant appeals to patriotism tapped cleverly into the neuroses of its target market.[31]

> **Germany** has splendid editions for *all* her classic musicians;
> **England** has the magnificent volumes of the *Musical Antiquarian Society*;
> **Spain** her superb collection the *Lyra sacro hispana*;
> **Belgium** has just set up a commission for the publication of the works of historic Belgian musicians;
> In **France**, alas, we still know only the names of our Great Old Masters, and **nowhere** do there exist *reductions* for **Piano and Voice** *of the* **Masterpieces** which contributed to the prosperity and have remained the glory of our **Académie Nationale de Musique.**
> It is to fill this gap that we have undertaken the publication of the **Chefs-d'oeuvre de l'Opéra français.** The project is an eminently **national** one and we are pursuing its realization with all speed.[32]

---

30. "ils sont à nous ces ouvrages puisque nous les avons inspirés." Review of Piccinni's *Didon*, *JD* 3 January 1809, n.p. See also my "A Dilettante at the Opéra."

31. I have inferred the timing from the dates of documents in which musicians and critics responded to Michaëlis's material, the earliest of which date from July 1880.

32. "L'**Allemagne** possède des Editions splendides de *tous* ses Musiciens classiques;
   L'**Angleterre** a les magnifiques volumes de la *Musical Antiquarian Society*;
   L'**Espagne**, sa superbe Collection de la *Lyra sacra Hispana* [sic];
   La **Belgique** vient d'instituer une Commission chargée de la publication des oeuvres des anciens Musiciens belges.

France, of course, was not alone in feeling culturally backward at this point in the nineteenth century, and in remaining that way for another twenty years or so. Michaëlis's appeal reappeared in only slightly altered guise in George Grove's *Dictionary* article of 1883 on Purcell. Germany, Belgium, and Holland, he wrote, had all produced complete editions of their great musicians, "while England has remained satisfied that Purcell should be little more than a name among us."³³ Nevertheless, perhaps Michaëlis had reason to fear foreign perceptions of France as a tail-ender in the race to monumentalize national composers: Grove made no mention whatever of French publications.

Perhaps to underline its national importance, Michaëlis invited endorsements of his project from the press and from the musical establishment (including the Institut, the Concerts Populaires, the Société Nationale, and Colonne's Association Artistique), which he then recycled in promotional leaflets. *Le Figaro* was no more gushing, or militaristic, than other papers:

> This collection will form a magnificent library, and we shall possess a musical monument which will be the envy of all other nations. . . . Our fervent wish is that artists and the public will accompany and support the editor in this campaign, one of the most justified and one of the most glorious which has ever been undertaken in honor of French music.³⁴

En **France**, malheureusement, nous ne connaissons encore nos Grands Maîtres anciens que de nom et il n'existe **nulle part** de *réductions* **Chant et Piano** *des* **Chefs-d'oeuvre** qui ont fait la prospérité et sont demeurés la gloire de notre **Académie nationale de Musique**.

C'est pour combler cette lacune que nous avons entrepris l'édition des

CHEFS-D'OEUVRE DE L'OPERA FRANCAIS . . .

L'OEuvre est éminement **nationale** et nous en poursuivrons sans relâche la réalisation."

Promotional form letter by Michaëlis (undated), bound with selected post-1879 editions in the *Chefs-d'oeuvre* series.

33. George Grove, "Purcell Society," in *Grove's Dictionary of Music and Musicians*, 1st ed., iii (1883), 53, cited in McHale, *A Singing People*, 48.

34. "Cette collection formera une magnifique bibliothèque et nous posséderons un monument musical que toutes les autres nations devront nous envier. . . . Nous faisons des voeux ardents pour que les artistes et le public accompagnent et soutiennent l'éditeur dans cette campagne, *une des plus légitimes* et des plus glorieuses qui aient été entreprises en l'honneur de la musique française." *Le Figaro*, cited in Michaëlis's promotional material. Michaëlis printed extracts from reviews in the following papers: *Le Figaro, L'écho du parlement, Gil Blas, L'indépendant, Journal officiel, La liberté, La paix, Le parlement, La patrie, Le petit journal, La presse, Le XIXᵉ siècle, Le siècle, Le soir, Le temps, L'union* and *Le Voltaire*, listing the *Journal officiel*'s responses first, doubtless to stress the fact that he had gained a positive response from the official government newspaper.

Writers for other papers hinted that it was a matter of duty to subscribe to such an edition. A writer for *Le siècle* even suggested that the ability or desire to read the scores was irrelevant: "Every musician, every music lover, every Frenchman, if only out of patriotism, should have this national publication in his library"—a tall order, given that the complete collection, even when discounted, was to cost 600F.[35] In *Le temps*, Weber argued that the project was so important that it deserved government support in the form of multiple subscriptions on behalf of provincial libraries.[36] The *Chefs-d'oeuvre*, presented in the general press variously as a "sacrifice" or a "campaign," and, perhaps in a deliberate throwback to the language of Louis XIV, as a monument to French "glory," turned Michaëlis into a battling hero worthy of national admiration.

He was also exhuming forgotten treasures, as several papers (including *Le siècle, La liberté, Le petit journal,* and *La république française*) noted. As such, his project contributed to the cultural regeneration of a battered and territorially depleted France in which the worship of ancestors and the idea of collective memory would soon be encouraged by Ernest Renan in his celebrated address of 1882, "What Is a Nation?" Michaëlis's project anticipated Renan's speech by half a decade and bespoke a similar desire for cultural memory—in this case a memory that needed to be washed clean of encyclopaedist derision for *ancien-régime* opera. For the past was to be constructed carefully and, ideally, agreed upon. Along with forgetfulness, said Renan, historical error was "essential for the creation of a nation."[37] Selectivity of various kinds, then, was key to both the "what" and the "why" of history. Michaëlis's choice of repertory reflected the "what," in that as a monument to the Opéra it shunned all comedies or works with dialogue; the preface to each work reflected the "why," since each argued the case for aesthetic value.

Each Michaëlis preface, prepared either by the editor of the score, or by an in-house team including Pougin, H. Lavoix *fils*, Adolphe Jullien, and Victor Wilder, reinscribed the glory and grandeur of French musical history. Longevity and popularity were emphasized as indicators of quality.[38] De Lajarte, who edited

---

35. "Tout musicien, tout amateur de musique, *tout français*, ne fût-ce que par patriotisme, devrait avoir dans sa bibliothèque cette publication." *Le siècle*, cited in Michaëlis's promotional material. The cost of a typical single volume was 15F. By contrast, Gérard's "popular" score of *Israel in Egypt* cost 3F50.

36. "Il serait facile à l'administration des beaux-arts de souscrire pour un certain nombre d'exemplaires, qu'elle distribuerait dans les bibliothèques de province, comme elle a coutume de le faire." *Temps*, 25 November 1879, n.p.

37. As quoted in Ben-Amos, "The Uses of the Past," 129. This key notion also heads McCrone's chapter "Inventing the Past: History and Nationalism," in his *The Sociology of Nationalism*, 44.

38. See De Lajarte's prefaces to *Bellérophon*, 4; *Proserpine*, 4; *Thésée*, 1; and *Les festes d'Hébé*, 3; and Pougin's prefaces to *Persée*, 8, and *Phaëton*, 6.

all the Lully, quashed potentially troublesome questions of political expediency in the case of "royal" prologues by asserting that they contained better music than the main body of each opera.[39] Indeed, he frequently made the generalized point that Lully's music for "accessory" scenes was better than his dramatic declamation—a view that resonated with the increasing focus on dance and the picturesque as the essential and praiseworthy qualities of la musique française. Signifiers of Frenchness had to be addressed, and they mirrored Lacome's emphasis on grace and dramatic expressivity. However, where Michaëlis's editors dissented was on the extent to which degrees of French nationality counted.

Lully's original nationality was a thorn in the side of "nation-génie" nationalists such as Pougin and Cohen, both diehard Ramistes; but for supporters of the "nation-contrat," such as De Lajarte, Lully was French because his training, naturalization, and sensitivity to French declamation made him so. Nevertheless, the unsullied Frenchness of Rameau, that largely self-taught Burgundian whose operatic career musicians such as Adolphe Adam and Arthur Pougin had described in terms of a Berliozian struggle against the establishment, would always trump that of the benign Florentine invader.[40] His originality was beyond question, and where Adam had suggested in 1852 that he was an inferior third party in a trinity including Bach and Handel, by the later 1870s his supporters were challenging that subordinate position. Even De Lajarte, whose musical sympathies lay with Lully, found Rameau's dramatic power an inspiration. He was wanting in harmonic subtlety, and (tellingly) De Lajarte preferred his dances to his music with voices. Nevertheless, he warned:

> Where the composer of Castor et Pollux is undoubtably and incontestably a master, is in the science of the theatre, in the musical development of a lyric scene. Before Rameau, the Lullian school knew nothing of what we would today call the shape, the construction of a number. . . . Let us not forget that Rameau's glory is an eminently French glory; consequently, it must be pure and untainted. So let us proclaim loudly: the composer of Castor et Pollux turns out to be the first of all the *dramatic* composers—dramatic in the highest sense of the word.[41]

---

39. See De Lajarte's prefaces to Thésée, 2; Bellérophon, 1; Proserpine, 2; Psyché, 3.

40. It was important that Rameau's style came from instinct more than from training (Lacome and Lavoix said the same of Destouches). See Adam, Derniers souvenirs, 42–46; and Pougin, preface to Poisot's "Michaëlis" edition of Zoroastre [1883], 1. In his biography of Rameau, Pougin also made much of the idea that Rameau's visit to Italy in 1701 had no discernible effect on his compositional style. See Pougin, Rameau, 16–17.

41. "là où l'auteur de Castor et Pollux est un maître incontestable et incontesté, c'est dans la science du théâtre, c'est dans le développement musical d'une scène lyrique. Avant Rameau, l'école de Lully ne savait rien de ce que nous appelons aujourd'hui la coupe, la facture d'un morceau, le développement d'une idée ou d'un rythme.

Rameau became, in Adolphe Jullien's striking words, the "father-nurturer" of French opera, and the direct link to Gluck.[42]

Where were Lacome's "fondateurs" in such a map of French operatic history? Had it not been for an audacious Vincent d'Indy, they would, once more, have become a lost generation. De Lajarte came close to dismissing Campra's *L'Europe galante* as a decadent mosaic, partly because of its distance from the grand tragic tradition; and Lavoix, in his preface to Destouches's *Omphale*, concluded that Destouches's instinctive ability and naturalness of expression could not sustain comparison with Gluck.[43] The demonstration of compositional lineages was crucial, however. Even if composers such as Campra and Destouches could not be defended as outstanding artists in their own right, they nevertheless needed to be integrated into a great tradition stretching from Lully to Rameau and beyond. D'Indy did all this and more.

His preface to the Lalande and Destouches's *Les éléments* (1883) was the most intellectually ambitious of all. He set out to impose a new vision on Michaëlis's subscribers, taking his preface well beyond the immediate context of *Les éléments* and writing a version of French operatic history designed to quash all thoughts of a musically dominant Germany. Perhaps taking up the *Lohengrin* cue from Lacome, he claimed that, long before Wagner, the French tradition had solved the problem of "dramatic" versus "musical" opera. His argument built logically, though unexpectedly in the context of the Michaelis collection itself, on the idea of the supremacy of dramatic verisimilitude in French opera from Lully onward:

> I shall perhaps surprise a good many readers in saying that I consider these *primitives* of the last century as the true precursors of Richard Wagner, and that the aesthetic applied in a systematic manner and in giant proportions by the German master seems to me to be essentially the same as that which worked, as it were unconsciously, in the minds of those such as Rameau and Destouches.[44]

C'est à Rameau seul que nous le devons.... N'oublions pas que la gloire de Rameau est une gloire éminemment française; par conséquent, il faut qu'elle soit pure et sans ombre. Aussi, proclamons-le bien haut. L'auteur de *Castor et Pollux* se trouve être, en date, le premier de tous les compositeurs *dramatiques*, dans la plus haute acception du mot." De Lajarte, preface to "Michaëlis" *Castor et Pollux* [1878/9], 2–3.

42. "père-nourricier." Jullien, *La cour et l'Opéra sous Louis XVI*, 90.
43. Preface to "Michaëlis" *Omphale* (1883), 7.
44. "J'étonnerai peut-être bien des lecteurs en disant que je considère ces *primitifs* du siècle dernier comme les véritables précurseurs de Richard Wagner, et que l'esthétique appliquée d'une manière raisonnée et dans des proportions gigantesques par le maître allemand me paraît essentiellement conforme à celle qui fer-

By equating French declamation with speech-melody, focusing on realist drama and de-emphasizing the music's virtuoso demands, D'Indy found similar principles underlying music over two centuries apart. His composers had written drama first and foremost, "frequently even subordinating the musical form, the *musical number*, to the demands of the dramatic tone and the dynamics of the plot."[45] The ploy was, by the mid-1870s, a common way of elevating Gluck,[46] but, despite hints in the early 1870s, not least from Lacome, it had not been systematically pushed further back.[47] In effect, D'Indy's preface to one of the last handful of Michaëlis scores to be published summed up the significance of all that had preceded it and then took the bold step of continuing the lineage into contemporary music. On the cusp of France's most intense period of Wagnerism, D'Indy argued two related cases: explicitly, that Wagner's roots lay in established French practice and, implicitly, that French practice would live on in new works adopting Wagner's developments of French traditions. Perhaps he had his own compositional projects in mind. Nevertheless, whatever his wider purpose, like Renan, D'Indy looked to the greatness of the past to feed the greatness of the future.[48]

But that future greatness was not to include the completion of this particular monument to French opera. Like Choron before him, Michaëlis had overestimated his market. The Alsatian Weber, one of his most loyal reviewers, pleaded with his readers in October 1883 not to let such a patriotic

---

mentait d'une façon pour ainsi dire inconsciente dans la tête des Rameau et des Destouches." Vincent d'Indy, preface to "Michaëlis" *Les éléments* [1883], 9.

45. "en subordonnant même fréquemment la forme musicale, le *morceau de musique* aux exigences de l'accent scénique et de la marche du drame." Preface to "Michaëlis" *Les éléments* [1883], 10.

46. Weber's summative review of the 1876 Bayreuth *Ring* stressed the French provenance of every possible element, even those of which Weber disapproved, such as "Grand-opera-spectacular" (*Temps*, 22 August 1876). Ernest Reyer's defence of Gluck as the source of Wagner's ideas was first published in the *Journal des débats* and was included in the Wagnerian chapters of his *Quarante ans de musique*, 148–51. Not surprisingly, D'Indy's historiographical link became institutionalized at the Schola Cantorum. At the end of the school's performance of *Castor et Pollux* at Montpellier in 1908, Bordes was reported to have said he felt moved as though he had just heard *Tristan*. See Charles Malherbe, "Le "Ramisme," *Courrier musical* (henceforth CouM), 11/10: 15 May 1908, 312.

47. The link had in fact been presented as a way of condemning French opera and Wagner together. In 1872 Mark de Thémines compared the monotony and over-use of recitative in Lully's stage works with that of an unnamed German school which he described as an "unhealthy utopia" [utopie malsaine]. Quoting Rousseau, he remarked on the extent to which his comments on eighteenth-century French music were applicable to that of Wagner. *RGM* 11/42: 17 October 1872, 325.

48. It is worth noting, however, that the *Cours de composition* attributes many of these "Wagnerian" qualities to Rameau alone, and that D'Indy may have changed his mind (somewhat like Lacome) or have been acting opportunistically in attributing them to Destouches in 1883. See my "En route to Wagner."

project fail for the sake of "a few thousand francs."[49] February 1884 saw a notice in the *Ménestrel* announcing the setting up of a committee to oversee the remaining 23 scores of the projected 60, and exhorting libraries, music societies, and artistic clubs, "all those, in fact, who care about our national glories," to send their subscriptions to the publisher.[50] Nevertheless, the project folded.

What was the significance of the efforts of Heulhard, Lacome, and Michaëlis to the rehabilitation of France's composers of *tragédies en musique* and *opéras-ballets*? Michaëlis's collection was, after all, the most enduring monument to early French operatic culture before the advent of the Rameau collected edition, begun by Durand in 1894–95. Available as a reprint and held in innumerable university libraries, it remains, even in the twenty-first century and despite its many flaws, the standard vocal-score source for the stage works it contains. It was not supported by the State to the extent that the project could be completed; nevertheless, the Ministère des Beaux-Arts bought 20 copies of the collection in 1886 for distribution via the Ministère de l'Instruction Publique, des Beaux-Arts et des Cultes to the libraries of regional conservatoires.[51] Along with the *Chronique musicale*, the collection represented a call to arms for the defence of one of the grandest manifestations of France's musical heritage. For both publications, price considerations would have ensured the most limited of private readerships, and in this sense the revival of interest may indeed be said to have been more symbolic than real, especially given the ambitious, "national" rhetoric that characterized each of them. Michaëlis was not providing a counterpart to Gérard's cheap Handel scores. Nevertheless, both he and Heulhard were, arguably, trying to provide the prelude to a national awakening by proving, in bookshelf feet if nothing else, that *la musique française* involved a substantial indigenous tradition strong enough to attract the services of foreign composers and worthy of celebration in its own right.

---

49. "quelques milliers de francs." *Temps*, 23 October 1883. According to Weber, Michaëlis needed another twenty subscribers to ensure the project's continuation.

50. "tous ceux enfin qui ont souci de nos gloires nationales." *Mén* 50/12: 17 February 1884, 95. The committee included several of the original "membres fondateurs," who had paid the entire subscription in advance. It included the comte and comtesse de Chambrun, the vicomtesse de Grandval, Pauline Viardot, Ambroise Thomas, Vaucorbeil, Saint-Saëns, Victorin Joncières, Laurent de Rillé, Guillot de Sainbris, Oscar Comettant, Jean-Baptiste Faure, Alexandre Guilmant, Ernest Guiraud, De Lauzières-Thémines, and Johannes Weber.

51. Notices to this effect are found on the pink slips in archives relating to the regional conservatoires. See AN Paris: Beaux-Arts F^{21}1317–23. The purchase of these twenty subscriptions, and the timing, suggest that the State did try to bail Michaëlis out.

Performance Problems

However, taking celebration beyond the merely symbolic meant encouraging performances, which in turn meant editing full scores (by contrast with Handel oratorio, there was no tradition of piano-accompaniment performances). Immediately, editors and critics seized on the problem of *remplissage* versus new orchestration, questioning the trustworthiness of the primary sources available to the editor, and the editor's decisions themselves.[52] At times, such as when Cohen attacked Weckerlin's orchestrations for extracts from *Les festes d'Hébé* in 1877, any hint of patriotic fervor was neutralized by editorial squabbling.[53] But was a performed revival, even of large excerpts, plausible? The evidence suggests not, even though the mid-1870s provided precisely the unprecedented run of complete performances that seemed to indicate a reversal of fortune for *la musique française*. Even here, however, traditional attitudes had to be suspended to make the music acceptable. In the 1850s and '60s, when the Opéra and the Comédie-Française first pooled their resources to mount Molière collaborations, press responses ranged from incredulity to derision. In 1852, Jules Janin described the sung numbers from Lully's *Le bourgeois gentilhomme* as "worthy of a Chinese concert."[54] Charpentier's *Le malade imaginaire* was "risible" as far as D. A. D. Saint-Yves was concerned.[55] Whereas literature of the *grand siècle* was "classic," its music was not, and, as an anonymous critic for the *Revue et gazette musicale* put it, referring to the 1852 *Bourgeois gentilhomme*: "we should heartily thank music for having made progress since [Lully's] time, because it was then no more than a heavy, sad kind of chanting in which one had difficulty recognizing a theme or any kind of melody."[56]

Tragedies fared just as badly. Immediately after the war, Republicans still found their monarchical origins disturbing. Weber, who was to change his mind in spectacular fashion in the late 1870s, described Lully's *tragédies en*

---

52. Certain figures were indefatigable on such questions, allowing them to dominate an entire review. Cohen and H. Moreno [Henri Heugel] were particularly trenchant.

53. See *AM* 16/3-4: 18–25 January 1877.

54. "dignes d'un concert chinois," Jules Janin, *JD* 19 January 1852, n.p. The previous week he had fulminated on the absurdity of the whole project to revive "ces vieilleries d'une cour amoureuse et galante." *JD* 12 January 1852, n.p.

55. "de la risible musique." *RGM* 27/5: 29 January 1860, 36.

56. "il faut remercier grandement la musique d'avoir fait des progrès depuis lui, car elle n'était alors qu'une lourde et triste psalmodie dans laquelle on pouvait à peine saisir une idée, un thème, un chant quelconque." *RGM* 19/2: 11 January 1852, 13.

musique, their vocal style especially, as "heavy and flat-footed, with a false air of grandeur"; for him, the whole amounted to nothing more than "pompous spectacles, princely pleasures."[57] To cap everything, the 1875 performance of most of Act I of *Callirhoé* flopped at the Concerts-Danbé. Advertized in glowing terms as "a marvel of grace and youthfulness," and supported financially by the Ministère des Beaux-Arts,[58] it was underrehearsed, and substandard singing did it no favors. Critics such as Pougin, Lacome's co-writer on *Le ménestrel*, tried to sound positive; a critic from the *Revue et gazette* (probably Charles Bannelier) disagreed, finding the work "an immense and monotonous recitative" and its composer rather "short-winded."[59] But Cohen, a Ramiste, was even harsher, highlighting orchestration that was "monotonous and tiring to listen to" and damning musical numbers with faint praise, as "crude, though effective," or "graceful, but insubstantial."[60] The point that *la musique française* suffered as much, if not more, from sectarianism among its supporters as from concerted opposition from its detractors could hardly be better illustrated than by Cohen's blasts against *remplissage* and pre-Ramiste composition.

Monotony, flat-footedness, and short-windedness: these were bywords in the criticism of French seventeenth- and eighteenth-century stage music, dating back to Rousseau and, beyond, to Raguenet's *Parallèle des Italiens et des Français* of 1702. Deeply entrenched in French discourse, their currency was sustained courtesy of theories of progress, selectively applied by music critics and literary critics alike. Arguably, Lully suffered most: Pougin championed Perrin and Cambert; Lacome, Campra and Destouches, then Rameau; Cohen, Rameau alone; even De Lajarte conceded Rameau's supremacy. Yet amid disparagement of his music from both within and outside the *musique française* lobby, it was indeed Lully (with a leavening of Charpentier) who emerged as the only composer whose stage music received near-complete performances at regular intervals during the second half of the nineteenth century. Most ironic of all, those performances were often given to full houses and to public acclaim. All this is counterintuitive enough to demand explanation.

---

57. "chant lourd et traînant, avec un faux air de grandeur . . . spectacles pompeux, plaisirs de prince." *Temps* 14 February 1871, n.p.

58. "une merveille de grâce et de jeunesse." Puff article from *L'entr'acte*, in *Mén* 41/13: 28 February 1875, 102.

59. "un immense et monotone récitatif"; "l'haleine du musicien est un peu courte." *RGM*, 42/10: 7 March 1875, 77.

60. "monotone et fatigant à entendre"; "rude, mais à effet"; "gracieux, mais étriqué." *AM*, 14/10: 11 March 1875, 76. He suggested that a *reprise* of Acts I and II of *Castor* would not have had the same effect (77), but the evidence suggests that his confidence in Rameau's ability to conquer was misplaced.

Incidental Music for Molière

The densest concentration appeared in 1875 and 1876 at the Théâtre de la Gaîté under the direction of, first, Jacques Offenbach, and then the violinist-conductor Albert Vizentini (b.1841), who was, by government decree, transforming the theatre into the new Théâtre-National-Lyrique. From January 1875 to 14 May 1876, the company, aided by actors from the Odéon, gave over twenty performances of Lully's *Le bourgeois gentilhomme* and *Monsieur de Pourceaugnac*, and Charpentier's *Le malade imaginaire*. Most took place in 1876 when the theatre was under Vizentini's direction; but it was Offenbach who inaugurated the series of "matinées classiques" for which they were prepared. Intended as family viewing, with an eye no doubt to the education and edification of the Third Republic's children (not to mention their parents), they took place on Sunday afternoons, beginning on 8 March 1873. Each comprised a masterpiece from the classical theatrical repertory and an *opéra comique* in the late eighteenth-century tradition of Monsigny, Dalayrac, Grétry, and Gaveau.[61] There was no mention in the press of presenting seventeenth-century plays with their original music. When Offenbach mounted *Monsieur de Pourceaugnac* in 1873, he did so using new music by Ernest Guiraud; it was only two years later that he used Lully's music for Act I of the play.[62] Contrary to what one might expect, Offenbach's Lully/Charpentier productions were not done on a shoestring. Production quality was high, houses were full.[63] When Offenbach's directorship of the Gaîté failed, Vizentini, his conductor, continued the tradition, commissioning new orchestrations of Lully's scores from his friend Weckerlin, who had ready access to primary materials at his place of work, the Conservatoire library.

Vizentini's performances, even more than Offenbach's, were a runaway success. Lavish forces—an orchestra of 80, and a chorus of 60, in addition to his dancers, actors, and solo singers—were marshaled by his conductor, Danbé.[64] Critics could not deny that his Lully/Molière productions "made waves," that they were rip-roaringly funny, and that the audiences seemed to enjoy them as much for the music as for the drama.[65] They correctly predicted extended runs—

---

61. *RGM*, 41/46: 15 November 1874, 366. See also Yon, *Jacques Offenbach*, 487.

62. Yon, *Jacques Offenbach*, 467 and 513. Yon does not suggest who might have prepared the performing versions of *Le malade imaginaire* or *Monsieur de Pourceaugnac*.

63. Yon calls the *Malade imaginaire* production "sumptuous" (fastueux). (*Jacques Offenbach*, 512). The point is confirmed in Genty, *Histoire du Théâtre National de l'Odéon*, 47.

64. Figures from the theater poster included in Weckerlin's annotated edition of the *Bourgeois gentlhomme*, BNF (Musique): Rés. 1841.

65. "grand bruit." Clément Caraguel, *JD* 31 January 1876. See also H. Moreno [Heugel], who told his

and even promotion to the evening schedule. Significantly, there was no recitative, and the musical numbers came in short, discrete bursts. Two things about their reception and their aftermath stand out: firstly, in the press there is not a single word of patriotic or nationalist hue on the choice or quality of the music (though there is plenty of discussion of Weckerlin's adaptation, his sources, and his use of them); secondly, once the new Théâtre-National-Lyrique was fully operational, Vizentini ceased his "matinées classiques" and did not produce Lullian repertory again. In addition, later performances of these same works, particularly the 1880 *Bourgeois gentilhomme* mounted for the bicentenary of the Comédie-Française, saw some of the old qualms return. For Clément Caraguel, theatre critic for the *Débats*, Molière's satire was as fresh as ever, but Lully's contributions appeared "rudimentary and primitive."[66] Both he and Francisque Sarcey, literary critic for *Le temps*, viewed the "complete" *Bourgeois gentilhomme* with all its accessories of music and dance, as a kind of historical curiosity or "archeological fantasy."[67] Neither judgement constituted an appeal to heritage. Despite bearing the outward signs of a nationalist revival, then, these performances of Lully's and Charpentier's music must be explained otherwise.

There was no overlap between the Lullian repertory of Lacome and Michaëlis and the works selected for complete performance in the latter half of the century. Anthologizers had concentrated on the heroic, mythological works (counterparts to the plays of Racine and Corneille); the works that appeared on stage were all, with the exception of the *tragédie-ballet Psyché*, incidental music to comedies. Tragedies, then, were applauded in theory; comedies in practice. But there was more to it than that. What happened at the Gaîté and elsewhere was a parasitical revival, feeding off a combination of Molière's cultural capital and the traditional museum culture in French drama. The impetus for using historical music came consistently from the theatrical, rather than the musical, side. For the Comédie-Française, inclusion of the incidental music to these Molière plays—which were usually performed with the bare minimum of (often

---

"lectrices" that Danbé's interpretation of *Le bourgeois gentilhomme* was so fine as almost to dispel the monotony of the music and to hold the public's interest (*Mén* 42/10: 6 February 1876, 76), and seemed similarly disappointed at the warm public reaction to the "wrinkles and rather senile appearance" [rides et . . . allure un peu sénile] of the music to *Monsieur de Pourceaugnac* (*Mén* 42/19: 9 April 1876, 147); Weber on *Monsieur de Pourceaugnac* as "a long belly laugh" [un long éclat de rire] (*Temps*, 4 April 1876); Lavoix on the audience's enjoyment of *Le bourgeois gentilhomme* (*RGM* 43/5: 30 January 1876, 34); and De Marenna, who called for the staging of new works, but enjoyed *Monsieur de Pourceaugnac* along with everyone else (*AM* 15/14: 6 April 1876, 110).

66. "élémentaires et primitifs." *JD* 1 November 1880, n.p.

67. "fantaisie archéologique." *Temps*, 25 October 1880. See also his (marginally) more conciliatory review of 1 November 1880.

new) music—simply turned a standard performance into a gala. Accordingly, such performances tended to close out a season; to mark Molière's birthday (15 January), which was celebrated, along with those of Racine and Corneille (21 December and 6 June, respectively) both here and at the Odéon; or to celebrate other events, such as the bicentenary in 1880 of the Comédie-Française itself. For such occasions the Comédie-Française had an agreement with the Opéra regarding the provision of solo singers and dancers. Typically, Conservatoire students made up the chorus.[68]

The 1852 *Bourgeois gentilhomme* at the Opéra seems to have revived a tradition originally dating from 1717, when the Opéra provided singers for a *reprise* at the Comédie-Française. It was mounted at the suggestion of Arsène Houssaye (director of the Comédie-Française from 1849) to celebrate Molière's birthday. Nestor Roqueplan, then Director of the Opéra, agreed so long as the Opéra could host the production,[69] but never took the logical step of having the score deposited in the Opéra's archives. Instead, as Weckerlin found to his dismay, it was abandoned in the Comédie-Française archives—symbolic of the Opéra's lack of interest.[70] The Gaîté's productions might seem to have been motivated by musical considerations, the initiative being taken under Offenbach's directorship. But the Odéon's director, Félix Duquesnel was equally involved, and, indeed, looking for employment for part of his company during an extremely successful season dominated by works that did not require their services.[71] Neither should we discount Offenbach's theatrical connections. Conductor at the Comédie-Française from 15 October 1850, he was in the post at the time of the 1852 *Bourgeois gentilhomme* and brought major changes to the theatre's traditions, not least the performance of extracts from the music of Lully, Rameau, and more modern composers during entr'actes.[72] What he brought to the Gaîté, therefore, was an outlook colored by his experience at one of the national theatres. The 1880s showed little change in general outlook: Lully's *Psyché* was performed thirteen times in 1887, starting on 11 April—not at the Opéra, but at the Odéon, under the directorship of Paul Porel.[73]

---

68. See the letters of 10 March 1863 and 20 February 1865 from Ed. Thierry, director of the Comédie-Française, to Emile Perrin, Director of the Opéra, reminding Perrin of this tradition as a prelude to requests for cooperation. AN Paris: AJ[13] 449, liasse 1, items 32 and 95.

69. See the news item in *RGM* 19/2: 11 January 1852, 13. Roqueplan apparently demanded "la primeur de cette reprise à frais communs."

70. See Weckerlin's manuscript annotations to his vocal score of *Le bourgeois gentilhomme*, prepared for Vizentini. BNF (Musique): Rés 1841, f. s^r.

71. Genty, *Histoire du Théâtre National de l'Odéon*, 47.

72. Yon, *Jacques Offenbach*, 101.

73. Genty, *Histoire du Théâtre National de l'Odéon*, 64.

Indeed, after that first joint performance of *Le bourgeois gentilhomme*, all joint performances of Molière's plays took place at the Comédie-Française rather than at the Opéra. The disproportionate size of the Opéra may have been to blame,[74] but the lack of enthusiasm of successive Opéra directors for *any* early stage repertory was palpable. Such inertia extended even to Emile Perrin, director of the Opéra from the end of 1862 to May 1871, who moved to the Comédie-Française that July and reinvigorated enthusiasm for the theatrical classics. It was Perrin who presided over the *Bourgeois gentilhomme* production of 1880; it was Perrin whom Sarcey later dubbed as devoted to the "cult of the old repertoire."[75] On the basis of his activities at the Opéra—even taking into account that his tenure coincided with the Second Empire and not the Third Republic—one would hardly have guessed it. "Old" at the Opéra, meant *Don Giovanni* and (exceptionally) Gluck's *Alceste*.

Contingencies of Revival

The incidental music of Lully and, to a lesser extent, Charpentier enjoyed a vicarious revival in the latter half of the nineteenth century, profiting from the Molière cult. As Lavoix wrote of Charpentier, "brought to us through the power of Molière's genius, his output has outlived his name": everyone knew the march from *Le malade imaginaire*, but who could name its composer?[76] Lully's position was not so precarious; nevertheless he did not earn his "revival" on his own terms. With the asymmetry between the attitude to the "classics" in theatre and stage music so pronounced, the reasons why certain works by Lully and Charpentier were revived, while Rameau's output was neglected, were brutally pragmatic. One kind of music was economically viable; the other was not (which essentially explains why the Opéra revived no *tragédies en musique* at all, whether by Lully or others). But even if Rameau had written incidental music for Voltaire, rather than collaborating in other genres, he would still not have been revived, because Voltaire was aesthetically (and probably ideologically) suspect at the Comédie-Française, his birthday "forgotten."

---

74. The disproportionate size of the Opéra was commented upon by Edmond Got, one of the actors in the 1852 performance. See Got, *Journal de Edmond Got*, i, 280.

75. "culte du vieux répertoire." *Temps*, 11 September 1882, n.p.

76. "portée jusqu'à nous par la puissance du génie de Molière, son oeuvre a survécu son nom. Chacun connaît par coeur la marche du *Malade imaginaire*; combien peu seraient capables aujourd'hui de nommer l'auteur de cette Marseillaise des apothécaires!" RGM 40/20: 18 May 1873, 157.

Rameau's stage music was thus reduced to performance as "trifles" throughout the nineteenth century, even though his stature and the public dissemination of his music through sheet music arrangements and performances increased steadily.[77] He was also the first, of course, to have a collected edition in full score devoted to him. Familiar rhetorics about forgotten heritage catalysed the project. They were both true and false: false because Rameau was not totally neglected; true because attempts at revival had not really succeeded. In March 1894, in his father's paper, Le Figaro, the young Albéric Magnard demanded recognition for this forgotten master of French composition; Paul Dukas echoed his demands in the Revue hebdomadaire five months later. To anyone associated with Michaëlis's edition, which was routinely disparaged by those connected with the new project, Magnard's nationalist call for a Rameau edition must have seemed rather familiar: "So, will a French editor ever be found who is capable of doing for our great masters—Rameau, for example—what Germany has done for Mozart and Beethoven, what Belgium has done for Grétry and England for Purcell?"[78]

The resulting collected edition, instituted with remarkable speed under the auspices of the Durand publishing house, involved, among others, Charles Malherbe as resident historian, D'Indy, and Saint-Saëns. Just days before the modern-day premiere of Hippolyte et Aricie at the Opéra in 1908, the self-serving Malherbe dated the "Rameau awakening" to 1895, the date of the new edition's first volume.[79] He was, of course, overconfident. Early twentieth-century performances of Rameau in Dijon, Montpellier, and Paris had been important in themselves, and had allowed the new Rameau edition to serve a practical purpose unavailable to Michaëlis. But they had not established Rameau in the operatic repertory. Instead, as the history of twentieth-century neo-classicism tells us, in addition to "trifles," it was primarily through the reinterpretations of generically "French" dances in new music—deriving as much from keyboard music as stage music—that a sustained "revival" of music of the French Baroque eventually took place, and through which a particular sense of Frenchness came to be expressed.

---

77. Girdlestone, *Jean-Philippe Rameau*, 569.

78. "Alors, il ne se trouvera donc jamais en France un éditeur capable de faire pour nos grands maîtres, Rameau par exemple, ce que l'Allemagne a fait pour Mozart et Beethoven, la Belgique pour Grétry, l'Angleterre pour Purcell?" Albéric Magnard, *Le Figaro*, 29 March 1894, cited by Malherbe in *CouM* 11/10: 15 May 1908, 311. Malherbe dismissed the Michaëlis collection out of hand as a waste of time and money, judging it naive, misconceived and misleading. However, if he thought the Durand editions would provide trustworthy texts and incontrovertible solutions to knotty questions (not least those of *remplissage*), he was mistaken. See Sadler, "Vincent d'Indy," 415–21.

79. "réveil de Rameau." *CouM* 11/10: 15 May 1908, 311.

The Struggle to Redefine Frenchness

In helping redefine the Frenchness of *la musique française* as a positive quality, discussions of this repertory had long-term importance. Debussy's famous observations of 1903 on the "tender delicacy," "clarity of expression ... terse and condensed form," equilibrium, and lack of affectation in Rameau's *Castor et Pollux* had their roots several decades earlier.[80] They were, however, somewhat tangled. From the 1850s onward a vocabulary of Frenchness was built up, centring on the perceived attributes of the dance and keyboard music of the French Baroque. Some such vocabulary appears designed to counter established prejudices, revealing the other side of familiar coins: "short-windedness" became "concision"; "heaviness," "nobility"; "pomposity," "grandeur"; "naive inanity," "charming naivety"; "simplistic" music, "fresh, direct, youthful" music. These and other descriptors also had valuable anti-German properties: "clarity," "concision," "directness," and "balance" were not perceived as part of Wagner's stock-in-trade. Grace, alertness, exquisite feeling, and elegance became key signifiers, alongside tenderness and vivacity. The critic Louis de Lassus drew many of these elements together when he wrote in 1870 of the adorable, graceful serenity of Rameau's "Dans ce doux asile" (as arranged by Adam) from *Castor et Pollux*: "Here we have one of those exquisite works which one never tires of hearing. What adorable serenity! Does this unified melody, which is without artifice and never lacks direction, not make one think of a fine river flowing quietly through balmy countryside?"[81]

Had supporters of *la musique française* tried to design a vocabulary that evoked a danced pastoral idyll they could hardly have done better. For the attributes of ballet—its symmetrical forms, lightness of movement, transparency of gesture, and artless expressivity—lay at the heart of all praising descriptions of this repertory. Concomitantly, *airs de danse* were ubiquitous among the examples of *ancien-régime* stage music selected for domestic use, in anthologies and music supplements. From an implicit link with dance could be inferred other crucial qualities that might act as talismans against decadence: natural strength, health, and grace in motion. Nevertheless, and by contrast with the 1890s, in the 1870s

---

80. Originally published in *Gil Blas*, 2 Feb. 1903; translated by B. N. Langdon Davies in *Three Classics in the Aesthetics of Music*, 36–37.

81. "C'est là une de ces oeuvres exquises que l'on ne se lasse pas d'entendre. Jamais mélodie plus douce ne s'épancha avec plus de grâce. Quelle sérénité adorable! Cette phrase toute unie, sans recherche, sans détour, ne fait-elle pas penser à quelque beau fleuve coulant sans bruit à travers une campagne embaumée!" Review of the Société Bourgault-Ducoudray, *FM* 34/22: 29 May 1870, 168–69, at 168.

the appeal to dance came at a cost. Indeed, the closer we look at the genres and styles that made up French Baroque stage music, the more fragmented and oppositional the signifiers become. As I have indicated, Lully suffered greatly in this regard. The most common compliments pointed to "grace" and "nobility" or "virile grace" in his music.[82] In 1878 Lavoix noted how the dances in *Armide* were "imprinted with charming elegance," and he lauded the "dramatic and touching pleas" of the abandoned Armide at its close[83]; in 1867 Ernest Thoinan described his operatic music as having a "naive and telling aspect."[84] That, however, was less than half the story.

Thoinan, in the above quotation, was making a clear distinction between Lully's incidental music to *Le mariage forcé* (a new edition of which he was reviewing) and what, by implication, he considered "real" Lully—the style of the *tragédies en musique*.[85] Others acted similarly. Lavoix dismissed all the Molière incidental music as too Italian because of the *buffo* nature of its comedy; Jullien concurred.[86] Critically, Lully's music thus appeared in a cleft stick. And as he became progressively sidelined by Rameau—the evidence for which lies in a growing tendency to emphasize precisely these Italian characteristics—the situation worsened. Works which remained in the repertory, as part of a nationalist theatrical tradition were deemed less national than those that would not reach the stage again until well into the twentieth century.[87]

In some respects, Rameau seemed different. As Adolphe Jullien put it, he had the "intuition and the brutal originality of genius. . . . he surprised the ears of lazy music-lovers by the unexpected novelty of his modulations, by the power of his harmony, by the expressive truth of his melodic lines, by the vigorous character of his recitatives."[88] But Rameau was also, as Jullien himself recognized,

---

82. Maurice Cristal [Maurice Germa] reviewing the Société des Concerts, *AM* 20/12: 24 March 1881, 90. He listed other qualities in Lully's *Armide*: "delicate, nimble, pungent and silky-smooth at the same time" [fine, déliée, piquante à la fois et suave]. H. Lavoix *fils* found that Lully's later ballets were "d'une grâce plus virile" than the early ones (Lavoix, *La musique française*, 100).

83. "empreints d'une élégance charmante"; "les plaintes dramatiques et touchantes d'Armide." *RGM* 45/44: 3 November 1878, 354.

84. "couleur naïve et pénétrante." *AM* 7/33: 18 July 1867, 261.

85. *AM* 7/33: 18 July 1867, 261.

86. See *RGM* 43/5: 30 January 1876, 33, and *RGM* 43/15: 9 April 1876, 116. In his review of Lecocq's edition of *Castor*, Jullien noted that *Le bourgeois gentilhomme*, recently published by Weckerlin, gave very little idea of the composer's style. *RGM* 44/43: 28 October 1877, 338.

87. A further layer of irony lies in the fact that Lully's Molière collaborations were tolerated, rather than celebrated, in theatrical circles; they were marginal to the Molière canon, earning their stage presence primarily on account of their utility as celebratory pieces.

88. "l'intuition et la hardiesse brutale du génie. . . . il étonnait l'oreille paresseuse des amateurs par la nouveauté imprévue des modulations, par la force de l'harmonie, par la vérité expressive de la mélodie, par l'accent vigoureux du récitatif." *RGM* 45/2: 13 January 1878, 10. In his *La cour et l'Opéra sous Louis XVI*, Jullien

capable of "exquisite tenderness."[89] Performances of extracts from *Les festes d'Hébé* never failed to elicit comments on the delicacy of the music, which tended to be feminized, either implicitly (Cohen in 1876, imagining the famous tambourin accompanied by the flirtatious dancing of ladies at Louis XV's court),[90] or explicitly (Gouzien in 1880, reviewing the Opéra's first *concert historique* and wondering at "so many feminine graces" in the music).[91] The wonderment would later work in reverse, as in the *Guide musical* of 1894: "[Rameau] appeared as of a singular grandeur unsuspected by those for whom [he] was just a composer of minuets and gavottes"; extracts from *Castor et Pollux*, and particularly the *air* "Tristes apprêts," "were a revelation for the public."[92]

Here was a composer who seemed to have two natures: the exquisite and the brutally challenging. That was a problem in the 1870s: critics appeared confused as to what to praise. Yet, with the exception of the "Trios des Parques" from *Hippolyte et Aricie*, the "Trio des Songes" from *Dardanus*, and "Tristes apprêts" from *Castor*, in the 1870s performed extracts were dominated by dances and the lighter of Rameau's operatic numbers—pieces from which Rameau's challenging style (which by general consent needed the space of entire scenes to be fully revealed) was absent. The cutting out, by arrangers such as Deldevez, of passages of declamation in favor of "music," only reinforced the effect. As we have seen in the case of Diémer and his predecessors, performers took a similar approach to Rameau's keyboard *ordres*, often excerpting single dances and mixing them with operatic extracts at concerts. And while writers such as Poisot waxed lyrical about the "masculine and powerful" style of *Zoroastre*, for instance,[93] performances of passages that displayed these qualities were outnumbered by those featuring Rameau's more "feminine" music.

The popularity of *ancien-régime* dance was, in the 1870s at least, a double-edged sword that created considerable critical ambivalence. One might argue that the split between dance as stereotypically decorative and feminine, and drama as (equally stereotypically) dynamic and masculine, is an anachronistic

---

compared the versions of *Dardanus* by Rameau and Sacchini. The former showed "strength and grandeur" [la force et la grandeur]; the latter, "nobility and grace" [la noblesse et la grâce] (89).

89. "tendresse exquise" (in *Castor*, specifically). See *RGM* 44/43:28 October 1877, 340.

90. Review of Weckerlin's arrangement, performed at the Concerts du Châtelet. *AM* 15/50: 14 December 1876, 396.

91. "tant de grâces féminines." *JM* 4 (no. 209): 29 May 1880, 1.

92. "Celui-ci est apparu d'une grandeur singulière, insoupçonnée de ceux pour qui Rameau n'était qu'un compositeur de menuets et de gavottes." "M.R.," on a concert by Bordes and the Chanteurs de Saint-Gervais, *GM* 40/6: 4 February 1894, 127.

93. "mâle et puissant." Poisot, preface to "Michaëlis" score of Rameau *Zoroastre*, 4.

interpretation. Perhaps in those references to Lully's "virile grace" there are indeed hints of the links at Louis XIV's court between ballet, self-control, fencing, and equestrian skill. But since nothing of that reaches the surface of critical prose at a time when demonstrating French masculinity counted for a great deal, it seems more likely to be an oxymoronic phrase full of the tensions that such phrases generally contain when they are not intentionally bathetic or sarcastic. In short, it is another example of the "père-nourricier" phenomenon. In any case, nineteenth-century ballet, from the 1830s at least, had become a thoroughly female-dominated phenomenon at the Opéra, with male dancers metaphorically "thrust to the margins of the stage": increasingly, men looked at women dancing.[94]

The legacy of this feminization of ballet is clear in De Lajarte's preface to his edition of Rameau's *Les festes d'Hébé* in the Michaëlis collection. Eleven years on, the line of argument mirrored that of Thoinan's condemnation of Lully's *Le mariage forcé*, this time using genre, not nationality, as its point of attack: the composer's "real" character is shown in the *tragédies en musique*; the ballet is a trifle. For De Lajarte, the episodic nature of the libretto/scenario "deprived the master's music of the dramatic aspect which seems to me ... to be the signal quality of Rameau's genius."[95] When critics wrote of Rameau's revolutionary streak or his integrity as an artist who steadfastly followed his own track in defiance of public opinion they were taking his operatic music, not his ballet music, as benchmarks. But other compositional elements feminized Rameau's music, too: his tendency to embellish pictorial words and to add ornaments to his dances was widely condemned as the tasteless addition of rococo decoration.[96] Worst of all, and whatever the merits of "concision" as opposed to quasi-Wagnerian prolixity, small-scale, nondevelopmental forms had been pejoratively feminized for most of the century.

As a result, in the years immediately following the Franco-Prussian War, the feminized nature of most of the early French stage music that was performed was a liability for those wishing to resurrect a "national" art form worthy of celebration alongside *grand siècle* plays. Racine, after all, had suffered in relation

---

94. Clark, "Bodies at the Opéra," 253. See also Smith, "About the House."

95. "a ôté à la musique du maître l'accent dramatique qui nous semble être ... la qualité maîtresse du génie de Rameau." De Lajarte preface to "Michaëlis" *Les festes d'Hébé* (1878), 2.

96. See Chouquet, *Histoire de la musique dramatique*, 131; De Lajarte, "Les airs à danser de l'ancienne école française," *CM* 4 (no. 23)–6 (no. 31): 1 June–1 October 1874, at 1 July 1874, 17; and De Lajarte's preface to *Castor et Pollux* (collection Michaëlis), 2–3, where he ranked Rameau's dances above his vocal music precisely because of his tendency to add ornaments which "deform" his melodic lines [déforment sa mélodie].

to Molière and Corneille from the Romantic period until the mid 1880s because the perception that he was primarily an analyst of the female heart had led to the notion that his art was itself "effeminate."[97] In the context of a well-developed museum culture such as that of French drama, such a precedent was ominous for *la musique française*. Among all the varied forms and styles of French stage music, including the *déclamation* that writers claimed to prize as a defining characteristic of its composers' Frenchness, it was the *accessoire* of ballet—the *divertissement* rather than the drama—that would prove most alluring. At the end of the century, what stole the show at the Opéra's *concerts historiques* was not grand tragic scenes (they were not programmed) but period-costume dance. And delicate femininity became a byword at the concerts of Van Waelfeghem, Diémer, and his colleagues in the 1890s, where the dance miniature in instrumental form reigned supreme. These concerts, set amid *belle époque* optimism, the beginnings of the *art nouveau* movement, and the celebration of arabesque, show us the trajectory among elite consumers of the French Baroque more generally at the end of the century; but of course they took place a world away from the anguished imperatives for French masculinity of twenty-five years before.

The problem with *la musique française* in the 1870s was therefore multilayered and dynamic. Until it became distilled into a celebration of dance as nostalgic *fête galante*, its stylistic components were hopelessly jumbled, their meanings constructed in such contradictory ways that as a whole it was rendered unusable for traditional nationalist purposes, whether educational or more generally civic. Music fought against declamation; Italy against France; femininity against masculinity; drama against *divertissement*; comedy against tragedy. And it was the wrong time for a "flat-footed" music to get up onto its points. As the final chapter of this book will demonstrate, one has only to compare the case of *la musique française* with that of Handel to see how different the post-war outcome might have been if its modes of reception had instead been either mutually complementary, or squarely rooted in notions of monumentality and masculinity, or (preferably) both. The fact that performance traditions showed increasing acceptance of the *buffo* (incidental music to comedies) and the feminine (dance) contravened the very symbolic values that were being carefully constructed elsewhere in French cultural life. It is no wonder that when French musicians of the 1870s experienced the nationalistic desire to reappraise the music of their national operatic heritage they immediately became mired in the implications of their research.

---

97. See Eustis, *Racine devant la critique française*, 107 and 118.

5

Sources of Frenchness

Origins matter. For French musicians and writers of the nineteenth century they were a constant source of fascination, their successful unearthing an inspiration to editors, historians, and performers alike. It is therefore unsurprising to find origins provoking especially heated debate when it came to making sense of some of the earliest musics they knew. The *chanson populaire* tradition, Adam de la Halle's *Le jeu de Robin et Marion*, and the Franco-Flemish polyphonic chanson all exemplify the importance and the nature of the search. These musics of the medieval and early modern eras lost none of their associations with issues of nationalism and national identity as the century progressed; indeed, such questions only gained in importance. A new intensification of regionalist historical study, combined with concern to demonstrate the authenticity, purity, and "popular" character of the musics that were valued most highly, all raised the ideological stakes in historical writings, editorial prefaces, and performance reviews. Active historical construction, with its attendant "collective forgetfulness," *à la* Renan, is particularly apparent in respect to the Franco-Flemish school, because "proving" that certain composers were indeed French, or finding ways to appropriate them legitimately as such, was a necessary prelude to their reintroduction into musical and liturgical life. And it was all the more important because of their accepted role as the avant-garde of musical development throughout Europe—Italy's music masters, no less.

To claim Franco-Flemish composers as French in the early

nineteenth century was nothing new. Charles Burney revealed as much in his *A General History* of 1789, writing of the appropriation of Ockeghem by Le Duchat in 1711: "I believe this assertion was hazarded more with the patriotic view of making Okenheim as much a Frenchman as possible, than from proof or conviction; for he was always spoken of as a Netherlander by his contemporaries."[1] Yet just five years after Burney's book appeared, the question became more important. The redrawing of borders in the wake of the French Revolution meant that the southern and southwestern parts of Flanders and the Hainaut, a central slice of the old North Burgundian lands of the fifteenth century, were, successively, part of Napoleonic France (1794–1813), occupied by the allied forces (1814–1815), part of the United Kingdom of the Netherlands (from 1815), and reintegrated into France (Treaty of Courtrai, 1820). With minimal changes, the border of 1820 between France and the United Kingdom of the Netherlands turned into the Franco-Belgian border of 1830, arbitrarily cutting Flanders in two, and leaving a rump of Flemish speakers in the northwestern-most corner of France. What, then, constituted historically French music? The French could perhaps claim composers born in parts of Flanders and Hainaut that had, after 1820, become France. But what about those born in areas of Northern Burgundy, such as Brabant and the more easterly parts of Flanders, that had been assimilated first into the United Kingdom of the Netherlands and then into Belgium? The question was emphatically not one of semantics, though semantic games often characterized answers to it.

On the grounds that it was Flemish or Burgundian, the French might have been able to claim most of the Franco-Flemish school as French with impunity had the most influential music historian of the middle of the century not been a nationalist Walloon, resident in Paris until 1833 and fascinated by this very period of musical history: Fétis. His 1829 *mémoire* on the merits and influence of "Netherlandish" music in the fourteenth, fifteenth, and sixteenth centuries was, of course, a patriotic response to a patriotic question posed by the Institute of Science, Literature and Fine Arts of the Kingdom of the Netherlands.[2] His opening gambit, in which he placed the birth of modern music in the Low Countries, bears comparison with Choron's view, expressed in an independent and unpublished study of the same subject, possibly written before Fétis's, and from a French perspective.[3] Choron, treating the same composers and

---

1. Burney, *A General History of Music*, vol. 1, 727.

2. The same question had been set twice: once in 1826, when the response was so poor that the competition was abandoned, then again in 1828.

3. BNF (Manuscrits): n.a.fr. 263 contains two versions of Choron's thoughts on the same subject. Their relative dates are, unfortunately, impossible to gauge.

theorists with a broader brush but using similar techniques, concluded that until the dawn of the Renaissance (by which he meant c.1560), "France was what Italy has since become: the general storehouse of European music,"[4] and the French school the origin of all Europe's contemporary schools of composition.[5] To both, the evidence revealed the domination of Europe by a single musical nation: the only question was, which one?

Both essays are historiographically important for their diametrically opposed interpretations of similar source material. Their influence, for obvious reasons, was unequal. Choron's study remained unknown; Fétis's *mémoire*, reviewed and referred to widely, became a touchstone of thought on the subject, partly because of his openness in discussing historical sources relating to composers' birthplaces and careers, but especially because he returned to many of the same ideas in the first edition of his *Biographie universelle* (1835–44). Three claims were particularly contentious, illustrating his determination to render the leaders of the Franco-Flemish school Belgian. The first told the story of his discovery, in a sixteenth-century manuscript auctioned in 1824 (it was, suspiciously, never traced thereafter), that Dufay came from Chimay, just inside the Belgian portion of the Hainaut district.[6] As Félicien de Ménil commented in 1894, Fétis "clung to this text with all his patriotic strength," despite the possibility that, in reading the manuscript quickly, and recording its contents from memory, he might have confused the Latin for Chimay with that for Cambrai.[7]

In the second, Fétis argued that Josquin—a prize scalp claimed variously by the Germans, the Italians, the French, and the Netherlanders—was born in the Belgian part of the Hainaut district, and that had he been born in Cambrai, as Perne argued in Fétis's own *Revue musicale*, it would still not have made him French because Cambrai was not declared French until Louis XIV's time. "This conquest," he wrote, "does not bring with it the right to consider as French those who were born before it happened."[8] The third contentious claim (later

---

4. "La France était alors ce qu'est devenu depuis l'Italie. Le Dépôt général de la Musique d'Europe." Choron, "De l'école française de musique et de son influence sur les autres écoles de ce même art en Europe." BNF (Manuscrits): n.a.fr. 263, f. 276.

5. BNF (Manuscrits): n.a.fr. 263, f. 280.

6. Fétis, *Quels ont été les mérites*, 13.

7. "se rattache de toutes les forces de son patriotisme à ce texte." De Ménil, *L'école flamande du XVᵉ siècle*, 19. First published in the *Revue du Nord* in 1894. De Ménil (b. 1860) had been trained at the Ecole Niedermeyer.

8. "Cette conquête ne peut donner le droit de considérer comme Français ceux qui étaient nés avant qu'elle se fît." Fétis, *Quels ont été les mérites*, 23. Perne's article dwelt on the absurdity of Forkel's appropriation of Josquin as German (*RM* [October] 1827, 265–72). Fétis did not, at this stage, query the evidence for his birth in Cambrai.

retracted) attacked the priceless belief that crowned the teleology of the French as masters of the Italians: that Goudimel had taught Palestrina. It replaced Goudimel with the Belgian Rinaldo del Mel.[9]

Fétis's chauvinism encouraged retaliation. Continuing irritation at his pulling of the historiographical carpet from under French historians' feet was palpable in a work as late as Weckerlin's *La chanson populaire* of 1886, where the author listed over 80 composers active at the end of the fifteenth century: "These names are all the more useful to cite, because 75 percent of them are French and omitted by Fétis, even though we possess their works. They provide abundant testimony to the existence of a French school—generally mentioned only in respect of the sixteenth century—[to place] beside the Belgian one."[10] However, progressively, the reasoning writers used to claim composers for their own nation fixed on a notion of regionalism centring on "Flanders" (the Northern French and Belgian areas, but not, interestingly, the Dutch) as a cultural unit. On a local level, this strategy was not a mere fudge. As historians of the region have observed, in Flanders the geographical, agricultural, social, religious, and economic similarities between the border regions of the two countries, together with their shared language, meant that the border was itself of administrative importance only,[11] with little effect on the lives of local inhabitants, who could in any case cross it unrestricted until as late as 1929.[12] This view was shared by one of the most prolific writers on Franco-Flemish music and musical writings before 1600: Edmond de Coussemaker. Born in Bailleul (in the Flemish-speaking and bilingual region of the West Hook) and resident in Lille for much of his life, De Coussemaker took an active interest in the cultural demographics of his region, publishing an analysis of the geographical distribution of French- and Flemish-speakers among its residents.[13] His treatment of Tinctoris provides a good example of his approach. De Coussemaker believed him to have been born in Poperinge, a half-day's country walk away (but on the other side of the Franco-Belgian border). He did not follow Choron, who in his bid of 1813 for a government-funded translation had claimed Tinctoris as French; but neither did

---

9. Fétis, *Quels ont été les mérites*, 45. I discuss the chauvinist mythology of Goudimel as Palestrina's teacher in chapter 6.

10. "Ces noms sont d'autant plus utiles à citer, que les trois quarts d'entre eux sont français et omis par Fétis, quoique nous possédons plusieurs de leurs oeuvres; ils témoignent surabondamment de l'existence d'une école française à côté de l'école belge, que généralement on mentionne seule pour le seizième siècle." Weckerlin, *La chanson populaire*, 81.

11. See, for instance, Baycroft, "Changing Identities," 419.

12. Baycroft, "Changing Identities," 424.

13. De Coussemaker, *Délimitation du flamand et du français*.

he describe him as born of the "fecund soil of Belgium," as Fétis's son Edouard had in 1859.[14] Instead of trying to place Tinctoris along rigid national lines, De Coussemaker consistently identified him as a native of their shared home region—West Flanders.[15] He did the same with Adam de la Halle, whose French nationality was never questioned, by placing him not only in the context of the Artois region, but among the wider community of Flanders *trouvères*.[16]

Among other historians we see considerable slippage between "French Flanders," "the North," and "Flanders," the first merging almost imperceptibly into the latter two, more general categories, without weakening the sense of France's claim. Writers also ignored the kind of argumentation that had enabled Fétis to deny French claims to any composer born in fifteenth- or sixteenth-century Cambrai. Once borders had been established in favor of the French, they were not to be rescinded; by contrast, where French territory had been reduced, it was reclaimed historiographically.[17] The French wanted the best of all possible worlds. In a single paragraph of his paper of 1851 on Josquin and the *maîtrise* of Saint-Quentin, local historian Charles Gomart moved from describing the seat of the fifteenth- and sixteenth-century polyphonic schools as "in Picardie, the Artois and French Flanders," to writing more generally about the economic and cultural richness of "Flanders" and its effect on musical progress in the "North."[18] Félicien de Ménil, another regionalist, writing on the Franco-Flemish school around forty years later, revealed the utility of appealing to the historical unity of North Burgundy as, effectively, part of "Northern France":

> [T]his territory, often broken up according to political necessity, after being an entity in itself, preserved its autonomy for a long time . . . today, despite the demarcations of the most recent treaties, the people who live there have conserved the same habits, the same traditions, similar customs and similar idioms and dialects, . . . so that the denomination French or Belgian, determined by a mere frontier, is often brought together under the simple description "of Flemish Race," comprising the ancient Belgii, who already had a well-defined character in Caesar's time.

---

14. "le sol fécund de la Belgique." Written for a Belgian readership in an article entitled "Musiciens belges," *GM* 5/14: 2 June 1859, n.p.

15. See especially his *Oeuvres théoriques de Jean Tinctoris*, introduction.

16. De Coussemaker, *Oeuvres complètes du trouvère Adam de la Halle*, vi.

17. Significantly, the concept of "natural borders" had led both Charles X and Napoléon III to consider the retaking or annexation of Belgium. See Robert Tombs, *France, 1814–1914*, 36, 43.

18. Gomart, "en Picardie, dans l'Artois et dans la Flandre française." "Notes historiques," 216.

Thus, during the period when Flanders made up part of the Duchy of Burgundy, an exceedingly famous school was founded in these regions of Northern France.[19]

It was this ahistorical sleight of hand, which stretched the legitimacy of the arguments attaching to residents of borderlands beyond what they could reasonably sustain, that characterized most of the post-1880 writing on the Franco-Flemish school, not least that of Tiersot, whose publications on the subject were extensive. It allowed the French to claim more than their share of key figures born outside France's contemporary borders: not only Lassus, born in Fétis's native Mons, but also Willaert, born in far-flung Bruges. Henry Expert's seminal anthology *Le maîtres musiciens de la Renaissance française* could thus open with volumes devoted to two Burgundians who were presented as equally French: Lassus (the French chansons) and Goudimel (the psalm settings).

Franco-Flemish Polyphony: A National Treasure?

Had the Franco-Flemish school been a backwater of musical historiography, French historians would doubtless have spared their efforts to claim its composers for themselves. But in the absence of information about contemporary developments in Italy (and England), there was no doubt in their minds that the old Burgundian lands had been the sole cradle of modern musical civilization. Only with Monteverdi (or possibly the Gabrielis) had Italian culture overtaken that of the French: this was the view of Choron, Fétis, and many of their successors. Yet, as we know, the music *qua* music was deeply problematic, and the sacred music, in particular, was rebarbative to almost everyone. Fétis had few opponents here: after engaging in protracted arguments about the birthplace of its composers, virtually all historians before Tiersot, and some after him, rejected

---

19. "ce territoire souvent morcelé par les exigences de la politique, après avoir fait un tout complet, a gardé longtemps son autonomie propre, et qu'actuellement encore malgré les délimitations des derniers traités, les peuples qui l'habitent ont conservé les mêmes habitudes, les mêmes moeurs, des coutumes semblables, des idioms pareils, des patois similaires, et que la démonimation de Français ou de Belges, déterminée par une borne frontière, se résume le plus souvent dans la simple appellation de *Race Flamande*, comprenant les anciens BELGII qui du temps de César déjà avaient un caractère nettement défini.
   Or, à l'époque où la Flandre faisait partie du duché de Bourgogne, une école musicale fort célèbre s'était fondée dans ces régions du Nord de la France." De Ménil, *L'école flamande du XVe siècle*, 7.

the music while lauding its composers. Why? The question is all the more pressing because the ultimate historiographical price of such impassioned rejection of France's own, and claimed, avant-garde, was to weaken the value of French influence on Palestrina. Two desired historiographies could not, seemingly, be reconciled: either one applauded the abuses from which Palestrina had saved sacred music (the Pope Marcellus Mass myth), or one consigned to aesthetic oblivion a set of national traditions that had been the envy of Europe for two centuries.

Choron and Fétis, the latter in his *mémoire* of 1829, had all but avoided comment on style in their surveys of Franco-Flemish music as the fount of modern music. Writings from 1828 and 1830, however, reveal how much distaste Fétis had concealed in his patriotic submission to the Netherlands Institute. In his own *Revue musicale* he regularly fulminated against a style which he perceived as lauding technique over expression and bringing disrespect to the Church. Palestrina, of course, emerged equally regularly as sacred music's savior. In 1830, an article on the history of ornamentation inspired nothing short of a tirade. Fétis presented chanson-based masses and motets as doubly secularized: first by the use of the chansons themselves, and then by the importation of secular ornamentation practices whose roots he traced to the chansons of Adam de la Halle. The passage is worth quoting at length for the sense of obsession that it conveys:

> Things reached the ridiculous point where, while three or four voices engaged in fugal counterpoint, full of imitation, canons and learned working of all kinds on the Latin words of the Kyrie or the Gloria, another voice—soprano, alto or tenor—continually sang "Kiss me my love," or "I am a little girl," while singing rapid scales, trills, leaps of all kinds, covering the entire range of the voice, from the bass to the treble, and producing at every instant consecutive fifths or octaves, inevitable consequences given the multitude of notes. The ridiculousness of such a practice is such that today it is difficult to believe that it ever existed, and yet it took a long time to destroy it. The complaints of men of taste and sensible writers, thunderbolts from the Church, the decrees of [church] Councils were not enough to overcome the pigheadedness of the cantors. Only a man of genius could achieve it, through the beauty of his works. That man was Palestrina.[20]

---

20. "Les choses en vinrent à ce point de ridicule que, tandis que trois ou quatre voix faisaient un contrepoint fugué, rempli d'imitations, de canons et de recherches de tout genre sur les paroles latines du Kyrie ou du Gloria, une autre voix de soprano, de contralto ou de tenore chantait continuellement *baysez-moi ma belle*, ou *or mi son giovinetta*, en faisant des gammes rapides, des trilles, des sauts de tout genre, embrassant toute l'étendue des voix depuis la basse jusqu'au dessus, et faisant entendre à chaque instant des quintes ou des octaves consecutives, choses inévitables dans une telle multitude de notes. Le ridicule d'un pareil usage est tel qu'on peut à

Individual articles of the *Biographie universelle* show more generosity, but Fétis was, as we have seen in his introductions to pieces performed at his *concerts historiques*, no defender of this music in practice, and his trenchant views, to which was added a widespread unease about the use of chansons as an indication of a lack of compositional imagination, appeared, explicitly or implicitly, in countless Francophone histories throughout the century. Several leitmotifs recur: logorhythmic composition, irreverence, the absence (because it was perceived to be irrelevant) of musical beauty or expression. The litany includes many of the key names in writing on sacred music. In the early 1830s, Castil-Blaze damned the Franco-Flemish use of chansons as an example of musical "fashion"[21]; Danjou echoed Fétis in 1839, dismissing Josquin's masses as written "in accordance with the ridiculous practice of his time."[22] In 1857, De Lafage, much more sympathetic to the repertory itself, struggled to defend it, not least by arguing that the bawdy texts of chansons were not sung in their new sacred context.[23] Josquin, as he wrote in 1853, was "a man of genius and imagination," whose contribution "to the art and in respect of melodic feeling" Baini in particular had underestimated: "it shines through at every instant in the midst of the artifices of every kind which he employs."[24] Yet the relief is palpable when in this annotated catalogue of his personal library De Lafage writes his only passage of aesthetic critique about a Josquin work, the penitential Mass "D'ung autre amour": "Here, Josquin completely abandons his usual compositional habits: the melody is almost syllabic, the parts move together all the time. Nothing is more majestic or better suited to the sense of the text."[25] Confining

---

peine concevoir aujourd'hui qu'il a existé, et cependant il fallût beaucoup de temps pour le détruire. Les réclamations des gens de goût et des écrivains sensés, les foudres de l'église, les décrets des conciles étaient insuffisans contre l'entêtement des chantres; un homme de génie put seul en venir à bout par la beauté de ses ouvrages: cet homme fut Palestrina." *RM* 10 July 1830, 309.

21. Castil-Blaze, *Mélanges littéraires* (album of reviews from the *Revue de Paris*, 1832–33), 29. BNF (Musique): 8° B. 2736.

22. "[c]onformément au ridicule usage adopté de son temps." *RGM* 6/5: 3 February 1839, 35. Danjou's "Archives curieuses" nevertheless contained the largest selection of Franco-Flemish polyphony yet published in France.

23. De Lafage, *Extraits du catalogue critique*, 113–14.

24. "homme de génie et d'imagination." De Lafage, *Extraits du catalogue critique*, 102; "à l'art et sur le sentiment mélodique qui, chez lui, perce à chaque instant au milieu des artifices de toute sorte qu'il emploie" (106).

25. "Josquin y sort complétement de ses habitudes de composition: le chant est presque syllabique, les parties marchent continuellement ensemble, rien de plus majestueux et de plus conforme au sens des paroles." De Lafage, *Extraits du catalogue critique*, 104.

his enthusiasm to music he considered unrepresentative, De Lafage condemned Josquin's most characteristic writing along precisely Fétisian lines.

Other writers made no concessions. Félix Clément was predictably damning in his history of sacred music in 1860, reiterating the key word "ridicule." Moreover, in his wish to elevate plainchant at the expense of all other liturgical music, he made sure that Palestrina himself was not exempt from criticism. In his "L'homme armé" mass (Clément knew only one), Palestrina had "accumulated the musical riddles and the combinations of which his contemporaries were so fond. It was only little by little that he abandoned this ridiculous system."[26] Ludovic Vitet, reviewing De Coussemaker, described the music as "a kind of cleverness, a game of patience."[27] In 1878 Bourgault-Ducoudray began his Conservatoire course in a patriotic vein with a study of French music, but even he found the sacred music of the Franco-Flemish polyphonists ungrateful, inert, and fundamentally restrictive, and likened its unyielding construction to the "walls of a chrysalis, from which melody, long-imprisoned, will emerge to fly skyward, like a joyful and multi-colored butterfly"[28]; in 1886, Weckerlin found works of Franco-Flemish sacred polyphony "at once serious and cringe-making," a form in which the sacred words were only an accessory.[29]

Behind all such interpretations of Franco-Flemish counterpoint lay a combination of puzzlement, moral indignation, and, perhaps above all, a deep suspicion of learned music in which artifice seemed to outlaw spontaneity. For spontaneity alone could yield the youthful freshness that French writers throughout the nineteenth century applauded in a wide range of music. Those who wished to rescue selected portions of such music from the taint of contrapuntal dryness tended to argue one of two cases, both of them easiest to defend in respect to sixteenth-century music: that fugal procedure had been sublimated into harmony (Palestrina and Goudimel); or that the composer's polyphony was itself freely melodic (Lassus). Both arguments allowed the possibility that polyphony and expressivity might be reconciled, even in pretonal music. They also applied to secular music (though secular music did not have so much of the additional baggage with which sacred music had to contend). Nevertheless, until the final two decades of the century, the deluge of derogatory critiques of pre-Palestrinian sacred music, almost all of which remained

---

26. "avait accumulé les énigmes musicales et les combinaisons dont ses contemporains raffolaient. Il n'abandonna ce système ridicule que peu à peu." Clément, *Histoire générale de la musique religieuse*, 327.

27. "une sorte d'industrie, un jeu de patience." *Journal des savants* (henceforth *JS*), June 1867, 381.

28. "comme l'enveloppe de la chrysalide, d'où la mélodie, longtemps prisonnière, sortira pour s'envoler vers le ciel, comme un papillon joyeux et diapré." *Mén* 45/2:8 December 1878, 10.

29. "en même temps sérieuses et grimaçantes." Weckerlin, *La chanson populaire*, 115.

unheard, undermined the nationalist fervor of the process—carried out by many of the same writers—of claiming its composers for the French nation.

Honorable Exceptions: Janequin and Lassus

For reasons that hold the key to an attempted reversal of both culture and practice by Tiersot and Weckerlin in the late 1880s, Janequin and Lassus emerged relatively early in the century as honorable exceptions to the rule that the compositional tastes of Franco-Flemish musicians deserved to be disparaged. The secret lay in the fondness of both for French chansons—those same pieces which were so vilified when they entered the church. Throughout the century, Janequin was known for one celebrated, nationalist, secular chanson (*La bataille de Marignan*) and two that were lesser-known but equally picturesque: *Les cris de Paris* and *Le chant des oiseaux*. The first two were introduced by Choron; the third by Moskova in the 1840s. Thereafter *La bataille* and *Le chant* in particular remained in the repertory through the concerts of most of the promoters of early choral music in Paris. His psalm settings and his *chansons spirituelles* were known about but undiscussed, as indeed were his masses and motets, including (ironically but inevitably) his mass "La bataille de Marignan."

In print and in performance, Lassus was known for a much wider range of works, comprising motets, French chansons, and his celebrated *Penitential Psalms*, extracts from which were a favorite of the Moskova society. His masses, however, remained virtually unknown in France until Bordes edited and promoted the mass "Douce mémoire"; the existence of his Italian madrigals and German lieder was not generally mentioned.[30] His two most frequently performed works were French chansons. These two works, frequently confused because they came to be known by the same title (*Les vendanges* or *Les vendangeurs*) comprised the fleet-of-foot counterpoint of "Fuyons tous d'amour le jeu" and the lively homophony of "Margot labouréz les vignes" (also known as "Vigne, vignolet," after the text of its second line). The reception of this small corpus of music throughout its performance history (from 1830 for the Janequin chansons; from 1844, "Fuyons"; from 1863, "Margot") contrasts utterly with that of Franco-Flemish sacred music of the same period (except in being as

---

30. Fétis performed one Italian madrigal at his *concert historique* of 1855; otherwise, I have found no reference to performances of Lassus works with texts other than Latin or French. Of course, in Germany attitudes to Lassus were different: the Cecilian Franz Xaver Witt highlighted Lassus's time in Munich as a way of rendering him spiritually Bavarian, especially in the wake of the unification of Germany in 1871. See Garratt, *Palestrina*, 145–46.

unified and internally consistent). Nationalist enthusiasm permeates almost every phrase; audience enthusiasm, too, was virtually guaranteed.

Choron made sure that the triumphalism of Janequin's portrayal of François I routing the Swiss at Marignan (1515) was well understood, printing notes to that effect in the programs to two of his concerts of 1830.[31] In the space of fourteen concerts between December 1829 and March 1830 he presented *La bataille* three times, and *Les cris* four, once by command of the duchesse de Berry.[32] More important, perhaps, was the inclusion of *La bataille* in two charity concerts of overtly nationalist music that Choron organized to benefit those bereaved and wounded in the July Revolution (24 August 1830) and the Belgian Revolution (21 November 1830). He also included music from Handel's oratorios: excerpts from *Judas* and *Samson* in August, and a complete performance of *Samson* in November. Janequin performed his customary function in both programs: as an entr'acte between the sections of more extended works. The August concert contained three such entr'actes: *La bataille*, a quick march by Choron himself, and *La Marseillaise*.[33]

From the outset, the nature of Janequin's *La bataille* as a nationalist expression of French superiority went uncontested. To that nationalist appeal was added lasting popularity of a kind that was unique for music dating from before 1600. The secret probably lay in the chanson's energetic pictorialism, its virtuoso demands, and its party-piece onomatopoeia: but, whatever the reasons, it was a hit. At its second performance by Moskova's Société des Concerts (8 April 1844), *La bataille* was encored; it had to be included in the final program of the season (15 May 1844) at the last minute—by audience demand. Needless to say, it was also featured in the first concert of the next season (10 February 1845). Most important of all, when programmed at the end of a concert, *La bataille* had the superhuman power of keeping society ladies in their seats until the very end. As Adolphe Adam noted with some astonishment: "not one of the noble spectators got up before the end to request her carriage."[34] During and after the débâcle of 1870–71, it became clear that the piece had lost none of its import: it was featured in an article on French battle music in the *Revue et gazette musicale* in 1870;[35] and when Bourgault-Ducoudray

---

31. See the listing by Anne Randier in Colette et al. (Ed.), *La musique à Paris*, 135, 137. The third performance of *La bataille*, and the fourth of *Les cris*, took place on 15 April (Randier provides no program). See Boettcher, *Les exercices publics d'Alexandre Choron*, 131.

32. Colette et al. (Ed.), *La musique à Paris*, 134.

33. Colette et al. (Ed.), *La musique à Paris*, 149, 151.

34. "pas une des nobles spectatrices ne s'est levée avant la fin pour demander sa voiture." *FM* 27 April 1845, 132, given in Campos, *La Renaissance introuvable?*, 124.

35. *RGM* 37/31–35: 31 July–28 August 1870 (unfinished due to suspension of the journal during the war).

programmed it alongside a Bach cantata at the popular (and cheap) Concerts-Danbé on 22 January 1874, it stole the show, its intended significance for the entire nation reinforced by the fact that it was sung not only by Bourgault-Ducoudray's amateur choir, but by *orphéon* singers from two of his associated societies: the Société Chorale Le Louvre and Les Enfants de Paris.[36] It was a staple of the Chanteurs de Saint-Gervais repertory, in Paris and on tour, and was included in their Exposition Universelle concert of 28 July 1900.[37]

What, then, was the appeal of the few Janequin chansons with which Parisians were familiar? Paul Scudo, whose dim view of Franco-Flemish sacred music was more extreme than most, was enchanted. The *Chant des oiseaux*, he wrote in 1846, was a "charming jest, full of rhythmic interest and caprices. There are pretty imitations of the cackling of birds; the ending especially has some fizz to it. It is a Gallic yarn in music. It was encored."[38] His approach was almost identical when he heard *La bataille* (which he had doubtless performed under Choron's direction) at the Society's next concert. Not only did the picturesque aspects of the piece attract him; so, too, did its combination of skill and imagination. The work was "at once an animated drama wherein there is also fantasy, and a kind of jesting."[39] Badinage/jesting, fantasy, imagination, caprice, the picturesque, piquancy, and rhythmic interest: these were the characteristics that were to become indelibly associated with the sixteenth-century French chanson and, by association, with "real" French music of the French Renaissance. Other attributes followed, all of them positive: "sève" [earthiness, vigor], "esprit" [spirit], verve, and a style that was "coloré" [richly colored] and "mouvementé" [eventful]. All could be perceived as qualities of healthy masculinity that contained no hint of decadence—attributes that became supremely important after 1870.[40] According to J.-B. Labat, who recalled the excitement of Choron's performances at a half-century's distance, modern French music owed all its finest characteristics to composers such as Janequin, in whose music he found "the purest and the truest reflection of our national character."[41]

This was a widespread view in the 1870s, as evidenced by Bourgault-

---

36. Henry Cohen in *CM* 3 (no. 15): 1 February 1874, 130–31.

37. Campos, *La Renaissance introuvable?*, 125.

38. "charmant badinage, plein de rhythme et de caprices. Il y a de jolies imitations du caquetage des oiseaux, la fin surtout est piquante. C'est un conte gaulois en musique. On l'a redemandé." Paul Scudo, unsigned notebook of reviews and articles: "Notes d'un critique musical, 1844–49" (Brussels, Bibliothèque Royale: ML 2916). Notes on the Moskova concert of 6 April 1846, [111]. Orthography regularized.

39. "c'est à la fois un drame animé où se montre aussi la fantaisie et une sorte de badinage." [Scudo], "Notes d'un critique musical," [117]. Notes on a concert of 2 May 1846.

40. On this question, see especially Fauser, "Gendering the Nations," 80–84.

41. "le reflet le plus pur et le plus vrai de notre caractère national." Labat, *Oeuvres littéraires-musicales*, vol. 1, 287.

Ducoudray's performances of 1874, which produced a dense constellation of reviews, most of which were variations on a theme. Those in the *Revue et gazette musicale* and *L'art musical* each used the Janequin work as the title of the review—an extraordinary decision given its length relative to the rest of the evening's program. The *Revue et gazette musicale* review of 25 January, by H. Lavoix *fils*, focused, perhaps wistfully, on the story of conquest, and on the heroism of François I in leading his men from the front. The work itself, wrote Lavoix, was strictly contrapuntal, but this could not be held against it because its counterpoint was handled with "a certain ease, remarkable for the period."[42] Lucien Augé, writing for *L'art musical*, also combined the nationalistic (he dwelt on the inclusion of "barbaric German" when the Swiss admitted their defeat) and the aesthetic. He wrote a poetic travelogue through the work, much in the tradition of 1830s *critique admirative*: the chanson, though three hundred years old, "flies as though carried along by an ever-youthful enthusiasm."[43] Henry Cohen of *La chronique musicale* piled on the acclamation: to call it a "work of genius" was not enough; it was a "masterpiece of genius."[44] In the same issue, the journal printed a piano reduction of *La bataille* as part of its historical series of French masterpieces intended for the edification of young pianists at home. But all were topped by an unsigned news snippet in *Le ménestrel*, which brought together a plethora of positive French signifiers.

> Through the boldness of his creations, through the intensity of his color-palette and his picturesque vivacity, he left his contemporaries way behind him. . . . *La bataille de Marignan* is a perfect model of the art of writing for voices. This piece, so full of invention and vigor, contains rhythmic effects unmatched by any modern composer. Moreover, it is an emanation of the genius of the sixteenth century. We find in it an overflowing sense of life which is seen as much in the proud surges of chivalrous ardor, as in the bubbling of a realistic and popular vitality. Through its music, through its political language, through the event that it celebrates, *La bataille de Marignan* is an essentially French work. Everything combines to give this work a strange historical and national flavor.[45]

---

42. "une certaine aisance, remarquable pour l'époque." *RGM* 41/4: 25 January 1874, 26–27.

43. "allemand barbare"; "vole comme emporté d'un enthousiasme toujours jeune." *AM* 13/4: 2 April 1874, 106.

44. "oeuvre de génie"; "chef-d'oeuvre de génie." *CM* 3 (no.15): 1 February 1874, 130.

45. "Par la hardiesse de ses conceptions, par la puissance de son coloris et sa verve pittoresque, il a laissé bien loin derrière lui ses contemporains. . . . La bataille de Marignan [sic] offre un modèle achevé de l'art d'écrire pour les voix. Ce morceau, plein d'invention et de sève, renferme des effets rythmiques qui n'ont été reproduits

After *Le ménestrel* of 18 January 1874, critics of *La bataille* could (and largely did) only repeat themselves.

Lassus presented a slightly different kind of challenge. Like Janequin, he had composed in embarrassing genres of sacred music (there are many more chanson-based masses than in Janequin's output). But he was also a cosmopolitan whose compositional horizons had reached well beyond the confines of the Low Countries: he had not only taken his own, Franco-Flemish, traditions to other parts of Europe; he had also absorbed traditions from elsewhere, in particular, the Italian madrigal and the German lied. Moreover, he was Palestrina's contemporary, and comparisons were unavoidable. Just as musicians compared Bach and Handel, so they compared Palestrina and Lassus. A final issue lay in his importance to Belgium, for his birthplace of Mons was never disputed. How was such an important figure, a Belgian Palestrina, to be appropriated for France? Part of the answer lay in the selectivity mentioned above. But Fétis himself provided an ideal solution to the Belgian "problem." His 1829 *mémoire* cast Lassus as inferior to Palestrina, but for significant reasons. Lassus's music was, given its date, "gracious and elegant," while Palestrina's had "more strength and gravity." Lassus's music was "more lyrical" and showed "more imagination," while Palestrina's was, by contrast, "much more learned."[46] Finally, he wrote: "In Palestrina's motets and madrigals there are massed effects which are admirable; but the French chansons of Lassus are full of the most interesting details."[47] In respect to sacred music these characteristics of Lassus's music remained signifiers of his inferiority to Palestrina. Yet for secular music they were, of course, entirely positive French signifiers. And it was an exasperated Fétis who sealed their identification as more French than Flemish.

There are few more memorable passages in the *Biographie universelle* than that in which Fétis, incensed beyond measure, defends his compatriot Lassus

---

par aucun compositeur moderne. C'est de plus une émanation vivante du génie du XVIe siècle. On y trouve une surabondance de vie qui se manifeste tantôt par les fiers élans d'une ardeur chevaleresque, tantôt par le bouillonnement d'une verve réaliste et populaire. Par la musique, par la langue politique, par le fait qu'elle célèbre, la bataille de Marignan [sic] est une oeuvre essentiellement française. Tout se réunit pour donner à ce morceau une étrange saveur historique et nationale." *Mén* 40/7: 18 January 1874, 54–55.

46. "gracieuse et élégante"; "plus de force et de gravité"; "plus chantante . . . plus d'imagination"; "bien plus savante." Fétis, *Quels ont été les mérites*, 45.

47. "Il y a dans les motets et dans les madrigaux de PALESTRINA des effets de masse qui sont admirables; mais les chansons françaises de Lassus sont remplies de détails très-intéressans." Fétis, *Quels ont été les mérites*, 45.

from the insults leveled at him in Baini's biography of Palestrina. Baini, intent on presenting his hero as on a different plane from all his contemporaries, adopted a policy of damning Lassus through ethnic stereotype: "Roland de Lassus. Flemish-born, Flemish in style—devoid of fine melody, lacking soul and fire."[48] "Flemish by birth" was an insult to Fétis himself, a fellow Walloon born in the same town of Mons. Provoked to write the opposite of what he said when Franco-Flemish unity was at stake, Fétis claimed that "language defines peoples."[49] Then Fétis effectively handed Lassus to the French:

> *Flemish in style!* This is a palpable error on Baini's part. The Flemish style, which became the model of the Italian style in the fifteenth, and the early part of the sixteenth, centuries, was composed of learned techniques that were more mechanical than truly artistic, based on the themes of popular songs whose melodies, and even the texts, produced, alongside the sacred texts, a monstrous assemblage in sacred music. By contrast, what particularly distinguishes Lassus's music, and what made his name, and gave his compositions both character and originality, was precisely that he distanced himself from this style and took on, in his sacred music, a simple and serious character, and, in his light compositions an elegant and easy style. . . . According to M. the abbé Baini, Lassus was *devoid of melody, lacking soul and fire!* Well! But it is exactly the opposite. For it was through melody (and here I mean melody according to the system of his time) that the master distinguished himself from his contemporaries, and it is the melodic lines of his compositions which lay at the root of his popular success.[50]

---

48. "*Roland de Lassus, Flamand de naissance, Flamand de style, stérile de belles mélodies, privé d'âme et de feu.*" Fétis, quoting Baini's *Memorie storico-critiche* in his *Biographie universelle*, 1st ed., vol. 6 (1840), 60. The italics are Fétis's.

49. "le langage fait la différence des peuples." *Biographie universelle*, 1st ed., vol. 6 (1840), 60.

50. "*Flamand de style!* Ceci est une erreur palpable de M. l'abbé Baini. Le style flamand, qui devient le modèle du style italien, au quinzième siècle, et dans la première partie du seizième, était composé de recherches plus mécaniques que véritablement artistiques sur des motifs de chansons vulgaires, dont les mélodies, et les paroles mêmes, faisaient dans la musique d'église un monstrueux assemblage avec les textes sacrés. Or, ce qui distingue particulièrement la musique de Lassus, ce qui fit ses succès, ce qui donna à ses ouvrages le caractère et de l'originalité, c'est précisément qu'il se sépara de ce style et prit dans sa musique d'église un caractère grave et simple, et dans ses compositions légères une manière élégante et facile. . . . Suivant M. l'abbé Baini, Lassus était *stérile de mélodies, privé d'âme et de feu!* Eh! Mais, c'est exactement le contraire; car c'est par la mélodie (j'entends ici celle du système de son temps) que ce maître se distingue de ses contemporains, et ce sont les chants de ses compositions qui ont fait la popularité de ses succès." *Biographie universelle*, 1st ed., vi (1840), 60.

Nationalist outrage caused Fétis to make a clear distinction, on language lines, between what did and did not constitute the Flemish component of sixteenth-century Franco-Flemish music. What remained once all Flemishness had been sieved out was, inevitably, French. Melodiousness, elegance, ease, character, and originality: these epithets stuck to Lassus's chansons, just as Fétis's view of the new gravity of Lassus's church music became attached to his motets and (unsurprisingly) his *Penitential Psalms*. Nevertheless, it was the national lineage of his French chansons that Fétis's description of Lassus had made clear, and later writers followed the trend. Scudo called "Fuyons tous d'amour" precisely what he was to call Janequin's *Chant des oiseaux*: a "charming jest" and a "lively conversation," without even stopping to mention its contrapuntal texture.[51] After hearing the chanson performed by Vervoitte's Société Académique in 1863, Denne-Baron described it in the *Ménestrel* as "ingeniously counterpointed, and rhythmically constructed with such grace and elegance."[52] As vice-president of the *Revue de musique sacrée, ancienne et moderne*, Denne-Baron was, of course, an insider (it was the Société Académique's mouthpiece journal). But outsiders agreed, as did the Society's audiences: "Fuyons" appeared to be an eternally youthful work, and it regularly produced a sensation.[53] Weckerlin, although he worried that learned writing in Lassus's chansons indicated their rather exclusive social status, nevertheless concurred that the composer had shaken free from restrictive counterpoint to give this piece "fantasy and inspiration" and a melodic contour that was "more direct, more alert" than anything that had preceded it.[54]

By the mid 1890s, the Chanteurs de Saint-Gervais's performances of Lassus chansons in sets of three or four had become one of their most popular concert items; Expert's volume of Lassus chansons rode the crest of a critical wave in which these works thrived on perceptions of their youthful energy and uncluttered grace. Simplicity combined with a certain earthiness now ranked among the greatest of French virtues. René de Brancour's review summed up the predominant view:

> How these old things are yet young! What warmth in the part-writing, in the manner of their interplay! The vocal polyphony plays freely and fully across these melodic lines taken, for the most part, from popular refrains—innocent, light-hearted, sometimes even

---

51. "charmant badinage"; "causerie vive." [Scudo], "Notes d'un critique musical," notes on Moskova concert of 5 March 1846, [104].

52. "ingénieusement contrepointé et rhythmée avec tant de grâce et d'élégance." *Mén* 30/27: 7 June 1863, 214.

53. See, for instance, Denne-Baron in *Mén* 30/23: 10 May 1863, 64; A. Lomon in *FM* 30/9: 4 March 1866, 62–63.

54. "fantaisie et inspiration"; "plus franc, plus alerte." Weckerlin, *La chanson populaire*, 74–75.

more than lighthearted. The rhythm is always marvellously appropriate to the subject—even more so, often, than is the melody.[55]

Class mattered too. Positive appraisal of the polyphonic chanson became increasingly dependent on evidence of the "popular," with the unpretentious simplicity of folk song becoming a mirror of the French musical spirit. Such trends had been detectable from the 1830s, becoming politicized in diverse ways as the century progressed. Writers such as Weckerlin represented a radical left-wing stance that championed the popular and the realist in the *chanson populaire*.[56] It is no surprise, then, to find him writing in the 1850s that even Lassus's chansons were simply "old-style counterpoint," with "undefined" melodic lines that bore no relation to the style of folk song.[57] In contrast, he pointed to the vitality of an oral tradition which, he believed, reigned from the thirteenth century onward, and in which "the people, this plural poet," instead of composing "insipid counterpoint," "developed works beyond the boundaries dictated by learning"—works which depended only on feeling and sincerity.[58]

Precisely what constituted a folk song, or a popular French song giving access to grass-roots Frenchness, was unclear, and different writers allowed different levels of mediation between the "people" and the composition as recorded. Although folk song collecting had received government support since 1852, when the Ministère de l'Instruction Publique published an appeal for its study, it was the Third Republic whose leaders were most anxious to capitalize on it as a means of uniting the inhabitants of diverse regions. A dedicated society, the Société des Traditions Populaires, was instituted in 1885; almost simultaneously, the history of the French *chanson populaire* was the subject chosen for the Institut's Prix Bordin—which Julien Tiersot won. Before that, a grey area covered several important corpuses of sixteenth-, seventeenth-, and eighteenth-century music: the *brunettes, romances and bergerettes* in the anthologies of Delsarte

---

55. "Que ces vieilles choses sont donc jeunes! Quelle chaleur dans le mouvement des parties, dans la manière dont elles s'alternent! La polyphonie vocale se joue à l'aise, se déploie dans tout son ampleur à travers ces chants pour la plupart écrits sur des refrains populaires, naïfs, légers, parfois même plus que légers. Le rythme est toujours merveilleusement approprié au sujet,—plus même que ne l'est souvent la mélodie." *PA* 19 (no. 963): 17 December 1896, 189.

56. See Fulcher, "The Popular Chanson." Weckerlin's collaboration with Gustave Courbet and Jules Champfleury on the *Chansons populaires des provinces de France* of 1860 (32) helps clarify the wider background to this attitude, which was also fundamentally anticlerical.

57. "l'ancienne forme de contrepoint"; "assez vague." Weckerlin, *Echos du temps passé*, ii, unpaginated preface.

58. "le peuple, ce poète multiple"; "insipide contrepoint"; "élabore ses oeuvres en dehors de l'état de la science." Weckerlin, *Echos du temps passé*, iii, unpaginated preface.

and Weckerlin[59]; the dances of Thoinot Arbeau's *Orchésographie*; the *chanson de geste* and the carol. Inevitably, there were disagreements about designations. Weckerlin was militant and aggressively bipolar, marginalizing and even deprecating anything that smacked of high art. Troubadour repertories, lays, and much of the polyphonic chanson corpus did not count as "popular": the two strands of musical culture were "divided, as different from each other as were the two major classes of the French population, the aristocracy and the people."[60] Tiersot, Weckerlin's subordinate at the Conservatoire Library, was more conciliatory. Writing on the same subject at the same time (it is highly likely that they competed against each other for the Prix Bordin), he could be more generous because his arguments about the provenance of folk songs were different. Folk songs, like the dances of Arbeau's *Orchésographie*, had been first "chased from cities by each new artistic current," then transformed by the people, and finally taken up again by composers of "la musique savante" in their polyphonic settings.[61]

But writers were consistent on one subject: the musics they themselves designated as "popular" embodied the French national psyche. As Louis Roger reminded readers of his *orphéon* journal *La réforme musicale* in 1868, "As is often said, the chanson is an obliging mirror which reflects with absolute fidelity the spirit and the features of a people" and its history.[62] In the case of one emblematic work, the *Jeu de Robin et de Marion*, the cultural significance of such a view could hardly have been greater.

In the Beginning Was the *Jeu*

Fétis's *Revue musicale* began with a discussion of it; most historical texts on French music came into focus with it; and it was the earliest single-author French work of any genre to be performed (in excerpts or complete) in nineteenth-century France. In the most fundamental of ways, French music, as far as many

---

59. See François Delsarte (Ed.), *Archives du chant*, and Weckerlin, *Echos du temps passé* and his later collections, including his *Chansons populaires des provinces de France* (1860), *L'ancienne chanson populaire en France: 16ᵉ et 17ᵉ siècles* (1887), and dedicated regional collections from the 1880s and 90s. On the *romance* tradition as "popular," see also Fétis in *RM* (November/December 1828), 409.

60. "scindées, aussi différentes l'un de l'autre que l'étaient les deux grandes classes de la population française, l'aristocratie et le peuple." Weckerlin, *La chanson populaire*, iv.

61. "chassée des villes par un nouveau courant artistique." Tiersot, *Histoire de la chanson populaire*, 349, cited in Pasler, "The *chanson populaire*," 204.

62. "La chanson, comme on l'a dit souvent, est un miroir complaisant qui réfléchit avec une fidélité rigide l'esprit et la physionomie des peuples." *RéfM* 13/17: 28 June 1868, n.p.

French writers were concerned, began with Adam de la Halle and the *Jeu de Robin et de Marion*. The work was iconic for musicians for much of the century because in 1827 Fétis, doubtless following Roquefort's *De l'état de la poésie* (1814), famously dubbed it the "oldest *opéra-comique* in existence."[63]

Fétis's view of the *Jeu*'s importance was taken up with remarkable speed and consistency: few writers in France could resist such a seductive version of operatic history, even if the *Jeu* was, as Léon Kreutzer and Edouard Fournier pointed out, an experiment that had no immediate influence.[64] By turns, and among others, Bottée de Toulmon (in the *Revue et gazette musicale*, 1836), Kreutzer and Fournier (*Essai sur l'art lyrique*, 1849), Théodore Nisard (in *Revue de musique ancienne et moderne*, 1856), De Coussemaker (*Oeuvres complètes du trouvère Adam de la Halle*, 1872), Weckerlin (edition of the *Jeu*, 1872), Chouquet (*Histoire de la musique dramatique*, 1873), Georges Becker (*Aperçu sur la chanson française*, 1876), Pougin (*La musique populaire*, 1882), and a host of reviewers for the 1896 performance in Arras, included this signal fact in their accounts of French musical history. But it was not just Fétis's label that mattered; it was his elevation of the monodic *Jeu* over Adam de la Halle's polyphonic works, which he had dubbed "still very crude" but "not without a certain elegance." They were also, of course, barbaric in their use of secular texts in sacred music.[65] However, when he came to introduce the *Jeu*, which he implied was previously unknown, his tone changed. Here was a work "which alone ought to have been enough to immortalize [Adam de la Halle]."[66] Fétis did not bestow lavish praise on the music itself but noted its distance from the "heavy psalmody" of the chansons of the Chastelain de Couci and other contemporaries, lauding its metrical regularity and its antecedent and consequent phrases. The result was "not ungraceful."[67] It was the formal innovation, one suspects, that counted more with Fétis than the musical content; but he had opened up a generic fissure in the composer's works which later writers exploited to the full, especially in relation to the barbarity of De la Halle's sacred and polyphonic music as against the folklike purity of his melodic writing in

---

63. "[le] plus ancien opéra-comique qui existe." *RM* spécimen: February 1827, 9. During the century the only competition came from Paul Lacome, who tried in 1878 to push the history even further back within the thirteenth century to embrace the refrain structure of the anonymous (and so potentially folk-influenced) *Aucassin et Nicolette*. This was not, however, a historiography that endured, and his series of music extracts still began with the *Jeu*. See his *Les fondateurs de l'opéra-comique*, ii–iii.

64. Kreutzer and Fournier, *Essai sur l'art lyrique*, 14.

65. "encore bien grossière"; "ne manquent pas d'une certaine élégance." *RM* spécimen: February 1827, 8–9. For an alternative reading of the monody/polyphony question, see Haines, *Eight Centuries of Troubadours*, 170–74.

66. "qui aurait dû suffire pour l'immortaliser." *RM* spécimen: February 1827, 9.

67. "lourdes psalmodies"; "pas dépourvue de grâce." *RM* spécimen: February 1827, 10.

the *Jeu*. The work's reception presents, in microcosm, the conflict in French musical historiography between learnedness and spontaneity, and between artifice and naturalness, especially when it came to defining the key qualities of a national music.

Even in 1836, the perception of the stylistic gap had widened. Bottée de Toulmon detected two distinct kinds of music in Adam de la Halle's output: music for the upper classes and music for the people. The former incorporated sacred music and the "wrong direction" of contemporaneous harmonic and polyphonic systems; the latter, the monodic *jeux* of which the *Jeu de Robin et de Marion* was one.[68] Two characteristics struck him: the force of "instinct," which drove De la Halle to write his melodies in modes close to modern tonality, then unknown as part of "what one might call their musical customs"; and the lyrical, simple [naïve] quality of the melodies themselves.[69] Significantly, naiveté is already a positive marker. He ended the article perplexed:

> Is it credible that the two types of music that I have just presented could have been the result of the same man's inspiration? The monodies are not devoid of lyricism; it is true that they are somewhat monotonous, but there is some naiveté there. Their very character has been preserved to this day in villages and mountains in the form of *complaintes* and *chansons*. By contrast, for the other music (destined for those people who claimed to be learned), only pedantry, which had demanded and welcomed it, could, alone, sustain it with any success until the moment when it was overturned by the definitive establishment of tonality, never to rise again.[70]

Separating Adam de la Halle's output into polar categories became a standard ploy after Fétis and Bottée de Toulmon. It quashed interest in anything other

---

68. "fausse route." "Adam de la Halle," *RGM* 3/51: 18 December 1836, 443; and 441. The article was taken from the *Encyclopédie catholique*.

69. "ce que l'on peut appeler leurs moeurs musicales." *RGM* 3/51: 18 December 1836, 442.

70. "Est-il croyable que les deux espèces de musique que nous venons de présenter aient été le résultat des inspirations d'un même homme? Les mélodies simples ne sont nullement dépourvues de chant; elles présentent, il est vrai, un peu de monotonie, mais on y rencontre de la naïveté; leur caractère même s'est conservé jusqu'à nos jours dans les villages et dans les montagnes sous la forme de complaintes ou de chansons. Pour l'autre musique, au contraire, destinée aux gens qui se prétendaient savans, le pédantisme seul, qui l'avait sollicitée et accueillie, put, seul aussi, la soutenir avec quelque succès jusqu'au moment où elle fut renversée par l'établissement fixe de la tonalité, pour ne se relever jamais." *RGM* 3/51: 18 December 1836, 445.

than his monodies. Eventually, even the corpus of monodic chansons was jettisoned as too mannered: by 1876, whereas the *Jeu* was "natural, easy and lyrical," De la Halle's monodic chansons had something "borrowed" and therefore unspontaneous about them. The polyphonic ones were, unsurprisingly, beyond the pale.[71] The *Jeu* thus became Adam de la Halle's signature, and only, work: known about yet hardly known, and burdened with an increasing load of cultural-nationalist baggage.

The earliest performance of the celebrated opening "air" "Robin m'aime, Robin m'a" was given not as part of one of Fétis's *concerts historiques*, as one might expect, but on 3 June 1846 at the Moskova society's last known concert. Thereafter it appears to have lain fallow until soon after the Franco-Prussian War, when a complete performance was given at the Comédie-Française, on 27 January 1872, of a version with piano accompaniment by Weckerlin. Notwithstanding the less-than-flattering portrayal of French peasantry (and particularly the weak-kneed Robin) in the *Jeu*, this was a nationalist move: the performance appeared as the opening session of an "Histoire du Théâtre de Musique" series organized under the aegis of the Société des Compositeurs de Musique, with a lecture by Edouard Fournier. It caused some embarrassment because of the unexpected presence of "ladies and even *young* ladies." Some of the bawdy language had to be toned down, and other passages cut altogether.[72] Weckerlin's score, replete with *opéra-comique* figurations, harmonized the work whose monody he was later to vaunt, his pastiche accompaniments making audible the historical link with eighteenth-century tradition on which the work's fame rested. No further performances took place until the Arras festival of 1896, organized by Tiersot, although a movement from the *Suite ancienne* for chamber orchestra by Paul Lacome based on "Robin m'aime, Robin m'a" was published in 1889.

Peasant-led modernity as expressed through the work's "tonality" provided the key to its soaring reputation, since it allowed prevalent paradigms of musical progress to be reversed. Introduced by Bottée de Toulmon, reinforced by De Coussemaker, and climaxing with Tiersot's statistical analysis of the extent of "tonality" in the *Jeu* and in a selection of *chansons populaires*, the idea seemed to demonstrate the prophetic nature of native French practice when unimpeded by art-music theory. Here was Bourgault-Ducoudray's butterfly, already out of its chrysalis. Moreover, as the Belgian organist and writer Théodore Nisard

---

71. "naturelle, facile et chantante"; "emprunté." Becker, *Aperçu sur la chanson française*, 13. On the *chansons* and the *jeux-parti* as "infinitely less clear and spontaneous" [infiniment moins nette et prime-sautière] than the *Jeu*, see also Tiersot, *Histoire de la chanson*, 420–22.

72. "des dames et même des demoiselles." *Mén* 38/10: 4 February 1872, 78 (unsigned).

argued in 1856, the singing of tunes similar to Marion's "Robin m'aime, Robin m'a" among Northern French peasant communities suggested that the work had an uninterrupted folk history.[73]

Such folk links were to be strengthened after the war. Charles Lévêque, reviewing Chouquet's monumental history of French opera, and Pougin, writing for families in his *La musique populaire*, each interpreted the fact that tunes from the *Jeu* had become folk songs as evidence of the work's fundamental character as "of the people."[74] For Lévêque, Chouquet's work had established the lineage that led, "by imperceptible degrees," from Adam de la Halle's "country songs" to the exquisite melodies of Mozart's *Le nozze*.[75] Pougin lauded music that he found fresh, seductive, gracious, artless, and spring-like.[76] Opera, tonality, and folk song links caused both authors to celebrate the *Jeu* as perhaps the most exceptional work in the French tradition. It turned the traditional (Fétisian) historiography of opera and musical expressivity on its head, since it was a tonal (and therefore, by definition, "expressive"), lyrical people's opera written in France by a Frenchman a heart-warming three centuries before Monteverdi.[77] All that was lacking, as Pougin himself admitted, was harmony and modulation. In other respects:

> One might say that, with a veritable genius of intuition, Adam de la Halle sensed and glimpsed the brilliant reform that, three centuries later, was to give dramatic music its power of expression, its power of expansion, its variety of expression, its pathetic color—which was, in a word, to make of it a modern and moving art, in bestowing it with three great capacities: pace, warmth and passion.[78]

Gradually, the "popular" ideology raised the question of cause and effect in the compositional process, prompting the suggestion that the composer might actually have borrowed from folk melodies rather than creating them. The

---

73. *Revue de musique ancienne et moderne*, October 1856, 599.
74. Lévêque in *JS* November/December 1875, 679; Arthur Pougin in *MPop* 2/22: 16 March 1882, 216.
75. "degrés insensibles"; "airs champêtres." *JS* November/December 1875, 674.
76. *MPop* 2/21: 9 March 1882, 207. He was, in part, quoting Théodore Nisard.
77. Fétis had suggested in 1827 that the *Jeu*, written in Naples, was influenced by Neapolitan culture. Not surprisingly, this particular interpretation had a limited shelf-life in the Francophone literature. *RM* spécimen: February 1827, 11.
78. "On peut dire qu'Adam de la Halle, avec un véritable génie d'intuition, a pressenti et entrevu la réforme éclatante qui, trois siècles plus tard, devait donner à la musique dramatique sa puissance d'expression, sa variété d'expression, sa couleur pathétique, qui devait, en un mot, en faire un art moderne et émouvant en lui communiquant ces trois grandes facultés: le mouvement, la chaleur et la passion." *MP* 2/23: 23 March 1882, 222.

ideological dangers of conceding that Adam de la Halle's melodies were not original could be avoided so long as it was clear that this was an opera written, effectively, by the "people." Weckerlin pondered the question, commenting that "one finds melodies which are so graceful, so superior to those which musicians had produced up to that time, that one asks oneself whether the Artesian trouvère did not borrow some elements from the popular muse."[79] Tiersot set out to prove it. Weckerlin's tactic was blatantly ideological: to appropriate Adam de la Halle for the people and to render him less of a learned musician; Tiersot's was less overtly ideological, and more far-reaching. His survey of the *chanson populaire* suggested that, far from being an original work, the *Jeu* was indeed composed of folk songs, and that it was the only work of its kind in Adam de la Halle's known output.[80] As far as he was concerned, that single fact explained its stylistic distance—noted by De Coussemaker (and others)—from De la Halle's other works.[81] Its value lay, therefore, not in originality, but in its quality as an anthology—a distillation, even—of the oldest French folk songs to have come down to the nineteenth century. As such it was "much more precious" than if it had indeed been the work of a single composer.[82] This historiographical realignment is evident in his *Histoire*. Though Tiersot titled the work as an *opéra-comique* in his edition of 1896, in 1889 he radically downplayed this traditional element of the piece's nineteenth-century signification, seeking to replace it with his new interpretation of its importance as an emanation of the French popular spirit. That is the most likely reason his main discussion of Adam de la Halle's *Jeu* is not in the portion of the book devoted to chanson and the theatre, but in that devoted to chanson and monody.

Hence the *Jeu* that the Arras audience heard in June 1896 was no re-creation of an eighteenth-century *opéra-comique*. Tiersot admitted that he had modernized the score, adding new verses to make it less fragmented, and interpolating an independent chanson, "En passant par la Lorraine." His orchestral accompaniment was, he claimed, free of futile attempts at historical authenticity (it could hardly have been otherwise), and "as discreet as possible."[83] What Tiersot did not say was that he had, by composing linking passages and relatively long orchestral introductions (one of which, featuring a flute as a symbol of Robin's flageolet, is used as a reminiscence motif), turned

---

79. "on trouve des mélodies tellement gracieuses, tellement au-dessus de ce que les musiciens avaient produit jusque-là, qu'on se demande si ce trouvère artésien ne faisait pas des emprunts à la muse populaire." Weckerlin, *La chanson populaire*, 60.

80. Tiersot, *Histoire de la chanson*, 422 (evidence presented on 424–25).

81. Tiersot, *Histoire de la chanson*, 422–23.

82. "bien plus précieux." Tiersot, *Histoire de la chanson*, 425.

83. "sans accuser aucune recherche de vaine archéologie"; "aussi discret que possible." Tiersot (Ed.), *Le jeu de Robin et de Marion* (1896), preface, n.p.

the *Jeu* into a miniature opera based not on the individual numbers of the old *opéra-comique*, but on the scene structures of through-composed opera. The dialogue remained, but the nature of the musical form had changed entirely. Like Weckerlin, Tiersot used drones to highlight the work's simple tonal character and to act as signifiers of its pastoral subject. But Tiersot's vision was very different. Some accompaniments merely underpinned the voice, in the style of folk song settings of the early nineteenth century; others were independent, using a wide accompanimental tessitura, and static chords above which the voice floated. The clearest example is his setting of Marion's "Trairideluriau, deluriau, delurère," which he asked to be sung "with a full voice and very freely, in the manner of an outdoor song," and which he accompanied in expansive style with long-held chords punctuated at the end of each phrase by hints at arpeggiation Weckerlin's interpretation could hardly have been more different. Rhythmically and metrically rigid, it follows the voice slavishly above its pedal bass, the acciaccaturas of the upper line adding little more than patterned hyperactivity (Fig. 5.1–2).[84]

Tiersot's version—more poetic, and less faithful to the original monody than Weckerlin's—realized the *Jeu* not so much as an *opéra-comique*, but as a folk opera. The spirit of Canteloube is not far away.

The Totality of Frenchness

Unsurprisingly, it was Tiersot, a friend of Bordes's and a champion of similar genres of music, who folded the arguments about the value of the *Jeu* as folk song back into an attempt to rehabilitate chanson-based masses. Tentative and inconsistent in the 1889 *Histoire*, after Bordes's reintroduction of Lassus's "Douce mémoire" on All Saints' Day 1893, he began to justify such works in a Republican spirit of nationalist secularization: they, too, were repositories of folk song. The combination of Catholic propaganda (Bordes) and Republican secularizing (Tiersot) is striking but characteristic of the Ralliement years, and emblematic of the complexity of ideological fracture lines in the history of the Schola Cantorum before D'Indy's takeover in 1903.[85]

An article for the *Tribune* in the summer of 1895 denounced Castil-Blaze, Fétis, Félix Clément, and even Charles Gounod (an avid supporter of the

---

84. "à pleine voix et très librement, dans le caractère d'un chant de plein air." Tiersot (Ed.), *Le jeu de Robin et de Marion*, 6.

85. Moreover, Jean-Pierre Noiseux has found that Bordes, though religious, was not a practicing Catholic during his Schola years. See Catrina Flint de Médicis, *The Schola Cantorum*, Chapter 2.

SOURCES OF FRENCHNESS 171

FIGURE 5.1. Adam de la Halle, *Ci commence le jeu de Robin et de Marion qu'Adam fit*, ed. Jean-Baptiste Weckerlin. Paris, 1872, p. 4. Courtesy of the Bibliothèque Nationale de France, Paris.

FIGURE 5.2A AND B. Adam de la Halle, *Le jeu de Robin et de Marion*, ed. Emile Blémont and Julien Tiersot. Paris, [1896], pp. 6–7. Courtesy of the Bibliothèque Nationale de France, Paris.

Chanteurs) for their denigration of the chanson-based mass and motet[86] and moved to a devastating critique of Haberl. In shame and embarrassment, implied Tiersot, Haberl had travestied the history of Palestrina's second, five-part "L'homme armé" mass by identifying its *cantus firmus* as a Gregorian

---

86. *TS-G* 1/5: May 1895, 1–3.

FIGURE 5.2B

melody.[87] Tiersot's alternative was to regard such masses, especially those in which the chanson was presented virtually intact as a *cantus firmus*, as a "precious and almost unique source" for the chansons themselves.[88] Yet he also subscribed to progress theories that militated against his museum spirit. Comparison of two of Bordes's chosen masses—Goudimel's "Le bien que j'ay" and Lassus's "Douce mémoire"—revealed how compositional procedure had become increasingly

87. *TS-G* 1/6: June 1895, 4–6.
88. "une source précieuse et presque unique." *TS-G* 1/5: May 1895, 4.

sophisticated during the sixteenth century, with fragmented entrances of the chosen melody replacing full (and recognizable) statements. The latter seemed preferable not only because from a religious point of view it rendered the secular source undetectable, but because it showed the individual composer mastering his material, rendering it "original": the Lassus mass belonged "as completely to Roland de Lassus as the Pope Marcellus Mass does to Palestrina."[89] In short, Tiersot had to use arguments potentially acceptable to radical Catholics to rehabilitate a repertory that he also wanted to retain as a secular museum for the vibrant French chanson tradition. Yet his arguments about composers mastering their material would have sounded, to those very Catholics, perilously close to a description of Renaissance man; and the individualism he sought to illustrate took him away from Republican celebration of an "authentic" folk song source.[90] It is no wonder that D'Indy, for instance, was both equivocal and evasive in his estimation of this repertory.[91] Despite their introduction of such works into the liturgy and in concert, the singing of chanson-based masses never became a major activity for the Chanteurs de Saint-Gervais, or of any other church choir whose activities were followed in the *Tribune*, during the nineteenth century. Neither would they ever be regarded, beyond their function as sources of French chansons, as repositories of Frenchness. The qualities of lightness, wit, piquancy, grace, and innocence would be forever denied them, while their chanson sources basked in those very epithets. Frenchness in music, as in Republican society, was ultimately secular, even during the Ralliement period of clerical and secular tolerance.

Tiersot is himself a curious figure. His *Histoire* was never to be matched, in originality or profundity, by his later writings. Quickly overtaken in his historical work by avowedly professional philologists such as Pierre Aubry, and archival historians such as Michel Brenet, he was, by 1900, effectively relegated to the ranks—to use Aubry's condescending term—of a mere musician writing about music.[92] Yet in the late 1880s and 1890s he was an important barometer of musical taste and ideology, and a crucial historiographical figure in the development of French neo-classicism because, unlike the more politically radical Weckerlin,

---

89. "aussi complètement à Roland de Lassus que la *Messe du Pape Marcel* à Palestrina." *TS-G* 1/5: May 1895, 4. The "originality" question probably comes from August Wilhelm Ambros's *Geschichte der Musik* of 1860–68 (the two texts share many similarities), in which Ambros lauded free composition over everything based on borrowed melodies, chant included, because it revealed the beginnings of a sense of compositional autonomy. For a brief discussion, see Kirkman, "From Humanism to Enlightenment," 456–58.

90. On the problem of Renaissance man, see chapter 6.

91. D'Indy found the use of chansons "profondément irreverencieux" (D'Indy, *Cours de composition musicale*, vol. 1, 146), even though in an earlier section of the treatise he describes chanson as a music emanating, ultimately, from plainchant (84).

92. For Aubry's "professional" manifesto, which includes his statement of commitment to freedom from doctrinal influence in the research of ecclesiastical history, see his *La musicologie médiévale*, v–vi, and 102.

he was prepared to underline the creative interrelationships between the aristocratic and folk traditions of France's music that reached back to the *Jeu*. In 1889 he gathered up great swathes of French music, from De la Halle to the *air de cour* to the *tragédies en musique* of Rameau, as expressive of the quintessence of musical Frenchness. Part of his eclecticism in this respect may be explained by the fact that he understood that much of the material that he recognized as folk song, and which he had presented as such for the Prix Bordin in 1885, was itself heavily mediated—taken from printings intended for the upper classes, and therefore adapted to their taste. Thoinot Arbeau's *Orchésographie*, he said, illustrated the interpenetration of the *chanson populaire* and court culture.[93] Later he argued that Ronsard was "the prince of poets and the poet of kings, but also sung by the people"[94]; and the extent to which Ronsard's texts turned up, unattributed, in sixteenth-century chanson collections indicated that he was "the most-sung French poet—before Victor Hugo."[95]

Tiersot's inclusivity thus ensured that devotion to *chanson populaire* did not necessitate the jettisoning of the multi-voice chanson, whether contrapuntal or homophonic. Quite the opposite: all could be celebrated as part of a unified chanson tradition that had enjoyed connections, at various points in its history, with the entire gamut of French society. The unifying instinct of Republicanism lies very close to the surface of his work. Like Weckerlin, Tiersot took the argument further, along the lines of Bourgault-Ducoudray's chrysalis metaphor, seeing in the *chanson populaire* a vital grass-roots culture of monody that would eventually break the stranglehold of polyphonic writing and lead not only to homophonic chansons, but also to opera. It was in this manner that he managed to forge a connection between the glories of sixteenth-century France and those of the *ancien régime* and to establish a sense of continuous filiation. For Weckerlin, chanson reached only to a limited extent into French opera (with Italian song bypassing the Florentine camerata entirely); nevertheless, in the early eighteenth century, he found unattributed melodies from Lully, Campra, Destouches, and even Rameau being published alongside street songs, which suggested a level of "popular" usage.[96] Tiersot embraced folk aspects of French opera more wholeheartedly, welcoming the popular elements in Lully and Collasse, but fixing their point of sublimation in the operas of Rameau,

---

93. Tiersot, *Histoire de la chanson populaire*, 348–50.
94. "prince des poètes et poète des rois, fut aussi chanté par le gens du peuple." Julien Tiersot, *Ronsard et la musique de son temps* [article originally printed in the *Société internationale de musique*, 1902–1903], 9.
95. "le poète de France qui ait le plus été chanté—avant Victor Hugo." Tiersot, *Ronsard et la musique de son temps*, 11.
96. Weckerlin, *La chanson populaire*, 147–48, 153.

whose music united all the characteristics and gifts of the French race. His stage works were

> in such marvellous accord with the most ancient and most permanent instincts of the nation that he himself became, in reality, a "popular" musician. His *airs de danse*, these airs which are so svelte, and band-box fresh, of which Diderot said that they would "last for ever," become chanson tunes. People adapt new words to them, and in this new form, they gain renewed success and lasting fortune.[97]

For Tiersot, a diehard Ramiste, the composer's importance lay in the fact that he embodied the popular spirit while not sacrificing his originality to it. A composer divorced from the ancient tradition of *chanson populaire* had nevertheless brought it to fruition in tragic opera, writing *chansons populaires* for the stage in the guise, tellingly, of *airs de danse*.[98] With this sublimation of the popular spirit in France's greatest composer of early opera, Tiersot reached the climax of his book's historical narrative.[99]

For the cultural historian, there is no better intellectual model than the work of Julien Tiersot for understanding the significance that Bordes and the early Schola Cantorum attached to the national repertories of sixteenth-century chanson and early French opera, and that Diémer and the Société des Instruments Anciens attached to French dance of the Renaissance and Baroque periods. Together, they formed a closed circle of musics that were at once popular and noble and contained the very sap of Frenchness. They included music from the reigns of two artistically celebrated monarchs—François I and Louis XIV—reaching back, in spirit, to the character of that first "anthology" of French chanson, Adam de la Halle's *Jeu de Robin et de Marion*, and forward to that of Louis XV. They illustrated the native wit, elegance, and vitality of a French tradition that could be traced from the late thirteenth century to contemporary rural culture, where parts of it remained alive and well, unaided by historians. Here was a patriotic, rather than a nationalistic, model of "collective

---

97. "est en si merveilleux accord avec les instincts les plus anciens et les plus permanents de la nation, qu'il devient lui-même, en réalité, un musicien populaire. Ses airs de danse, ces airs si sveltes et si pimpants, à propos desquels Diderot disait qu'ils dureraient éternellement, deviennent des airs de chansons. On y adapte des paroles et, sous cette forme nouvelle, ils obtiennnent un nouveau succès et font une fortune durable." Tiersot, *Histoire de la chanson populaire*, 508–509.

98. Tiersot, *Histoire de la chanson populaire*, 509.

99. His final chapter, on nineteenth-century uses of folk song, acts as a coda on the vitality of French folk-song-based composition (equalled only by the Russians). Tiersot, *Histoire de la chanson populaire*, 528–36.

memory" that clearly differentiated French culture from that of both Italy and Germany, without "othering" either, and which could fundamentally change the historiographical meaning of *la musique française*. For the first time in the nineteenth century, a solution had been found to the dead-end of describing French music as the *juste milieu* between two dominant foreign cultures. It was not for nothing that in 1902 Lionel Dauriac, then professor of musical aesthetics at the Sorbonne, found "France's musical soul" in Tiersot's *Histoire*.[100]

---

100. "l'âme musicale de la France." *La revue latine*, 1/1: 25 January 1902, 61. The article was entitled "Avons-nous encore une Musique française?"

6

Defining Palestrina

Fétis called it *"fashionnable"* as early as 1827 but remained skeptical of its value as expressive music.[1] By the beginning of the twentieth century it was enshrined, second only to Gregorian chant, as an appropriate vehicle for the Catholic liturgy in the *Motu proprio* of Pope Pius X on 22 November 1903.[2] Counter-Reformation polyphony was a focus for debate throughout the period, its revival geographically widespread and uneasily shared between church and concert hall. Palestrina himself held a special place, as indeed he had since Hoffmann's essay "Alte und neue Kirchenmusik" of 1814. Canonized as the savior of sacred music because the Pope Marcellus Mass had changed the course of liturgical music history, his importance to the French was elevated still higher through the idea, not reversed until 1895, that he was Goudimel's pupil.[3] As part of the liturgy, Palestrinian music appeared sporadically during the July Monarchy, gathered momentum in the pro-Catholic climate of the Second Empire, and thrived during the Third Republic (despite anticlerical attacks) until the advent of Emile Combes's government in 1902. From the point of

---

1. *RM* 1 (no. 7): March 1827, 188. Italics original.
2. For the text of Pius X's edict, see Hayburn, *Papal Legislation on Sacred Music*, 195–249.
3. These two myths were retold and elaborated in almost every biographical article on Palestrina, from the "proto-musicological" to the "coffee-table," and in many reviews. They were the foundation on which his fame rested. For a detailed examination of famous myths and stories in musical biography more generally, see Wiley, *Re-writing Composers' Lives*.

view of certain Catholic musical reformers, the timing of Pius X's *Motu proprio* was thus poignant indeed, serving to institutionalize Gregorian chant and Palestrinian polyphony in the Catholic liturgy at precisely the point when relations between the Vatican and the French government were frayed beyond repair. Combes would break off diplomatic ties with the Vatican in July 1904; the law formalizing the separation of Church and State, with its attendant funding cuts and its appropriations of church property, was passed (now under Maurice Rouvier's ministry) the following year.

The ideological, religious, and aesthetic modes of reception that attended Palestrinian music had far-reaching implications. Modes of performance were, until the 1890s, intimately related to Fétisian historiographical theories concerning the aesthetic implications of a shift, at the end of the sixteenth century, from what he termed the *ordre unitonique* of modal music to the *ordre pluritonique* of tonal harmony.[4] For Fétis this shift constituted progress; for French pro-Palestrinians and liturgical reformers (as for many of their German counterparts), the questions, as we shall see, were more complex.[5] From this shared starting-point, French writers developed often contradictory arguments relating to the repertory's aesthetic, liturgical, and political significance. Palestrina's totemization as a symbol of mystical purity and sanctity was quickly established, underpinned by nationalist myth and a selective approach to repertory that winnowed out ideologically inappropriate works. Yet there were crosscurrents. From the 1830s, when liturgical reform was of paramount importance among Ultramontane Catholics anxious to return to the fold of Roman tradition, Palestrinian music became a contested area, its claims to liturgical appropriateness hampered by its popularity as concert music and measured disadvantageously against those of Gregorian chant.[6] Whereas Romantics had described Palestrina as in some sense "gothic" and, therefore, "medieval,"[7] radical Ultramontanes began to seize on his "newness" and antitraditionalism in order to designate him a "Renaissance man." In doing so they followed a tradition in art and architectural history which, stemming from the medievalism of Chateaubriand's *Génie du Christianisme* of 1802, presented the late fifteenth and sixteenth centuries as a decadent period of rampant individualism and—

---

4. Fétis's notion was a theoretically enriched version of the historical narrative presented by Choron and Fayolle in 1810. See their *Dictionnaire historique des musiciens*, vol. 1, xxxiv–xliv, esp. xxxiv.

5. On German responses, see Garratt, *Palestrina*, esp. 36–42 and 57–61.

6. In France the tradition begins, of course, in 1833 with the establishment of a Benedictine community at Solesmes under the guidance of Dom Prosper Guéranger. For an excellent comparative study of the Catholic revival in England, France, and Germany (which does not, however, give music more than a cursory glance), see Franklin, *Nineteenth-Century Churches*.

7. See Haar, "Music of the Renaissance," and Vendrix, "'La musique montait'," esp. 22–26.

crucially—secularization.⁸ In contrast to Protestant Germany, for instance, where comparisons with a golden age of Renaissance art (that was itself dignified by its evocation of ancient Graeco-Roman sublimity) tended to blend several centuries into a homogeneous period of Middle-Ages naiveté, the French created a politicized divide.⁹ The 1890s provided a historiographical corrective that was equally political: pro-Palestrinians wrenched their hero back into the medieval era, now defining the musical "Renaissance" as a belated cultural flowering that began only with Italian monody of c.1600. Palestrina thus returned to being the culmination of the "medieval" period—safe from the nefarious influences of humanism, Protestantism, and individualism. Such historiographical rupture only underlines the extent to which musical interpretations were driven by ideological, rather than aesthetic, concerns.

The relationship of the French Palestrina revival to the classic Gallican/Ultramontane divide is equally complex, not least because although Palestrina's reputation was inseparable from considerations of national pride, his natural supporters were Ultramontanes (and of course Ultramontanes, pledging allegiance to the Vatican first and to Parisian/French episcopal governance second, were not obvious patriots). Following the Ultramontane gains of the 1830s and '40s, under Louis-Napoléon the Roman Rite replaced local Gallican liturgies in numerous cathedrals and parish churches; by the time of the vote, in 1869/70, on Papal Infallibility at the First Vatican Council, Gallican bishops were in a small (though in many cases determined) minority.¹⁰ Only with the new patriotism of the Third Republic did the Ultramontane cause—now almost synonymous with "the Catholic cause"—experience significant setbacks, on account of basic Republican anticlericalism on the one hand and perceptions of lack of patriotism on the other. It would take the clergy/army coalition of the Dreyfus Affair in the late 1890s to cement Ultramontanism and patriotism.¹¹

In line with most other French musicians, however, Gallican reformists did not champion the music of Gallicanism's most glorious period—Lalande and Rameau. In fact, while radical Ultramontanes invariably favored Gregorian chant as the sole legitimate music for liturgical use, reformist Gallicans

---

8. See Bullen, *The Myth of the Renaissance*, 59–90.

9. See Garratt, *Palestrina*, 47–49. For a Viennese Catholic interpretation, that of August Wilhelm Ambros in vol. 3 of his *Geschichte der Musik* (1868), see Perkins, "Published Editions," 110–13.

10. Gough, *Paris and Rome*, v.

11. Ralph Gibson, "Why Republicans and Catholics Couldn't Stand Each Other," 116. However, in his account of separatism before Dreyfus, Gibson crucially omits reference to the Ralliement years of the early 1890s, when monarchists (many of them Catholic) and conservative Republicans were just as likely to join forces against radicals on the Left as to battle along traditional party lines. For a detailed account of relations between the Vatican and Paris in the 1890s under Pope Leo XIII, see Larkin, *Religion, Politics and Preferment*, esp. 53–58.

and moderate Ultramontanes tended to club together in favor of Palestrinian and *stile antico* music as the necessary complement to chant. Indeed it is a measure of the level of disparagement of *la musique française* (and potentially its royalist connections) that the moderate Ultramontane preferences should have won over Gallicanism's traditional chauvinism in this regard. However, it also explains why some of the key cathedrals of the Palestrinian revival had Gallican bishops (Blanquart de Bailleul at Rouen in the 1850s; Marguerye at Autun in the late 1860s), and why we find Gallicans acting as patrons of the Société des Concerts de l'Ecole de Musique Religieuse on its foundation in 1872 (Le Courtier, Bishop of Montpellier; Dupanloup, Bishop of Orléans). Likewise, at Langres, where a Roman revival was instituted by the Ultramontane Mgr Parisis (Bishop of Langres, 1835–51), the cathedral continued its Palestrinian traditions under the moderate Gallican Mgr Guérrin, diocesan bishop from 1852 to his death in 1877.

The Goudimel Connection

Questions of national pride helped ensure that the Palestrina works to achieve greatest popularity were either predominantly homophonic works tied to the solemn festivals of Holy Week, works with the allure of harmonized chant, or those that were more antiphonal than polyphonic. This stylistic preference was actually pan-European, resulting, as I have noted, in the irony that certain inauthentic works, such as the Ingegneri responsories for Holy Week (misattributed), and the homophonic "Adoramus te" (fake), became Palestrina's most celebrated compositions in Germany, France, and England. However, the French had more reason than either the Germans or the English to value homophony. The further removed from Franco-Flemish "fracas" Palestrina could appear, the better; hence the ideological fervor of the emphasis on the calm nobility of pure harmony, to which I shall return.[12] The French approach was thus the opposite of that of, for example, Kiesewetter and Ambros in Vienna, who sought both to emphasize and to celebrate Palestrina's northern European (specifically Netherlandish) ancestry.[13] It was the characteristic element of harmony, said Choron and Fayolle in 1810, that distinguished Palestrina's style from the fugal practice of his predecessors.[14]

---

12. Choron and Fayolle, *Dictionnaire historique des musiciens*, vol. 1, xlvii and ii, 117–18
13. See Perkins, "Published Editions," 106 and 114.
14. Choron and Fayolle, *Dictionnaire historique des musiciens*, vol. 1, xlvii. For obvious reasons, the fact that Palestrina, the composer of the purest, most seraphic music imaginable, had written two "L'homme armé"

Nevertheless, one predecessor had to function as a bridge between the untouchable and the saintly. That predecessor was Goudimel: Palestrina's French teacher.

The problem of identifying Palestrina's teachers had troubled historians since the seventeenth century. Everyone had to return to the reference to "Gaudio Mell, fiamingo" by Antimo Liberati (1685) and to find him a plausible identity. And while Hawkins (1776) had mocked the idea that it might have been Goudimel (on account of his Protestantism), Burney (1789) expressed doubt and suggested alternatives but left the case open. Choron and Fayolle also hedged their bets: their Goudimel entry proclaimed him as Palestrina's teacher; the Palestrina entry plumped for an unnamed Franco-Flemish master.[15] However, after Giuseppe Baini's mammoth biography (1828) and its French summary by his pupil Adrien de Lafage, there was to be no doubt in French minds but that Goudimel had taught Palestrina in Rome. As De Lafage put it, Baini "refutes the opinion of Burney and of all those who have confused Goudimel with a Claudio Mell, of whom nothing is known; with a Renauld de Mel, who came to Rome only in 1580, [or] with René de Mel, who by all accounts never set foot there."[16]

The extent of what was at stake becomes clear if we look at the Belgian side of the historiography. In his 1829 *mémoire*, Fétis claimed that Palestrina's teacher was not Goudimel, but that very same Rinaldo [Renauld] del Mel, a Belgian from Liège, the preface to whose 1588 book of madrigals indicated that he had indeed taught in Rome at the relevant time. By contrast, wrote Fétis in 1829, Goudimel had never been in Rome.[17] Goudimel was, in any case, a "mediocre" composer, in terms of his learning.[18]

Fétis's search for an alternative to Goudimel was prompted by Burney's surmise that Goudimel was already Huguenot when in Rome and that it was therefore implausible for him to have taught Catholic musicians. But Fétis soon decided that the evidence of Goudimel's Catholic compositions from the

---

masses tended to be downplayed in nineteenth-century accounts of his music. I have yet to find any mention of a nineteenth-century French performance of either of them. The stock term "le style palestrinien" (which I invoke here and elsewhere in the interests of hermeneutic fidelity) was thus slippery, endowing Palestrina's music with a false homogeneity.

15. Choron and Fayolle, *Dictionnaire historique des musiciens*, vol. 1, 285 (Goudimel); vol. 2, 117 (Palestrina).

16. "... réfute l'opinion de Burney et de tous ceux qui ont confondu Goudimel avec un Claudio Mell, dont on n'a aucune connaissance; avec Renaud de Mel, qui ne vint à Rome qu'en 1580, avec René de Mel, qui, selon toute apparence, n'y a jamais mis le pied . . . ," *RM* September 1829, 197. De Lafage never finished this mammoth review of Baini's *Memorie storico-critiche*. On Baini's hagiography of Palestrina, see Kirkman, "'Under such heavy chains'," esp. 96–102.

17. Fétis, *Quels ont été les mérites*, 45.

18. "médiocre." Fétis, *Quels ont été les mérites*, 45.

late 1580s militated against this interpretation. In a rare admission of error, he retracted his 1829 account in the *Biographie universelle* entry of 1837, conceding (wrongly, as it happens) that Goudimel had worked in Rome,[19] and restoring, in the articles on Goudimel and Palestrina respectively, both the traditional historiography of his Roman school and his teaching of Palestrina. Moreover, in 1837 he did not present Goudimel's psalms of 1565 as liturgical music—instead, he described them as destined for private Catholic devotion. They were therefore unthreatening. And toward the end of the article Fétis even attempted to save Goudimel from the taint of Protestantism by claiming that he became Huguenot almost without realizing it, and only belatedly, in 1565.[20] Finally, the composer was no longer mediocre, but "undoubtedly a learned musician and a good teacher," whose purity of harmony offered a pre-echo of the Pope Marcellus Mass.[21] The ideological imperative was clear: now that he had "established" that Goudimel had indeed taught Palestrina, Fétis had to make this Franco-Flemish musician worthy of the honor.

After 1829, French writers did not need to employ such compensatory tactics: most of them simply treated Palestrina's master with unusual respect. De Lafage had himself quoted Liberati's view that Goudimel's style was "full of grace and sweetness."[22] But that Goudimel was John the Baptist to Palestrina's Messiah came through most strongly in Danjou's "Archives curieuses de la musique" (1839–40). Here, in his evolutionary journey through early music history, Danjou placed a chorale by Goudimel (the score headed "maître de Palestrina") next to that of his famous pupil (ironically, the fake "Adoramus te"), noting in his commentary, "The regeneration of sacred music today depends on detailed study and knowledge of these great models."[23] The fact that the Goudimel and "Palestrina" items that he selected were each almost entirely homophonic was crucial to the implicit point. This was an illustration of how far Goudimel had brought Palestrina from the "ridiculous" practices of Josquin. What characterized this "eminently religious" music was its "noble and majestic character."[24]

Perhaps the most telling evidence for such an interpretation is the lack of emphasis and the almost complete lack of adverse comment given to Goudimel's conversion, an uncomfortable historical fact for many supporters

---

19. Fétis, *Biographie universelle*, 1st ed., vol. 4 (1837), 379, 382.
20. Fétis, *Biographie universelle*, 1st ed., vol. 4 (1837), 380–81.
21. "certainement un musicien instruit et un bon professeur." Fétis, *Biographie universelle*, 1st ed., vol. 4 (1837), 381–82, and vol. 7 (1841), 144.
22. "plein de grâce et de douceur." *RM* September 1829, 197.
23. "La régénération de la musique sacrée depend [sic] aujourd'hui de l'étude approfondie et de la connaissance de ces beaux modèles." *RGM* 6/47: 15 September 1839, 376 and supplement.
24. "éminemment religieuse"; "caractère noble et majestueux." *RGM* 6/47: 15 September 1839, 376.

of Palestrina's music, not least because for almost all of them the story of the Pope Marcellus Mass underpinned Palestrina's status as the savior of musical Catholicism.[25] Not surprisingly, as radical Ultramontanism gained ground this position of evasion became increasingly fraught. For although Goudimel's conversion dated from the late 1550s or early 1560s (well after his supposed teaching of Palestrina), his perceived contribution to the retreat from Catholic excess could also be interpreted as the polluting influence of someone already predisposed to the extremes of the Reformed church. The Third-Republic Protestant version of the Counter-Reformation myth, for instance, identified precisely this connection but proffered the opposite conclusion: that Palestrina's music was good because it was so "reformed" as to be effectively Protestant.[26] Moderate Ultramontanes found themselves caught between these two positions. They had to protect Palestrina from all hint of Protestantism; yet they had no option but to side with Protestant historiography on the question of the necessity of musical reform. After all, they were themselves using Palestrina to bring about a second purging of secular practices from liturgical repertories— a re-enactment of the Counter-Reformation project.

As we have seen, in 1837 Fétis was loath to admit that Goudimel's conversion was either historically certain or willed. Goudimel's four-part psalm settings of 1565 proved nothing, he claimed, about his supposed intention to abandon Catholicism: "but it is to be expected that after the success of this collection of psalms, French Protestants would have made every effort to recruit an artist of such great renown, and that the composer might have found himself engaged in the new religion almost without knowing it."[27] Goudimel was thus excused the embarrassment of having exercised free will, but only at the price of being portrayed as spectacularly naïve. Fétis did not discuss Goudimel's religious beliefs in his *Biographie universelle* entry on Palestrina. In the 1840s, Delécluze insulated Palestrina from any hint of proto-Huguenot influence by making it clear that Goudimel's conversion took place well after his Rome years.[28] By contrast, Bellaigue was silent on the subject of Goudimel's religious leanings in his 1894 biographical article on Palestrina. Instead, he presented the general "severity" of the epoch in which Palestrina lived, combined

---

25. Delécluze, "Palestrina," *Revue de Paris* (henceforth *RP*), October 1842, 315; Bellaigue, *RDM* 15 October 1894, 849.

26. Douen, *Clément Marot*, vol. 2, 369–70.

27. "mais il est vraisemblable qu'après le succès du recueil des psaumes, les réformés de France auront fait des efforts pour attirer à eux un artiste de si grande renommée, et que le compositeur se sera trouvé engagé presque sans le savoir dans la nouvelle religion." Fétis, "Goudimel," *Biographie universelle*, 1st ed., vol. 4 (1837), 381. This passage appears unchanged in the second edition of 1860–65.

28. *RP* October 1842, 261.

with his exposure to Franco-Flemish tradition, as factors that produced his uniqueness as "the musician of a particular Italy, but not of Italy herself."²⁹ Palestrina's training and formative experiences had made him more sober, more inward-looking, and more philosophical than the typical Italian (graphic) artist as described by Hippolyte Taine in his *Philosophie d'art*; his music presented a mixture of what Taine had described as quintessentially German and Italian features. Drawing on Taine's theory of "race, milieu, moment," Bellaigue universalized Palestrina, arguing in true Ultramontane fashion that he stood "outside, if not above" his race, while also emphasizing his French connections.³⁰ In line with a long intellectual tradition that perceived Frenchness in music as a judicious balance between the extremes of the Italian and the German, and in which figures such as Gluck, Piccinni, and Meyerbeer were appropriated into the national canon, he all but claimed Palestrina as a composer of French music, his Italian ebullience tempered by the sobering (but not ostensibly proto-Huguenot) influence of Goudimel's teaching.³¹

Among Palestrina's supporters, historical, historiographical, and nationalistic elements converged to make many of these outcomes predictable. For many, it was only by disengaging Palestrinian repertory from the taint of both Franco-Flemish contrapuntalism and the Protestant chorale that the composer's status as the savior of Church music could be ensured. Nevertheless, it was by focusing on the sublimity of Palestrina's harmony rather than the detail of his counterpoint that the Romantics in particular (and they included Catholics) were able to invest it with a grand expressivity that chimed with their own preferences.³² For them it was the paradoxical combination of evenness and unpredictability, newness and antiquity in the music's harmonic progress, that contributed so powerfully to its otherworldly allure.

---

29. "le musicien d'une certaine Italie et non d'Italie." *RDM* 15 October 1894, 870. In view of the vexed relationship between the Vatican and Italy after unification this comment might also, of course, be barbed. The Vatican did not (and does not) belong to Italy.

30. "en dehors, peut-être au-dessus de sa race." *RDM* 15 October 1894, 871. This was, of course, a French-inflected variant of the idea, given in Ambros's *Geschichte der Musik* (vol. 3) of 1868, that Palestrina's Italian nature had been tempered by Netherlandish severity. See Perkins, "Published Editions," 111.

31. Only the following year the historian Marie Bobillier, writing as Michel Brenet, stopped this kind of debate in its tracks by arguing that there existed no evidence for Goudimel's Roman school. With characteristic perspicacity and directness, Bobillier detailed the pro-Palestrinian and anti-Catholic arguments surrounding his activities and prepared to flick down the entire house of cards: what would become of such arguments, she wrote, if one day it turned out that Goudimel had never been in Rome? *GM* 41/4: 27 January 1895, 75–77, at 75.

32. On the implications of this opposition, see my "Berlioz, the Sublime, and the *Broderie* Problem." Garratt notes that German Romantics saw in Palestrina a classicized sublime which they also detected in eighteenth-century German traditions—thereby distancing them from the taint of the (French) Enlightenment. See Garratt, *Palestrina*, 45–46, and 55–56.

Palestrina as a Mystical Monument

In concert, the Palestrinian revival was effected spasmodically, through private groups whose directors often had strong church connections, and in schools of sacred music. It was a revival headed by enthusiasts: Choron in the 1820s and '30s, Moskova and De Lafage in the 1840s, Joseph Régnier in Nancy in the 1850s, Niedermeyer from the 1850s onwards, Vervoitte in the 1860s, Lefèvre (again at the Ecole Niedermeyer) in the 1870s, and Bordes in the 1890s. Slow, soft, tender, and sung by large choirs was how nineteenth-century Parisian audiences first heard this music. Choron's choir set a trend that was broken only rarely in the ensuing half century, and which Fétis described with admiration as "a hundred singers performing, in *piano*, a long, legato, unaccompanied choral piece."[33] Moskova, Niedermeyer, and Vervoitte continued the tradition; only Bordes, seemingly, dissented from the custom of massed singing *à demi-voix*.[34] As Choron described it, there was "something supernatural" about the sound of a large choir singing quietly.[35] The outcome must have been a veiled monumentality in which the staggering of individual singers' breathing—which Moskova, for instance, explicitly requested—contributed to the production of a velvety sound of almost orchestral continuity.[36]

On his deathbed, Choron reportedly situated Palestrina's music as the junction between "one immense ocean whose waves roll calmly and with majesty" and another, "whose furious waves reach to the sky and then suddenly plunge down into the abyss."[37] If the report is accurate, then he was, in addition to appealing to a stock trope of the Romantic sublime, placing Palestrina squarely in a Fétisian historiographical tradition whereby modern tonality was a prerequisite for conventional musical expressivity. Yet he was also blurring a crucial issue: if Palestrina's music formed the junction between two styles, what was its relationship to each? Was it not a peculiarly elusive form of *juste*

---

33. "cent chanteurs qui exécutent *piano* un longue morceau à voix soutenue sans accompagnement." *RM* February 1827, 91.

34. For more detail, see my "Palestrina et la musique dite 'palestrinienne,'" 159–69.

35. The full text reads: "Exécuté de cette manière, elle produit un effet extraordinaire, qui a réellement quelque chose de surnaturel et qui justifie la qualification de genre sublime, que les maîtres de tous les temps ont exclusivement et unanimement décernée au style de Palestrina." Choron, "Observations préliminaires" to his *Collection de pièces de musique religieuse* [1820], n.p.

36. Moskova, preface, *Recueil des morceaux de musique religieuse*, n.p.

37. "un immense océan dont les flots roulent avec calme et majesté"; "dont les vagues furieuses s'élèvent jusqu'au ciel, puis tout à coup s'enfoncent dans l'abîme." Given in Hippolyte Réty, *Notice historique sur Choron*, 19. See also Gautier, in his *Eloge d'Alexandre Choron*, 97.

milieu, rather than a fully medieval, or fully modern, style? The question vexed even Fétis, whose melodramatic likening in 1859 of the "feeling of terror" that characterized Palestrina's *Stabat mater*, and the rending of the temple curtain on the death of Christ (Matthew 28: 51), contradicted the majority of his evaluations of what he himself categorized as inferior, pretonal, music.[38] The tensions in Fétis's thinking are evident in the writings of several critics and musicians when they attempt to define the distinction between Palestrinian music and "dramatic" music, while preserving for Palestrina the aesthetic dignity of expressivity. Despite his own fascination with early music and his eclectic, Cousin-inspired philosophy, Fétis was, like so many others, seduced by the Comtian idea that civilization progressed towards a state of perfection.[39] Monteverdi's "discovery" of the dominant seventh marked the beginning of a music capable of expressing human emotion. That, for him, was welcome; for Ultramontane Palestrinians and Romantics looking to recapture the otherworldliness of the gothic, it was not. So when Fétis characterized Palestrina's religious music as "devoid of worldly passions," others followed, but often in order to overturn his value judgements.[40] The question of "dramatic passion" (with its implications of humanist individualism) or its absence (with concomitant implications of medieval collectivism) lay accordingly at the heart of Palestrina's reception throughout the century.

Among the writers who inverted Fétis's evaluations, members of the Couturier family, at Langres cathedral, were among the most fanatical.[41] For them, Monteverdi's break from ecclesiastical modes was an abhorrent act of violence against sacred music, forcing its composers into the world of the emotions. It was "a violation of form, which rightly caused Monteverdi to be attacked passionately by the partisans of the old harmonic system, Artusi in particular. A complete and generalized violation, which one of the most learned theorists of the nineteenth century calls the *annihilation* of the old harmony, the *death* of the old tonality."[42] In 1835 Fétis had used the same word "anéantir" to describe

---

38. "sentiment de terreur." *RGM*, 26/38: 10 September 1859, 311.

39. See my *Music Criticism*, 33–45.

40. "dépouillé de passions terrestres." Fétis, *Biographie universelle*, 1st ed., vol. 1 (1837), ccx.

41. The Couturiers prepared their own editions of music for the *maîtrise*, printed at the Cathedral "zincographie." Several pieces are works *alla Palestrina* signed N.-M. Couturier; the collections also contain most of the works of Palestrina, Lassus, and Victoria (both authentic and misattributed or fake) that were known in the 1860s.

42. "violation formelle, qui a valu à Monteverde les vives attaques des partisans de l'harmonie ancienne, d'Artusi en particulier. Violation complète, violation totale, que l'un des plus savants théoriciens du XIXe siècle appelle l'*anéantissement* de l'ancienne harmonie, la *mort* de l'ancienne tonalité." Couturier and Couturier, *Décadence et restauration*, 17–18.

the tonal revolution for which he crowned the same Monteverdi; it is difficult not to conclude that, in 1862, the Couturiers were deliberately turning his words back on him.⁴³ In secular circles, and in relation to the border area of *mondaine* societies dedicated to moral regeneration, we find the same ideas (mostly without the attendant anger) throughout the century—up to and including the *Motu proprio* of 1903.

The absence of conflicts, of compositional extremes, of climactic gestures and of apparent individuality in, specifically, Palestrina's music, is interpreted in a similar vein by the majority of critics of the period. In a sketchbook dating from 1844–49 in the hand of Paul Scudo, Palestrina's music is praised as the embodiment of "serenity, calm, elevation and grandeur."⁴⁴ But this pure and reflective music offered its listeners something more: critics wrote as though it were a new therapy to help them cope with the stresses of modern urban life, lulling them into a state of meditative bliss perilously close to sensual pleasure. For Henri Blanchard, this tranquil and easily flowing music contained no element that might disturb the soul—on the contrary, Palestrina's works were a music of reassurance and comfort. The Pope Marcellus Mass, he wrote in 1856, "lulls one in a kind of divine ideality."⁴⁵ Choron's biographer Hippolyte Réty detected "something chaste, pure, tranquil, which consoles the Christian soul and cradles it in a celestial embrace"⁴⁶; for Delécluze in 1842 such music brought to his soul "a feeling of well-being, a state of sweet ravishment, in which one would like to stay for ever"⁴⁷; even Berlioz admitted that "the music's purity and tranquility lulls one into a state of suspended animation that has a charm of its own."⁴⁸ Whereas the perception of cool chasteness was fueled by various versions of the Pope Marcellus Mass story, the myth also revealed Palestrina's skill as a composer negotiating a middle way between self-indulgence and abstinence: no wonder it was during the July Monarchy, with its *juste milieu* values and politics, that Palestrina's reputation was secured. And no wonder that Lassus and Victoria remained secondary in terms

---

43. Fétis, *Biographie universelle*, 1st ed., vol. 1, ccxxiii. However, it is worth remembering that in the *Allgemeine musikalische Zeitung* of 1834 Karl Emil Schafhäutl (writing as "Pellisov") had described the unprepared seventh chord rather pithily as "like an evil spirit among the heavenly host." See Garratt, *Palestrina*, 140.

44. "la sérénité, le calme, l'élévation et la grandeur." [Paul Scudo], "Notes d'un critique musical," Bibliothèque Royale Albert Iᵉʳ, Brussels (ML 2916), 103.

45. "vous berce d'une sorte d'idéalité divine." *RGM* 23/28: 13 July 1856, 222.

46. "quelque chose de chaste, de pur, de tranquille, qui console l'âme chrétienne et la berce dans un céleste ravissement." Réty, *Etudes historiques sur le chant religieux*, 138, given in De Rohan-Csermak, "La canonisation de Palestrina," 208.

47. "un bien-être, un ravissement doux, où l'on voudrait toujours se maintenir." *RP* October 1842, 326.

48. Berlioz, *Memoirs*, 218. For a discussion of Berlioz's paradoxical view of Palestrina, see Lespinard, "Berlioz et la restauration de Palestrina."

of compositional "purity": the first too dramatic and the second too emotional. Yet, like Louis-Philippe's version of constitutional monarchy, the *juste milieu* oxymoron of Palestrina's passionless expressivity was never convincingly resolved. For those not enamored of the style, its purity could make it too elusive: in comparison with Handel's full-blooded music, Maurice Germa (writing in 1875 as Maurice Cristal) found Palestrina's to be characterized by "the monastic coolness and the languid pallor of nuns in the cloister."[49] Nevertheless, the trope was given new impetus in the wake of Bordes's Holy Week services, from 1892 onward, at Saint-Gervais. The trusty Bellaigue's comments of 1894 are typical: that the Palestrinian style expressed "the idea, and not the form"; that it "never contained anything of the picturesque or exterior"; and, even more significantly, that "the body and the flesh are absent from this art."[50]

Such responses had partly to do with the music's combination of modality and elements that were perceived as proto-tonal. In 1810 Choron had noted that in Palestrina's music, the feeling of modern tonality made itself felt in the most decisive of ways, without however making him forget that of the ancients.[51] Fétis's word *"fashionnable"* of 1827 conveys the same novelty, together with an explicit sense of the passing phase. But as a sense of tradition became increasingly important to artists and musicians alike, symbolic meetings of minds caused more profound comment. One such "meeting" took place on 28 April 1864 at the funeral of the painter Hippolyte Flandrin, who had himself helped to rekindle interest in religious art of the sixteenth century. Adrien Gros, *maître de chapelle* at Saint-Germain-des-Prés, programmed two extracts from a Palestrina mass alongside music by Ambroise Thomas. In including the Palestrina, perhaps he intended to present music that closely mirrored Flandrin's own interests; at least one critic thought so. Here, wrote an ecstatic Louis Roger, was a homage "well rendered"; Palestrina and Flandrin appeared as an "image of living tradition": hand in hand across history, they provided a model of veneration for young artists.[52]

In practice, that veneration also encouraged a tendency, especially before the advent of Bordes, to hear all Palestrinian music as harmonic rather than

---

49. "la froideur monacale et la pâleur alanguie des religieuses dans le cloître," *CM* 8 (no. 43): 1 April 1875, 31.
50. "l'idée et non la figure"; "n'a jamais rien de pittoresque ni d'extérieur"; "le corps et la chair sont absents de cet art." *RDM* 15 October 1894, 863, 865, 866.
51. Choron and Fayolle, *Dictionnaire historique des musiciens*, vol. 1, xlvii.
52. "adroitement rendu"; "une image de la tradition vivante"; "Ils se donnent la main dans l'histoire." Review in *RMSAM* 5/7: 15 May 1864, col. 204. Roger's account of Meyerbeer's funeral, which followed that of Flandrin's, provides a striking contrast.

contrapuntal. Using more imagery derived from Choron mythology, Roger wrote of the music's "great and sovereign harmony," which sent out its "austere waves" into the church.[53] Berlioz described the "Popule meus" of the *Improperia* as representative of the Palestrinian style[54]; using unusually classical imagery, Delécluze likened his chordal progressions to the strains of an Aeolian harp[55]; for Jules Carlez, comparing *Stabat* settings by Palestrina, Pergolesi, and Rossini, Palestrinia's "majestic consonant chords" offered respite from the "enervating harmonies of dramatic music."[56] All these writers were perfectly aware of the contrapuntal processes at work in the majority of Palestrina's music then available in print; they prefered, however, to typecast it as a succession of nonfunctional harmonies.

Two streams of thought—one Ultramontane, one Romantic—contributed to such modes of listening. Community, as against (Gallican) individualism, was central to Ultramontane visions of a new Catholicism, so it is hardly surprising that supporters of Palestrina as an ideal of church music should have alighted on the music's harmonic, rather than its contrapuntal, aspects. For only in its guise as a series of consonances could it easily fulfil the condition of a music that embodied concerted action.[57] In addition, the timbral homogeneity of interpretation favored by Choron and others would have encouraged the same conclusion, smoothing out vocal entries and rendering contrapuntal detail inaudible in all but the most intimate performing spaces. The music, frequently described as sublime in the sense that it was a music comprising vast expanses of unadorned simplicity, was rendered so by an Ultramontane performance style that became dominant in both liturgical and concert culture. It was, moreover, presented as medieval by an anachronistic comparison with styles of architecture (such as at the cathedrals of Notre-Dame, Rouen, and Bourges) that antedated the music by up to three centuries.

Crucial also were Romantic images of distance, both historical and spatial. One of the most striking features common to critiques of Palestrinian music is that of disembodied sound emanating from the semidarkness of large churches. As early as 1838 we find an educational text comparing Palestrina's music to incense: its harmony, rising in clouds, likewise symbolizes the carrying of prayers

---

53. "grande et souveraine harmonie"; "ondes sévères." *RMSAM* 5/7: 15 May 1864, col. 204.
54. Berlioz, *Memoirs*, 218.
55. *RP* October 1842, 326.
56. "ces majestueux accords consonnants"; "énervantes harmonies de la musique dramatique." *RMSAM* 5/9: 15 July 1864, cols. 271, 270.
57. On the drive toward communitarian worship shared by all brands of new Catholic in the early nineteenth century, see Franklin, *Nineteenth-Century Churches*, esp. 15–21.

to heaven.[58] Such views were commonplace among interpreters of Palestrina's work and historical significance, including those who would not have counted themselves as enthusiasts. Paul Lacome, for example, wrote in *L'art musical* in 1868:

> It is in the evening, beneath the vast naves and plunged in semi-darkness, that one should hear it; it requires that its crude chords and strange harmonies climb the length of the fluted surfaces of spindly columns and wing their way to lose themselves in the shadows of the vaulted ceilings. Its mystical accents ally well with these emaciated stone saints, whose elongated feet run bizarrely along the walls.[59]

Maurice Germa used almost identical turns of phrase in a review of Holy Week music in 1875: "Palestrina's choruses attain their divine expression of mystical and monastic ecstasy only in the immense naves of cathedral churches; otherwise, they make no sense and lose their interest."[60] Writing in 1894, Bellaigue wanted to hear Palestrinian music, but not to see it: "A few voices suffice for this music—a few hidden voices."[61] He doubtless had in mind the practice of Bordes and his Chanteurs de Saint-Gervais, where the choir, split between the two upper galleries of the church, was out of sight of the listeners.[62] Bellaigue described the effect in quasi-Wagnerian vein:

> Between the altar and the nave [Palestrinian music] interposes neither a group of strangers nor a mass of instruments. It does not allow the agitated silhouette of a conductor to break up the noble

---

58. "l'harmonie large et majestueuse de cette composition remplit la voûte de l'église en montant vers le ciel comme la fumée de l'encens, image de la prière fervente des vrais fidèles agenouillés." Damour, Burnett and Elwart, *Etudes élémentaires*, 309 (on the *Stabat mater*).

59. "C'est le soir, sous les nefs immenses et plongées dans une demi-obscurité qu'il faudrait l'entendre; il faudrait que ses accords frustes, que ses harmonies étranges montent le long des faisceaux de colonnettes grêles, et s'aillent perdre dans l'ombre des voûtes. Ses accents mystiques conviennent bien à ces saints de pierre aux formes émaciées, dont les longs pieds courent bizarrement dans le sens du mur."*AM* 8/20: 16 April 1868, 155.

60. "Les choeurs de Palestrina n'atteignent leur divine expression de mystique et de monacale extase, que dans les nefs immenses des cathédrales; ailleurs, ils n'ont ni sens ni intérêt." *CM* 8 (no. 43): 1 April 1875, 32.

61. "Quelques voix lui suffisent, et quelques voix cachées." *RDM* 15 October 1894, 861. Bellaigue was almost unique in his fondness for a small choir singing such repertory.

62. The "hidden voices" were probably as pragmatic as they were aesthetic: Bordes was breaking with Papal desiderata by using women's voices in his choir. He was not, however, alone in using women singers in church.

perspective of the church, and to conceal from the eyes the sight of the sacred rites, the gestures which bless and consecrate.⁶³

Lacome, too, was expressing an almost Wagnerian idea when he linked the mystical aspect of Palestrina's music to its immateriality, almost lost in darkness. Yet such comments have much in common, of course, with earlier German Romantic traditions established by Jean Paul and Hoffmann, among others, in which darkness and the invisible performer were linked with sublimity and transcendence. Descriptions, such as that of Ernest Legouvé, of Liszt playing Beethoven in private soirées of the 1830s and '40s, dramatized those very elements as markers of artistic spirituality.⁶⁴ Critics appealed to the mystical quality of Palestrina using similar criteria, even though they were dealing with texted music. For it was effectively only half-texted, just as it was only half-tonal. In large spaces it was impossible for listeners to decipher the words of a polyphonic work, and difficult even with a homophonic one. On the cusp of, but distanced from, dramatic expressivity, Palestrina was also released from the restrictions of conventional signification; indeed, celebrating his lack of dramatic expressivity was a way of highlighting this very point. His was quasi-absolute music that opened a window onto a supernatural, incorporeal world.⁶⁵ And that was one of the ways in which it was used and appreciated in French concert halls. For those reasons it was also, for Palestrina's radical-Ultramontane detractors, worryingly close to an expression of art for art's sake, and therefore inappropriate as liturgical music.

Palestrinian Music Within the Liturgy

Debates between rival groups of Ultramontanes intensified in the second half of the century against a backdrop of increasing secularization and (particularly after 1879) repressive state policies that would eventually drive an unbreachable wedge between the Republic and the Catholic church. The secular/aesthetic question of whether Palestrinian music was dramatic or incorporeal was increasingly replaced by that of whether he, as the figurehead of a larger group

---

63. "Elle n'interpose entre l'autel et la nef ni un groupe d'étrangers ni un amas d'instruments. Elle ne souffre pas que la silhouette agitée d'un batteur de mesure rompe la noble perspective de l'église, et dérobe aux yeux la vue des rites sacrés, des gestes qui bénissent et consacrent." *RDM* 15 October 1894, 861–62.

64. For Legouvé's celebrated description, see his *Soixante ans de souvenirs*, vol. 1, 297–98. Adrian Williams translates in *A Portrait of Franz Liszt*, 42–43.

65. Compare Hoffmann and Tieck as discussed in Garratt, *Palestrina*, 53–54.

of Renaissance polyphonic composers, had written music that was both liturgically appropriate and accessible to ordinary congregations. Such emphasis on participation, equality, and democracy in liturgical music is inseparable from debates sparked by the liberal Catholicism of Lamennais (who had tried to be both Ultramontane and social-democratic) and by the new Catholicism of Solesmes—in part a reaction to Lamennais's failure. It also, later in the century, underpinned Pope Leo XIII's moves toward "Christian democracy" during a reign (1878–1903) characterized by unusual sensitivity to the plight of the peasant and working classes. The accession of Pius X in August 1903 marked a decisive elitist, antimodernist and right-wing shift within the Papacy. Nevertheless, the compromise position of the *Motu proprio*, which lauded both chant and Palestrina, may have been intended to help neutralize the antagonisms of both the pro- and anti-Palestrinian camps within a now overwhelmingly Ultramontane French clergy.[66] For Bordes, who in addition to evangelizing on behalf of Palestrinian repertory had close personal and institutional links with the monks at Solesmes Abbey (at which the Schola held summer schools), the terms of the *Motu proprio* of 1903 could hardly have represented a greater ideological triumph. However, whether he supported the right-wing causes that such returns to tradition came to symbolize at the Schola is open to question. The religious politics of toleration of the Ralliement—the precise period when Bordes began trying, through the Chanteurs de Saint-Gervais, to tempt old-fashioned *maîtres de chapelle* away from their operatic adaptations and to persuade the radical Ultramontane camp away from its extremist Gregorian position—could hardly have been further removed from those which attended the Dreyfus affair and the accession of Pius X.[67]

The question of a musical "Renaissance" as antagonistic to the Medieval period, was also central. If, for Voltaire, the Middle Ages represented a period of darkness from which civilization was rescued by scientific humanism, for French Ultramontanes of the early nineteenth century the reverse was true. The gothic revival that began in France and spread to England was from the outset inextricable from religious politics because its main reference point was Voltaire's anticlericalism. As Bullen explains, Chateaubriand did not actively intend to denigrate the Renaissance in his *Génie du Christianisme*; nevertheless,

---

66. On Pius X's reforms, see Chadwick, *A History of the Popes*, 332–405.

67. On D'Indy's right-wing sympathies and their influence at the Schola, see Fulcher, *French Cultural Politics & Music*, 50–51, and Huebner, *French Opera at the "fin de siècle,"* 301–7. Bordes was forced to resign from direction of the Schola Cantorum in 1903; D'Indy, who saw the school as a rival to the republican Conservatoire and who regularly reported on its activities to the right-wing Ligue de l'Action Française, took over its direction (Fulcher, 73).

ambivalence, seized upon and intensified by later writers, was the inevitable by-product of a work written against Voltaire's heinous *Essai sur les moeurs*.[68] Charles Nodier introduced "a new note of nationalism" into the Gothic revival, emphasizing the role of the French monarchy within Gothic civilization.[69] Finally, and well before Edgar Quinet and Jules Michelet presented the Renaissance as a vital, energized period of cultural emancipation, Hugo's *Notre Dame de Paris* of 1831 served to illustrate the inevitability of its negative force: the Renaissance not only destroyed the idea of the artisan and the organic relationship of the arts within the liturgical environment but also celebrated imitation of the antique (i.e. artistic insincerity) rather than offering something true to its own "génie."[70] Though these ideas came from the pen of a man who was neither a Catholic nor a royalist, they became rooted in the myth of the Renaissance at the very moment when French Catholic reformers advancing ideas of collectivity and communitarianism from a liturgical viewpoint were making headway. It is hardly surprising that the two streams of thought came together in writings on sacred music.

The problem of the Renaissance for French Catholics—a problem articulated around the axes of elitism, secularism, sensuality, and Protestantism—provided essential fuel for pro-Gregorianists, who decided that the Palestrinian style was so tainted with the anti-Catholicism of the Renaissance period that it deserved to be sidelined in liturgical practice. The category of the musical "Renaissance" became an object of ideological contention almost as soon as it was born, since radical Ultramontanes had a particular interest in separating the Christian "Medieval" period from the secular "Renaissance." Palestrina belonged to the latter.[71] To differing degrees, D'Ortigue, Danjou, Clément and the *Univers* critic Antoine Dessus, *dit* Super, contributed loudly to this debate. Dissenting voices of the 1890s, such as those of Bellaigue and D'Indy, did not appear in a vacuum, therefore. As part of a discourse akin to that which surrounded architecture, painting, and the restoration of historical monuments, there emerged a (vilified) "musical Renaissance" against which to posit a new interpretation of the periodization of musical style.

Plainchant's simplicity, combined with its stubborn resistance to secularization (it would never become concert music), lay at the heart of the Medieval/Renaissance split. As D'Ortigue wrote in 1836, setting up an opposing

---

68. Bullen, *The Myth of the Renaissance*, 66–67.
69. Bullen, *The Myth of the Renaissance*, 68.
70. Quinet, *Les révolutions d'Italie* (1849); Michelet, *Histoire de France*, vii (1855). Bullen, *The Myth of the Renaissance*, 72–75. Hugo's novel was set in 1482.
71. See Campos, *La Renaissance introuvable?*, 218–29; and Vendrix, "'La musique montait,'" 25–27.

paradigm to that which sustained Palestrina, plainchant's qualities echoed the sublimity of God: immutability, eternity, and infinity [72] Moreover, the musically untrained could sing it, whether in unison or with the kind of *fauxbourdon* harmonization that Danjou tried to introduce in the mid 1830s. Tempted by the idea of a collective return to Gregorian purity, previously moderate Ultramontanes such as Danjou himself began to harden their position on Palestrina's music, even when it was nearly homophonic. In 1839 Danjou had written warmly, and in traditional vein, of Palestrina's sacred music as performed liturgically by Choron :

> The sublime harmony, the heavenly chords of Palestrina's music have often sounded beneath the arches of the [church of the] Sorbonne; we were able to judge the immense effect, the truly religious impression which this kind of music produces, and yet the cathedral and the other Paris churches have continued to perform works which are entirely devoid of taste and merit.[73]

Yet, in the four volumes of his *Revue de la musique religieuse, populaire, classique* (1845–54) Palestrina's name figured only twice[74]; and general articles on sixteenth-century polyphonic repertory, too, were scarce. A rare statement of support (for Lassus's *Penitential Psalms* in 1846) was predicated in large part on his "majestic chords"[75]; the more general context was stark. The "populaire" of his journal title was no accident: Danjou reached the conclusion that polyphony was devoid of liturgical merit. He was, he wrote, able to recommend the first volume of Carl Proske's collection *Musica divina* (1853–86) to readers but warned them that the works published therein were "very complicated and often unsingable" and that he would have preferred to see simpler, more "popular" works of the same period, in whose homophonic textures he might discern "a truly religious cachet."[76]

Within radical Ultramontanism, then, the problem with Palestrina was counterpoint. For counterpoint, stretching from Josquin to the Counter-Reformation,

---

72. *L'univers religieux*, 10 February 1836, given in L'Ecuyer, "Berlioz, d'Ortigue et la musique religieuse," 101.

73. "La sublime harmonie, les célestes accords de Palestrina ont souvent retenti sous les voûtes de [l'église de] la Sorbonne; on a pu juger de l'effet immense, de l'impression vraiment religieuse que produisait ce genre de musique, et cependant la cathédrale et les autres églises de Paris ont continué à exécuter les oeuvres les plus dépouvrues de goût et de mérite." *RGM* 6/20: 19 May 1839, 155.

74. *Pace* De Rohan-Csermak, Danjou's journal did not reflect the idea that the Palestrinian style was the "true" religious style (De Rohan-Csermak, "La *canonisation* de Palestrina," 201); the situation was not static.

75. "les accords majestueux." *RMRPC* 2 (1846), 337.

76. "très-compliquées et souvent inexécutables . . . un cachet vraiment religieux." *RMRPC*, 4 pt. 2 (1854), xiv–xv.

was itself a sign of incipient paganism because it smacked of self-aggrandizement rather than communication:

> The pagan reaction in music did not start with sensualism [i.e. Monteverdi]; it began through the abuse of learning and of spiritualism. The most celebrated composers of the fifteenth and sixteenth centuries did not set their sights on dramatic effect, but on ingenious [polyphonic] combinations, on kinds of mind games in which the difficulty overcome constituted the principal merit . . .
>
> The true character of Christian music is, by contrast, equally removed both from the pedantry which seeks nothing but to interest the mind, and the materialism which seeks only to impress the senses.[77]

This was the political, as opposed to the aesthetic, problem with Franco-Flemish sacred music. In contrast to Fétis, who saw it as primarily antimusical, Danjou condemned it, Palestrina included, for being antireligious. The shift from a vertical to a horizontal conception of Palestrinian style decisively marked its downfall; it ceased to be a collective, medieval music. As Joseph Régnier commented in *Le choeur*: after the most promising of beginnings, Danjou's *Revue* "ended up by allying itself with more extreme opinions, which no longer asked for the regeneration, but now asked for the banishment of great organs and the death of all church music except plainchant."[78] It was a stance inspired by the general call for congregational participation—active understanding, rather than bystanding—that characterized the Catholic revival across Europe.

As the Ultramontane cause gained in power under Napoléon III, so the rhetorics of its radical wing became more extreme. They were epitomized by

---

77. "La réaction païenne dans la musique n'a pas commencé par le sensualisme, elle a commencé par l'abus de la science et du spiritualisme. Les auteurs les plus célèbres du XVe et du XVIe siècle ne visaient pas à l'effet dramatique, mais à des combinaisons ingénieuses, à des sortes de jeux d'esprit dont la difficulté vaincue faisait le principal mérite. . . .
Le véritable caractère de la musique chrétienne est, au contraire, également éloigné et du pédantisme qui ne cherche qu'à intéresser l'esprit, et du matérialisme qui ne cherche qu'à frapper les sens." *RMRPC*, 4 pt. 2 (1854), xv.

78. "finit par se rallier à [des] opinions plus hardies, qui demandaient non plus la régénération, mais le bannissement des grandes orgues et la mort de toute musique d'église autre que le plain-chant." Untitled, unsigned editorial undoubtedly by Régnier, *Le choeur* 6 (February 1854), 1–12, at 6.

Clément, who, like Danjou, hardened his views considerably as his career progressed. Early tolerance came via the presentation of Palestrina's style through the traditionally distorted lens of "Harmony in perfect triads."[79] But Clément's official *Rapport* on the state of sacred music in France (1849), which would help lead to the founding of the Ecole Niedermeyer in 1853, revealed a new decisiveness. Palestrinian music was "inherently unpopular" because of its counterpoint, which was no better than newer melody and accompaniment styles as a solution to the problem of representing equality within a choir.[80] Accordingly, in his later writings (here the 1860s) Clément preferred simply to typecast the entire repertory as elite chamber music, best heard "in a chapel, . . . performed by very accomplished artists and directed by a learned master, . . . appreciated by an elite audience prepared through a distinguished education and through regular contact with the arts."[81] This, for Clément, was *l'art pour l'art*—and in terms strikingly reminiscent of Pierre-Joseph Proudhon's *Système de contradictions économiques* of 1846 he condemned such elevation of form over function.[82] Difficulty of performance and textual incomprehensibility (even in the Pope Marcellus Mass), Clément claimed, made this music elitist; and Tridentine structures had failed to eradicate the "labored puerilities" of fifteenth-century counterpoint.[83] Palestrina, then, had jeopardized the piety of the masses by composing a metaliturgical music whose signification could be appreciated only by the educated and which caused the people to be alienated from the liturgical experience itself. Clément was also, arguably, frightened by the music's self-contradictory power, and trapped within its *juste milieu*. On the one hand he found the style "cold and monotonous" in church[84]; on the other,

79. "L'harmonie en accords parfaits." Clément, *Notice sur les chants de la Sainte-Chapelle* [1875], 14. This pamphlet, originally written in 1849, formed the preface to a new edition of thirteenth-century music from manuscripts in Sens and Paris which Clément had (significantly) harmonized in block chords and presented in religious/ceremonial contexts more than a dozen times between 1849 and 1875. The first presentation of this repertory of medieval music was, significantly, at the "Fête de la Justice" of 3 November 1849, at which Napoléon III's judiciary were sworn in at the Sainte-Chapelle. I am grateful to Gwendolyn Trietze for alerting me to this event.

80. "d'une facture impopulaire." Clément, *Rapport sur l'état de la musique religieuse en France*, 8 and 37.

81. "dans une chapelle . . . exécutée par des artistes très-habiles et dirigés par un maître savant, . . . goûtée d'un auditoire d'élite préparé par une éducation distinguée et par la culture habituelle des arts." Clément, *Histoire générale de la musique religieuse*, 328.

82. Clément, *Histoire générale de la musique religieuse*, 329. Cf. Proudhon's complaints about the futility and dissolute nature of art for art's sake (Proudhon, *Système*, 226). This paradoxical closeness to Proudhon, who equated God with Evil, highlights the extent to which socialist thinking of various kinds (and varying degrees of secularism) permeated French religious politics of the century. A line stretching from Lamennais via Danjou, Clément, Super [Dessus], and even Bellaigue (see below) is detectable in this regard.

83. "laborieux enfantillages." Clément, *Histoire générale de la musique religieuse*, 327.

84. "froid et monotone." Clément, *Histoire générale de la musique religieuse*, 328.

he found it too luxuriant in the decadent tradition of gilded ecclesiastical art of the sixteenth-century Renaissance.[85] The combination of opposites—golden coolness—suggests that he, too, was seduced by the ambiguous allure of a style which appeared to be at once pure and sensual.

Further intensification of the anti-Palestrina campaign came in the midst of Third-Republic anticlericalism, not least because the battle had to be waged on two fronts: against the propagation, by moderate Ultramontanes, of Palestrinian music in the liturgy because it was aesthetically appropriate; and against its retention by moderate Republicans on account of its heritage value. For radical Ultramontanes, the government debates of 1883–84 must have been particularly galling. There were threats to downgrade plainchant into a teaching tool and to turn the liturgical performance of Palestrina into a *concert historique*.[86] And that was the rescue package, not the main attack. For when, in January 1884, the Ministère de la Justice et des Cultes recommended withdrawing funding to major Palestrinian institutions including Langres and Moulins, the Ministre de l'Instruction Publique protested: "The Commission's goal, and mine, is to prevent the teaching of plainchant from perishing altogether and, uniquely in the interests of the art of music, to come to the aid of those rare institutions at which the great traditions of the Palestrinian school have been preserved with [such] success."[87]

Whatever the political imperatives that led to such presentation of France's cathedrals as secularized museums conserving culture, for radical Ultramontanes the valuing by a Republican government of Palestrinian music as a matter of aesthetics rather than liturgy proved its irreligious nature beyond all doubt. No wonder that when in the aftermath of this same rash of anticlerical reforms Langres cathedral was required to affiliate itself to the Académie des Beaux-Arts to conserve "the taste for and study of classic music" and to submit to biennial government inspections if it wished to receive its 4000F of state funding, its radical Ultramontane bishop Mgr Bouange resisted. It was only after his death that Nicolas Couturier was able to secure a state-funded future for

---

85. Clément, *Histoire générale de la musique religieuse*, 330.
86. A comparison of performances of sacred music by Durante, Jommelli, and Pergolesi at the early *exercices* of the "Republican" Conservatoire is pertinent here.
87. "Le but de la commission, le mien, c'est de ne pas laisser périr tout à fait en France l'enseignement du plain-chant et de venir en aide, uniquement dans l'intérêt de l'art musical, aux rares institutions où se sont conservées avec éclat les grandes traditions de l'école palestrinienne." AN Paris: F[21]1328A, given in Rannaud, *La maîtrise de la cathédrale de Moulins*, 20. For an analysis of the transformation of the French cathedral into a site of cultural and patrimonial memory, see Vauchez, "The Cathedral."

the *maîtrise*.[88] The price, of course, was the institution of a museum-church precisely in the spirit of Clément's *l'art pour l'art*.

Such secularization, characteristic of Palestrina concert performance since Choron's *exercices* and the concerts of the Moskova society, combined in radical Ultramontane minds with heightened sensitivity to questions of exclusivity on musical and class grounds. It spilled over in the 1890s, which saw the most heated debates of all. The abbé Antoine Dessus, writing as A. Super, saw secular performances of Palestrina's works—in particular those of Bordes and his Chanteurs de Saint-Gervais—as proof that the composer was too much of an artist to create true liturgical music.[89] Amidst a strong tradition of the hagiographical treatment of heroes, his 1892 book on Palestrina was a rare exercise in biography as character assassination. Here, Quinet was ridiculed for seeing Palestrina as inherently religious; and Goudimel was "outed" as a Protestant heathen who failed to teach his students plainchant and turned his young protégé's head.[90] To make his point, Dessus counterpointed his attacks on Palestrina with a sustained attack on Bordes, who had just started his Holy Week services, in the footnotes. Most tellingly of all, he yoked Bordes's work to that of Liszt, who was a "virtuoso mason" and author of a "*Messe dramatique*" conducted by "a Jew, M. Judas, otherwise known as Colonne."[91] In comparison, Palestrina got off rather lightly. Nevertheless, paraphrasing D'Ortigue from thirty years before, Dessus claimed that in his music, "The more the musician is in evidence, the more the Christian is effaced and disappears from view."[92] The collective ideal had been shattered. Dessus had no option but to disavow a composer whose ego had, he believed, led him to misunderstand the nature of his duty: "Palestrina failed to understand that polyphony is by its very nature restricted and exclusive. It is chant, but only chant sung in unison, as conceived and organized by Saint Gregory, that the people, all the faithful, will accept. It is the only [music] which can act as an instrument of love and of union."[93] He

---

88. "le goût et l'étude de la musique classique." Noël and Roussel, *M. l'abbé Nicolas Couturier*, 26–27.

89. Super [Dessus], *Palestrina*, 71–74. Hardly surprisingly, Dessus was scandalized by Bordes's use of women's voices for concerts taking place in a church (74).

90. Super, *Palestrina*, 8–9.

91. "maçon-virtuose"; "un juif, M. Judas, dit Colonne." Super, *Palestrina*, 71. The attack on Bordes runs pp. 71–74. Catrina Flint de Médicis has recently found documents revealing that a large proportion of the Chanteurs de Saint-Gervais was Jewish. See her *The Schola Cantorum*, chapter 3.

92. "*Plus le musicien se montre, plus le chrétien s'efface et disparait*" (original emphasis). Super [Dessus], *Palestrina*, 47. D'Ortigue's formulation "plus le musicien se montre, plus le chrétien disparaît" appears in a *Maîtrise* article of April 1860 defending plainchant. The article was reproduced in D'Ortigue's *La musique à l'église*, 347–76.

93. "Palestrina n'a pas compris davantage que la polyphonie est par nature, restreinte, exclusive. C'est le chant, mais le chant à l'unisson, conçu et organisé par saint Grégoire, que peuvent seul admettre le peuple, tous les fidèles. C'est le seul qui puisse être instrument d'amour et d'union." Super [Dessus], *Palestrina*, 39.

provided Palestrinian historiography with another oxymoron, this time a damning mix of Renaissance Italian and Medieval French that described his reputation as that of "a maestro mystérieux": the semblance of mystery, in other words, and an architect of deceit.[94] Through polemic and insult Dessus tried to convince his readers that Palestrina was himself a fake, or at least a charlatan.

It is hardly surprising to find Bordes in a conciliatory role. At the Rodez liturgical congress of 1895 he began his first paper by distinguishing between the roles of the two kinds of liturgical music that were central to his vision: chant and "figured music." Admittedly, he said, Palestrinian music was not truly popular because its performance demanded training. Yet it remained accessible to the humblest church singer and was less difficult than was commonly believed: "Written within the normal tessitura of the voice and made up of frequently reproduced formulae, flowing along easily, Palestrinian music presents no obstacle to a relatively experienced choir school."[95] He suggested that choirmasters should work in tandem with their local *orphéons* to form *a cappella* choirs for their churches.[96] For many of his contemporaries—musicians and writers alike—Bordes's idea would have seemed implausible, especially given the unfortunate results of earlier attempts of this kind in Paris. But he proved his point at Rodez, where his choir was drawn from local choir schools, seminaries and *orphéons*; and he had already done so in Paris, where his Chanteurs de Saint-Gervais included around a dozen members of the *orphéons* Les Enfants de Paris and Les Enfants de Lutèce.[97] Similar attempts around the country were enthusiastically written up in the *Tribune*.

If Bordes succeeded in weakening the idea that advanced musical training and high breeding were necessary conditions for understanding Palestrina, he could offer no solution to the objections of Clément and Dessus that the music itself was secular and individualistic. It was the supportive voice of Camille Bellaigue that offered such a perspective in an attempt to rebut radical Ultramontane arguments via a return to quasi-Mennaisian appeals to equality: that this music was immanently egalitarian, collective, democratic, and nonegotistical.[98] He tried, in short, to reconcile counterpoint and medievalism. By contrast

---

94. Super [Dessus], *Palestrina*, 72.

95. "Ecrite dans la tessiture normale des voix et composée de formules souvent reproduites, d'un débit coulant, aisé, la musique palestrinienne n'offre aucun obstacle à une maîtrise un peu exercée." Bordes, "De l'emploi de la musique figurée," 149.

96. Bordes, "De l'emploi de la musique figurée," 152–53.

97. Ginsty, in Anon. (Ed.), *Congrès diocésain de musique religieuse*, 26–27, and De Castéra, *Dix années d'action musicale religieuse*, 13. Significantly, both *orphéons* had been associated with the Société Bourgault-Ducoudray.

98. *RDM* 15 October 1894, 868–69.

with functional harmony, he found no hierarchy of voices in Palestrinian counterpoint; neither was there a tradition of solo passages or melody and accompaniment. Reciprocity (rather than collective action) reigned. If "modern" music represented individual passions, that of Palestrina represented the generality of humanity. In this Mennaisian view, *fraternité* emanated from the choir to the nave and, though congregations were unable to participate in such music, they were nevertheless represented within it:

> All other sacred musics from Bach, Mozart and Beethoven to that of Verdi or Gounod, seem to recognize in their use of a few soloists the privileged interpreters of the thought and speech of everyone else: the Palestrinian art admits no such distinctions or prerogatives. In the brotherly concert of which it is constituted, no voice dominates or disdains the others; pride and the sense of self are effaced here. . . .
>
> Impersonal in its form, Palestrinian art is also impersonal as regards the composer himself. In other words, there is in this music, as in gothic architecture, something general and I would say even anonymous.[99]

Bellaigue's celebration of the choir as a microcosm of the congregation and, by extension, of society, offered a close paraphrase of Clément's arguments of 1849, as indeed did his comments on the "equality" of counterpoint as distinct from soloistic music.[100] However, most important here was the idea of an anonymous Palestrina whose personality was effaced by the need to represent

---

99. "Toute autre musique religieuse depuis celle de Bach, de Mozart, de Beethoven, jusqu'à celle de Verdi ou de Gounod, semble reconnaître en quelques solistes les interprètes privilégiés de la pensée et de l'oraison commune: l'art palestrinien n'admet ni distinctions ni prérogatives. Dans le fraternel concert dont elle est faite, aucune voix ne domine ou ne dédaigne les autres; l'orgueil et le sens propre s'effacent ici . . .
Impersonnel par son objet, l'art palestrinien l'est aussi chez le compositeur ou par le compositeur lui-même. En d'autres termes, il y a dans cette musique, comme dans l'architecture gothique, quelque chose de général et je dirais presque anonyme." *RDM* 15 October 1894, 869.

100. Clément, *Rapport sur l'état de la musique religieuse en France*, 37, given in De Rohan-Csermak, "La canonisation de Palestrina," 212. The section of Bellaigue's essay under discussion here is openly aimed at Clément's ideas, despite the fact that he had been dead for nine years when it was published, and despite its resonances with Bellaigue's earlier work. Bellaigue moved increasingly to the right during his career as a critic: in 1886 he acclaimed D'Indy's *Chant de la cloche* of 1886 as "music of the masses instead of music of the individual . . . music of democratic socialism replacing subjective, aristocratic or heroic art" [la musique-foule au lieu de la musique-individu . . . la musique de la démocratie socialiste remplaçant l'art aristocratique, héroïque ou subjectif] (*RDM*, given in Vallas, *Vincent d'Indy*, vol. 1, 290); in the 1890s his views (and his critical tone) became more conservative. He appears to have made decisive shifts to the right throughout and after Pius X's reign.

the entire people. This was a riposte to men such as Dessus, couched in language that would have been understood by radical Ultramontanes going back to Danjou and D'Ortigue.

By denying that Palestrina was an egotist, Bellaigue was, in part, returning to a French Romantic conception of musical history in which the Middle Ages and the Renaissance were not clearly differentiated. Bordes, too, implied as much by using the term "maîtres primitifs" in the title of his anthologies of sacred polyphony. Within the earlier historiography of the Renaissance in French writings on music, Delécluze had, because of his painter's background, been unusual in arguing that the Renaissance in music spanned only the period between the Counter-Reformation and the birth of opera.[101] More traditionally musicological was De Lafage, who continued a well-established custom in both Germany and France of placing Palestrina in "the second part of the Middle Ages, or the Renaissance."[102] For pro-Palestrinian Church reformers of the nineteenth century, the fact that the composer formed part of a musical "renaissance" (in the sense of revival) had been a *sine qua non*, since it was in emulation of Palestrina's own "revival" of the quality of Church music that they based their own. The spirit of that "renaissance," however, had been almost invariably a late-medieval one.

Bellaigue's strategy was different. In 1894, he removed the impious taint of the Italian Renaissance from Palestrina by claiming that since there were no surviving examples of musical antiquity to emulate, the Renaissance *per se* had bypassed music altogether: the individualist Raphael was a quintessential Renaissance man, but Palestrina was the most elevated representative of the end of the Middle Ages.[103] However, two years after this Palestrina essay, Bellaigue shifted his historiographical ground to even more spectacular effect. Adapting the ideas of Julien Tiersot on the use of popular melodies in pre-Counter-Reformation music, he attempted to rehabilitate the entire Palestrinian oeuvre, including the previously embarrassing "L'homme armé" masses, by arguing that the use of secular chansons as the basis for sacred music was evidence of

---

101. *RP* October 1842, 329. His intention was to distance Palestrina's pre-Marcellus compositions, and those of his predecessors, from the later, "purer" tradition. Following his belief that from around 1080 there existed a succession of Renaissances, each centering round a particular figure, Delécluze presented Palestrina as the single "great man" of the Renaissance in music, which took place toward the end of his historical continuum of Renaissances, succeeded only by that of science (Galileo and Francis Bacon). See Baschet, *E.-J. Delécluze*, 365–66. In a review of Michelet, Delécluze was critical of his chronologically limited conception of the Renaissance (*JD* 2 May 1855).

102. "la seconde partie du moyen âge ou la renaissance." De Lafage, *Histoire générale de la musique et de la danse*, xiii. Given in Haar, "Music of the Renaissance," 128.

103. *RDM* 15 October 1894, 860.

sacred polyphony's deep roots in the collective memory of popular culture: "The popular element invades music to an increasing extent. Until the Council of Trent's reforms, the liturgical offices are constantly sung on dance tunes, battle songs, even love songs and cabaret songs."[104] It was not until the birth of opera, argued Bellaigue, that such collective expressions in music were overturned, replacing the contrapuntal voice of the people with the voices of individuals, and moving from the public to the private sphere. Echoing the historiography outlined in Ambros's *Geschichte*, he declared that the musical Renaissance therefore started with monody.[105]

> Then came the Renaissance. It arrived later for music than for the other arts, but it arrived in the same manner. Everywhere it substituted, for the principle of association and of groups, the principle of individualism; and the music which, like man himself, had existed for so long in a collective form, reappeared in a private and individual form. First recitative, then, and especially, melody, rediscovered and as if created anew by Italian genius, divorced itself from vocal counterpoint: but in the pride of its newly-conquered beauty, it turned away from the crowd which it had once so loved, and the most popular of the arts became the most aristocratic and the most worldly.[106]

Bellaigue thus provided a sociohistorical defence of late sixteenth-century counterpoint that answered the vast majority of the pro-Gregorian camp's objections. In slightly altered form it became the historiographical orthodoxy of the Schola Cantorum, to which Bellaigue had always been close, appearing in the Schola Cantorum's composition curriculum as devised and taught by

---

104. "L'élément populaire envahit de plus en plus la musique. Jusqu'aux réformes du concile de Trente, les offices liturgiques se chantent couramment sur les thèmes de danse, de guerre, quand ce n'est pas d'amour ou de cabaret." *RDM* 1 May 1896, 84.

105. For an excellent analysis of Ambros's historiographical dilemmas in respect to a post-Burkhardtian musical "Renaissance," see Kirkman, "The Invention of the Cyclic Mass," esp. 31–36.

106. "Puis la Renaissance vint. Elle vint plus tardive pour la musique que pour les autres arts, mais elle ne vint pas différente. Au principe de l'association et du nombre, elle substitua partout le principe de l'individualisme, et la musique qui, depuis longtemps, ainsi que l'homme même, n'existait plus que sous la forme collective, reparut sous la forme particulière et individuelle. Le récitatif d'abord, et puis, et surtout, la mélodie, rétrouvée et comme créée à nouveau par le génie italien, se dégagea du contrepoint vocal; mais dans l'orgueil de sa beauté reconquise, elle se détourna de la foule que jadis elle avait tant aimée, et le plus populaire des arts en devint le plus aristocratique et le plus mondain." *RDM* 1 May 1896, 84–85.

D'Indy from April 1897. Permeated by attacks on Protestantism (which he saw as a defining feature of the Renaissance), D'Indy's *Cours*, too, presented the sixteenth century as a period of rampant individualism, but dated the musical Renaissance from the first attempts at monody.[107] Like Bellaigue, D'Indy celebrated Palestrina's contrapuntal style but protected the purity of the composer's Catholicism in an impious and increasingly Protestant age. Perhaps expanding on Bellaigue, he did so by arguing that musical style tended to lag behind movements in other arts by around a century.[108] However, there are crucial differences between the two accounts. D'Indy celebrated the anonymity of the medieval artist in a collective age, but omitted all reference to egalitarianism and democracy in sixteenth-century polyphony. Moreover, he drew explicit parallels between the sins of the artistic Renaissance—particularly pride and self-advancement—and those of the Reformation. His arguments thus folded straight back into the series of Catholic debates over painting and architecture that had been catalysed by Chateaubriand in 1802:

> Subdued by the Christian faith, that formidable enemy of man, Pride, rarely showed itself in the soul of an artist in the Middle Ages. But with the weakening of religious belief, with the spirit of the Reformation applying itself almost at the same time to every branch of human learning, we see Pride appear, and watch its veritable Renaissance.[109]

A revisionist move such as that of Bellaigue was not unprecedented outside of music history: in 1855, the very year that Michelet's rehabilitation of the

---

107. D'Indy, *Cours de composition musicale*, vol. 1, 216–18. The first two volumes contained not only D'Indy's work but also notes taken during classes by his pupil Auguste Sérieyx. Guy de Lioncourt compiled volume 3 alone. Sérieyx's notes for volume 1 were taken during the 1897–98 academic year. Fulcher discusses D'Indy's view of the Renaissance as decadent but does not point out the crucial historiographical twist on which it is predicated (Fulcher, *French Cultural Politics and Music*, 49–50).

108. D'Indy, *Cours de composition musicale*, i, 216.

109. "Dominé par la foi chrétienne, le redoutable ennemi de l'homme, l'Orgueil, s'était rarement manifesté jusqu'ici dans l'âme de l'artiste. Mais, avec l'affaiblissement des croyances, avec l'esprit de Réforme appliqué presque en même temps à toutes les branches du savoir humain, depuis le langage usuel jusqu'aux théories philosophiques et religieuses, nous verrons reparaître l'Orgueil, nous assisterons à sa véritable Renaissance." D'Indy, *Cours de composition musicale*, vol. 1, 215. Translation from Romain Rolland's appreciation of Vincent d'Indy in the *Revue d'art dramatique* of 5 February 1899, given in Rolland, *Musicians of Today*, 117. Rolland's analysis of the nature of D'Indy's right-wing Catholicism as shown in the *Cours de composition* and his inaugural lecture of 1900 to the newly enlarged Schola (published in the *Tribune de Saint-Gervais* of November 1900) is exceptionally perspicacious, and not just the product of the two men's opposing political ideals.

Renaissance had appeared, with a celebration of Leonardo da Vinci's humanism at its centre, the Catholic reformer A. F. Rio had published a biography of Leonardo, the scourge of the medievalists, that "vainly strove to demonstrate that Leonardo, far from being the prophet of moral relativism and uncertainty, was in fact a pious Catholic and leader of the 'mystic school' of religious artists."[110] But Bellaigue's was more effective because it returned Counter-Reformation polyphony to its former, lauded, place, rather than trying to create a new niche for it. For reasons entirely unconnected with Romanticism, the arguments of both D'Indy and Bellaigue brought the Palestrinian historiography full circle in presenting the repertory as a culminating point and a lost paradise. Indeed, at the end of the century, Palestrina's reception in France displayed a tenacious set of givens which could be adapted to diverse ideological purposes. With the exception—significantly, given the revisionist line—of his description of Palestrinian music as "horizontal," Gounod's remembrances of his experience of music in the Sistine Chapel are as typical of the period in which the experience took place (1839–42) as of that in which they appeared as part of his memoirs (1895–96). In particular, the shadow of Choron's marine metaphor looms large:

> This severe, ascetic music, horizontal and calm like the Ocean, monotonous by dint of its serenity, anti-sensual and yet of a contemplative intensity which sometimes reaches to ecstasy . . . Palestrinian music seems to be a sung translation of Michelangelo's vast poem . . . . There are no disturbances on the way, and at the end of the journey one finds oneself raised to prodigious heights.[111]

Moreover, characteristics of the music and of its nineteenth-century revival were themselves conflated. When, as part of his heroizing of Palestrina in 1894, Bellaigue lauded the composer's preference for "soft sounds and half-tints" rather than "noise" in the performance of his music, he had no evidence whatever: he was relying entirely on his confidence in the authenticity of a seventy-year-old performing tradition of collective *piano*.[112] Memory, history, and entrenched modes of reception converged to a historiographically telling point. In borrow-

---

110. Bullen, *The Myth of the Renaissance*, 182.

111. "Cette musique sévère, ascétique, horizontale et calme comme la ligne de l'Océan, monotone à force de sérénité, antisensuelle et néanmoins d'une intensité de contemplation qui va parfois à l'extase . . . la musique palestrinienne semble être une traduction chantée du vaste poème de Michel-Ange . . . Rien ne frappe en route, et au bout du chemin on se trouve porté à des hauteurs prodigieuses." Gounod, *Mémoires d'un artiste*, 99–104, given in Lespinard, "Berlioz et la restauration de Palestrina," 112.

112. "demi-sonorités et demi-teintes"; "bruit." *RDM* 15 October 1894, 864.

ing its rhetoric from liberal Catholicism of the 1830s, Bellaigue's 1896 description of Palestrina as the people's representative—one of the last democrats in the history of music—gave his myth of heroic purity a new twist, his music becoming once more a symbol of collectivity and churchly perfection. Yet sectarianism was only just under the surface, and even within Schola circles Bellaigue's inclusive vision would soon be tempered by the content of D'Indy's *Cours de composition*, in which one heard a version of the Palestrina story that gave that perfection an antagonistic edge. Palestrina remained a moving target, his "in-betweenness" a perpetual invitation to appropriation and redefinition. He was lauded as a symbol of religious purity, but religious politics gave his music a distinctly cloudy historiography.

7

Baroque Choral Music: The Popular and the Profound

> Happy shall I be if the publication of this work, by recalling to my countrymen the memory of a great master whom they know too little of, shall suggest to them the regular performance of his immortal works. . . . There can be little doubt that the French public would not be slow to reward such an effort. So long as France deprives herself of the oratorios of Handel, there will be found within her a great deficiency in the culture of Musical Art.[1]

Victor Schoelcher's words, the closing gesture of the preface to his 1857 *Life of Handel*, were either prophetic, or an extraordinarily effective call to action. A Republican in exile from Louis-Napoléon's France, Schoelcher had, as he put it, taken consolation in Handel's oratorios while in England. In them he had discovered a sense of noble warmth and stability, pervasive grandeur, and a focus for community music-making that his beloved France lacked.[2] For despite all the attempts of proselytizers such as Choron, a mixed choral society culture had never really taken off in France; Beaulieu's Association Musicale de l'Ouest

---

1. Schoelcher, *The Life of Handel*, xxiv.
2. "Grandeur is the distinctive characteristic which dominates over all the compositions of Handel." Schoelcher, *The Life of Handel*, 387.

was exceptional. From 1834 and the closure of Choron's school, those institutions that might have been flagships remained technically fragile (the Société des Concerts choir) or uninterested in the wider community (the Moskova Société des Concerts, Edouard Rodrigues's group, and, later, Vervoitte's Société Académique). Oratorio composition had dwindled to almost nothing, for lack of an audience or the possibility of a hearing.[3] Second-Empire attempts at a choral revival centred on Handel (during the mid 1860s) seemed doomed to failure. Yet the years from 1868 to 1875 saw such difficulties triumphantly surmounted in Paris in precisely the terms that Schoelcher had outlined over a decade earlier. We witness a concerted attempt to naturalize a mixed choral culture, primarily via Handel but also via Bach, among the French people. At first sight such a phenomenon—the applauding of Germanic culture in the wake of defeat by Germanic culture—might seem counterintuitive, particularly given the loud appeals to *ars gallica* after the humiliation of the Franco-Prussian War and the continued occupation of Paris by Prussian forces. But the cultural weave is more complex, threaded through with a deep-seated sense of musical inferiority in respect to Germany and other Protestant nations that boasted the cultural capital of thriving amateur choral societies.[4] The stakes concerned democratization and national musicality, not compositional prowess. As Arthur Pougin put it in 1873: "In France we have no idea what it is to have great musical festivals such as take place annually on the other side of the Channel, the other side of the Rhine or the other side of the Meuse."[5] In a bid for heightened self-respect as a musical nation, earlier allegiances to Italian (Catholic) vocal and choral music—Pergolesi and Marcello—were all but put aside in favor of the grander products of northern Protestantism.

The emergence, across the decade punctuated by the Franco-Prussian War, of Handel the oratorio composer as a musical symbol of idealized Republican nationhood was a defining episode in the history of early music in France. However it is also inextricably linked, following the long-standing tradition of pairing "rival" composers, with the career of Bach as the tortoise to Handel's hare. For it was indeed Bach's choral music—perceived in the late 1860s as

---

3. No new oratorio by a Frenchman was performed in France between 1815 and 1843. The years 1843 to 1865 yielded just 12 works. Smither, *A History of the Oratorio*, vol. 4, 532.

4. For another aspect of this complex nationalist weave, see Strasser, "The Société Nationale."

5. "Nous ne savons pas en France ce que c'est que de grandes fêtes musicales, telles qu'il s'en donne annuellement de l'autre côté de la Manche, de l'autre côté du Rhin, ou de l'autre côté de la Meuse." Pougin, *A propos du Messie*, 12.

overbearingly Protestant and Germanic—that was appropriated into acceptability at Handel's expense two decades later.[6]

The first signs of a new attitude toward monumental Baroque choral music can be traced to around 1860, hot on the heels of Schoelcher's Handel biography, the first third of which was serialized in *La France musicale* in 1860–62.[7] But early plans to perform such repertory never bore fruit. The Société des Concerts du Conservatoire committee, which reportedly considered putting on oratorio performances for several years before 1863, never did so[8]; David and Saint-Etienne's project for a Société du Grand Concert resulted in several new editions of Handel's works in 1865, but no performances.[9] Although Weckerlin and his Société Sainte-Cécile initiated the Paris revivals of Baroque choral music with their 1866 performance of Handel's *Ode for St Cecilia's Day*, the decisive impact did not come until 1868–69, from Pasdeloup and Bourgault-Ducoudray. Enthusiasm grew in the years immediately following the Franco-Prussian War, reaching maximum intensity with Charles Lamoureux's six performances of *Messiah* in the winter of 1873–74, followed by the St Matthew Passion and *Judas Maccabaeus* (both 1874) and a further *Messiah* series in January 1875.[10] Thereafter, Parisian conductors' interest in Handel waned to such an extent that even in late 1875 writers began questioning whether the "revival" would stall.

But if Handel's popularity in Paris was short-lived, it was nevertheless the necessary condition for the composition of a host of new works, by Dubois, Franck, Gounod, Massenet, and Saint-Saëns—some of them very Handelian indeed.[11] Finally, the Handel revival underpinned the emergence in the 1880s of the late, now-lamented Berlioz as the quintessential French composer of monumental choral music, and the rise of Bach, the trajectory of whose choral music performance offers a striking contrast with that of Handel. Here, interest

---

6. For a detailed discussion of "pairings" in musical biography of the nineteenth and early twentieth centuries, see Wiley, *Re-writing Composers' Lives*. For important background to Bach in France, see Corten, Le "procès de canonisation," summarized in his "La réemergence de J.S. Bach." See also Fauquet and Hennion, *La grandeur de Bach*.

7. Broken off after 39 installments, halfway through chapter 5. The remainder was never published in French, though the all-important chapter 12 on Handel's character appeared in *La France musicale* in 1870, followed by individual "essays"—versions of five sections taken from intermediary chapters of the book. No reason was given for breaking off publication in 1862. The sheer length of the biography is a plausible one; however, state muzzling is another. Schoelcher's French-language writings during his exile were otherwise published in Geneva or Brussels, not Paris.

8. Charles Coligny in *FC* 2 (no. 46): 1 February 1863, [2].

9. See the notice in *UM* 3/11–12: August 1864, 185.

10. None was complete, but all presented over 50 percent of the work concerned.

11. The last 35 years of the century yielded 21 new French oratorios, 13 of them clustered around the years 1867 to 1880. Smither, *A History of the Oratorio*, vol. 4, 532.

gathered momentum over a longer period, beginning with two "false starts" in 1868 and 1874 (Pasdeloup's and Lamoureux's performances of the St Matthew Passion) and culminating in the Société des Concerts du Conservatoire's performances of the B minor Mass under Jules Garcin (1891) and the cantata cycles of the Chanteurs de Saint-Gervais (from 1893).

Press response to almost all such ventures focused on the idea of regeneration through the democratization of good music. Saint-Etienne described his own Handel editions of the 1860s as cheaply bought masterpieces which might offset the pernicious effect of "so many useless works, mediocre and short-lived efforts, which invade *café concerts* and even salons every day."[12] Pasdeloup's St Matthew Passion (Part I and closing chorus only) of May 1868 was performed to more than six thousand people in the Panthéon and sent Mathieu de Monter into raptures of hope.

> The project so magnificently inaugurated by Pasdeloup three days ago, will live on and increase. Such prosperity, this extension into the popular [domain], is very important; it is, in my humble opinion, a contribution to the elevation, the substance, I would say even to the health, almost, of serious musical study in our country. The sublime harmonies . . . must not, in abating suddenly, leave emptiness or doubt behind them. They must rise up again soon, even more brilliantly, and resound often, so that, from these classical heights, they spread over Paris, over France.[13]

The poetic vision betrays fear as much as it conveys enthusiasm. Why was the nation's musical health at risk? Why should this particular concert have national significance? Why might "emptiness" ensue if Pasdeloup's venture failed? Had De Monter written these lines after the disaster of 1870, the reasons—centring on France's need to compete with Teutonic culture and

---

12. "tant de morceaux futiles, de productions médiocres et éphémères, qui chaque jour envahissent les cafés chantants et même les salons," *UM* 3/15–16: 16 October 1864, 238.

13. "L'oeuvre si magnifiquement inaugurée, il y a trois jours, par Pasdeloup, vivra et grandira. Cette prosperité, cette extension populaire importe beaucoup, c'est du moins mon humble avis, à l'élévation, à la substance, je dirais presque à l'hygiène des hautes études musicales dans notre pays. Ces harmonies sublimes, qui ont réveillé les échos endormis du temple national et retenti jusque dans la nuit des tombeaux illustres, ne sauraient, en s'éteignant subitement, laisser après elles le vide, le doute, l'oubli. Il faut qu'elles s'élèvent bientôt, plus éclatantes encore, qu'elles résonnent souvent, que, de ces hauteurs classiques, elles se répandent sur Paris, sur la France." *RGM* 35/19:10 May 1868, 146.

education at all levels—would be more easily explicable. But his comments are symptomatic of the extent to which French musicians, even during the heyday of the Second Empire, sensed a crucial lack of seriousness in French musical culture and education. The disparagement of Second-Empire frivolity, so common a form of self-flagellation during the Third Republic, in fact dates from the Second Empire itself. From the early 1860s enthusiastic reports of foreign choral festivals appeared regularly in the musical press, but by the mid-1860s the need for France to find a "national institution" to compare with such traditions was a pressing one. For various reasons, the spotlight fell on Handel as the ideal vehicle.

Handel vs. Bach

The idea, initiated by Pasdeloup and pursued by Lamoureux, of following large doses of Bach with a leavening of Handel, encouraged comparisons that worked to Bach's disadvantage. Reviews of Pasdeloup's Panthéon concert in 1868 and its immediate successors already reveal a telling dichotomy: Louis Roger found Bach arid and Handel supple,[14] while for Jules Carlez, Bach's melodic aridity—music born more of the head than the heart—took on national significance, since he regarded it as characteristic of Germanic melody, even though he detected in it a poetic dreaminess.[15] Arthur Pougin, reviewing Lamoureux's St Matthew Passion of 1874 (performances of which concluded with familiar numbers from *Messiah*) found Bach inward-looking and only indirectly expressive, especially in comparison with the brilliance and fire of Handel's music.[16]

Comparisons between Handel and Bach invariably portrayed Handel as closer to the French spirit. Towards the end of the century the contrast was often intended as purely factual. For instance, when René de Récy [pseud. J. Trezel] described Bach as German and Handel as cosmopolitan in his 1885 biography of Bach, he was merely recognizing in Handel a composer who worked in three countries and wrote music to suit a variety of national and religious tastes.[17] A similar contrast (used to elevate Bach) appears in William Cart's 1899 comparison of the two German composers as polar opposites: the

---

14. *La réforme musicale* (henceforth *RéfM*) 15/12: 17 April 1870, n.p.
15. *La semaine musicale* (henceforth *SM*) 3 (no. 108): 31 January 1868, n.p.
16. *Mén* 40/18: 5 April 1874, 139.
17. *RDM* 15 November 1885, 224. For the attribution of this article, see Corten, *Le "procès de canonisation,"* 71.

one a gothic Romantic, the other closer in spirit to classical antiquity.[18] But earlier critics had other agendas, emphasizing Handel's distance from Teutonic traditions specifically in order to Latinize and appropriate him, and to provide reasons to sideline Bach as part of a living repertory. After 1870 and the foundation of the new Republic which was to symbolize a return to the noble ideals of Greek and Roman antiquity, such rhetorics of Latinizing became commonplace, contributing to the idea of France as a "new Rome."[19]

Yet the Latinizing of Handel took place well before it became a political imperative, bringing with it a valuable distancing from Protestant and Germanic values. Indeed, Handel was received in largely non-Christian terms, irrespective of the nature of the work involved. His Christian devotion was not doubted; it simply remained a biographical fact rather than an element which French critics perceived to be a driving force behind his music. *Messiah* and *Judas Maccabaeus* consistently drew epithets such as "epic," "vast," "heroic," or "of grandiose majesty," inspiring little comment on their character as religious works. By the mid-1860s, enough of their closeness to secular musical traditions in Britain was known to render them worldly, public works as far as the French musical intelligentsia were concerned. Moreover, the popularity, in the late 1860s and early 1870s, of smaller-scale works such as *Alexander's Feast* and *Acis and Galatea*, served to fuel other non-Christian critical rhetorics. Reviewing Bourgault-Ducoudray's *Alexander's Feast* of March/April 1870, Louis de Lassus described a Grecian sublime. Handel's music, in which there were "no false jewels, no superfluous decorations, no verbiage . . . everything that is needed and nothing except that which is required," resembled the "grandeur, power, solidity, beauty and even grace" of a Greek temple.[20] The following week, with Bourgault-Ducoudray's recent performances in mind, he portrayed Handel as entirely Latin, characterized by "that prodigious fertility of mind, that facility of improvisation which seems granted only to the Latin races."[21] Also inspired by these performances, the conductor Jules Cressonnois called Handel a "pagan Greek" whose musical nature was "strength in all its serenity."[22] The subject-matter of *Alexander's Feast* notwithstanding, such comments—all dating from before the Franco-Prussian War—created a "Mediterranean" Handel; and

---

18. Cart, *Etude sur J.-S. Bach*, 259.
19. See Fauser, "Gendering the Nations," 82.
20. "Pas de faux brillants, pas d'enjolivements superflus, pas de verbiage; il y a tout ce qu'il faut et rien que ce qu'il faut. . . . Grandeur, force, solidité, beauté, grâce même." *FM* 34/15: 10 April 1870, 110.
21. "cette fécondité d'esprit prodigieuse, cette facilité d'improvisation qui semble n'être dévolue qu'aux races latines." *FM* 34/16: 17 April 1870, 118.
22. "un païen, un païen grec"; "la *force* dans toute sa sérénité." *La France orphéonique* (henceforth *FO*) 2/7: 10 April 1870, n.p.

the knowledge that he had written Italian operas worked to similar effect. It was little wonder, then, that in a postwar period replete with rhetoric about a new Republic built on Graeco-Roman models and freed from the decadence of the Second Empire, a secular and Latin Handel would triumph over the musical Protestantism of Bach's choral music.

Alongside images of a Latin Handel we find gendered rhetorics of particular importance in a society which was, especially in the aftermath of a lost war, questioning the strength, character, and virility of its men. There were other factors, too: calls for equality in education, in the workplace, and in civic life from Second-Empire feminists such as Juliette Lamber, Julie Daubié, and Jenny d'Héricourt had provoked fierce debate on the question of whether French women should still, more than 50 years on, be trapped within the confines of the Napoleonic Code Civil of 1804. Women's increasing demands for education and opportunity contained, as far as their opponents were concerned, both the threat of masculinization in women and a rejection of their traditional submissive, domestic role. After the defeat of 1870, such perceptions intensified, since the French army's failure seemed to be symbolic of a loss of masculine authority not only over French territory, but over their property, women included.[23] From the perspective of the early 1870s, the Second Empire seemed a decadent, effeminate age which, depending on one's viewpoint, the superior values of either the new Republic or a return to a Catholic monarchy would consign to a salutary past. Nevertheless, since the sense that the Second Empire had lost its moral way—that it had rendered men less than "real" men and made women aspire to be more than "real" women—was already deeply rooted in 1860s cultural perceptions, the gendered rhetoric with which Bach and Handel were evaluated in the 1860s and '70s provides an important and fascinating reflection, within musical life, of debates about ways to "remasculinize" culture.

Essentialism was pervasive. Witness the scathing tones of Johannes Weber in 1869, when he complained that the soprano Christine Nilsson had "sighed Handel's music in such vaporous and amiable fashion that the female portion of the audience, especially, demanded an encore."[24] True, Weber was writing in

---

23. The Code Civil states: "La femme est notre propriété." For an indication of how long-lived and widespread men's insecurities were about the related problems of defeat by Prussia and potential "defeat" at the hands of noncompliant women, see Berenson, *The Trial of Madame Caillaux*, esp. 114–17, and, on fencing and the duel as a form of ritual military re-masculinization during the *Belle époque*, 186–98, and Nye, *Masculinity and Male Codes of Honor*, 148–71.

24. "a soupiré la musique de Haendel d'une façon si vaporeuse et si amiable que la partie féminine surtout de l'auditoire lui a redemandé le morceau." *Temps* 27 April 1869, n.p.

portentous mode at the time (he saw musical decadence everywhere and attributed it to poor education nationwide); nevertheless, he saw in such spineless singing of music from *Judas Maccabaeus* not only an insult to Handel, but also an indication that the austere traditions of the Société des Concerts du Conservatoire now risked being brought closer, through this "feminine" element (as he put it), to those of the Opéra or the Théâtre-Italien.

In fact, both Bach and Handel, as choral composers, were perceived to display a potentially redeeming virility. Several critics who attended Pasdeloup's St Matthew Passion in 1868 said as much. For Sextius Durand, the closing chorus combined admirable gravity and splendor, with the "sovereign brilliance" of the chorus parts set in relief by the "masculine harmonies" underpinned by the low-lying cello and bass part. Closing his review of the Bach, he could not resist comparing such music to the vapidity of modern ephemera.[25] "B.D." (Bougault-Ducoudray?), in *Le ménestrel*, wrote that the St Matthew Passion was "the work of a giant, which in its austere and even rough language, in its Herculean structure, in its gigantic proportions, is disconcerting to our musical taste, which has been flattered by the infinite suppleness, the caressing wheedling and the voluptuous refinements of modern art!"[26]

The dichotomy between the hearty maleness of the old and the decadent femininity of the new could hardly have been spelt out more clearly. Moreover, as this critic further argued, whereas modern music seeks effects of sonority to flatter the listener's ear and keep his or her interest alive, in Bach "All the effect lies in the strength of the musical invention itself, in the justness of expression and in [the] power of conception."[27] The familiar trope of surface (feminine) versus substance (masculine) appears here, linked to the equally familiar conception of masculinity as defined in part by the sustained mental power (a capacity denied to women) that subjugates decoration to essence.

Yet Bach was manifestly more "feminine" than Handel, not least because his music appeared more varied in style. He was not immune to the charge (even from a supporter such as Charles Bannelier) of writing indulgent vocal ornamentation at the expense of musical expression, and was excused such lapses only because they were "imposed" on him by eighteenth-century musical tastes.[28] Ernest Reyer, also an ardent supporter of Bach as against Handel, saw

---

25. "éclat souverain"; "mâles accords." *FM* 32/20: 17 May 1868, 150.

26. "oeuvre de géant, qui déroute, par un langage austère et même rude, par sa structure herculéenne, par ses gigantesques proportions, notre goût musical flatté par les souplesses infinies, les cajoleries caressantes, et les raffinements voluptueux de l'art moderne!" *Mén* 35/24:10 May 1868, 187.

27. "Tout l'effet consiste dans la force de l'invention musicale proprement dite, dans la justesse de l'expression, et dans [la] puissance de conception." *Mén* 35/24:10 May 1868, 187.

28. Article previewing Lamoureux's first St Matthew Passion. *RGM* 41/13:29 March 1874, 100.

in his music the "pure and fortifying" flow of the stream indicated by Bach's name. But while Bach's work left him "overwhelmed by the grandeur and unity of this style, by the power and variety of these inspired songs," he also found his melodic lines "unctuous and tender"; and that "fortifying stream" was also both stereotypically feminine ("full of sweet murmurs") and stereotypically masculine ("bursting its banks; a stream larger than a river, more impetuous than a torrent").[29] There were also pieces in which Bach's gentler side dominated. In January 1874, when Danbé programmed an unidentified church cantata alongside Janequin's *La bataille de Marignan* and excerpts from Rameau's *Hippolyte et Aricie*, Pougin (a Handelian where choral music was concerned) waxed lyrical, but using a rhetoric usually destined for the genderless Palestrinian school. It was, he said, "a calm, somewhat restrained work, which is notable for a heavenly kind of grace and a sweetness full of suavity." He also compared it, *à la* Palestrina, to the great monuments of religious painting.[30]

Arguably, Bach's range was his undoing in the competition with Handel. In the 1870s the latter's music became more popular precisely because of its more easily definable character, its narrower emotional appeal, and its more straightforward construction. Notwithstanding moments such as the "Pastoral symphony" from *Messiah*, in Handel the French saw the essence of virility in music: robustness, solidity, healthy energy, forcefulness and a complete absence of the overrefinement that spelt incipient decadence. Moreover, his chosen texts were replete with military images, especially in the Old Testament subjects of the oratorios. The allegorical import of Handel's *Judas Maccabaeus* in particular was not lost on the French, whose favorite (and ubiquitous) chorus was "See, see, the conq'ring hero comes." Even texts such as Dryden and Hamilton's *Alexander's Feast*, which were not particularly triumphalist, became so in French translation: Victor Wilder's version of "Happy, happy, happy pair / None but the brave deserves the fair," became "Gloire à toi, Gloire à toi, Prince puissant, roi triomphant" in the popular Heugel edition which dated, inopportunely, from early 1870.[31]

For postwar French critics, the four-square diatonicism of Handel's music suggested desirable characteristics for French society. Twice in the same review

---

29. "ébloui par la grandeur et l'unité de ce style, par la puissance et la variété de ces chants inspirés"; "ces mélodies onctueuses et tendres"; "ruisseau dont l'onde est pure et fortifiante, ruisseau plein de doux murmures et de débordements, ruisseau plus large qu'un fleuve, plus impétueux qu'un torrent." *JD* 31 May 1868, n.p.

30. "une oeuvre calme, recueillie en quelque sorte, qui se fait remarquer par une grâce toute céleste et par une douceur pleine d'onction." *Mén* 40/8: 25 January 1874, 61.

31. As indicated by a note on the contents page, this translation was first performed by the Société Bourgault-Ducoudray on 31 March 1870.

of Lamoureux's *Messiah* of December 1873, Pougin described his music as containing "severe and masculine beauties"[32]; in a retrospective essay on the significance of Lamoureux's first performance, published in his family magazine *La musique populaire* (1881–82), he argued that every society needed activities that (like singing Handel) were "healthy, virile and comforting."[33] The element of comfort is particularly interesting, since it might be perceived as indicating emotional weakness. But as described in 1872 by Guy de Charnacé, the anti-Wagnerian son-in-law of Liszt and Marie d'Agoult, the comforting nature of Handel's music was created by powerful means: diatonicism and clearly directional harmony. He was reviewing Bourgault-Ducoudray's *Acis and Galatea* of 1 May 1872:

> Our modern ears, accustomed to chromaticism, are surprised hearing music in an almost entirely diatonic style. That is a fact. But what is equally true is the tonal power of Handel's music, a power so great that the ear never experiences indecision or doubt, and so fine that it [the ear] never becomes lost.
>
> This great musician is of a time that knew neither our dreams, nor our sadnesses, nor our complex aspirations, and still less our emotional vapidities. His language is thus necessarily the expression of uncomplicated, direct, strong, natural sentiments—the language which responds best to [the expression of] clearly-defined ideas.[34]

The comfort Handel offered was thus a cloak of self-confidence that, temporarily at least, expunged doubt because its harmonic language offered no riddles. Had De Charnacé written only the first paragraph, we might be tempted to read his views as simply those of another conservative anti-Wagnerian (although Lamoureux's status as both a Wagnerian and a Handelian/Bachian

---

32. "beautés mâles et sévères"; "mâles beautés." *Mén* 40/3: 21 December 1873, 19, 20.

33. "saines, viriles, réconfortantes." Pougin, revision of *A propos du Messie*, published in his own *La musique populaire* (*MPop*), 1/6: 24 November 1881, 87.

34. "Nos oreilles modernes, habituées aux éléments chromatiques s'étonnent en entendant une musique d'un genre presque exclusivement diatonique. Cela est vrai. Mais ce qui n'est pas moins vrai, c'est la puissance tonale chez Handel, puissance telle qu'il n'y a jamais d'indécision, de doute pour l'oreille, si bien qu'elle ne s'égare jamais.

Ce grand musicien est bien d'un temps qui ne connaissait ni nos rêves, ni nos mélancolies, ni nos aspirations compliquées, et encore moins nos mièvreries sentimentales. Sa langue est donc bien l'expression nécessaire aux sentiments simples, francs, sains, forts, naturels, la langue qui répond le mieux aux idées définies." De Charnacé, *Musique et musiciens*, vol. 1, 148–49.

makes the drawing of clear dichotomies insecure); it is his shift from music per se to the manner in which music reflects society that helps situate his critique as part of a wider search for a music that embodied successful aspiration and was unencumbered by the pressures of the present.

Such qualities were much needed in a society racked by self-doubt regarding its military prowess and, by extension, the strength and virility of its manhood. But within French discourse the model for De Charnacé's image of Handel dates from considerably earlier—back to Maurice Germa's long biographical article in the *Revue contemporaine* of 1866, which was itself a review of Handel biographies, Schoelcher's included. It detailed Handel's struggles in England and his success in producing a genre that reflected the character of "this valiant, austere and liberal nation."[35] Not only was Handel a "masculine and proud" genius, but his project to institute opera in English was a "virile and national" exercise.[36] Inevitably, though, Germa's focus was the oratorios, discussion of which formed a natural climax to the biographical narrative and led to a peroration comparing Handel's contribution to religious music with that of the angelic Palestrina.

For Germa, Handel had humanized religious music, turning it into a vehicle to express the drama of humanity's relationship to God. But more than that, because of the personal struggles of their creator—which Germa presented as a military campaign during which the composer conquered England and the English—Handelian oratorio became a symbol of determination, personal and collective resistance in the face of attack, and permanence.

> Filled with indomitable perseverence against ever-threatening hostilities, he erects impregnable ramparts, built on rock and capable of fending off the winds of the sky, the waves of the sea and the attacks of man. He imprinted on his compositional style a massive solidity which remains unaffected by time and changing fashion. His scores carry the stamp of a valiant nature that nothing can overcome, a tenacity which exhausts that of any obstacle, and his oratorios, in which are melded all art, all sacred melody, all the operatic and

---

35. "cette nation vaillante, austère et libérale." *Revue contemporaine*, 2d series, 23: September/October 1866, 616. It was, of course, precisely this image of Handelian oratorio as national allegory that the English themselves had cultivated since the genre's earliest days. See Buch, *Beethoven's Ninth*, 14–16.

36. "mâle et fier génie"; "virile et nationale." *Revue contemporaine*, 2d series, 23: September/October 1866, 610, 606. I have yet to find comparably gendered interpretations of Handel in Francophone writings before Germa. The closest comparable article, by Fétis, dwells on Handel's clarity and his massive choral effects [*Biographie universelle*, 2d ed., vol. 4 (1862), 137–38] but takes the evaluation no further.

dramatic inspiration of a nation, are monuments of granite and iron which will live on for so long as England remains standing.[37]

In 1866 Germa had effectively written the script of postwar Handelian reception. His Handel contained all the requisite features of a successful warrior nation: positive on the attack and steely in defence. The nature of his music as raw material—with its granite- and iron-like qualities—is also alluded to in comments such as de Charnacé's description in 1872 of Handelian rhythms as "beaten by bronze hammers."[38] Germa had of course read Schoelcher's peroration of 1857, in which Handel was referred to as a "great conqueror" and a man of "indefatigable perseverance," "moral courage," and "indomitable will"[39]; he was undoubtedly influenced by Schoelcher's graphic metaphor of each section of a Handelian chorus as a "battalion marching to the assault."[40] But the references to territory and the elements, and the projection of composer onto people, appear to be his own. Moreover, when Germa re-used this passage in 1875, in a review of Holy Week concerts that had featured both Handel and Palestrina, the resonances were entirely different and the implication blunt: had France been blessed with men like Handel in 1870, she would not have had to cede Alsace-Lorraine to Germany.[41] In Germa's vision, therefore, virility, confidence, strength in simplicity—all these elements now familiar in the reception of Handel's choral music—combined with the image of massed delivery to climax in the irresistible image of a disciplined, unified and indomitable warrior nation singing its own, indomitable music. It is no wonder that Handel pro-

---

37. "Plein d'une persévérance indomptable, contre les hostilités toujours menaçantes, il élève des remparts inexpugnables, assis sur le rocher et capables de braver les vents du ciel, les flots de la mer, l'attaque de l'homme. Il a imprimé à sa facture et à son style un solidité massive, qui n'a point à compter avec le temps et avec les modes changeantes. Ses partitions portent l'empreinte d'une vaillance que rien ne dompte, d'une ténacité qui fatigue l'obstacle, et ses oratorios, dans lesquels s'absorbent tout l'art, toute la mélopée religieuse, toute l'inspiration lyrique et théâtrale d'une nation, sont des monuments de granit et de fer qui subsisteront tant que l'Angleterre sera debout." *Revue contemporaine*, 2d series, 23: September/October 1866, 615.

38. "frappé par des marteaux de bronze." De Charnacé, *Musique et musiciens*, 147 (from his 1872 review of *Acis*).

39. Schoelcher, *The Life of Handel*, 398.

40. Schoelcher, *The Life of Handel*, 388. Germa extended the idea: "les compositions de ce grand homme gagnent à être mises en relief par d'énormes armées orchestrales et chantantes. Dompter les masses, les rallier dans l'idée biblique, telle est la virtualité de l'oratorio et le caractère du génie d'Haendel." *Revue contemporaine*, 2d series, 23: September/October 1866, 615; *CM* 8 (no. 43): 1 April 1875, 32.

41. There is, of course, another element, post-1870, to the comparison with a liberal and friendly England: it was well known that the British prime minister, William Gladstone, had tried to dissuade Bismarck from his plan to annex Alsace and Lorraine and that he had attempted to form a coalition with other neutral European powers for this purpose. See Magnus, *Gladstone*, 205; and Roy Jenkins, *Gladstone*, 330.

vided French musicians with an enviable model for the revitalization of their own moribund choral culture, and that no indigenous tradition appeared equal to it.

The People's Handel?

Rhetorics of directness and masculine vigor contributed significantly to perceptions of Handel's popular accessibility. Reviewers of Pasdeloup's concerts noted it in 1868[42]; by the 1880s, the idea of his choral music as accessible to "the people"—not just "le public," but also the masses ("la foule")—had become received wisdom. In 1882, Pougin summed up the prevailing view: "More accessible, perhaps, to the crowd than the great Bach himself, more radiant, more easily comprehensible, exciting the masses and impressing them with all the power of his genius, his memory remains brilliant: he dominates the art with all the grandeur of a magnificent and overflowing inspiration."[43]

The popular appeal of Lamoureux's Handel performances of the 1870s had been documented in the same way: Reyer wrote of "an attentive crowd, excited and full of enthusiasm" flocking to the Cirque des Champs-Elysées for *Judas Maccabaeus*.[44] As a committed Bachian, he even found Handel's popularity suspicious, hinting that the music therefore showed little of the sophistication that characterized great art[45]; but for other writers, the combination of Handel's uncomplicated style and foreign traditions of massed performance suggested that his music was ripe for adoption beyond the confines of Paris's high-bourgeois and aristocratic choral societies. It was imperative for Handel to break free from the Salle Herz and, even, the Cirque des Champs-Elysées. Here, two defining strands of the composer's reception—the perception of his music as both accessible and gigantic—became weapons in a wide-ranging ideological battle to bring Handel, and Handel specifically, to the people of France.

It was Bourgault-Ducoudray whose performances came at the most propitious time: from 1869 to 1874. To his supporters they appeared to be a prelude

---

42. See especially Sextius Durand's review in *FM* 32/20: 17 May 1868, 151.
43. "Plus accessible peut-être à la foule que le grand Bach lui-même, plus rayonnant, plus facilement compréhensible, remuant les masses et les frappant de toute la puissance de son génie, son souvenir reste éclatant, il domine l'art de toute la grandeur d'une inspiration magnifique et débordante." *MPop.* 2/44: 17 Aug. 1882, 390.
44. "une foule attentive, émue, enthousiasmée." *JD* 24 Nov. 1874, n.p.
45. Toward the end of his review of Lamoureux's St Matthew Passion he quipped that Lamoureux had ended the concert with the most "saisissantes, je devrais dire saisissables" passages of *Messiah* (the Hallelujah chorus). *JD* 21 April 1874, n.p.

to a great flowering of Handel oratorio in France, during which choral societies would progress beyond *Acis* and *Alexander's Feast* to the full-scale works sung by enormous choirs. This was undoubtedly Louis de Lassus's agenda when in April 1870 he expressed the wish that, through Bourgault-Ducoudray's activities, Handel should belatedly be accorded "droit de Patrie" in France.[46] It was also Louis Roger's, when in the same month he dubbed Bourgault-Ducoudray's society an "institution nationale."[47] The general public needed to be educated to appreciate Handel, and immediately after the war Bourgault-Ducoudray appeared to be the conductor best qualified to do it. The critic A. de Bory wrote a lyrical appreciation of his work after a performance of *Acis*, exhorting him to embark on a crusade of artistic enfranchisement: "Will you, M. Ducoudray, please be Handel's advocate. Initiate us completely—and especially the masses, who are so often disinherited in matters of art—as regards these great choral compositions."[48] De Bory was encouraged by the recent decision of the Directeur des Beaux-Arts to subscribe to Gérard's cheap score of *Acis* and to distribute it to all state-run conservatoires and regional philharmonic societies: it seemed to indicate that serious attempts were being made to democratize good music and (as in Victorian England) to offset the pernicious influence of lower-class musical entertainments such as farce and the *café-concert*.[49]

It is therefore not surprising to find De Bory at the centre of a move to spread the Handelian word around the nation's amateur choral societies and to enable them to emulate the great traditions of Germany and England. In spring 1873, he, Bourgault-Ducoudray, and De Lajarte met in Paris to discuss how Handelian repertory might be imported into the male-voice *orphéon* tradition.[50] The group's vision was a distilled version of that put forward from the early 1860s by another reformer—Louis Roger—who later used his *orphéon* journal *La semaine musicale* as a platform for the argument that the *orphéon* should change course. As he asked in 1862, why could *orphéons* not prove that the popularization of music did not necessarily mean a decline in artistic standards?

46. *Mén* 34/16: 17 April 1870, 118.
47. *RéfM* 15/11: 10 April 1870, n.p.
48. "Soyez, vous, monsieur Ducoudray, l'homme de Handel, initiez-nous complétement, et surtout les masses, si souvent déshéritées des choses de l'art, à ces grandes compositions chorales." *La nouvelle France chorale* (henceforth *NFC*) 5/8: 16 April 1873, n.p.
49. *NFC* 5/8: 16 April 1873, n.p.
50. As reported in an article co-written by Charles Coligny and De Bory in *NFC* 5/9: 1 May 1873, n.p. Bourgault-Ducoudray had used *orphéon* singers in 1872, for his *Acis* of 1 May. Thereafter, they shared program credits with Bourgault-Ducoudray's own society for performances of (among other concerts) *Alexander's Feast* on 28 January and 16 March 1873, and *Acis* on 6 April 1873.

I do not want to start redrawing the map for choral societies. I say simply to those who direct them: there is much still to be done and you have as yet done nothing at all. You are behind in respect of early music, and you are no less so in respect of modern music. Orlandus Lassus awaits; so do Handel, Haydn, Cherubini and Mendelssohn.[51]

Roger's outburst was probably motivated as much by the new sense of possibility as by lingering frustration. It was not enough to popularize *music*; what was necessary was the popularization of "classic" music.[52] By contrast, and entirely in line with prevailing ideologies relating to the emulation of English and Germanic choral traditions, the 1873 group narrowed the field of favored composers to Handel, Bach, Haydn, and Beethoven, with Handel given pride of place. As for involving the lower classes: Bourgault-Ducoudray had already shown the way forward by enlisting the services of men from the *orphéons* Le Louvre and Les Enfants de Lutèce from 1872. For while his society was relatively small and performed mostly to elite audiences in the Salles Herz and Pleyel, his aspirations for its public utility were not. He intended it to serve as a small-scale model for larger gatherings that would, once France's system of public musical education had been improved, be accessible to all.[53] His teaming up with two *orphéon* societies was thus symbolic of his determination, after the lost war with Prussia, to illustrate how all strata of French society could be brought together in harmonious alliance and participate together in a form of music-making that was traditional in other nations—not least Germany.

For various reasons, co-opting the *orphéon* on a national scale was an obvious ambition in 1873. Since its inception in the mid-1830s under the direction of Bocquillon Wilhem, it had become a national movement, comprising both male-voice choirs and wind or brass bands. In 1855 there were three hundred choirs nationwide (though unevenly spread); seven hundred by 1860; twelve hundred by 1864; and in 1870, more than two thousand.[54] The *orphéon* followed

---

51. "Je ne veux pas entreprendre de tracer un plan aux sociétés chorales. Je dis seulement à ceux qui les dirigent: il y a beaucoup à faire et vous n'avez encore rien fait. Vous êtes en retard avec la musique ancienne; vous ne l'êtes pas moins avec la musique moderne. Orlando Lassus vous attend à l'oeuvre; Haendel, Haydn, Cherubini et Mendelssohn vous y attendent également." *RéfM* 6/49: 12 January 1862, n.p., reprinted in Roger's own *La semaine musicale* 2 (no. 61): 1 March 1866, n.p.

52. *SM* 2 (no. 61): 1 March 1866, n.p.

53. This is the burden of the brochure *Société Bourgault-Ducoudray*, which set out the society's rationale, traced its history, and touted for new members.

54. Gerbod, "Vox populi," 233.

an annual cycle which culminated in a competitive festival season stretching from June to August, during which towns across the country would host visiting choirs and bands for a three-day orgy of performances, street processions, prize-givings, and a final banquet for hosts and judges. In the eyes of their higher-class organizers at least, the *orphéon* movement had always brought its participants a combination of artistic and social benefits. Music's civilizing effects were married to militaristic, patriotic, and faintly religious texts which were intended to inspire a potentially insurgent lower class with devoted loyalty to family and nation. Whatever the more sinister aspects of social control it embodied, the *orphéon* movement, which involved members of the artisan as well as the working classes, was originally intended to provide structured leisure activity that could give France's male population a taste of disciplined learning through art under the banner of brotherhood and the oft-cited "spirit of association." It was perhaps a fitting by-product of the movement's success that in the festival season it demanded such protracted absences of the men from their family homes and workplaces: for the *orphéon* was, with few exceptions, an all-male phenomenon that aped the characteristics and adopted the trappings of military life, from battle against strangers on a foreign field to the sparkling epaulettes of participants' uniforms, the gilt-edged processional banners, and, of course, medals.

However, as Roger had intimated, surface bustle no longer indicated a healthy tradition even by the early 1860s. For many commentators, some of them regular jury members, the balance between artistic and social goals had shifted such that the movement was no longer fulfilling any meaningful musical function. Standards of singing at regional and national competitions were often lamentable; many societies remained musically illiterate and clung to a small repertory of well-known, short, pieces.[55] From the late 1860s onward, writers for the *orphéon* press followed the Paris oratorio revivals closely and began to measure the movement's choral decadence against the rising stars of the capital's elite amateur societies. Charles Coligny saw the decadence as early as 1863: the *orphéon* had to be saved from itself. If Marcello were still alive, he wrote, he [Coligny] "would beg him to help us chase away from the *orphéon* the buffoons who dishonor it."[56] Six years later, F. Gillet, editor of *La France orphéonique* (and prob-

---

55. For repertory lists of the Paris Orphéon up to around 1880, see Di Grazia, *Concert Societies*, 132–33 and 157–59. It should be noted, however, that under the leadership of Gounod, Pasdeloup, and Bazin this *orphéon* was unusually experienced in the "classique."

56. "le supplierais de nous aider à chasser de l'Orphéon les bouffons qui le déshonorent." *FC*, 2 (no. 46): 1 February 1863, n.p.

ably a member of the Gillet oboists' dynasty) wrote of an unmistakable and widely observed decline in the "temperature" of the choral *orphéon* tradition,[57] claiming that the most important reasons were musical illiteracy and the misconceived ideals (travel and the excitement of competitions) that lay behind the institution of the newest choral societies.

The consequences of illiteracy prompted reformers to advocate a more overtly pedagogical approach, turning education into a hotly debated issue long before defeat brought the conviction that the Prussians' victory owed much to superior systems of training at all levels.[58] With respect to musical culture the French sense of inferiority was in any case already acute, with much ink spilt on discussions of whether the Germans were an innately musical nation. But the most common counterarguments—that their superior musicality was due to musical education from infancy, or that the Lutheran chorale tradition provided an aural/harmonic training that French plainsong practices could not hope to equal—merely intensified the perceived need for educational reform at all levels. More worryingly, they also prompted the thought that Catholic nations were necessarily held back by their tradition of singing chant—"an incomplete music which has neither melodic span, nor key, nor rhythm, nor harmony, and melody so rarely that it's hardly worth mentioning."[59] As late as 1899, William Cart advanced a similar argument when he wrote that in the wake of the Thirty Years' War Protestant traditions were the most potent vehicles for cultural regeneration, and that Catholic states had taken considerably longer to re-establish themselves.[60]

Such comments, which form an important subset of the plethora of laments about France's musical backwardness, had limited effect on those *orphéon* traditionalists who clung to the movement's social ideals.[61] While

---

57. "thermomètre de l'Orphéon français." *FO* 1/10: 10 December 1869, n.p.

58. See, esp., Digeon, *La crise allemande*. As Digeon notes, the notion that the Germans were better equipped, intellectually and spiritually, than the French, was not born of defeat, "Mais la défaite incite, impérativement, l'imitation" (365).

59. The complete passage is a blistering condemnation of the effects of plainchant singing on music education: "Or, voilà trois siècles que les protestants ont renoncé au plain-chant, et quand nous aurons comme eux, pendant plusieurs générations, entendu et exécuté de la musique harmonisé et rhythmée, il sera temps alors de constater qui aura fait le plus de progrès dans l'usage de la vraie musique." [Plainchant is] "une musique incomplète, qui n'a ni l'étendue, ni la tonalité, ni le rhythme, ni l'harmonie, et si rarement la mélodie qu'il en faut à peine parler . . . Pour surcroit de désastre artistique, dans le grand nombre des communes de France, on laisse chanter faux au lutrin. Voilà ce qui nous retarde." Guimet, *La musique populaire*, 12–13.

60. Cart, *Etude sur J.-S. Bach*, 2–3.

61. Meaning, in practice, the persuasion of the have-nots that they were "integrated" in society.

reformers from within and commentators from without argued that France's status as a civilized nation was at stake, *orphéon* men such as Ernest Gebaüer found the artistic and chauvinistic benefits of better musical education irrelevant because the French, with their underdeveloped educational system, could not possibly hope to compete with centuries of Lutheran training. Moreover, he argued, "The *orphéon* is not a school; it is an institution whose primary goal is the fusion of different classes in society, and in which the moralizing aspect must take precedence over the musical one."[62] Musical literacy classes, he claimed, were for the conservatoires, not the *orphéons*. It was hardly surprising that after 1870 such debates should intensify and become imbued with anxiety about the nature of "real" men and the need to cultivate a healthy mass culture that could compete with those of stronger military nations such as England and Germany. After all, in the name of fraternity and social cohesion the summer competitions saw thousands of Frenchmen dress up for a quasi-military pageant and apparently waste their efforts on unworthy music. As Gustave Francolin, founder of a journal dedicated to musical literacy, observed in an article entitled "The Errors of the *Orphéon*": "The French *orphéon* . . . has not taken the manly decision to engage in serious study; still less has it developed a taste for great works; it tackles the magnificent oratorios of the classic masters no more than it ever did."[63] Like so many manifestations of feminized culture, from salon music to the popular novel, the movement appeared to prioritize surface over substance.

It was in this climate, with the debate already a decade old, that De Bory, Bourgault-Ducoudray, and De Lajarte met in 1873 to discuss the artistic future of the *orphéon*. Yet nothing substantive had happened in the interim, and so what De Bory and his colleagues were suggesting was nothing short of a complete overhaul. Even those (notably the composers Camille de Vos and Charles Coligny) who were enthusiastic and prolific in their writings on Handel, were resistant to the idea. The proposed change of repertory from unaccompanied male-voice works to orchestrally accompanied works (potentially requiring the teaming-up of *orphéons* and local philharmonic societies) represented not so much a reform as a takeover bid by bourgeois and amateur musicians among whose own class there were too few willing singers to create the massive effects

---

62. "L'Orphéon n'est pas une école: c'est une institution ayant surtout pour but la fusion des diverses classes de la société, et où le côté moralisateur doit primer essentiellement le côté musical." *L'écho des orphéons* (henceforth *EO*) 6/4: 20 February 1866, 1.

63. "L'orphéon français . . . n'a pas pris la résolution virile d'étudier sérieusement; il n'a pas pris davantage le goût des grandes oeuvres; il n'aborde pas plus qu'avant les magnifiques oratorios des maîtres classiques." *Journal populaire de musique et de chant* 4 (no. 42): August 1873, 72.

Handel's music demanded. Coligny approved of the co-option of *orphéon* singers to bourgeois societies for their oratorio performances, but he recoiled at the idea of destroying the unique character of the *orphéon* itself.[64] De Vos was in a more embarrassing position because as chief editor of *La nouvelle France chorale* he had, from 1870 to April 1873, written concert reviews that were paeans to Handel, to the exclusion of almost all other composers (Wagner excepted) being performed in Parisian concerts. He had also emphasized the extent to which Handel's music demanded enormous performing forces.[65] Nevertheless, perhaps fearing for his own career as a successful composer of *orphéon* choruses, he limited his support for restructuring to the establishment of mixed *orphéons* singing dedicated, unaccompanied music.

Participation, too, was different from competition: the celebratory and socially cohesive type of festival became, in the mid 1860s, preferable to the potentially divisive pageant of competition.[66] The monumental numbers involved in the *orphéon* movement inspired ideas of a new choral festival culture that would cut across class divisions and present, through a single chorus, a microcosm of society. In 1868 the official Government paper, the *Moniteur universel*, printed a Utopian picture of English festival customs in which class differences were erased and one saw "excited ladies singing their part alongside humble middle-class women."[67] The allure of such monumental solidarity, before but particularly after the war, was that it could suggest a unified nation and that it offered possibilities as the music of civic ceremonial. As early as 1866, Louis Roger had written that for state celebrations or other important events in the civic calendar: "we might convene in Paris or elsewhere one or two hundred orpheon societies to perform a masterpiece. This would constitute [a truly] popular art, worthy of a fine and wealthy nation."[68] It was precisely the image of the singing nation, evoked most powerfully in Germa's seminal Handel article of the same year, that drove Republican-inspired reformists to try to import Handel into the *orphéon* tradition after 1870. The Handelian project also encouraged comparison with the musical styles of the late 1700s, and in its ambition, its rooting in a spirit of educational *fraternité*, its implicit

---

64. *Journal populaire de musique et de chant* 4 (no. 42): August 1873, 72.

65. See, for instance, his "Bulletin" in *NFC* 2 (no. 26): 16 April 1870, n.p.; his "Bulletin-Chronique" in *NFC* 3 (no. 47): 16 March 1872, n.p.; and his review of Lamoureux's *Messiah*, *NFC* 6 (no. 1): 1 January 1874, n.p.

66. French writers did not deny that the Germans and the British also had their competitive festivals for male-voice choirs; they simply chose to ignore them in favor of a model that offered more obvious social solidarity.

67. "de fièvres ladies chanter leur partie à côté d'humbles bourgeoises," given in the *RMSAM* 9/8: July/August 1868, 58.

68. "on convoquât à Paris ou ailleurs cent ou deux cents sociétés orphéoniques pour l'exécution d'un chef-d'oeuvre. Ce serait l'art populaire, digne d'une belle et riche nation." *SM* 2 (no. 83): 2 August 1866, n.p.

anticlericalism, and its intended nationwide application it was indeed a project in the classical Republican tradition, dating back to the aftermath of 1789, of unifying the nation by giving it access to a common sense of, and right to, secular citizenship.[69] Indeed, hopeful sketches of scenes akin to the massed gatherings of Revolutionary festivals appeared throughout the musical press; and the monster concert, gathering participants from entire *départements* was the necessary goal, as is attested by the almost obsessive precision with which the number of performers in foreign festivals was reported (even down to the numbers in each choir section).

Society, however, includes women; and by far the most radical demand of the 1873 project was that *orphéon* culture should embrace them. Although many choirs included children, the movement's overwhelmingly male culture was, of course, a major obstacle. As early as 1869, F. Gillet had suggested the inclusion of women as a means of saving the *orphéon*[70]; opponents of reform pointed acidly to the absence of "l'élément féminin" as a decisive reason why the *orphéon* could not change artistic direction.[71] However, in other contexts the issue had already received significant publicity, with the prudishness of French societal rules about the mixing of the sexes criticized as a factor that was fatally hindering France's chances of competing musically with Protestant countries. Such problems were not restricted to French choirs or indeed to *orphéons*: an excited report of the Brussels festival *Messiah*, which involved thirteen hundred singers and five hundred instrumentalists, trumpeted that the problem of persuading four hundred women "of a certain station" to participate alongside persons of whose character and social status they were ignorant had finally been overcome.[72] And one senses the frustration (ambivalent though it was) of Camille de Vos's compliment of 1874 to Guillot de Sainbris on his success in bringing together his Société Chorale des Amateurs—a choir of fifty men and fifty women.

> In sum, from this society we hear works which could not be performed by any other society, because those which are known to us manage to put a few pieces together only by dint of desperate

---

69. On the "Republican tradition" during the nineteenth century and beyond, see Hazareesingh, *Political Traditions in Modern France*, 65–89.

70. *FO* 1/10: 10 December 1869, n.p.

71. See, for instance, Ernest Gebaüer's comment about the plausibility of *orphéon* choirs tackling *Elijah*, which I interpret as a sarcastic retort to the evangelizing of his rival journal editor Louis Roger. *EO* 10/3: 5–9 February 1870, 1.

72. "d'un certain rang." *L'écho du parlement*, given in *RéfM*, 14/37–38: 10–17 October 1869, n.p. A portion of this report, which contains some telling plagiarism of Germa's militaristic Handel imagery from his *Revue contemporaine* biography of 1866, is also given in *AM* 9/45: 7 October 1869.

measures to bring together male and female singers who have no other reason to meet—which therefore renders all contact between them impossible.[73]

The problem was thus surmountable within the leisured classes (De Vos's gloom may actually be an exaggeration born of his immersion in lower-class music-making, with its rather different *mores*). But fear of inappropriate class mixes still prevailed, as Bourgault-Ducoudray found when his levels of female recruitment dwindled after the arrival of his *orphéon* men.[74]

It may have seemed to De Bory and his associates that it would be easier to co-opt lower-class and rural women to *orphéon* choirs than to struggle against various levels of bourgeois Catholic *mores*. In practice, it was not. As Peter McPhee has argued, relative economic prosperity in the decades after 1850 produced widespread changes in rural life, not least among which was a progressive *embourgeoisement* especially noticeable in rural communities situated close to towns.[75] Of course, with that *embourgeoisement* came closer attention to patriarchal codes wherein men and women would ideally inhabit the separate spheres of the public and the domestic, and where chaperones and tightly controlled encounters with members of the opposite sex became the rule once girls reached marriageable age. Within bourgeois urban society, we see the system at work. The statutes of amateur choral societies such as the Société Académique made provision for the presence of non-subscribing parents (implicitly chaperones) at rehearsals; and, with a regularity that went beyond the need for preparatory sectional rehearsals, separate rehearsals for men and women were common in choral societies of the period. In that same spirit of idealist/realist tension born of a need to keep up appearances, some examples of mixed choirs in the 1870s actually represent the bringing together of separate societies of men and women respectively (Poisot's in Dijon, for instance). Neither would anticlerical Republicanism bring major changes in this respect, since Republican ideals did little more than substitute Marian devotion with devotion to a secular version of family and motherhood, disseminated nationwide via an equally

---

73. "En somme on entend des oeuvres dans cette société que l'on ne pourrait exécuter dans aucune autre société, car celles que nous connaissons n'arrivent à mettre quelques morceaux sur pied qu'à force de tambouriner pour rassembler des chanteurs et des chanteuses qui n'ont aucune raison pour se rencontrer ce qui rend, par conséquent, toute association impossible." "C.V." [Camille de Vos], *NFC* 6/4: 16 February 1874, n.p.

74. Detailed in my "A Tale of Two Societies."

75. McPhee, *A Social History of France*, 234–35.

effective education system in which gender-specific primary-school texts replaced the catechism. It is arguable, then, that in terms of changing social *mores* (rather than political change), the 1860s and 70s were an extraordinarily *unfavorable* time to attempt the kind of long-term change De Bory and his colleagues had in mind.

In his 1873 review of Lamoureux's first *Messiah*, Pougin lamented women's absence from virtually any form of singing except opera.[76] Two years later, perhaps on the strength of the ideas of De Bory and his team, the Paris Conseil Municipal issued a policy for "la musique populaire" that instituted a prize for female *orphéons* and in the same breath attributed the lamentable absence of regular performances of Bach and Handel choral music specifically to the lack of female choirs.[77] Yet two years after that, a certain De Moonen, writing anonymously to the *orphéon* leaders François Bazin and H. Simon, is found pleading for the musical education of lower-class women, through all-female choirs led by female conductors if necessary, since they needed music's moralizing influence just as much as did their men. The popularization of good music in France, he claimed, depended on "the introduction of the feminine element in popular musical events."[78] Familiar complaints were reiterated in 1890, when Louis de Romain published a collection of his criticism. His essay "Nous et les autres" brought together discussion of the ills of the *orphéon* repertory, the woman problem (rendered a stalemate by a male-female conspiracy in which patriarchal rules went unchallenged by women who feared for their daughters' futures), and the embarrassing issue of French frivolity in matters of art. "Les autres"—so aptly named—were the Protestant countries. Ironically, they included England, "the ultimate anti-musical and prudish nation," but one where it seemed as though "women's reputations did not hang by a thread, so easily snapped,"[79] and where female participation in choral music was perfectly normal. For de Romain, the problem lay not so much with societal morals as with the absence of an artistic will strong enough to overcome them in the pursuit of a higher goal.

---

76. *Mén* 40/3: 21 December 1873, 19.

77. Article 5 of the Conseil Municipal document, cited and discussed by Léon Escudier in *AM* 14/35: 2 September 1875, 273: "C'est parce que nous n'avons pas en France des choeurs de femmes amateurs que nous ne pouvons pas exécuter d'une manière régulière les chefs-d'oeuvre des grands maîtres: Bach, Haendel, etc., qui ont écrit pour des masses chorales mixtes." Escudier draws attention to the suppression of the word "oratorio" in this anticlerical, Republican, document.

78. "l'introduction de l'élément féminin dans les solennités musicales populaires." M. de Moonen, "L'orphéon," 8.

79. "nation anti-musicale et prude par excellence . . . la réputation de femmes ne tient pas à un fil, si facile à casser." De Romain, *Essais de critique musicale*, 200.

Aspirations

That higher goal was nothing less than a clone of the choral culture of France's neighbors. Within musical writings, the density of debate on this aspect of French inferiority, its causes and possible cures, compares only with that on Wagner during the same period. The attempt to integrate Handel into a newly mixed *orphéon* tradition was not just a salvage attempt on the *orphéon* movement itself, but an opportunity for France to save face through massed displays of cultural capital.[80] During the period 1866 to 1875, Handel was the most widely discussed of all Baroque composers—and not just composers of choral music—in the French press and in pamphlets of all kinds. Symbolic of so much to which the French Republicans aspired in the early years of the Third Republic, earlier modes of reception meant that by the time of France's defeat of 1870, the level of hope for regeneration invested in his music meant that the momentum was unstoppable: indeed, the match between prewar interpretive paradigms and the cultural needs consequent upon defeat actually served to intensify and accelerate the process. The revival of Handelian oratorio in Paris was inextricable from the perceived social and cultural health of the French nation. The obverse of a narrowly nationalist revival elevating indigenous culture, it was in fact its necessary complement, demanding that the French prove to themselves (and to others) that they could equal or better the Germans on their own traditional ground. That they saw it in such terms, and discussed it explicitly as a competition that France was losing, says much about the profundity with which it was felt. But such profundity is hardly surprising, especially given the Republicanism of the Handel revival's main proselytizers. Until 1873 Paris was still being "protected" by Prussian soldiers—a fact which many Republicans were unwilling to accept as "atonement" for Imperial sins; until early 1876, while the Republicans in government were in the minority, Catholics enjoyed the "Moral Order" years, during which attempts to strengthen the Church's hold on education were extremely successful. The Handel debates, then, kicked against enemies both without and within.

The revival itself was short-lived. Indeed, where Handel is concerned, Lamoureux's concerts may actually be seen as an endpoint. Why? At this level the reasons seem to be as much pragmatic as ideological; but they stem from a key moment when the Société des Concerts program committee refused to listen to the very arguments about Baroque oratorio and national pride that

---

80. Concomitantly, Lamoureux's Handel choirs could never be too big—or big enough.

underpinned the debate. By their refusal to sanction Lamoureux's "patriotic" plan of 1872 to add oratorio concerts to the Société des Concerts' series, the Conservatoire authorities had sown the seeds of failure for the Handel revival in Paris, since they denied the revival its best opportunity for state recognition, state funding, and international publicity.[81] In Paris, the Société des Concerts' decision effectively turned the revival into a private venture in which conductors of independent means, unable to co-opt amateur singers in large numbers to form balanced choirs, had to rely on professionals or on wealthy amateurs combined with (and strengthened by) paid singers.[82] Conversely, the failure of the attempt to co-opt the *orphéon* meant that nonprofessional performances remained relatively small: hence the disappointment of critics who craved an equivalent to the English "Handel Festival" experience.

By 1875 worries were surfacing in the Paris press: was the revival stalling? Low audience numbers for Lamoureux's charity performance of *Messiah* on 14 January 1875 were in stark contrast to the overflowing crowds of his 1874 Handel concerts. Expense could not have been the only factor, concluded Henry Cohen: the applause among those who *were* there was distinctly muted, even for the Hallelujah chorus.[83] Lamoureux himself had abandoned his Handel concerts after this January series of *Messiah*s, even though he had advertised forthcoming performances of a new work: *Israel in Egypt*. After three years of Handelian silence, broken only by a single attempt by Pasdeloup to re-establish his position as a promoter of choral repertory, another *Art musical* critic, L. Kerney, despaired of a lasting revival. All would be lost if Lamoureux stopped performing Handel—which he appeared to have done, his idea "dead, abandoned."[84]

Kerney was right. Later in 1878, when Pasdeloup secured a grant of 25,000F per year from the Ministère de l'Instruction Publique to cover the cost of mounting choral works, he did not promote Handel; instead he concentrated, when increasingly difficult finances permitted, on modern works. Lamoureux, too, was shifting his interest to modern oratorio and, increasingly, Bach. The bicentenary was hardly noticed. That the only society in the capital to commemorate Handel in 1885 was Ernest Deldevez's ultraconservative

---

81. See the minutes of the committee of the Société des Concerts du Conservatoire, BNF (Musique): D 17345 (8); and Deldevez's *La Société des Concerts*, 270–76.

82. In preparing his application for government subsidy in 1878, Pasdeloup estimated that hiring a chorus of 140 nearly doubled the wage bill for an orchestra concert. Given in *Journal de musique* (henceforth *JM*) 2 (no. 90): 16 February 1878, 2.

83. *AM* 14/3: 21 January 1875, 19.

84. "morte, abandonnée." *AM* 17/2: 10 January 1878, 12.

Société des Concerts—in a concert containing "selections" only—was a sure sign that the revival was in terminal decline. Symbolic events, too, lost their symbolic power. There is an echo of the Republican Handel in performances of *Messiah* at that most symbolic of Expositions Universelles, in 1889. But the reviews reveal that the Republican "moment" for Handel had gone. Tiersot rehearsed the "Republican/popular festival" rationale for programming *Messiah* as though 1870s propaganda had never happened: "At first it is difficult to see what relation there might be between the Exposition and Handel's music," he wrote. "Looking more closely, one can understand that the two things go well together."[85] Outlining the architectural and triumphal nature of Handel's music, he emphasized its grandeur and its majestic accessibility but also, in contrast to earlier comparisons with ancient Greek sublimity, found it to be "decorative" music.[86] Worse followed, since Tiersot was writing in a journal one of whose other contributors, Amédée Boutarel, found the Hallelujah chorus too militaristic and the work as a whole too lacking in variety to command the attention fully.[87]

The anti-Handel trend continued: in 1891, tickets for the second and final performance of *Israel in Egypt* by the aristocratic-Republican Société des Grandes Auditions had to be sold at half price;[88] and Lamoureux's *Messiah* performances of 1896 provoked little more than press nostalgia and the belated recognition that the opportunity of a generation before had been lost. The fate of Victor Schoelcher's voluminous Handel collection, given to the French nation in three tranches after Schoelcher's return from exile, was in many ways emblematic of the failure of the specifically Handelian face of the French

---

85. "L'on ne voit pas bien au premier abord quelle relation il peut y avoir entre l'Exposition et la musique d'Haendel. A y regarder de plus près, l'on finit par s'apercevoir que les deux choses vont bien ensemble. La musique d'Haendel est surtout extérieure. Soit par la beauté architecturale et décorative, par la grandeur de ses proportions, soit par le relief de la ligne mélodique, elle frappe au premier abord et apparaît dans un essor majestueux et triomphal." *Mén* 55/24: 16 June 1889, 188. For more detail on the 1889 *Messiah*, see Fauser, *Musical Encounters*, chap. 1.

86. "décorative." *Mén* 55/24: 16 June 1889, 188.

87. Boutarel wrote that the Hallelujah chorus "manque le caractère spécial qui devrait distinguer un hymne religieux d'un chant guerrier. Le morceau d'Haendel aurait pu servir à recevoir au Capitole un général victorieux de l'ancienne Rome, mieux encore qu'à célébrer l'avènement pacifique du Messie. Comme impression d'ensemble on peut dire que l'oeuvre, malgré la variété réelle des formes musicales, devient à la longue un peu monotone." *Mén* 55/24:16 June 1889, 192.

88. As noted by Ernest Reyer, *JD* 7 June 1891, n.p.

choral revival and of its architects' aspirations for official recognition both by the government and its musical agent, the Conservatoire. After 1872 (the date of the first donation), cataloguing and the release of the collection into the public domain were delayed, with the result that the entire Handel revival of the 1870s in Paris took place while the most important collection of Handeliana in western Europe lay hidden in boxes.[89]

Back to Bach

Bach's fate was different, and the bicentenary year holds clues as to why. Although 1885 did not see a marked increase in Bach concerts, the celebratory performance organized by the indefatigable (and Protestant) Henriette Fuchs and Concordia in April of that year was part of a general intensification of interest in Bach's choral music, particularly the cantatas, dating from the early 1880s.[90] Bach would never be potential *orphéon* material; as such he would never be politicized in the manner of Handel. He superseded Handel among Parisian choral amateurs only after an interregnum during which nationalist sentiment encouraged more appreciation of and confidence in France's own cultural products, both old (*chanson populaire* and, to a lesser extent, early stage and keyboard music) and new or recent (the Société Nationale de Musique; Colonne's lionization of Berlioz). It is, moreover, no coincidence that Bach's rehabilitation coincided with the rise of Wagnerism, his bicentenary conveniently occurring the year the *Revue wagnérienne* was founded. Among prominent musicians and critics, Reyer, Gouzien, Benoît, and Lamoureux himself all promoted both composers' music; as Walter Corten has pointed out, the filiation of contrapuntal technique from Bach to Wagner had been commented upon by Wagner's supporters and detractors at least since Théophile Gautier's (ghosted?) comments of 1857 that Wagner's music represented a "return to the old fugal styles."[91] It was, of course, this illustrious pairing that Bellaigue lampooned in his "Tedium in Music" of 1888. But the connection had existed on many levels since the 1860s (Pasdeloup was as

---

89. See King, "The *fonds Schoelcher*," 706–7. There was no attempt, even on Weckerlin's part, to give priority to the Handelian part of the collection (the initial donation): the second donation (miscellaneous English music) was catalogued first (706).

90. His music in other genres had, of course, enjoyed increasing favor in admittedly intimate circles throughout the Second Empire.

91. "retour aux anciennes fugues." *Moniteur universel*, 29 September 1857, given in Corten, *Le "procès de canonisation,"* 173–74.

much a Wagnerian as a lover of Bach; Lamoureux, too). And among the eccentrics of high society the coupling of the two composers was neatly epitomized by the comte and comtesse de Chambrun: she who died on her way back from Bayreuth; he who underwrote editions of Bach's choral music and held private performances in the 1890s, much in the manner of Edouard Rodrigues's Handel half a century earlier.

The link was made explicit in two contrasting ways in 1892, the year after the Conservatoire's first B minor Mass. First, Julien Tiersot compared the Christmas Oratorio, intended to be sung over the course of six days, to the *Ring*.[92] Then, for Holy Week, the brothers Paul and Lucien Hillemacher presented an alternative to the St Matthew Passion at the Théâtre du Châtelet: Ed. Haraucourt's play *La Passion* (1891), with incidental music for orchestra adapted from the *Well-Tempered Clavier*, various organ pieces, and the famous "Pentecost" aria. The whole was put together according to Wagner's leitmotif system. Henry Eymieu's detailed description of the piece is the only aspect of it that has come to light thus far; but his report, which has the allure of a program note for pilgrims to Bayreuth, is revealing for its casual use of Wagnerian terminology in respect to this Bach *pasticcio*. The terms "motive" and "leitmotif" permeate the text, and individual motives are even given official names in the manner of published guides to the *Ring*:

> When Judas counts the price of his treachery on the very table on which Christ has just broken the bread with his apostles, the theme of the F minor fugue (which we might call the "Judas leitmotif") returns in the orchestra.
>
> The motive from the E minor organ fugue serves as the prelude to the Garden of Olives tableau.... At the moment when Judas kisses Christ the characteristic theme described above returns, and at the end of the scene the "Virgin's Theme" [from tableau I] (prelude in F minor), which intermingles with the Judas leitmotif.[93]

---

92. Review of the Société des Grandes Auditions Musicales's performance. *Mén* 58/5: 31 January 1892, 35.

93. "Au moment où Judas compte le prix de sa trahison sur la table même où le Christ vient de rompre le pain avec les apôtres, le thème de la fugue en fa mineur, qu'on pourrait appeler le leitmotive de Judas, revient à l'orchestre. Le motif de la fugue en mi mineur des pièces d'orgue sert de prélude au tableau du jardin des Oliviers.... Au moment où Judas embrasse le Christ revient le thème caractéristique dont nous parlons plus haut, et à la fin de la scène la Phrase de la Vierge (prélude en fa mineur) qui se mêle au leitmotive du Judas." *MS* 15/9: April 1893, 70.

The Hillemachers' provision of a funeral march emanating from the crucifixion scene (complete with a final statement of the "Judas" theme) further strengthens the association of their Christ with Siegfried. Such Wagnerian adaptation of Bach—and explicitly Bach the polyphonist—struck Eymieu as the work of "marvellous artisans" creating a new relationship with the great master's music.[94] But in terms of the cultural construction of Bach, La Passion also provides insights into the composer's changing image. For there appears to be no other example in nineteenth-century France of such double translation—of the updating of early music according to the stylistic norms of a third party who is himself associated with the ultramodern.

In combination with the progressive acceptance of the most Catholic and overtly expressive of the choral works—the "Actus Tragicus," the Magnificat, and the B minor Mass—the association of Bach with the saturated expressivity of Wagner also allowed him to begin to escape the charge of overlearned calculation and to attain a mystical aura which effectively overturned 1870s complaints that his church music was too unemotionally Protestant or learned.[95] Reviewing bicentennial biographies, René de Récy [J. Trezel] even argued that he was more Catholic than Protestant, and that the Magnificat and the B minor Mass were entirely Catholic in spirit.[96] Later writers nuanced such sentiments: for Benoît in 1891, the absence of chorales and recitatives in the B minor Mass rendered it universally Christian, a quality which gave it, for Cart, a special place in Bach's output, since it transcended both denominations while nevertheless revealing how significant were the remnants of Catholicism in the early eighteenth-century Lutheran rite.[97] Just as French supporters of Handel transformed his Protestantism in order to appropriate him in the late 1860s, so too—and not just in the spirit of Gounod's dressing-up of the C-major Prelude as an "Ave Maria"—did Bach's champions claim the Catholic side of his output for themselves over twenty years later. This was the last stage in a Catholic appropriation of Bach that had, since the 1840s, seen institutions such as Langres Cathedral and the Ecole Niedermeyer claim his organ works as an extension of the Palestrinian lineage.

Texts for the program book for Concordia's 1888 St Matthew Passion reveal the beginnings of the change. There were strong links, wrote the Wagnerian

---

94. "merveilleux artisans." *MS* 15/9: April 1893, 70.

95. See Corten, *Le "procès de canonisation,"* 175–77. In contrast to Corten, who sees the concert performances of 1868 as the beginning of the end of Bach's "learned Kantor" image, I would place this transformation considerably later, first with the Guilmant concerts, and then with the establishment of the Bach/Wagner association.

96. *RDM* 15 Nov. 1885, 414 and 416.

97. Benoit, *La grande messe en si mineur de Jean-Sébastien Bach*, 5–6; Cart, *Etude sur J.-S. Bach*, 221–24. On Bach chez D'Indy, see my "En route to Wagner."

Edouard Schuré, between Bach and Palestrina. Both appealed neither to the senses nor the intellect. Instead, in their "virile and chaste tenderness," they reached directly to the soul. Using language that had been commonplace in the evocation of a Palestrinian mysticism since the 1830s, Schuré claimed the "half-light of a gothic cathedral" as the natural home for Bach's sacred music and, with more Palestrinian resonances, imagined it rising, incense-like, to the heights of the nave.[98] J.-G. Fréson, writing on the Wagnerian aesthetic in 1893, compared *Parsifal* to the St Matthew Passion, and the polished leitmotif treatment of the composer's late style to the *Art of Fugue*; but he then, via an apparent paraphrase of Choron, traced the roots of Wagner's contrapuntal practice further back, again to Palestrina. "Musically," he wrote, "we float between all tonalities; as in the masses and motets of Giovanni Pierluigi da Palestrina, the sea of harmony extends to the horizon, in a series of infinitesimal gradations."[99] Fréson's aim was to emphasize the distance between *Parsifal* and opera; but the result, in terms of a longer historiographical trajectory, was to make Wagner the direct descendent of sacred-music composition in the severe style and to cement Bach's place at its historical centre.

But where Bach ultimately trumped Handel in the last two decades of the nineteenth century was in perceptions of his profundity, his subtlety, his variety of mood, and his old-fashioned Romantic isolation from the compromises entailed in carving out a career in the musical marketplace. As we have seen, in 1874 Reyer somewhat resented Handel's capacity to please the crowd; by contrast, from the 1880s Bach's commentators provided their readers with a quiet philosopher of music. For René de Récy in 1885, Bach was the official medium for Protestant expressions of religious mysticism: a reflective, unworldly genius in whose work the outside world found only "dim reflections."[100] Tiersot, writing at the time of Garcin's first performance of the B minor Mass, praised a self-taught composer of extraordinary depth, who appeared to shun both publicity and the wider public. Quoting Mme de Staël's definition of the German artist as a figure whose inwardness contrasted with French artists' sensitivity to

---

98. "tendresse mâle et chaste"; "le demi-jour d'une cathédrale gothique." Program booklet for Concordia's St Matthew Passion, 16 May 1888: "Notices et texte," 11–12 [BNF (Musique): Fonds "Programmes: Concordia"].

99. "Musicalement, nous flottons entre toutes les tonalités; comme dans les messes et les motets de Jean Pierluigi da Palestrina, la mer de l'harmonie s'étend à perte de vue avec une série d'insensibles dégradations; les vagues du rhythme ne la soulèvent ni l'agitent; et toutes les souffrances terrestres semblent se dissoudre dans l'Amour sans bornes du Christ souffrant pour nous." Freson, *L'ésthétique de Richard Wagner*, vol. 2, 217.

100. "de lointains reflets." *RDM* 15 November 1885, 414.

public tastes, he presented the mismatch between Bach's humble communitarianism and his genius as a signifier of artistic integrity:

> He cared little about the public; he composed his greatest masterpieces to be performed once only in the presence of a few friends and parishioners.... Not seeking to please the public, Bach thus concentrated on expressing what he felt, and he did it so much more spontaneously and naturally because he had not "legislated" anything and because he seems, in his writing, to have followed only the vague and obscure principles to which his genius (much more than his will) had given powerful illumination.[101]

By the later 1890s, mention of Bach's profundity, his lack of ambition, and his purity of artistic spirit was a commonplace that served to relegate Handel to the inferior position of a great but ultimately opportunistic artist who "was there for his own apotheosis" and whose compositions were tainted with theatricality and conventionality.[102]

Bach's need to provide weekly cantatas and generally fulfil employers' requirements seems to have escaped his supporters' notice, though detractors seized on its artistic consequences. "Rameau" of *Le monde artiste*, for instance, exposed the self-borrowing within the B minor Mass in an explicit attempt to dent the myth of the composer's much-vaunted "sincerity"[103] and perhaps to slow a process of artistic beatification according to which the composer could be described, even if half-jokingly, as "our holy Father."[104] He failed. Reviewing the Chanteurs de Saint-Gervais at the Concert Guilmant of 26 April 1899, Hip-

---

101. "Le public, il n'en avait cure: ses plus beaux chefs-d'oeuvre, il les composa pour être exécutés une seule fois en présence de quelques amis et des paroissiens de son église ... Ne cherchant pas à plaire au public, Bach se bornait donc à exprimer ce qu'il sentait, et il le faisait d'autant plus spontanément et naturellement que lui non plus a point 'légiféré' et qu'il semble, en écrivant, n'avoir obéi qu'à des principes vagues et obscurs que son génie, bien plutôt que sa volonté, a puissamment illuminés." *Mén* 57/11: 15 March 1891, 81. Tiersot was referring to De Staël's discussions of German artistic character in her *De l'Allemagne* of 1810.

102. "assista à son propre apothéose." Hippolyte Barbedette, reviewing what turned out to be Lamoureux's last *Messiah* series. *Mén* 62/13: 29 March 1896, 101.

103. "Sincérité." *MA* 31/11: 15 March 1891, 169. Nevertheless, the journal's critics still favored Bach over Handel when they made the comparison; "Tic-Tac," writing sarcastically of the Société des Grandes Auditions' *Israel in Egypt* of 3 June 1891, used precisely the traditional comparison of the commercial Handel as against the "purist" [le puriste] Bach, composing only "for himself" [pour lui-même]. *MA* 31/23: 7 June 1891, 368.

104. "notre saint père Bach." From a comment of Eugène de Bricqueville on the motet "Jesu meine Freude," sung (probably complete) by the Société des Concerts on 5 March 1899. *Mén* 65/11: 12 March 1899, 84.

polyte Barbedette reported the enthusiasm of the five-thousand-strong audience and, in respect to the cantata "Jesu der du meine Seele," wrote the now-traditional Bachian encomium: "Bach has expressed everything: no human emotion is unknown to him. He is perfect, from the slightest fugue to those colossal pieces the Mass in B minor and the St Matthew Passion."[105]

Given the conditions in which it arose, it is difficult to see how a specifically Handelian choral revival in France could have succeeded in the long term. He was after all an outsider—a double foreigner whose music was appropriated to a nationalistic cause and then dropped when its political attractiveness had waned and once the works of indigenous heroes (with Berlioz at their head) were able to replace it. Yet for as long as the French needed a musical weapon against Prussian culture, a pagan, Republican, and Mediterranean Handel was ideal. For all the rhetoric that placed Bach and Handel as twin pillars of the eighteenth-century oratorio tradition, at the beginning of the Third Republic Bach was still too difficult, too Protestant, too chromatic, and ultimately too German to be pressed into service as a popular nationwide repertory. Moreover, the fact that by 1871 Handel was already favored over Bach provided an opportunity to enjoy the best of (almost) all worlds: one could argue for the creation of a singing nation to rival that of Germany through the medium of a de-Germanized composer whose music was identified with an even greater military power, the British Empire.

Saint-Saëns was chillingly accurate when in 1879 he called performances of Handel oratorio a "blip" lacking the institutional bedrock of performances abroad.[106] Yet he was also myopic, since the "death" of Handel did not mean the death of attempts to found a choral culture. Rather, hindsight renders Handel the choral composer a transitional figure who (the Germanic traditions of Alsace aside) was the necessary condition for a reappraisal of Bach, and who made possible the flowering of French choral music in composition and nationwide performance during the last quarter of the century. This was an episode in French concert history that was predicated on reaching out to more sectors of French society than any before it, Choron's attempts excepted: an idealist vision that embraced all generations and both sexes; amateurs and professionals; all social strata from workers and artisans to aristocrats; Republicans,

---

105. "Bach a tout exprimé: aucun sentiment humain ne lui est étranger. Il est parfait, depuis la moindre fugue jusqu'à ses oeuvres colossales que sont la Messe en si mineur et la Passion de Saint-Mathieu." Mén 65/18: 30 April 1899, 140.

106. "un accident." Saint-Saëns, "Les festivals de Birmingham" (1879), in Harmonie et mélodie, 151.

Protestants, pagans, and even (moderate) Ultramontanes. Though the architects of the Baroque choral revival failed in their immediate goals, the entire episode nevertheless marks not just a defining period in the history of early music in France, but a defining period in the history of French musical culture. The music of the monumental Baroque—Handel especially—was more important for prompting crucial questions than for providing all the answers.

Conclusion

Researching the activities of a dedicated minority is methodologically risky because pursuit of the exceptional can seduce one into losing sight of its distance from the normal. All the more so in the case of early music, now that the cultural practices of our own time are so thoroughly saturated with a love of the past and now that heritage has produced its own service industry. Routine familiarity potentially distorts our lens on the past by eliminating the foreignness that can in other circumstances act as a check, separating historians from their objects of study and encouraging them to keep re-attuning their expectations. Nevertheless, there is also a difference between normality as fact and normality as perception, and whereas it would be difficult to argue that any one kind of early music became ubiquitous in nineteenth-century France, certain early musics did indeed reach beneath the surface of people's lives. Hence the mid-century fears about proliferation; hence the 1890s jokes about the saintly Bach; hence the clinging on to cherished biographical myths, Palestrinian and otherwise, in popular and educational material; hence the intertextual evocation of past styles in new music; hence the allure of the fake piece or adaptation that mediated teasingly between past and present.

In terms of operatic life, for instance, early musics remained marginal for the entire century. Revivals of stage plays with incidental music, such as *Le bourgeois gentilhomme, Monsieur de Pourceaugnac,* and *Le malade imaginaire,* though important for what they reveal about cultural attitudes, did nothing to render seventeenth- and eighteenth-century stage music viable in its guise as an operatic experience. The fact that the 1895 revival of *Dardanus* (*chez* Polignac) was private and unstaged highlights the role of economics in this matter, as does the early twentieth-century history of revival in respect to Rameau and Monteverdi stagings before the Opéra's *Hippolyte* of 1908: all were under the aegis of the Schola Cantorum and used mostly student performers. Because of its status as France's prime historical operatic genre, *tragédie en musique* cried out to be revived at the Opéra. But except for dance numbers for its *concerts historiques* it was never, under even the most historically sympathetic of its directors (Perrin and Vaucorbeil), taken further back than Gluck.

Yet there was another way of bringing eighteenth-century stage music, in particular, to the French nineteenth-century opera-goer: the tradition of *couleur locale*. Meyerbeer is famous for his archaizing use of Lutheran chorale in *Les Huguenots* of 1836; but at this stage his approach was itself the exception rather than the rule in French opera, where *couleur locale* meant primarily geographical, not historical, color. We might expect Niedermeyer, for instance, to have imbued his *Stradella* of the following year with stylistic references to early music; although recent research has uncovered certain links, to one of his contemporaries at least it appeared rather too contemporary.[1] Nevertheless, following Gounod's lead in works such as *Le médecin malgré lui* (1858), later composers, particularly during the Third Republic, showed different priorities. Increasingly, historical subjects encouraged composers to write historical pastiche, especially in respect to the "refurbishing" of historical dance styles for ballet sequences[2]: Massenet's *Manon* (1884), set in early eighteenth-century France, is a touchstone in this regard, with an entire sequence of Baroque dances in the Act III *divertissement*. And if we are to believe Alfred Bruneau's interpretation of his friend Gustave Charpentier's *Louise* (1900), the meanings newly attached to early music eventually became part of opera's arguments, subjected to anachronistic use in the service of modern social themes. Charpentier's allusion to Janequin's *Les cris de Paris* to portray the street vendors of Act II allowed the *chanson populaire* to be reinterpreted as a signifier of the grit of working-class life in industrial Paris at the turn of a new century.[3] If early

---

1. Berlioz complained that the score contained "too many twists and turns that belong to our own time" [trop de tournures propre à notre temps]. Unsigned review, *RGM* 4/10: 5 March 1837, 80. For more on historicism in *Stradella*, see Sarah Hibberd, "Murder in the Cathedral?"

2. For further discussion of this point, see Lacombe, *The Keys to French Opera*, 169–71.

3. Bruneau, *La musique française*, 50. This point is noted in Fulcher, *French Cultural Politics & Music*, 44, though it is unclear whether Fulcher thinks that Charpentier himself intended to make such a connection. Moreover, as an indicator of class divides, street cries and Baroque dance had already been combined in Massenet's *Manon* (Act III).

opera, then, as a complete, staged, experience, was doomed to remain exceptional in the nineteenth century, opera as a genre did not remain immune from revivals of early music more generally.

Nevertheless, it was as a part of concert life that early music per se eventually became mainstream. In Paris, not only did a continuing (though weakening) tradition of "miscellaneous" recital programs allow the presentation of individual, short pieces; but the trend towards more homogeneous programs epitomized by those, for instance, of Colonne (his Thursday orchestral series), or of Ysaÿe and Pugno, coincided with a significant intensification of interest in early repertories and increased acceptance of such music in large portions. With respect to the choral music of Handel and Bach, Pasdeloup, Weckerlin, Lamoureux, and Bourgault-Ducoudray had prepared audiences for precisely this kind of concentrated exposure. As far as explaining the greater representativeness of these repertories is concerned, the economics of amateur performance play an important role. Choral music, though expensive if one used paid choirs with orchestra, became cost-effective in amateur hands, especially if it was music *a cappella*. After the state-funded initiatives of Choron, concert receipts, subscriptions and, more often than not, the personal wealth of the conductor, allowed increasing numbers of amateur societies to lead the concert revival of sixteenth- to eighteenth-century music. The same holds for the numerous chamber music societies (of professional musicians, mainly) that pepper the century. At home, music supplements for piano reflected increasing interest in early musics as vehicles for education and enjoyment. New music, too, contributed increasingly to the embedding of a sense of historicism in composers and public alike. As Debussy commented strikingly on his manuscript of the song that would become the minuet of the *Petite suite*, this was "Louis XIV music with formulae from 1882."[4]

Normality and Conservatism

Amateurs and concert musicians, with music publishers in their wake, had embraced early musics very quickly in the 1830s and '40s, and had by that time, with few exceptions, introduced all the genres of music that would be considered "early music" by 1900. Such cultural indicators illustrate the extent to which early musics permeated concert life and, later, liturgical practice. While music

---

4. "Musique Louis XIV avec formules de 1882." The song, to a poem by Théodore de Banville, was the *fête galante* "Voilà Sylvandre et Lycas et Myrtil."

written before c.1760 never became predominant in the nineteenth century, it benefited from a move toward conservation and canonization (with their attendant secularizing tendencies) that substantially increased the average age of the musical fare offered to audiences. The idea of splitting concert programs into a first part of "musique ancienne" (meaning pre-1800 for the most part) and "musique contemporaine" dates from around 1860 (Weckerlin's Société Sainte-Cécile). The system, though it remained unusual, persisted for the rest of the century, not least—and this is perhaps most significant of all—to act as a defence against the charge that, in their dedication to the masterworks of the past, conductors were neglecting more recent, or even living, composers.

It was thus that attachments to early music became closely intertwined with questions of cultural conservatism. In Paris there is little sense of such a link until the late 1840s; on the contrary, the association of early musics with novelty and fashion is predominant, summed up in the critic Pierre Borel's quip, in a review of D'Ortigue's *Le balcon d'opéra*, that in order to be up-to-date one had to immerse oneself in the past.[5] As I have argued, during the Second Republic and Second Empire, critics' reservations as to its place in musical culture served as an indication that early music had begun to be perceived as more than an idle diversion. During the *belle époque* years, nostalgia for an idealized and irrecoverable past became an important part of the enthusiasm for early French music in particular. Within the Catholic Church, too, the Cecilian and Ultramontane traditions, aided by moderate Gallicans, thrived in high-profile *maîtrises* across the country.

Yet the association of revivalist activity and conservatism is not, at this level at least, uncomplicated. While there are plenty of examples of musicians and critics who display diehard fidelity to early music as part of a more general musical appreciation limited to pre-Romantic styles (Scudo, Mongin, Pougin, De Lafage, the Farrencs, Méreaux, Bordes, Fétis, Weckerlin, Heulhard, Bellaigue), others, especially in the middle of the century, were just as likely to be committed modernists. Most striking, perhaps, is the combination of Wagnerism and enthusiasm for eighteenth-century musics that we find in Pasdeloup (Bach, Handel), Lamoureux (Bach, Handel), Jullien (Rameau), Tiersot (Rameau, Bach), D'Indy (Bach, Rameau, Monteverdi), Saint-Saëns (a temporary Wagnerite; Bach, Rameau), Benoît (Bach), and Wilder (Handel). Moreover, among soloists we can detect an increasing eclecticism where early repertories appear as part of an ever-widening continuum of music available for recital use. By the 1880s it was customary for pianists to cover musical periods from 1720 to the

---

5. *L'artiste* (1833), 198. Given in Simms, *Alexandre Choron*, 156.

present in their recitals, even if their pre-1760 material consisted only of a two-minute piece of Bach. Early music specialists such as the pianist Mongin were rare indeed. For all his early music activity, Diémer was just as well known as an interpreter of nineteenth-century music as he was for his *clavecin* music; the same holds for Pugno and for the plethora of organists whom Guilmant inspired. But the idea that early music simply became a natural extension of the contemporary repertory comes across most strongly in respect to orchestral wind players such as Taffanel and Gillet, and string players, whether card-carrying virtuosi such as Ysaÿe, or orchestral and chamber players, such as Baillot, Alard, and Parent. Nevertheless, as Scott Messing has intimated, once Wagner ceases to be a byword for challenging modernity in composition— from the mid-1890s—it becomes more difficult to find early music enthusiasts who combine their interest with a commitment to avant-garde music: Debussy, Ysaÿe, and Rolland stand out for this very reason.[6] Modernism, like conservatism, is never static, and never absolute.

However, conservatism of another kind is evident throughout the century. Some of the most deep-rooted pieces of early music in nineteenth-century France were totemic works or extracts that, for all their popularity, failed or took some time to catalyse interest in the music surrounding them, even when editions were available. Despite the popularity of Marcello's "I cieli immensi narrano," his psalm settings were neglected; despite much of his harpsichord music appearing in the *Trésor des pianistes,* Daquin was known only by "Le coucou"; the same applied, to a lesser extent, to Palestrina's motet and mass music and to Couperin's *clavecin* works. Function and genre account for much: function in the sense of ritual (the obligatory Pergolesi or Durante at the *concerts spirituels* early in the century); and genre as a guarantor of a certain type of musical experience, as examples from Baroque instrumental music illustrate. Throughout the century, Handel's harpsichord suites were represented by variations—either the "Harmonious Blacksmith" variations or the G minor passacaglia (Suite no. 7). Corelli's solo violin music meant *La follia*; Bach's meant the chaconne; other popular music for violin included *La romanesca* and, later, the Vitali chaconne. Here, as elsewhere in the early instrumental music that became popular in nineteenth-century France, dance is a conspicuous presence. And while the solo instrumental music that reached the concert platform went well beyond dances and variation sets (and their combination in the guise of chaconnes), these musics never lost their appeal. In vocal music, concert life outside of specialist societies showed similar narrowness. After Choron and before the revival of the late

6. Messing, *Neoclassicism in Music*, 17–18.

1860s and early 1870s, Handel oratorio was represented overwhelmingly by just two pieces: the Hallelujah chorus and "See, see, the conqu'ring hero comes." Even during the revival itself, there was almost total reliance on those works which Mozart had reorchestrated, the exception being *Judas*. The examples could be multiplied in respect to earlier music (Josquin and Victoria, and Palestrina and Lassus as secular composers, for instance).

Complacency and familiarity account for much of this regression to a mean. In the contemporary press, complaints abound regarding the former and the stagnation it encouraged; audience reaction and the incidence of encores give us an insight into the latter. But wider ideological concerns are at least, if not more, significant in establishing why certain genres or pieces are revived, and then kept—whether in the medium or long term—in the repertory.

Ideology, Revival, and Neglect

To what extent, then, can we map political and religious ideologies onto the resurgence of interest in early musics? It is a measure of the complexity of the historical situation that no clear-cut answers appear satisfactory. Undeniably, certain genres of early music held particular associations and were either revived or reviled on account of them. It was entirely predictable, for instance, that *La bataille de Marignan* should be newly championed and enjoy increased popularity after 1870: it had always been associated with expressions of national pride. Similarly, it was predictable that in an increasingly Ultramontane environment after around 1830, French Catholics would have little time for the tradition of the *grand motet* or other quasi-operatic styles of eighteenth-century French church music. And since there was no prospect of Gallican or anti-Ultramontane *maîtres de chapelle* abandoning their more modern, opera-based repertories for this Gallican music, it was predestined to remain neglected— entirely in accordance with the non-nationalist (or, rather, pro-Italian) focus of the Ultramontane movement. With only a few exceptions, mostly relating to regional pride in local composers of the Midi, it was not until the Rameau complete edition (begun in 1894) forced the issue of the composer's sacred music that any of this repertory gained significant recognition. Given its availability in old prints, and the extent to which the secular music of Lalande, Destouches, Charpentier, Lully, and Rameau either clung to a place in the repertory, or was revived through theatrical production, neglect of the sacred repertory can only have been deliberate. Even Rameau's late nineteenth-century proselytizers, from Adam's biography of 1852 onward, hardly mentioned his sacred music. The encomia of Castil-Blaze and J.-J.-B. Laurens of the 1820s and later on behalf of Lalande as a composer of sacred music are all the more striking for appearing in a near-total vacuum.

Religious and political considerations affected the Baroque oratorio revival that became a characteristic and influential feature of the musical landscape from the late 1860s, both in the regions and in Paris. Alsace's musical culture, as evidenced in Strasbourg, was clearly divided between Protestant and Catholic, and much more active on the Protestant side. It was in this environment that the sacred choral music of Bach and, to a lesser extent, Handel, was first regularly performed in France. Niort, also in a highly Protestant area of the country, was not far behind. When Paris played host to a revival of both composers' oratorios and secular odes in the years after 1865 (and particularly from 1868), questions of nationalism and religious affiliation became central, and Protestant countries a force to be emulated by a backward, Catholic France. Soon after 1870, the music of the "Latin, dramatic, accessible" Handel came to sideline that of the "Germanic, learned, elitist" Bach as an intended symbol of musical regeneration for the French people. The idea of a "people's Handel," frequently reiterated in the musical and general press, conformed closely to Republican ideals for non-Catholic cultural regeneration after France's defeat in the Franco-Prussian War. No one at the Schola Cantorum made Handel oratorio a central plank of the school's concert repertory (Guilmant's performances of Handel organ concertos were a different matter), and no wonder. It was surely symbolic that the most famous Handelian of all was Victor Schoelcher, a Republican prodigal son returned after the war from his exile under Napoléon III; symbolic, too, is the fact that when it became less necessary to fight hard for Republican causes in general (by the late 1870s, for instance), the need for Handel subsided.

Nevertheless, the waters are muddied at several turns. It was the same, arch-Republican Schoelcher who, in the anticlerical climate of 1884, headed a commission that recommended that cathedral *maîtrises* renowned for their Palestrinian music should retain their state funding. And the Republican democratizing zeal of a Handelian such as Bourgault-Ducoudray did not preclude his championing (to a far lesser extent, admittedly) Palestrinian music as concert fare, or his appearing, alongside Guilmant and the prince de Polignac, as one of the three Presidents of the Schola Cantorum on its foundation in 1894.[7] We are not, therefore, necessarily dealing here with impermeable binary oppositions

---

7. The supplement to an issue of the *Tribune de Saint-Gervais*, some time before Easter 1895, gives details of the founding committee, first elected on 15 June 1894 and reelected unanimously on 2 December the same year. Bourgault-Ducoudray was also listed among the teaching staff in 1896 (*T S-G* 2/3: March 1896, 43).

between Catholic and Protestant, Republican and Monarchist, Republican and Catholic, or left-wing and right-wing. Across the century (certainly until the Dreyfus Affair erupted) the situation was both more fluid and less consistent. This is not to say either that music was apolitical during the period (far from it) or that there were not antagonistic factions throughout the century. Certain gestures in the revival of early music do indeed suggest a single ideological interpretation: the programming of Candeille's *Castor et Pollux* at the Opéra in December 1814 is a prime example. But that interpretation says more about general political exigency than it does about the ideological stance of the Opéra's director, who was merely a civil servant working under a particular régime.

The potential for disjunction is at its most striking in the last third of the century, particularly in the years immediately following Sedan and preceding the Dreyfus Affair. Just because *ancien-régime* court music is associated with the Bourbon monarchy does not mean that its revival is supported only by royalists after 1870 (in this respect at least, the case mirrors that of Molière). The greater cause of national pride complicates matters a great deal. We can, as Charles B. Paul has attempted for Rameau reception in the late nineteenth and early twentieth centuries, point to some dichotomous tendencies in the reception of such music[8]; but the presence of almost as many exceptions as proofs means that we cannot fully systematize those patterns. Henri Blanchard's plays were censored on account of their radical Republican content; yet (and this despite his general worries about the prevalence of early music) he was one of the most supportive critics of French harpsichord music in the 1840s and '50s. The fate of Rameau's stage music from the 1870s to the end of the century would have been far less rosy had it not been for the activity of younger Republicans, such as Pougin and Tiersot. Similarly, after complaining about the aura of privilege around *ancien-régime* stage music in *Le temps*, Johannes Weber (a Republican critic for a Republican paper) became, in the late 1870s, a staunch supporter of the *Chefs-d'oeuvre classiques de l'Opéra français*, welcoming each volume to the bitter end.

The above analysis assumes, of course, that during the nineteenth century the signification of a particular music retained a broad, stable core of characteristics, despite accretions (and this irrespective of whether contemporaries considered its characteristics to be qualities or weaknesses). And while this was indeed the case with *ancien-régime* stage music, which remained "royal" while becoming progressively "national" and "historic," it was not so elsewhere. Fraught religious politics were never far away from the reception of

---

8. Paul, "Music and Ideology."

early sacred music, rendering it a particularly contested area. After several decades during which his Protestantism was a byword, the argument for a mystical, universally Christian Bach in the 1880s and 1890s helped effect the composer's overturning of Handel in the oratorio stakes after 1885. Yet it was also a mode of reception with strong links to earlier Ultramontane practice, in which Bach's organ works appeared alongside Palestrinian polyphony as the "next stage" in the history of sacred music, neatly overstepping the more operatic styles of eighteenth-century Italy and France. Practices at Langres Cathedral and at the Ecole Niedermeyer (this latter founded, of course, by a Calvinist) provide the best evidence of this prototype of Bach the universal Christian; it was simply one more step to apply the idea to the composer's texted sacred music. For a committed anti-Protestant such as D'Indy, it was essential to the acceptance of Bach's music into the teaching canon at the Schola Cantorum; moreover, it provides an insight into why, in the 1890s, we find Bach's cantatas being championed by a choir (admittedly a highly various one in terms of its members' religious affiliations) attached to a major Catholic parish church and otherwise known for its "propagande palestrinienne"—Charles Bordes's Chanteurs de Saint Gervais.

Palestrina's own fate was more complex still. The performance style initiated by Choron in the 1820s helped cement the meaning of Counter-Reformation polyphony as expressive of a mystical religious ecstasy—an interpretation that held for the entire century but which came under repeated attack from the 1840s, with opposing factions aiming to appropriate, downgrade, or even discredit it. Here, divisions according to religious ideology are relatively clear: the three responses above correspond, broadly, to the actions of moderate Ultramontanes, Protestants, and radical Ultramontanes, respectively. But the extent of Gallican involvement in the revival of Palestrinian usage in educational establishments and in cathedrals around France complicates matters: the bishops and archbishops Blanquart de Bailleul (Rouen), Marguerye (Autun), Dupanloup (Orléans), Le Courtier (Montpellier), and Guérrin (Langres) were all involved in instituting or maintaining such traditions. Similarly, it is useful to bear in mind the extent to which this music had been secularized since the 1820s, presented as a key part of music's heritage (and indeed of the heritage of French-inspired music), and brought into the concert hall by religious reformers and secular concert conductors alike. As we have seen, its artistic quality was accepted in cultural circles to the extent that during a wave of 1880s anticlericalism it could seriously be posited, by a Republican minister in a parliamentary debate, that certain *maîtrises* be spared funding cuts simply because they acted as curators of an important part of music's heritage.

National Inferiority, National Pride, and National Identity

The above examples leave bipolar Republican/Catholic hatreds (as traditionally described) in fluctuating states of contingency and inconsistency where early musics are concerned. Time and again, discussions of musical artworks reveal authorial tension between perceptions of a work's artistic quality on the one hand, and its signification (and the implications of that signification) on the other. Nineteenth-century musicians and commentators in France were far less likely to be swayed in their attitude to early musics by questions of party politics than by those of liturgical politics or—even more important—national pride. This latter, especially in evidence after 1870, appears as a leitmotif in polemics, appreciations, and examples of sales pitch in respect to both French and foreign music throughout the century. More often than not it is a defining factor in the question of whether a genre of early music is, or is not, accepted. The complexity of reception displayed by the main exceptions before around 1885—Franco-Flemish polyphony and *ancien-régime* music—merely provides negative proof of national pride's centrality in this respect. From Choron's influential introduction to the *Dictionnaire des musiciens* onward, the bolstering of France as the most civilized of nations is the common appeal of proselytizers. The appeal was necessary because of a strong underlying conviction that France had slipped to second and then third place in the league of European musical nations. And while following Italy was acceptable so long as it was simply a prelude to another turn at leadership (music histories had impressed on nineteenth-century minds the see-sawing of influence between the two countries), to find her behind and then defeated by Germany was devastating.

Most of the time, the music of Spain (except as an exotic other), Belgium (except as an adjunct to France), and England (except in terms of musical consumption) did not feature on the French musical map. Yet in several key aspects of early music activity, these countries, alongside Germany (but not, this time, Italy), were manifestly ahead of France. It hardly seemed to matter which aspect was in question—concert societies, literature on the history of music, collected editions of national composers, music education, the democratization of "classic" music—all, in turn, exposed France's backwardness. Paris was in a paradoxical position: a city that could plausibly claim to be the cultural capital of Europe, but in which a growing sense that musical imports were outnumbering exports sapped the patriotic confidence of the musical intelligentsia. The aftermath of the *guerre des bouffons*, and its effect on the status of French music of the *grand siècle*, was important here: while Germany rediscovered a performing tradition of Bach, and the English continued to claim Handel as their own, the French were happier continuing to embrace Italian, rather than French, traditions. Thus it was, through the Napoleonic years and the Restoration, that Italian eighteenth-century styles predominated, alongside Rousseau's Italianate *Devin*, as the staple early-music fare available to French audiences.

But in respect to earlier music, France also lost ground through the internationalism of her revivalists. While Palestrina could be claimed as French-influenced, the more general Ultramontane cause that nurtured the revival of his music was in no way patriotic. The results of such national *laissez-faire* became clear later in the century, when it came to matter a great deal. The Belgians and Spanish published anthologies of their Renaissance masterpieces some fifty years before Expert's patriotic *Les maîtres musiciens de la Renaisssance française* formed a natural pendant to the (equally belated) Rameau complete edition. The English and the Germans were decades ahead with their collected editions of Handel and Bach respectively. In drawing some of these precedents to his potential subscribers' attention, Théodore Michaëlis was using the same kind of marketing ploy that had characterized earlier appeals to museum culture when musical institutions of the July Monarchy sought state funding; but it was also born of a real feeling that France had somehow, and soon, to place her heritage on the musical map. The alternative was to lose further ground in a race in which she already found herself among the trailing group. It is hardly surprising that despairing cries lamenting France's seeming inability to compete musically with her neighbors occur at regular intervals from Choron's time onward.[9] And, as the example of Handel oratorio showed, that despair was not restricted to the promotion and performance of French music; it extended much more widely, to the question of socially cohesive musical practices emblematized by the success, in England, Germany, and latterly Belgium, of the amateur choral tradition.

Throughout the nineteenth century French musicians had agonized over the character and extent of their own Frenchness, as expressed in their contemporary music. Whether one took the view of certain post-1870 writers, that foreign (i.e. German) influences should be purged entirely, or whether one accepted, along more traditional lines, that the history of French music had always involved the creative assimilation of foreign influences, there was no escaping the sense that the qualities of Frenchness in music were sometimes ill-defined and had been consistently undervalued, first in favor of Italian styles and then, from the 1830s, in favor of German ones. France's most exportable commodity in contemporary music, grand opera, was itself a mixture of national

---

9. Though of course Choron was a major force in the continued denigration of *la musique française*.

styles and had regularly been portrayed in the terms of July Monarchy eclecticism as the golden mean, the *juste milieu*, between the Italian and the German. Beyond that, what was specifically French about the musical language of French grand opera could not be easily defined. Yet the contemporary music that *was* manifestly French, and available as a model, belonged to the *genre mineur* of *opéra-comique*; and the most familiar French music of olden times was an embarrassment.

Even with the intensified patriotism after 1870, the old antagonisms toward such music persisted, though they were countered with progressively greater success; moreover, while the dance music associated with the French stage and the French harpsichord became popular during this very period, its popularity came at the price of being perceived largely as a collection of graceful, feminine miniatures. For so long as a desired sense of national identity remained stereotypically masculine (the "indomitable Handel" model), *la musique française* was vulnerable. However, the French *chanson populaire*—a source of grassroots Frenchness epitomized equally by Janequin and the *Jeu*—suffered no such taint. Despite also comprising miniatures, it appeared to embody a rustic energy, wit, and spirit. It also shared enough characteristics with courtly dance to enable the two to be regarded, toward the end of the century, as complementary. From the point of view of musical heritage, then, salvation of national pride was to come through a reappraisal of the attributes which French musicians considered theirs alone, and which had characterized French instrumental music and *chansons* for several centuries: directness, concision, rhythmic vitality, naturalness, and lack of pretension.

The complexity of the "official" view at the end of this story is neatly summed up in parts of Alfred Bruneau's "report" on the concerts of 400 years of French music at the 1900 Exposition Universelle: *La musique française* (1901). The title, a celebratory appropriation of a once-pejorative moniker, tells us much. The contents as a whole are an ideological minefield, the ability to untangle the various historical layers essential if we are to understand Bruneau's agenda and the more general import of his document. For the book's anticlerical Republican author, who was no historian, silently interwove received wisdom, recent historical research (sometimes travestied), and personal opinion in his account. Some of his ideas were nearly a century old; most dated back at least 70 years, to the time of Fétis; others can be traced to the work of fellow Republicans such as Weckerlin and Tiersot in the 1880s and 1890s. By way of a coda to a century-long study, then, let us circle back and revisit the "museomania" of Expo 1900.

Bruneau stressed two related notions in the history of French music: a sense of continuous tradition, and a sense of musical–national identity in which (in circular fashion) the characteristics of the French race were reflected in truly French music. Forging connections between the musical personalities of Clément Janequin and Gustave Charpentier, between Beaujoyeulx, Cambert, and Saint-Saëns (the ploy was, ironically, a favorite of his nemesis, D'Indy), Bruneau outlined a history that had its roots in popular culture and which emphasized the freshness, grace, and unpretentious directness of "national" music. From its chronological starting-point with the *Jeu de Robin et de Marion*, Bruneau's history moved straight to Josquin before touching on the sixteenth century (Goudimel, Janequin) and then focusing on the operatic legacy of the seventeenth and eighteenth centuries: the music of Lully, Rameau, and Gluck. With the exception of Josquin and Goudimel, this was a historical map that many music-loving Parisians would have recognized from popular histories, music supplements, and performances. The same was true of many of his historical interpretations.

Bruneau's enthusiasm for Adam de la Halle's *Jeu*, and his description of it as France's first *opéra-comique*, derived from Fétis (1827) and, beyond that, from Roquefort's history of early French poetry (1814); his denigration of the composer's sacred polyphony in favor of his secular monodies also derived from Fétis. An enraged D'Indy saw the latter as part of a specifically anticlerical agenda,[10] and doubtless it was; but in this case anticlericalism could easily be hidden under the cover of tradition. Predictable, too, was the nationalist enthusiasm Bruneau showed for the chansons of Janequin, which contained "extraordinary gaiety and malice, [and] an often delicious poetry,"[11] and which had appeared on concert programs since 1829 with no appreciable interruptions. His silent appropriation of Josquin, whose birthplace was unknown, was an equally nationalist gesture, mirroring that of French historians who had expended extraordinary amounts of energy trying to prove the French nationality of Franco-Flemish polyphonists, with Josquin and Dufay at their head.

So far, so conventional. But in discussing Josquin's sacred music, along with that of Goudimel and Palestrina, Bruneau exceeded his brief in ways that encourage reflection on the occupational hazards of historiography and cultural history. None of this music was performed at the Exposition's official concerts.

---

10. Review in *Revue d'histoire et critique musicales* 1/3: March 1901, 110–19. See Fulcher, *French Cultural Politics & Music*, 45. I follow her attribution of this unsigned article to D'Indy, whose intellectual fingerprints show clearly through the initial "X" and who identified himself as a former member of the Exposition's music committee. His central objection to the content of the report (though he did not say so explicitly) was that Bruneau was abusing his power: his work would be read as an authoritative description of current public taste (*Revue d'histoire*, 110) when in fact it was an attempt to cement a Republican orthodoxy.

11. "une gaieté, une malice extraordinaires, une poésie souvent délicieuses." Bruneau, *La musique française*, 14.

There was no reason for him to mention it, except that its signification for the general public (meaning the relatively shallow stratum of society that would read his work) was, in his view, in need of revision. Before Tiersot, generations of writers had complained with exceptional unanimity of the dryness of Josquin's counterpoint and the impropriety of his use of secular melodies in church. Despite the liturgical battles, generations had, by contrast, elevated the music of Palestrina to ecstatic heights of purity, promoted the myth (unchallenged until 1895 and current even later) that he was taught by Goudimel and therefore French by education, and had swept the existence of the "L'homme armé" masses under the historiographical carpet. Yet in this "official" report Bruneau denigrated Counter-Reformation Palestrina as a representative of the dark ages of music, as an imprisoning musical force, and as an instrument of Catholic musical repression.[12] In return, he celebrated Josquin's sacred music for bringing an ironic echo of the French street into the church and for its "arabesques of charming fantasy, of utter grace."[13] More than that: he presented both historiographies as though they were unremarkable, when they were actually extraordinary. In the case of Josquin, he appropriated the arguments of a moderate Republican and a Schola supporter—Julien Tiersot—in bad faith; in the case of Palestrina he revealed the extent of radical Republican/Protestant closeness at the turn of the century, and explicitly turned the tables on 1890s attempts—notably by Bellaigue—to "save" Palestrina from the radical Ultramontanes by making him medieval again.

While Tiersot was indeed, in musical circles, regarded as the originator of the idea that chanson-based masses were important as repositories of written-out folk tunes, he would never have suggested that they were intended to be ironic or subversive, and that their value lay therein. That was a far more radical agenda than even Weckerlin had pursued when discussing the chanson-based mass in his *La chanson populaire* of 1886. Neither would Bellaigue have characterized Palestrina's "medieval" period in Voltairean terms, as the "dark ages." Silently twisting the thought of the Schola Cantorum's closest allies, Bruneau wrote wilful history. It is no wonder D'Indy was incensed enough to write the anonymous rejoinder in which he attacked Bruneau's selection of composers and the rampant secularism of his interpretations; yet he, too, misrepresented the historiography underpinning much of the report, by allowing it to be inferred that Bruneau's history was all newly minted fable intended to serve radical Republican ends. Catholic and Republican traded conflicting

12. Bruneau, *La musique française*, 18.
13. "arabesques de fantaisie charmante, de grâce extrême." Bruneau, *La musique française*, 13.

ideologies under the cloak of historical probity, demonstrating yet again that the contents of the early music museum were dictated by their current significations, and that both their inclusion and their meanings were worth fighting over.

Meanings, then, are the central issue, because they disclose ideologies that are themselves the foundations on which aesthetics are built, and because people—in this case large numbers of bourgeois music lovers—invest in them and act out their implications. Those meanings, accessed by analyzing the ways people use, abuse, and debate music, are keys to an understanding of complex and shifting relationships between style and ideology, genre and politics. They reach from entire repertories to the individual work or performance. They remind us that musical silences speak as loudly as musical sounds, demanding just as much explanation. They have the power to help us ground our own musical readings sensitively, without falling into false universality. By highlighting the "for whom, and why" of musical culture, and the disjunctions between culture and practice, they also illuminate the problem that without an understanding, even a partial one, of what musics mean to different social groups—with all their inconsistencies of cultural, political, and religious allegiance—we cannot know what to make of the patterns of musical performance that traditional historical research uncovers, nor how to evaluate their historical significance. Most important of all, for those of us studying the century that tried so hard to render music autonomous, they are emblems of music's inextricability from questions of context and identity.

Personalia

(Further information may be found according to the sigla cited below. Entries with no such sigla have been compiled piecemeal from primary sources.)

Sigla: NG2   *New Grove Dictionary of Music and Musicians*, 2d ed., ed. Stanley Sadie and John Tyrrell. London: Macmillan, 2001.

19^eS *Dictionnaire de la musique en France au XIXe siècle*, ed. Joël-Marie Fauquet. Paris: Fayard, 2003.

Désiré [Martin-]Beaulieu (1791–1863): Winner of the Prix de Rome (taught by Méhul) in 1810. Founded Société Philharmonique (1827) and choral society Association Musicale de l'Ouest (1835) in his native Niort. In Paris, helped found a similar mixed choral society (Société de Chant Classique: Fondation Beaulieu, 1860–1912), but died before it could gain significant momentum. (*NG2*, *19^eS*)

Camille Bellaigue (1858–1930): Prize-winning pianist (pupil of Marmontel) turned critic. Criticism dates from 1884; the following year he succeeded Henri Blaze de Bury (son of Castil-Blaze) at the *Revue des deux mondes*. Most significant in the history of early music for his pro-Palestrinian activity. Conservative musical tastes; pro-Italian; anti-German. Became a radical right-winger after 1900. Developed and maintained close connections with the Schola Cantorum, with the Benedictines at Solesmes (where he went for retreats) and Pope Pius X; was even claimed, in Louis Gillet's celebratory obituary for the *Revue des deux mondes*, as a plausible co-author of the *Motu proprio* of 1903. By the beginning of 1906 he had had seven papal audiences. (*19^eS*)

PERSONALIA

Charles Bordes (1863–1909): One of Franck's last Conservatoire pupils; also a piano pupil of Marmontel. *Maître de chapelle* at Nogent-sur-Marne (1887–90), then at Saint-Gervais in Paris (1890–?1903). Introduced Counter-Reformation polyphony at both churches. Began famous series of "Sistine Chapel" Holy Week services 1892; founded the Chanteurs de Saint-Gervais 1892; co-founded the Schola Cantorum 1894. Founder/editor of the *Tribune de Saint-Gervais* (from 1895); editor of several anthologies of sixteenth-century vocal music. Also a champion of vocal/choral works of Bach, Schütz, Lassus, and Janequin, and of early French stage music. (*NG2, 19ᵉS*)

Louis-Albert Bourgault-Ducoudray (1840–1910): Prix de Rome winner 1862, after which his Italian sojourn inspired enthusiasm for Palestrina. In Paris from 1868; founded amateur choral Société Bourgault-Ducoudray (1869–74), with emphasis on Handel; founder member of the Société Nationale de Musique (1871) and the Schola Cantorum (1894). Chair of Music History at Paris Conservatoire (1878–1908). (*NG2, 19ᵉS*)

Michel Brenet, *pseud.* [**Marie Bobillier**] (1858–1918): Highly respected music historian specializing in French and Flemish music before 1700. Her work of the 1890s on Goudimel and Palestrina was iconoclastic and influential. Supported work of the Schola in the late 1890s as Tiersot had done earlier. Joint founder in 1911 of *L'année musicale*. (*NG2, 19ᵉS*)

Alexandre-Etienne Choron (1771–1834): Pioneer of early music editing and performance. Contributed with François Fayolle to France's first biographical dictionary of musicians (1810–11); founder and director of a celebrated singing school (1817–1834) whose concerts included much early music. A "vulgarisateur" and moderate Ultramontane committed to the reform of liturgical music via Roman chant, Palestrina, and *stile antico* repertory. (*NG2, 19ᵉS*)

Félix Clément (1822–1885): Music historian, organist at the Collège Stanislas and the Sorbonne; radical Ultramontane viewed with dismay among pro-Palestrinians. Mounted controversial concerts of thirteenth-century sacred music sporadically from 1849 until 1870s. Closely connected with church reform under Napoléon III; his *Rapport sur l'état de la musique religieuse en France* (1849) led to the founding of the Ecole Niedermeyer (opened 1853). (*NG2, 19ᵉS*)

Félix Danjou (1812–1866): Organist at Notre-Dame-des-Blancs-Manteaux (1831–34); Saint-Eustache (1834–44); Notre Dame de Paris (1840–47). Discovered the Montpellier Codex (1847). Founder of the *Revue de la musique religieuse, populaire, classique* (1845–48, 1854). Ultramontane church music reformer from at least 1839 (his earliest known writings); became progressively more radical. (*19ᵉS*)

Louis Diémer (1843–1919): Studied with Benoist (organ) and Marmontel (piano) at Paris Conservatoire, showing proclivities for early music as early as the 1850s.

Championed French harpsichord music and helped reintroduce the instrument itself. Joint founder of the Société des Instruments Anciens in 1895. His editions up to and beyond 1900 focused on the French harpsichordists. (*NG2*, *19ᵉS*)

Alexandre Guilmant (1837–1911): Organist, composer, music editor. Virtually self-taught, with some guidance from Lemmens, who introduced him to the Bach organ tradition. In demand for organ inaugurations, European/USA tours from the 1860s. Organist at La Trinité, Paris, from 1871. Famous for Bach and Handel performances at Trocadéro for over 20 years from 1878. Co-founder of Schola Cantorum, 1894; organ professor at Conservatoire, 1896–1911. Editions include organ works from 1600 to 1800; Campra stage works for the Michaëlis *Chefs-d'oeuvre* edition. (*NG2*)

Arthur Heulhard (1849–1920): Independently wealthy journalist and bibliophile with what he himself described as an important art collection. A member of the Fourchette Harmonique club of bibliophiles. Moved from political to arts journalism after the Franco-Prussian War, writing for *L'art musical* and *La France chorale*. Worked on a history of the "first" French *opéra-comique* (doubtless De la Halle's *Jeu*) but never published it.

Adolphe Jullien (1845–1932): Studied law before training in music and entering journalism. From 1869 contributed to almost all major music periodicals. Critic of *Journal des débats* from 1893 to 1932, succeeding the composer and Bachian Ernest Reyer. Modernist (Berlioz, Wagner, Debussy) and music historian of French eighteenth century. (*NG2*, *19ᵉS*)

Paul Lacome [Paul-Jean-Jacques Lacome d'Estalenx] (1838–1920): Primarily an operetta composer, with 20 such works between 1870 and 1900. Dedicated to early French stage music (published major collections and editions in the 1870s). Wrote journalism for children's and family journals. Awarded the Légion d'honneur in 1891. (*NG2*)

Adrien de Lafage [Juste-Adrien Lenoir de Lafage] (1805–1862): Disciple of Perne, Choron, and Baini. Palestrinian, though it is unclear whether he used such repertory liturgically at Saint-Etienne-du-Mont or Saint-François-Xavier (his first church posts, 1829–33). Edited collections of Palestrina masses and motets with Launer in the 1840s; substantial book and early music collection. Chief editor of *Le plainchant*, 1860–61. (*NG2*, *19ᵉS*)

Théodore de Lajarte (1826–1890): Composer turned editor and librarian. Trained at the Paris Conservatoire. From 1873, served as archivist of the Paris Opéra under Charles Nuitter; became the Opéra's librarian in 1882. Prepared the Lully editions for the *Chefs-d'oeuvre classiques de l'Opéra français* and a major edition of *ancien-régime* dance music. (*NG2*, *19ᵉS*)

Jean-Joseph-Bonaventure Laurens (1801–1890): Artist, musician, antiquarian, with an extraordinary personal collection of early music that rivaled those of De Lafage and

Farrenc, if not Fétis. Travels in Germany and exposure to the work of Anton Friedrich Justus Thibaut made him an early Bach enthusiast. (*19^eS*)

Jean-Amédée Méreaux [Le Froid de Méreaux] (1802–1874): Solo pianist and teacher based in Rouen from 1835. As a young man, an acquaintance of Mme Récamier and Chateaubriand; pianist to the Duke of Bordeaux from 1828. His important anthology of French harpsichord music (1867) earned him the Légion d'honneur the following year. (*NG2, 19^eS*)

Joseph-Napoléon Ney, *dit* **prince de la Moskova** (1803–1857): Statesman, composer. Founder of the Jockey Club; avid collector of seventeenth-century manuscripts. Ultramontane revivalist of Palestrina's music, through his Société des Concerts de Musique Vocale Religieuse et Classique. The society also regularly sang Janequin, Lassus, Victoria, Handel, and Haydn. (*NG2, 19^eS*)

Louis Niedermeyer (1802–1861): Swiss Protestant composer, editor, teacher, whose career in France culminated in founding of the Ecole Niedermeyer, a state-funded, Catholic, national *maîtrise*, in 1853. Studied in Vienna and in Italy, where he was exposed to sixteenth-century vocal music. Closely associated with the prince de la Moskova's society; may have edited or helped edit the society's printed anthology of 1843–46. (*NG2, 19^eS*)

Joseph d'Ortigue (1802–1866): Student of Castil-Blaze and Castil-Blaze's father in their native Cavaillon. Trained in law. In Paris from 1829, began writing for religious and music journals. Ultramontane, progressively more radical. Joint founder of *La maîtrise* (with Niedermeyer) and the *Journal des maîtrises* (with the radical Ultramontane Félix Clément). Staunch supporter of Choron in the 1830s. (*NG2, 19^eS*)

Arthur Pougin (1834–1921): Pursued journalism after first career as a violinist. Contributed to most of the major musical papers; among daily papers, wrote for those on the far left. Staunch supporter of early French music, writing several monographs on aspects of the subject. Member of the bibliophile club La Fourchette Harmonique. Served on the teaching committee of the Ecole Niedermeyer, acting as Secretary in 1878. Author of the supplement to Fétis's *Biographie universelle* (2d ed.). (*NG2, 19^eS*)

Louis Roger (1824–?): Organist, music educationalist (Galin-Paris-Chevé school), *orphéon* director, and journalist. After *orphéon* and educational work in Rouen in the 1850s, came to Paris in 1860. Described himself as a founder of the Société Académique de Musique Sacrée, against whose elitism he later turned. From 1860, took over direction of the *Revue de musique sacrée, ancienne et moderne* from De Lafage; from 1863, replaced Stéphen de la Madelaine at *L'univers musical*; directed *La semaine musicale* from 1865. A member of the bibliophile club La Fourchette Harmonique.

Julien Tiersot (1857–1936): Musicologist; editor. Studied with Massenet, Franck, and Bourgault-Ducoudray at Paris Conservatoire. Became assistant librarian there in 1883; head librarian in 1909. His history of the French chanson won him the Prix Bordin in 1885. Eclectic tastes: folk song, Wagner, Berlioz, contemporary Scandinavian/Eastern European music, wide range of early music, especially French. Founder of the Société des Traditions Populaires in 1885; staunch supporter of Bordes. (*NG2, 19ᵉS*)

Charles Vervoitte (1822–1884): *Maître de chapelle* at Rouen Cathedral, 1847–59, where he introduced early music, Palestrina included, into concert and probably liturgical use; from 1859 *maître de chapelle* at St-Roch, Paris. Moderate Ultramontane. Director of the Société Académique de Musique Sacrée (1861–72), after which he returned to Rouen and became involved in local music-making. (*19ᵉS*)

Jean-Baptiste Weckerlin (1821–1910): Studied at Paris Conservatoire; became its head librarian, 1876–1909, having served as clerk from 1863. Director of the refounded amateur choral Société Sainte-Cécile, 1865–68. Champion of early French stage music (performing editions of Adam de la Halle, Lully, Cambert). Author of a history of the French chanson (pub. 1886); editor of major folk-song collections. (*NG2, 19ᵉS*)

Bibliography

PRIMARY SOURCES

Archive and Manuscript Sources

Archives Nationales, Paris: Series AJ^{13} (Opéra); AJ^{37} (Conservatoire); F^{21} (Beaux-Arts)
Archives Municipales de Dijon: Series 1M XVI (Statue de Rameau); 2R (Conservatoire)
Bibliothèque Inguimbertine, Carpentras: Collection Laurens
Bibliothèque Municipale et Médiathèque de Niort: Collection Désiré-Martin Beaulieu
Bibliothèque Nationale de France (MSS): n.a.fr. (papiers Brenet, Choron, Fétis, Viardot)
Bibliothèque Nationale de France (Musique): l.a.; n.l.a; Fonds Montpensier; Archives de la Société des Concerts; Fichier Peyrot; papiers Bottée de Toulmon, Diémer, Farrenc, De Lafage, Weckerlin.
Bibliothèque Nationale de France (Opéra): lettres autographes; dossiers d'artistes; Journal de l'Opéra
Bibliothèque Municipale de Rouen: papiers Amédée Méreaux.
Bibliothèque Royale Albert Ier, Brussels: Collection Fétis; series ML.

Music Editions

[Adam de la Halle]. *Oeuvres complètes du trouvère Adam de la Halle (poésies et musique) publiées sous les auspices de la Société des Sciences, des Lettres et des Arts de Lille*, ed. Edmond de Coussemaker. Paris: A. Durand & Pédone-Lauriel, 1872.
Adam de la Halle. *Ci commence le jeu de Robin et de Marion qu'Adam fit.* Pre-

mier essai d'Opéra-Comique par Adam de la Halle (1275), ed. J.-B. Weckerlin. Paris: Durand & Schoenewerk, 1872.

———. *Le jeu de Robin et Marion. Opéra-comique en un acte. XIIIe siècle*, ed. Emile Blémont (text) and Julien Tiersot (music). Paris: E. Fromont [1896].

Alard, Delphin (Ed.) *Les maîtres classiques du violon. Collection de morceaux choisis dans les chefs-d'oeuvre des plus grands maîtres classiques italiens, allemands et français avec le style, le phrasé, l'expression, les doigtés et les coups d'archet propres à l'interprétation traditionnelle de ces oeuvres*. Paris: E. Gérard, then A. O'Kelly [1861–85?].

A.M.D.G. *Concerts spirituels ou Recueil de motets [. . .] sur la musique de Gluck, Piccini, Sacchini, Mozart, Rossini, Beethoven, Weber & d'autres maîtres célèbres*. Avignon: Saguin aîné, 1832.

Anon. (Ed.) *Echos d'Italie*, 6 vols. Paris: Flaxland; later Flaxland, Durand, Schoenewerk & Cie, 1851–1874.

———. (Ed.) *Echos du monde religieux*, 7 vols. Paris: Flaxland; later Flaxland, Durand, Schoenewerk & Cie, 1857–1901.

Bach, J. S. *30 variations pour le piano-forte*. Paris: Navoigille, 1804.

———. *Collection complète pour le piano, avec et sans accompagnement, des oeuvres de J. S. Bach*, 10 vols. Paris: Launer, 1843 (based on Czerny ed.).

———. *La Passion. Oratorio*, ed. Maurice Bourges. Paris: G. Brandus & S. Dufour [1843].

———. *La passion selon Saint Matthieu*, ed. and trans. Charles Bannelier. Collection Litolff. Seul texte conforme à l'exécution des concerts d'Harmonie sacrée dirigés par M. Charles Lamoureux. Paris: Enoch père & fils [1874].

———. *La passion selon Saint-Jean. Oratorio en deux parties*, trans. Maurice Bouchor. Bibliothèque du Comte de Chambrun. Paris: Durdilly & Cie, 1895.

Bordes, Charles (Ed.) *Anthologie des maîtres religieux primitifs des quinzième, seizième et dix-septième siècles [. . .] Edition populaire à l'usage des maîtrises et des amateurs en notation moderne avec des clés usuelles, nuances et indications d'exécution et réduction des voix au clavier par Charles Bordes*, 6 vols. Paris: Au siège de l'association des chanteurs de Saint-Gervais, 1893–95.

Bourdeau, Emile (Ed.) *Renaissance du chant religieux. Oeuvres remarquables avec accompt. de piano ou orgue*. Paris: Arouy [1869].

Castil-Blaze, Henri (Ed.) *Théâtres lyriques de Paris. Recueil de musique (de 1100 [1550] à 1855)*. Paris: Castil-Blaze, 1855.

Chefs-d'oeuvre classiques de l'Opéra français, 33 vols. Paris: Michaëlis, 1877–84.

Choron, Alexandre-Etienne (Ed.) *Collection générale des ouvrages classiques de musique [Raccolta generale delle opere classiche musicali]*. Paris: Auguste Leduc et Cie [1807–c.1809].

——— (Ed.) *Principes de composition des écoles d'Italie adoptés par le gouvernement français pour servir à l'instruction des élèves des maîtres des cathédrales . . .* Paris: Auguste Leduc & Cie [1808].

——— (Ed.) *Collection des pièces de musique religieuse qui s'exécutent tous les ans à Rome, durant la semaine-sainte dans la chapelle du souverain pontife*. Paris: chez l'éditeur [1820].

Clément, Félix (Ed.) *Chants de la Sainte-Chapelle, tirés des manuscrits du XIIIe siècle et mis en parties avec accompagnement d'orgue par Félix Clément. Avec une introduction par Didron aîné* . . . Paris: Victor Didron, 1849.

Couperin, François. *Pièces de clavecin*, ed. "Un artiste antiquaire" [J.-J.-B. Laurens]. Paris: Vve Launer, 1841. Reprinted as *Pièces choisies pour piano par F. Couperin* (no preface). Paris: S. Richault [1856].

Damour, Burnett, and Elwart. *Etudes élémentaires de la musique depuis ses premières notions jusqu'à celles de la composition*. Paris: Au bureau des études élémentaires de la musique, 1838.

Danjou, Félix (Ed.) *Archives curieuses de la musique*. Paris: Schlesinger (music suppl. of the *Revue et gazette musicale de Paris*), 1839–40.

Delaborde, Eugène. *Cadence pour le finale du concerto pour clavecin en ré mineur de J. S. Bach*. Paris: Hartmann, 1872.

Deldevez, E.-M.-E. (Ed.) *Pièces diverses choisies dans les oeuvres des célèbres violonistes-compositeurs des XVIIe et XVIIIe siècles, avec parties concertantes ajoutées au texte original des auteurs et réalisées pour piano et violon*, Op. 19. Paris: S. Richault, 1857 and 1869.

——— (Ed.) *Pièces diverses choisies dans les oeuvres des célèbres compositeurs des XVIe, XVIIe et XVIIIe siècles, avec parties concertantes ajoutées au texte original des auteurs et réalisées pour chant et orchestre*. Paris: S. Richault, 1869.

Delsarte, François [and Rosine]. *Archives du chant. Répertoire des chefs d'oeuvre lyriques des XIVe, XVIIe et XVIIIe siècles accompagnés de chants du Moyen âge et precédés d'une riche collection de hymnes, proses et antiennes de l'Eglise disposées conformément au type harmonique consacré par les plus anciennes traditions*. 3 vols. Paris: F. Delsarte, 1855–64.

Diémer, Louis (Ed.) *Les Clavecinistes français*. 4 vols. Paris: Durand & Schoenewerk (vol. 1); A. Durand & fils (vols. 2-4), 1887–1912. (Vol. 4 edited by Saint-Saëns, D'Indy, Dukas, Guilmant, G. Marty, and Th. de Lajarte.)

Dietsch, Louis (Ed.) *Répertoire de musique religieuse de l'Eglise de la Madeleine de Paris*. Paris: S. Richault, 1854–57.

Dubois, Théodore. *Collection de 9 motets extraits des oeuvres des grands maîtres*. Paris: Graff, 1878.

———. *Illuxit dies tertia. Motet solennel pour le jour de Pâques sur le Psaume 18ème de B. Marcello. Texte latin composé d'après les vers originaux italiens de Giustiniani par R. Moissenet, maître de chapelle de la cathédrale de Dijon. Transcription musicale pour quatre voix S. A. T. B. avec G^d orgue alterné*. Paris: A. Peregally & Parvy fils [1899?].

Durante, Francesco. *Litanies à quatre voix, deux violons, alto et basse*. Paris: Porro, 1804.

Expert, Henri (Ed.) *Les maîtres musiciens de la Renaissance française*. 22 vols. Paris: Alphonse Leduc, 1894–1908.

Farrenc, Aristide, and Louise Farrenc (Eds.) *Le trésor des pianistes*. Paris: A. Farrenc, 1861–74.

Guilmant, Alexandre (Ed.) *Répertoire des concerts d'orgue du Trocadéro*. 3 vols. Paris: Schott, 1884–92; new ed. 2 vols. Paris: Durand [1894].

Handel, G. F. *Il convito d'Alessandro* [Italian version by S. Pazzaglia]. Paris: Carli [c.1827].

———. *Messiah*, trans. Gasse. Paris: Gasse, 1827.

———. *Choeurs de Haendel. Grande partition avec paroles françaises et accompagnement arrangé pour le piano, par J. Pasdeloup*. 2 vols. [*Judas Maccabaeus, Theodora, Joshua*]. Paris: Sous le patronage de Monsieur Edouard Rodrigues par Martinet, 1839.

———. *Judas Maccabée*, trans. Edouard Rodrigues. Paris: S. Richault, 1846.

———. *Cantate pour le jour de Sainte Cécile*, trans. Sylvain Saint-Etienne. Paris: E. Gérard & Cie [1865].

———. *Israël en Egypte*, trans. Sylvain Saint-Etienne. Paris: E. Gérard & Cie [1865].

———. *Salomon*. Paris: E. Gérard & Cie [1865].

———. *Acis & Galatea*, trans. Sylvain Saint-Etienne. Paris: Gérard, 1872.

———. *La fête d'Alexandre ou Le pouvoir de la musique*, trans. Victor Wilder. Paris: Au Ménestrel, 1870; new ed. Paris: H. Gautier, 1872.

———. *Messiah*, trans. Victor Wilder. Paris: Au Ménestrel, 1875 (based on W. T. Best, ed., London: Novello).

Jommelli, Nicolo. *Offertoire [. . .] tiré du répertoire de la Chapelle Sixtine, exécuté par les Conservatoires d'Italie, de France, aux Concerts de l'Odéon, &c*. Paris: Pierre Porro, 1811.

Lacome, Paul (Ed.) *Les fondateurs de l'Opéra français*. Paris: Enoch père & fils, 1878 (first published in *La chronique musicale*, 1873).

——— (Ed.). *Les fondateurs de l'opéra-comique*. Paris: Enoch père & fils, 1878.

Lajarte, Théodore de (Ed.) *Airs à danser de Lulli à Méhul, transcrits d'après les manuscrits originaux de la Bibliothèque de l'Opéra de Paris*. Paris: Durand & Schoenewerk, 1876 (first published in *La chronique musicale*, 1874).

Lully, Jean-Baptiste. *Le bourgeois gentilhomme*, ed. J.-B. Weckerlin. Paris: Durand, Schoenewerk & Cie, 1876.

Marcello, Benedetto. *Cinquanta salmi musica del celebre Marcello con accompagnato di Piano Forte composto da Francesco Mirecki Polacco* . . . Paris: Carli [1820].

———. *Psaumes de Marcello*. 2d ed. 4 vols. Paris: Mme Vve Launer, 1841.

Méreaux, Amédée. *Les clavecinistes de 1637 à 1790. Histoire du clavecin. Portraits et biographies des célèbres clavecinistes avec exemples et notes sur le style et l'exécution de leurs oeuvres*. Paris: Heugel [1864–67].

Moskova, [Joseph-Napoléon Ney], prince de la (Ed.) *Recueil des morceaux de musique ancienne exécutés aux concerts de la Société de musique vocale religieuse et classique, fondée à Paris en 1843*. . . . 11 vols. Paris: Pacini, 1843–45.

Nouveau répertoire de l'orphéon. Collection de choeurs adoptés par la Commission du chant de la Ville de Paris. Paris: E. Gérard [1859].

Palestrina, G. P. da. *Cinq messes tirées du répertoire de la chapelle sixtine à Rome*, ed. Adrien de Lafage. Paris: Vve Launer [1844].

———. *Vingt motets tirés du répertoire de la chapelle sixtine à Rome, composés par Jean Pierluigi da Palestrina*, ed. Adrien de Lafage. Paris: Vve Launer, n.d.

Pergolesi. *Stabat mater [. . .], arrangé pour le forte-piano ou l'orgue par M. M.* [Martini Il Tedesco]. Paris: Pleyel, 1803.

Rameau, J.-P. *Castor et Pollux* [1737], ed. Charles Lecocq. Paris: Legouix, 1877.

———. *Oeuvres complètes*, ed. Camille Saint-Saëns et al. Paris: Durand, 1895–1924.

Stamaty, Camille. *Concerts du Conservatoire. 18ᵉ Psaume de Marcello, "I cieli immensi narrano" paraphrasé pour piano et dédié à son élève Mad^lle Adelina Vautier*, Op. 26. Paris: Heugel & Cie, 1856.

Szarvády, Wilhelmine (Ed.) *Trois morceaux de piano tirés des programmes de concert de Mme W. Szarvády*. 3 vols. Paris: J. Maho, 1863–64.

Tiersot, Julien. *Ronsard et la musique de son temps: oeuvres musicales de Certon, Goudimel, Janequin, Muret, Mauduit etc.* Leipzig: Breitkopf & Haertel. Paris: Fischbacher [1903].

Weckerlin, J.-B (Ed.) *Echos du temps passé. Recueil de chansons, noëls, madrigaux, brunettes, etc., du XIIᵉ au XVIIIᵉᵐᵉ siècle, suivis de chansons populaires*. Paris: G. Flaxland, 1853–57.

NEWSPAPERS AND PERIODICALS (PARIS)

L'art musical	(1860–94)
La chronique musicale	(1873–76)
La correspondance des amateurs musiciens	(1802–05)
Le courrier musical	(1898–1914)
L'écho des orphéons	(1861–1905)
L'encyclopédie pittoresque de la musique	(1833)
Le Figaro	(1854→)
La France chorale	(1861–69)
La France orphéonique	(1869–70?)
La France musicale	(1837–70)
Le journal de musique	(1876–82)
Le journal des débats	(1800–1914)
Le journal des savants	(1665–1938)
Le journal populaire de musique et de chant	(1869–74)
La maîtrise	(1857–61)
Le ménestrel	(1833–1940)
Le mercure de France	(1800–1818)
Le mercure du dix-neuvième siècle	(1827–32)
Le monde artiste	(1862–1914)
Le monde musical	(1889–1940)
La musique populaire	(1881–90)
La nouvelle France chorale	(1869–98)
L'orphéon	(1855–1939?)
La presse théâtrale et musicale	(1855–65)
Le progrès artistique	(1878–1908)

La réforme musicale	(1856–70)
La renaissance musicale	(1881–83)
La revue contemporaine	(1852–70)
Revue de la musique religieuse, populaire, classique	(1845–54)
La revue de musique sacrée, ancienne et moderne	(1861–70)
Revue de Paris	(1829–45)
La revue des deux mondes	(1829–1944)
La revue d'histoire et de critique musicales	(1901–12)
La revue du monde musical et dramatique	(1878–84)
La revue et gazette des théâtres	(1855–67)
La revue et gazette musicale de Paris	(1834–80)
La revue latine	(1902–08)
Revue musicale	(1827–35)
La revue musicale	(1920–40)
La semaine artistique et musicale	(1888–89)
La semaine musicale	(1865–67)
Le temps	(1861–1942)
La tribune de Saint-Gervais	(1895–1922)
L'union musicale	(1864–66)
L'univers musical	(1853–64?)

NEWSPAPERS AND PERIODICALS (REGIONAL/FOREIGN)

L'almanach du Comtat	(Carpentras, 1882–?)
Le bien public	(Dijon, 1868–1944)
Le choeur	(Nancy, 1848–60)
La chronique de Rouen	(1854–87)
Le conciliateur de Vaucluse	(Carpentras, 1849–72)
La Côte d'Or	(Dijon, 1868–83)
Le guide musical	(Brussels and Paris, 1855–94)
Le journal de Rouen	(1791–1944)
Musica sacra	(Toulouse, 1874–1901)
Le progrès de la Côte d'Or	(Dijon, 1869–1944)
La revue de musique ancienne et moderne	(Rennes, 1856)
La revue littéraire de l'Ouest	(Niort, 1836–38)
La semaine religieuse de l'Archidiocèse d'Aix	(Aix-en-Provence, 1879–1944)

BOOKS, PAMPHLETS AND ARTICLES

Anon. [Désiré-Martin Beaulieu] *Association Musicale de l'Ouest. Congrès de Niort. Année 1843*. Niort: Robin & Cie [1844].

———. *Concordia. Assemblée générale du 3 décembre 1887* [privately printed].

———. *Concordia. Société chorale. 2ᵉ exercice, 1880–1881. Statuts.* [privately printed].

———. *Congrès diocésain de musique religieuse et de plain-chant tenu à Rodez les 22, 23 et 24 juillet 1895. Compte rendu.* Rodez: E. Carrère, 1895.

———. *Notice sur la Société des concerts de chant classique. Fondée par M. Beaulieu.* Paris: Imp. Jules Juteau & fils [1872].

———. *Rameau. Sa vie, ses oeuvres.* Dijon: H. Grigne, 1876.

———. *Société académique de musique sacrée. Séance générale du 15 janvier 1864.* Paris: Morris, 1864.

———. *Société Bourgault-Ducoudray.* Paris: Imp. Louis Edmonds, 1873.

———. *Société chorale des amateurs.* Paris: J. Claye, 1872.

———. *Statuts de la Société des concerts de chant classique. Fondation Beaulieu.* Paris: Imp. Jules Juteau & fils, 1863.

Adam, Adolphe. *Derniers souvenirs d'un musicien. Nouvelle édition.* Paris: Michel Lévy frères, 1871.

Aldin, Félix, and Louis Roger. *Société académique de musique sacrée. Constitution de la société, 16 décembre 1861.* Saint-Germain-en-Laye: L. Toinon & Cie [1862].

Aubry, Pierre. *Les fêtes musicales d'Avignon et l'oeuvre de Saint-Gervais (3, 4 et 5 août 1899).* Paris: De Soy & fils, 1899.

———. *La musicologie médiévale: histoire et méthodes. Cours professé à l'Institut catholique de Paris, 1898–1899.* Paris: H. Welter, 1900.

Becker, Georges. *Aperçu sur la chanson française (du XIᵉ au XVIIᵉ siècle).* Geneva: Ziegler & Cie, 1876.

Bellaigue, Camille. *L'année musicale, 1887–1888.* Paris: Charles Delagrave, 1889.

———. *Pie X et Rome. Notes et souvenirs, 1903–1914.* 3d rev. ed. Paris: Nouvelle Librairie Nationale, 1916.

Benoît, Camille. *La grande messe en si mineur de Jean-Sébastien Bach.* Paris: Imprimerie de l'art, 1891.

[Berlioz, Hector]. *Memoirs,* trans. David Cairns. St Albans: Granada Publishing, 1970.

———. *Correspondance générale.* Vol. 1, ed. Pierre Citron. Paris: Flammarion, 1972.

Bertrand, Gustave. *Les nationalités musicales étudiées dans le drame lyrique.* Paris: Didier & Cie, 1872.

Blondeau, Pierre-Auguste-Louis. *Notes sur Palestrina–MS XIXᵉ s.* Rome: A. Blondeau, 1809.

———. *Histoire de la musique moderne depuis le premier siècle de l'ère chrétienne à nos jours.* 2 vols. Paris: Tantenstein & Cordel, 1847.

Bonnassies, Jules. *La musique à la Comédie-Française.* Paris: Baur, 1874.

Bordes, Charles. "De l'emploi de la musique figurée et spécialement de la musique palestrinienne dans les offices liturgiques." *Congrès diocésain de la musique religieuse et du plainchant. Rodez, 22, 23 et 24 juillet 1895. Compte rendu.* Rodez: E. Carrère, 1895, 146–53.

Bottée de Toulmon, Auguste. *De la chanson musicale en France au Moyen Age*. Paris: Imp. de Crapelet, 1836.

———. *Rapport sur une publication de musique ancienne fait au Comité historique des arts et monuments*. Paris: Imp. de Paul Dupont, s.d. [1843].

Brenet, Michel [Marie Bobillier]. *Claude Goudimel: essai bio-bibliographique*. Besançon: Paul Jaquin, 1898.

———. *La musique sacrée sous Louis XIV. Conférence prononcée le 12 janvier 1899 dans le grand amphithéâtre de l'Institut catholique*. Paris: Bureau d'édition de la Schola Cantorum, 1899.

———. *Palestrina*. Paris, 1906; 5th ed. Félix Alcan, 1919.

Bruneau, Alfred. *La musique française: rapport sur la musique en France au XIIIe au XVe siècle. La musique à Paris en 1900 au théâtre, au concert, à l'exposition*. Paris: Charpentier, 1901.

Burkhardt, Jacob. *The Civilization of the Renaissance: An Essay* [1860]. London: Phaidon, 1965.

Burney, Charles. *A General History of Music from the Earliest Ages to the Present Period* [1789], ed. Frank Mercer. 2 vols. London: G. T. Foulis, 1935.

Cart, William. *Etude sur J.-S. Bach, 1685–1750*. New ed. Paris: Fischbacher, 1899.

Castéra, René d'Aveyrac de. *Dix années d'action musicale religieuse, 1890–1900*. Paris: Au Bureaux de la Schola Cantorum, n.d.

Castil-Blaze [François-Henri-Joseph Blaze, *dit*], *Chapelle-musique des rois de France*. Paris: Paulin, 1832.

Charnacé, Guy de. *Musique et musiciens*, 2 vols. Paris: Pottier de Lalaine, 1873.

Choron, Alexandre-Etienne. *Considérations sur la situation actuelle de l'Institution royale ou Conservatoire de musique classique*. Paris: Imp. de Ducessois [1834].

Choron, Alexandre-Etienne, and François Fayolle, (Eds.) *Dictionnaire historique des musiciens, artistes ou amateurs, morts ou vivans*. 2 vols. Paris: Valade, Lenormant, 1810–11.

Chouquet, Gustave. *Histoire de la musique dramatique en France depuis ses origines jusqu'à nos jours*. Paris: Didot frères, fils & Cie, 1873.

Clément, Félix. *Rapport sur l'état de la musique religieuse en France*. Paris: Imprimerie archéologique de Victor Didron, 1849.

———. *Histoire générale de la musique religieuse*. Paris: Adrien le Clere & Cie, 1860.

———. *Notice sur les chants de la Sainte-Chapelle*. Paris: Imp. Victor Goupy [1875].

Colomb, Casimir. *La musique*. Paris: Hachette, 1878.

Coussemaker, Edmond de. *Délimitation du flamand et du français dans le nord de la France*. Dunkirk: Typ. Benjamin Klein, 1857.

——— (Ed.), *Oeuvres complètes du trouvère Adam de la Halle (poésies et musique) publiées sous les auspices de la Société des sciences, des lettres et des arts de Lille*. Paris: A. Durand & Pédone-Lauriel, 1872.

——— (Ed.), *Oeuvres théoriques de Jean Tinctoris d'après les manuscrits de Bruxelles, de Bologne et de Gand*, 2d ed. Lille: Lefebvre-Ducrocq, 1875.

Couturier, C[laude], and N[icolas] M[ammès?]. *Décadence et restauration de la musique d'église*. Paris: E. Repos, 1862.

Dandelot, Arthur. *La Société des concerts du Conservatoire, 1828–1923*, ed. Philippe Gaubert. Paris: Delagrave, 1923.

David, Ernest. *G.-F. Händel. Sa vie, ses travaux et son temps*. Paris: Calmann Lévy, 1884.

[Debussy, Claude]. *Three Classics in the Aesthetics of Music*. New York: Dover Publications, 1962.

Decourcelle, Maurice. *La Société académique des enfants d'Apollon (1741–1880)*. Paris: Durand, Schoenewerk & Cie, 1881.

Decourcelles, Charles. *Monographie de la musique. Utilité des recherches propres à faciliter l'étude de la musique ancienne, et importance de cette étude*. Paris: P. Duport, 1847.

Deldevez, E.-M.-E., *La Société des concerts, 1860 à 1885 (Conservatoire national de musique)*. Paris: Firmin-Didot & Cie, 1887, ed. Gérard Streletski. Heilbronn: Lucie Galland, 1998.

———. *Mes mémoires*. Paris: Le Puy, 1890.

Dent, Edward J. *Alessandro Scarlatti: His Life and Works*. London: Edward Arnold, 1905.

Dessus, Antoine [see also Super, Antoine]. *Restauration du chant liturgique*. Paris: Librairie de la Société Bibliographique, 1882.

Douen, Orentin. *Clément Marot et le psautier huguenot. Etude historique, littéraire, musicale et bibliographique*. 2 vols. Paris: Imprimé par autorisation du gouvernement, à l'Imprimerie Nationale, 1878–79.

[Dukas, Paul]. *Les écrits de Paul Dukas sur la musique*, ed. Gustave Samazeuilh. Paris: SEFI, 1948. Republished as *Paul Dukas: chroniques musicales sur deux siècles, 1892–1932*. Paris: Stock, 1979.

Duprez, Gilbert. *Souvenirs d'un chanteur*. Paris: Calmann Lévy, 1888.

Elwart, Antoine. *Histoire de la Société des concerts du Conservatoire impérial de musique*. Paris: Castel, 1860.

———. *Histoire des Concerts populaires de musique classique*. Paris: Castel, 1864.

Fétis, François-Joseph. *Quels ont été les mérites des Neerlandais dans la musique, principalement aux 14e, 15e et 16e siècles; et quelle influence les artistes de ce pays qui ont séjourné en Italie, ont-ils exercés sur les écoles de musique, qui se sont formés peu après cette époque en Italie?* Amsterdam: J. Müller, 1829.

———. *Biographie universelle des musiciens*. 1st ed., 8 vols. Paris: H. Fournier (vols. 1–4), Brussels: Meline, Cans & Compagnie (vols. 5–8), 1835–44.

———. *Biographie universelle des musiciens et bibliographie générale de la musique*. 2d ed., 8 vols. Paris: Firmin Didot frères, fils & Cie, 1860–65. Supplément et complément ed. Arthur Pougin, 2 vols. Paris: Mesnil, 1878–80.

Freson, J.-G. *L'esthétique de Richard Wagner*. 2 vols. Paris: Fischbacher, 1893.

Fuchs, Mme Henriette. *Le bi-centenaire de Bach: "La Passion selon Saint Matthieu" à Bâle le 31 mai 1885*. Paris: Fischbacher, 1885.

Gautier, Léon-E. *Eloge d'Alexandre Choron*. Paris: Derache, 1845; Caen: Hardel, 1845.

Gobineau, Joseph-Arthur de. *La renaissance*. Paris: E. Plon, 1877.

Gomart, Ch. "Notices historiques sur la maîtrise de Saint-Quentin et sur les célébrités musicales de cette ville," *Société académique de Saint-Quentin. Annales agricoles, scientifiques et industrielles du Département de l'Aisne*, series 2, vol. 8 ("Travaux de 1850"). Saint-Quentin: Ad. Moreau, 1851, 212–79.

Got, Médéric. *Journal de Edmond Got, sociétaire de la Comédie-Française, 1822–1901.* 2 vols. Paris: Plon-Nourrit & Cie, 1910.

Gounod, Charles. *Mémoires d'un artiste,* 3d ed. Paris: Calmann-Lévy, 1896.

Grégoir, E.-J.-G. *Souvenirs artistiques. Documents pour servir à l'histoire de la musique.* 3 vols. Brussels: Schott frères, 1888–89.

Guimet, Emile. *Cinq jours à Dresde. Relation de la grande Fête des chanteurs du 22 au 26 juillet 1865.* Lyon: Charles Méra, 1865.

———. *La musique populaire. Discours de réception à l'Académie des sciences, belles-lettres & arts de Lyon.* Lyon: Association Typographique, 1870.

Guyot, François-Xavier-Joseph, Marquis de Maiche. [Untitled notice on Goudimel], *Séances publiques de l'Académie des sciences, belles-lettres et arts de Besançon. Séance du 28 Jan 1826.* Besançon: Ve Daclin [1826], 67–71.

Indy, Vincent d'. *Cours de composition musicale* [with Auguste Sérieyx], and Guy de Lioncourt, 3 vols. Paris: Durand & fils, 1909–50.

[———]. *Ma vie. Journal de jeunesse. Correspondance familiale et intime, 1851–1931,* ed. Marie d'Indy. Paris: Séguier, 2001.

Jullien, Adolphe. *La cour et l'Opéra sous Louis XVI. Marie-Antoinette et Sacchini, Salieri, Favart et Gluck.* Paris: Didier & Cie, 1878.

Kreutzer, Léon, and Edouard Fournier. *Essai sur l'art lyrique au théâtre depuis les anciens jusqu'à Meyerbeer.* Paris: Imp. Vve Bouchard-Huzard, 1849.

Labat, Jean-Baptiste. *Oeuvres littéraires-musicales.* 2 vols. Paris: J. Baur, 1879–83.

Lafage, Adrien de. *Histoire générale de la musique et de la danse.* Paris: Au Comptoir des Imprimeurs Unis, 1844.

———. *Extraits du catalogue critique et raisonné d'une petite bibliothèque musicale.* Rennes: H. Vatar, 1857.

———. *Essais de dipthérographie musicale, ou Notices, descriptions, analyses, extraits et réproductions de manuscrits rélatifs à la pratique, à la théorie et à l'histoire de la musique.* 2 vols. Paris: O. Legouix, 1864.

Lajarte, Théodore de. *Bibliothèque musicale du théâtre de l'Opéra: catalogue historique, chronologique, anécdotique.* 2 vols. Paris: Librairie des Bibliophiles, 1878; Hildesheim: Olms, 1969.

———. *Les curiosités de l'Opéra.* Paris: Calmann Lévy, 1883.

[Laurens, Jules]. ("XXX.") *Jean-Joseph-Bonaventure Laurens: sa vie et ses oeuvres.* Carpentras: J. Brun & Cie, 1899.

Lavoix fils, Henri. *La musique française.* Paris: Libraires-Imprimeries réunies [1891].

Legouvé, Ernest. *Soixante ans de souvenirs,* 4th ed., 2 vols. Paris: J. Hetzel, 1886.

[Leo, Sophie Augustine]. "Musical Life in Paris (1817–1848): A Chapter from the Memoirs of Sophie Augustine Leo," trans. W. Oliver Strunk, *Musical Quarterly,* 17 (1931), 259–403.

Loth, abbé Julien. *Notice sur M. Charles Vervoitte. Membre de l'Académie de Rouen.* Rouen: Imprimerie de Espérance Cagniard, 1885.

Lucas, Eusèbe. *Les concerts classiques en France.* Paris: Sandez & Fischbacher, 1876.

Mallortie, de. "Théâtre français au moyen âge: Adam de la Halle," *Mémoires de l'Académie des sciences, lettres et arts.* 2e série/xxii. Arras: Imp. Rohard-Courtin, 1891, 307–38.

Martine, [Jacques-Daniel]. *De la musique dramatique en France.* Paris: Dentu, 1813.
Mayeur, J.-M. *Histoire religieuse de la France, XIXe, XXe siècles.* Paris: Beauchesne, 1975.
Ménil, Félicien de. *L'école flamande du XVe siècle.* Paris: La revue du Nord, 1895.
Méreaux, Amédée. *Variétés littéraires et musicales. Pages d'histoire, critique, portraits à plume.* Paris: Calmann-Lévy, 1878.
Michelet, Jules. *Histoire de France.* 15 vols. Paris: Hetzel & Cie, 1833–65.
Moonen, M. de. "L'orphéon et la popularisation de la bonne musique." Privately published pamphlet, 1877.
Niedermeyer, Louis-Alfred. *Vie d'un compositeur moderne (1802–1861).* Paris: Fischbacher, 1893.
Nisard, Théodore. *Giovanni Pierluigi da Palestrina.* Le Mans: Imp. de Beauvais, n.d.
———. *Monographie de Dieudonné Denne-Baron.* Paris: E. Repos, n.d.
Ortigue, Joseph d'. *La musique à l'église.* Paris: Didier & Cie, 1861.
Pougin, Arthur. *A propos du Messie de Haendel au cirque des Champs-Elysées le 19 décembre 1873.* Paris: Imp. Centrale des Chemins de Fer. A. Chaix & Cie, 1873.
———. *Rameau: essai sur sa vie et ses oeuvres.* Paris: Decaux, 1876.
———. *Les vrais créateurs de l'opéra français: Perrin et Cambert.* Paris: Charavay frères, 1881.
Proudhon, Pierre-Joseph. *Système des contradictions économiques, ou Philosophie de la misère* [1846]. Paris: Rivière, 1939.
Radet, Edmond. *Lully: homme d'affaires, propriétaire et musicien. Notes et croquis à propos de son hôtel de la rue Saint-Anne et de son mausolée aux Petits-Pères.* Paris: Librairie d'Art, 1891.
Régnier, Henri. *Mémoire sur le mantien de la musique d'église* [from *Le correspondant*, 10 Sept. 1846]. Paris: A. René & Cie, 1846.
Renan, Ernest. *Qu'est-ce qu'une nation?* 2d ed. Paris: Calmann Lévy, 1882.
Réty, Hippolyte. *Etudes historiques sur le chant religieux.* Paris: Bray & Retaux, 1870.
———. *Notice historique sur Choron et son école* [Académie de Macon. Séance du 22 novembre 1872]. Paris: Douniol & Cie, 1873.
Reuchsel, Maurice. *La musique à Lyon (aperçu historique).* 2d ed. Lyon: P. Legendre & Cie, 1903.
Reyer, Ernest. *Notes de musique.* Paris: Charpentier & Cie, 1875.
———. *Quarante ans de musique.* Paris: Calmann-Lévy [1909].
Robert, Gustave. *La musique à Paris [1894–1900].* 6 vols. Paris: Ch. Delagrave, 1895–1900.
Rolland, Romain. *Les origines du théâtre lyrique moderne. L'histoire de l'opéra en Europe avant Lully et Scarlatti.* Paris: E. Thorin, 1895.
———. *Musicians of Today* [1908], trans. Mary Blaiklock. 2d ed. London: Kegan Paul, Trench, Trüber & Co Ltd., 1915.
———. *Haendel.* Paris: F. Alcan, 1910.
Romain, Louis de. *Essais de critique musicale.* Paris: Alphonse Lemerre, 1890.
Sabattier, J.-B. *L'opéra et la symphonie, ou l'Idée générale de la musique.* Paris: C. Marpon & E. Flammarion, 1879.
Saint-Saëns, Camille. *Harmonie et mélodie.* Paris: Calmann-Lévy, 1885; 9th ed., 1923.

———. *Ecole buissonnière: notes et souvenirs*. Paris: Pierre Lafitte & Co. [1913].
———. *Au courant de la vie*. Paris: Dorbon aîné [1914].
Schoelcher, Victor. *The Life of Handel*, trans. James Lowe. London: Trübner & Co., 1857.
Scudo, Paul. *Critique et littérature musicales (deuxième série)*. Paris: Hachette, 1859.
Super, Antoine [pseud. for Antoine Dessus]. *Palestrina: étude historique et critique sur la musique religieuse*. Paris: Victor Retaux & fils, 1892.
Tiersot, Julien. *Histoire de la chanson populaire en France*. Paris: Plon, 1889.
Vaucorbeil, Auguste-Emmanuel. *Mémoire présenté à l'Assemblée Nationale par la Société des compositeurs de musique*. Paris: Imprimerie Administrative de Paul Dupon, 1874.
Vervoitte, Charles. *Société académique de musique sacrée. Séance générale du 15 janvier 1864*. Paris: Typ. de Morris, 1864.
Weber, Johannes. *La situation musicale et l'instruction populaire en France*. Leipzig and Brussels: Breitkopf & Härtel; Paris: V. Durdilly & Cie, 1884.
Weckerlin, Jean-Baptiste. *Bibliothèque du Conservatoire national de musique et de déclamation. Catalogue bibliographique . . . avec notices et reproductions musicales des principaux ouvrages de la Réserve*. Paris: Firmin Didot, 1885.
———. *La chanson populaire*. Paris: Firmin Didot, 1886.
———. *L'ancienne chanson populaire en France, 16ᵉ et 17ᵉ siècle. Avec préface et notices*. Paris: Garnier frères, 1887.
———. *Nouveau musiciana*. Paris: Garnier frères, 1890.

SECONDARY SOURCES

Anon. (Ed.) *Mélanges Couperin*. Paris: Picard, 1968.
Albanese, Ralph Jr. "The Molière Myth in Nineteenth-Century France," *Pre-Text, Text, Context: Essays on Nineteenth-Century French Literature*, ed. Robert L. Mitchell. Columbus: Ohio State University Press, 1980, 239–54.
———. *Molière à l'école républicaine: de la critique universitaire aux manuels scolaires (1870–1914)*. Saratoga: Anma Libri, 1992.
——— "Molière républicain: la réception critique et scolaire de son oeuvre au dix-neuvième siècle," *Homage to Paul Bénichou*, ed. Sylvie Romanowski and Monique Bilezikon. Birmingham, Ala.: Summa Press, 1994, 307–22.
———. "Corneille à l'école républicaine," *Papers on French Seventeenth-Century Literature*, 46 (1997), 145–55.
Applegate, Celia, and Pamela Potter (Eds.) *Music and German National Identity*. Chicago: University of Chicago Press, 2002.
Ardouin, Laurence. "La musique ancienne au Conservatoire: évocations de la pratique d'un répertoire," *Le Conservatoire de Paris: regards sur une institution et son histoire*, ed. Emmanuel Hondré. Paris: Association du Bureau des Etudiants du CNSMDP, 1995, 173–84.
Bar-Tal, Daniel, and Ervin Staub (Eds.) *Patriotism in the Lives of Individuals and Nations*. Chicago: Nelson-Hall, 1997.

Baschet, Robert. *E.-J. Delécluze: témoin de son temps, 1781–1863.* Paris: Boivin & Cie, 1942.
Baycroft, Timothy. "Changing Identities in the Franco-Belgian Borderland in the Nineteenth and Twentieth Centuries," *French History*, 13 (1999), 417–38.
Becker-Derex, Christiane. *Louis Diémer: pianiste, claveciniste, professeur, compositeur (1843–1919).* 2 vols. Ph.D. diss., Paris, Conservatoire National Supérieure de Musique, 1983.
Bèges, Alex, and Janine Bèges (Eds.) *Alexandre Guibal du Rivage: oeuvres littéraires & musicales.* Béziers: Centre International de Documentation Occitaine, 1978.
Belin, E. (Ed.) *La Société chorale de Dijon de 1870 à 1900. Directeur: Arthur Deroye.* Dijon: Imp. Jacquot & Floret, 1905.
Ben-Amos, Avner. "The Uses of the Past: Patriotism between History and Memory," *Patriotism in the Lives of Individuals and Nations*, ed. Daniel Bar-Tal and Ervin Staub. Chicago: Nelson-Hall, 1997, 129–47.
Berenson, Edward. *The Trial of Madame Caillaux.* Berkeley and Los Angeles: University of California Press, 1992.
Bergeron, Katherine. *Decadent Enchantments: The Revival of Gregorian Chant at Solesmes.* Berkeley: University of California Press, 1998.
Boettcher, Tilmann. *Les exercices publics d'Alexandre Choron à travers la presse de l'époque.* Maîtrise, Université de Paris–Sorbonne (Paris IV), 1995.
Boghossian, Irma. *Catalogue du fonds musical de l'ancienne maîtrise de la Cathédrale Saint-Sauveur [Aix-en-Provence].* Aix-en-Provence: ARCAM/EDISUD, 1990.
Bordachar, l'abbé. *Charles Bordes et son oeuvre.* Pau: E. Marrimpouey jeune, 1922.
Brenet, Michel. (pseud. Marie Bobillier). *Les Concerts en France sous l'ancien régime.* Paris: Fischbacher, 1900.
Buch, Esteban. *Beethoven's Ninth: A Political History*, trans. Richard Miller. Chicago: University of Chicago Press, 2003.
Bullen, J. B. *The Myth of the Renaissance in Nineteenth-Century Writing.* Oxford: Clarendon Press, 1994.
Caballero, Carlo. "Patriotism or Nationalism? Fauré and the Great War," *Journal of the American Musicological Society*, 52 (1999), 593–625.
Caillet, Robert. *Les vêpres de Saint-Siffrein à Carpentras. Bribes d'histoire Comtadine,* 2d ed., trans. from original Provencal by author. Cavaillon: Imp. Mistral, 1956.
Campos, Rémy. "'Mens sana in corpore sano': l'introduction de l'histoire de la musique au Conservatoire," *Le Conservatoire de Paris: regards sur une institution et son histoire*, ed. Emmanuel Hondré. Paris: Association du Bureau des Etudiants du CNSMDP, 1995, 145–71.
———. *La Renaissance introuvable? Entre curiosité et militantisme: La Société des concerts de musique vocale religieuse et classique du prince de la Moskowa (1843–1846).* Paris: Klincksieck, 2000.
Cannone, Belinda. "L'éclipse de la musique baroque au début du 19e siècle," *Dix-huitième siècle*, no. 26 (1994), 523–38.
Castéra, René de (Ed.) *La Schola cantorum: son histoire depuis sa fondation jusqu'en 1925.* Paris: Bloud & Gay, 1927.

Chadwick, Owen. *A History of the Popes, 1830–1914*. Oxford: Oxford University Press, 1998.
Chartier, Roger. *Cultural History: Between Practices and Representations*, trans. Lydia G. Cochrane. Cambridge: Polity Press, 1988.
Clark, Maribeth. "Bodies at the Opéra: Art and the Hermaphrodite in the Dance Criticism of Théophile Gautier," *Reading Critics Reading: Opera and Ballet Criticism from the Revolution to 1848*, ed. Roger Parker and Mary Ann Smart. Oxford: Oxford University Press, 2001, 237–53.
Colette, Marie-Noëlle, et al. (Eds.) *La musique à Paris en 1830–1831*. Paris: Bibliothèque Nationale, 1983.
Combarnous, Victor. *L'histoire du Grand-Théâtre de Marseille, 31 octobre 1787–13 novembre 1919*. Marseille, 1927; reprint Marseille: Lafitte, 1980.
Compagnon, Antoine. "Proust's *Remembrance of Things Past*," *Realms of Memory: The Construction of the French Past*, vol. 2: *Traditions*, dir. Pierre Nora, ed. Lawrence D. Kritzman, trans. Arthur Goldhammer. New York: Columbia University Press, 1997, 210–46.
Cooper, Jeffrey. *The Rise of Instrumental Music and Concert Series in Paris, 1828–71*. Ann Arbor: UMI Research Press, 1983.
Corten, Walter. *Le "procès de canonisation" de Sébastien Bach en France au 19e siècle*. Unpublished diss., Université Libre de Bruxelles, 1978.
———. "La réemergence de J.S. Bach au XIXe siècle et en particulier dans le romantisme français," ed. Walter Corten et al. *Conférences Jean Sebastien Bach: "Pôle Nord," janvier-fèvrier 1985*, Bruxelles: Pôle Nord, 1985, 3–24.
Devriès, Anik, and François Lesure. *Dictionnaire des éditeurs de musique français*, 2 vols. Geneva: Minkoff, 1979–1988.
Digeon, Claude. *La crise allemande de la pensée française (1870–1914)*. Paris: PUF, 1959.
Di Grazia, Donna M. *Concert Societies and their Choral Repertories, c.1828–1880*. Ph.D. diss., Washington University, St Louis, 1993.
Donakowski, Conrad. *A Muse for the Masses: Ritual and Music in an Age of Democratic Revolution, 1770–1870*. Chicago and London: University of Chicago Press, 1977.
Doret, Monique. *Le théâtre de Dijon et l'opéra de Jean-Philippe Rameau*. Unpublished diss., Université de Dijon, 1980.
Dubled, Henri. "Le fonds musical de la Bibliothèque Inguimbertine et des musées de Carpentras," *Exposition musicale. Fonds de la Bibliothèque Inguimbertine et des musées de Carpentras, 16 juin–30 octobre 1979*. Carpentras: Musée Comtadin, 1979.
Dukas, Paul. "Charles Bordes," *La revue musicale* 5/10: 1 August 1924, 97–103.
Earp, Lawrence. "Machaut's Music in the Early Nineteenth Century: The Work of Perne, Bottée de Toulmon, and Fétis," *Guillaume de Machaut*, ed. Jacqueline Cerquiglini-Toulet and Nigel Wilkins. Paris: Presses de l'Université de Paris—Sorbonne, 2001, 9–40.
Eigeldinger, Jean-Jacques. *L'univers musical de Chopin*. Paris: Fayard, 2000.

Ellis, Katharine. *Music Criticism in Nineteenth-Century France: "La revue et gazette musicale de Paris," 1834–1880*. Cambridge: Cambridge University Press, 1995.

———. "Female Pianists and their Male Critics in Nineteenth-Century Paris," *Journal of the American Musicological Society*, 50 (1997), 353–85.

———. "Palestrina et la musique dite 'palestrinienne' en France au XIXe siècle: questions d'exécution et de réception," *La Renaissance et sa musique au XIXe siècle*, ed. Philippe Vendrix. Paris: Klincksieck, 2000, 155–90.

———. "A Dilettante at the Opéra: Issues in the Criticism of Julien-Louis Geoffroy, 1800–1814," *Reading Critics Reading: Opera and Ballet Criticism from the Revolution to 1848*, ed. Roger Parker and Mary Ann Smart. Oxford University Press, 2001, 46–68.

———. "Berlioz, the Sublime, and the *Broderie* Problem," *Hector Berlioz: Miscellaneous Studies*, ed. Fulvia Morabito and Michela Niccolai. Ut Orpheus Edizioni, Bologna, 2005, 29–59.

———. "Vocal Training at the Paris Conservatoire and the Choir Schools of Alexandre-Etienne Choron: Debates, Rivalries and Consequences," *Musical Education in Europe (1770–1914): Compositional, Institutional, and Political Challenges*, ed. Michael Fend and Michel Noiray. Berlin: Berliner Wissenschafts-Verlag, 2005, 125–44.

———. "En route to Wagner: Explaining D'Indy's Early-Music Pantheon," *Vincent d'Indy et son temps*, ed. Manuela Schwartz. Liège: Mardaga, forthcoming, 2005.

———. "A Tale of Two Societies: Class, Democratisation and the Regeneration of Choral Musics in France, 1861–74," *Les sociétés de musique en Europe, 1700–1920: Structures, pratiques musicales et sociabilités*, ed. Hans Erich Bödeker and Patrice Veit. Berlin: Berliner Wissenschafts-Verlag, forthcoming.

———. "Rameau in Late Nineteenth-Century Dijon: Memorial, Festival, Fiasco," *French Music, Culture, and National Identity: 1870–1939*, ed. Barbara Kelly. Rochester, N.Y.: University of Rochester Press, forthcoming.

Eustis, Alvin A. *Racine devant la critique française, 1838–1939*. Berkeley: University of California Press, 1949.

Fauquet, Joël-Marie. "Rameau après Rameau: la mort des dieux?" *L'avant-scène opéra*, 46 (*Les Indes galantes*) (December 1982), 70–74.

———. *Les sociétés de musique de chambre à Paris de la Restauration à 1870*. Paris: Aux amateurs de livres, 1986.

——— (Ed.) *Dictionnaire de la musique en France au XIXe siècle*. Paris: Fayard, 2003.

Fauquet, Joël-Marie, and Antoine Hennion. *La grandeur de Bach: l'amour de la musique en France au XIXe siècle*. Paris: Fayard, 2000.

Faure, Michel. *Musique et société du Second Empire aux années vingt*. Paris: Flammarion, 1985.

———. *Du néoclassicisme musical dans la France du premier XXe siècle*. Paris: Klincksieck, 1997.

Fauser, Annegret. "Gendering the Nations: The Ideologies of French Discourse on Music (1870–1914)," *Constructions of Nationalism: Essays on the Ideology of European Musical Culture, 1800–1945*, ed. Michael Murphy and Harry White. Cork: Cork University Press, 2001, 72–103.

———. *Musical Encounters at the 1889 Paris World's Fair.* Rochester, N.Y.: University of Rochester Press, 2005.

Ferguson, Wallace K. *The Renaissance in Historical Thought: Five Centuries of Interpretation.* Cambridge, Mass.: Houghton Mifflin, 1948; reprint New York: AMS Press, 1981.

Fitzpatrick, Brian. *Catholic Royalism in the Department of the Gard, 1814–1852.* Cambridge: Cambridge University Press, 1983.

Flint de Médicis, Catrina. "The Schola Cantorum, Early Music, and French Cultural Politics," unpublished paper read at the conference "Nationalism and Identity in Third Republic France," Keele University, July 2001.

———. "Nationalism and Early Music at the French *fin de siècle*: Three Case Studies," *Nineteenth-Century Music Review*, 1 (2004), 43–66.

———. *The Schola Cantorum, Early Music, and French Cultural Politics from 1894 to 1914.* Ph.D. diss., McGill University, 2005.

Flynn, Timothy Scott. *A Study in Music Criticism and Historiography: Sacred Music Journals in France, 1848 to 1870.* Ph.D. diss., Northwestern University, Evanston, Illinois, 1997.

François-Sappey, Brigitte. *Alexandre P. F. Boëly (1785–1858): ses ancêtres, sa vie, son oeuvre, son temps.* Paris: Aux Amateurs de Livres, 1989.

Franklin, R. W. *Nineteenth-Century Churches: The History of a New Catholicism in Württemberg, England, and France.* New York and London: Garland Publishing, 1987.

Fulcher, Jane F. "The Popular Chanson of the Second Empire: 'Music of the Peasants' in France," *Acta musicologica*, 52 (1980), 27–37.

———. *French Cultural Politics & Music: From the Dreyfus Affair to the First World War.* New York and Oxford: Oxford University Press, 1999.

Gagnepain, Bernard. "A la recherche du temps passé: du rôle de quelques précurseurs dans la renaissance du patrimoine musical français," *Echos de France et d'Italie: liber amicorum Yves Gérard*, ed. Marie-Claire Mussat, Jean Mongrédien, and Jean-Michel Nectoux. Paris: Buchet/Chastel, 1997, 119–28.

Galerne, Maurice. *L'Ecole Niedermeyer: sa création, son but, son développement.* Paris: Margueritat, 1928.

Galteaux, Paul. *Un musicien niortais. Martin-Beaulieu. Grand Prix de Rome. Fondateur de la Société des concerts de chant classique (1791–1863).* Niort: G[eorges] Clouzot, 1912.

Garceau, Hélène. "Notes sur la presse musicale religieuse en France de 1827 à 1861," *Periodica musica*, 2 (Spring 1984), 6–13.

Garratt, James. *Palestrina and the German Romantic Imagination: Interpreting Historicism in Nineteenth-Century Music.* Cambridge: Cambridge University Press, 2002.

Genty, Christian. *Histoire du Théâtre national de l'Odéon (Journal de bord) 1782–1982.* Paris: Fischbacher, [1982].

Gerbod, Paul. "Vox populi," *La musique en France à l'époque romantique (1830–1870)*, ed. Joseph-Marc Bailbé et al. Paris: Flammarion, 1991, 231–55.

Geyer, Myriam. *La vie musicale à Strasbourg sous l'empire allemand (1871–1918).* Strasbourg and Paris: Société savante d'Alsace/Ecole Nationale des Chartes, 1999.

Giazotto, Remo. "La congrégation de Sainte-Cécile et le retour à la culture classique

dans la Rome musicale du début du XIXème siècle," *Revue belge de musicologie*, 26/27 (1972–73), 7–13.
Gibson, Ralph. "Why Republicans and Catholics Couldn't Stand Each Other in the Nineteenth Century," *Religion, Society and Politics in France since 1789*, ed. Frank Tallett and Nicholas Atkin. London: The Hambleden Press, 1991, 107–20.
Gildea, Robert. *The Past in French History*. New Haven: Yale University Press, 1994.
Girdlestone, Cuthbert. *Jean-Philippe Rameau: His Life and Work*. London: Cassell & Co, 1957.
Gosselin, Guy. *L'âge d'or de la vie musicale à Douai, 1800–1850*. Liège: Mardaga, 1994.
Goubault, Christian. *La critique musicale dans la presse française de 1870 à 1914*. Geneva and Paris: Slatkine, 1984.
Goudail, Agnès. *Art, savoir et pouvoir. L'Académie des beaux-arts sous le Premier Empire. Présentation et édition critique des procès-verbaux (1811–1815)*. Ph.D. diss., Ecole Nationale des Chartes, 1995.
Gough, Austin. *Paris and Rome: The Gallican Church and the Ultramontane Campaign, 1848–53*. Oxford: Clarendon Press, 1986.
Gumplowicz, Philippe. *Les travaux d'Orphée: 150 ans de vie musicale amateur en France. Harmonies–Chorales–Fanfares*. Paris: Aubier, 1987.
Haar, James. "Music of the Renaissance as Viewed by the Romantics," *Music and Context: Essays for John M. Ward*, ed. Anne Dhu Shapiro. Cambridge, Mass.: Department of Music, Harvard University, 1985, 126–44.
———. "The *conte musical* and Early Music," *La Renaissance et sa musique au XIXe siècle*, ed. Philippe Vendrix. Paris: Klincksieck, 2000, 191–208.
Haine, Malou. "Concerts historiques dans la seconde moitié du XIXe siècle," *Musique et société: hommages à Robert Wangermée*, ed. Henri Vanhulst and Malou Haine. Brussels: Editions de l'Université de Bruxelles, 1988, 121–42.
Haines, John. "Généalogies musicologiques: aux origines d'une science de la musique vers 1900," *Acta musicologica*, 73 (2001), 21–44.
———. "Paraphrases musico-théâtrales du *Jeu de Robin et Marion*, 1870–1930," *Revue d'histoire du théâtre*, 54, 4 (2002), 281–94.
———. *Eight Centuries of Troubadours and Trouvères*. Cambridge: Cambridge University Press, 2004.
Haskell, Harry. *The Early Music Revival: A History*. London: Thames & Hudson, 1988.
Hayburn, Robert. *Papal Legislation on Sacred Music, 95 AD to 1977 AD*. Collegeville, Minnesota: The Liturgical Press, 1979.
Hazareesingh, Sudhir. *Political Traditions in Modern France*. Oxford: Oxford University Press, 1994.
Hibberd, Sarah. "Murder in the Cathedral? Stradella, Musical Power, and Performing the Past" (unpublished paper).
Himmelfarb, Constance. "L'interprète à travers la presse musicale," *Charles-Valentin Alkan*, ed. Brigitte François-Sappey. Paris: Fayard, 1991, 23–57.
———. "'Dans le genre ancien': Charles-Valentin Alkan (1813–1888) et la musique du passé," *Sillages musicologiques: hommages à Yves Gérard*, ed. Philippe Blay and Raphaëlle Legrand. Paris: CNSMDP, 1997, 25–35.

Hirschberg, Jehoash. "Berlioz and the Fugue," *Journal of Music Theory*, 18 (1974), 152–88.
Holoman, D. Kern. *The Société des Concerts du Conservatoire, 1828–1967*. Berkeley and Los Angeles: University of California Press, 2004.
Hondré, Emmanuel, ed. *Le Conservatoire de Paris: regards sur une institution et son histoire*. Paris: Association du Bureau des Etudiants du CNSMDP, 1995.
Honegger, Geneviève. *Le Conservatoire et l'Orchestre philharmonique de Strasbourg*. Strasbourg: Oberlin, 1998.
———. "Le Conservatoire de Strasbourg et ses liens avec le Théâtre et l'Orchestre muncipal (1855–1918)," *Musical Education in Europe (1770–1914): Compositional, Institutional, and Political Challenges*, ed. Michael Fend and Michel Noiray. Berlin: Berliner Wissenschafts-Verlag, 2005, 676–97.
Huebner, Steven. *French Opera at the "fin de siècle": Wagnerism, Nationalism, and Style*. New York and Oxford: Oxford University Press, 1999.
Jenkins, Roy. *Gladstone*, corr. ed. London: Pan Books, 2001.
Julian, Philippe. *The Triumph of Art Nouveau: Paris Exposition 1900*. London: Phaidon, 1974.
Kahan, Sylvia. *Music's Modern Muse: A Life of Winnaretta Singer, princesse de Polignac*. Rochester, N.Y.: University of Rochester Press, 2003.
King, Richard G. "The *Fonds Schoelcher*: History and Contents," *Notes*, 53, 3–4 (1997), 697–721.
Kirkman, Andrew. "From Humanism to Enlightenment: Reinventing Josquin," *Journal of Musicology*, 17, 4 (1999), 441–58.
———. "'Under such heavy chains': The Discovery and Evaluation of Late Medieval Music before Ambros," *Nineteenth Century Music*, 24, 1 (2000/2001), 89–112.
———. "The Invention of the Cyclic Mass," *Journal of the American Musicological Society*, 54, 1 (2001), 1–47.
Kottick, Edward L. *A History of the Harpsichord*. Bloomington: University of Indiana Press, 2003.
Lacombe, Hervé. *The Keys to French Opera in the Nineteenth Century*, trans. Edouard Schneider. Berkeley and Los Angeles: University of California Press, 2001.
Larkin, Maurice. *Church and State after the Dreyfus Affair: The Separation Issue in France*. London: Macmillan, 1974.
———. *Religion, Politics and Preferment in France since 1890: La Belle Epoque and its Legacy*. Cambridge: Cambridge University Press, 1995.
Latreille, André, et al. *Histoire du catholicisme en France: la période contemporaine*. Paris: Spes, 1962.
L'Ecuyer, Sylvia. "Berlioz, d'Ortigue et la musique religieuse: un document inédit," *Echos de France et d'Italie: liber amicorum Yves Gérard*, ed. Marie-Claire Mussat, Jean Mongrédien, and Jean-Michel Nectoux. Paris: Buchet/Chastel, 1997, 95–104.
Leech-Wilkinson, Daniel. *The Modern Invention of Medieval Music: Scholarship, Ideology, Performance*. Cambridge: Cambridge University Press, 2002.
Lespinard, Bernadette. "Berlioz et la restauration de Palestrina en France," *Echos de France et d'Italie: liber amicorum Yves Gérard*, ed. Marie-Claire Mussat, Jean Mongrédien, and Jean-Michel Nectoux. Paris: Buchet/Chastel, 1997, 105–117.

Lesure, François. *Dictionnaire musical des villes de province.* Paris: Klincksieck, 1999.
Leterrier, Sophie. *La musique historique. Histoire de la musique ancienne au XIXe siècle.* Dossier d'habilitation, Université de Versailles, 2002.
Lévêque, A. "Le Conservatoire de musique de Dijon.–La Maîtrise de la cathédrale.–Les principales sociétés de musique de Dijon," *Dijon et la Côte d'Or en 1911. 40e congrès de l'Association française pour l'avancement des sciences.* Vol. 3. Dijon: Imp. Eugène Jacquot, 1911, 272–78.
Magnus, Philip. *Gladstone* [1954], new ed. Harmondsworth: Penguin Books, 2001.
Malignon, Jean. *Jean-Philippe Rameau.* Paris: Editions du Seuil, 1960.
Massip, Catherine. "La bibliothèque du Conservatoire (1795–1819): une Utopie réalisée?" *Le Conservatoire de Paris: des Menus-Plaisirs à la Cité de la Musique,* ed. Anne Bongrain and Yves Gérard. Paris: Buchet/Chastel, 1995, 117–31.
———. "Berlioz and Early Music," in *Berlioz: Past, Present, Future,* ed. Peter Bloom. Rochester, N.Y.: University of Rochester Press, 2003, 19–33.
McClellan, Andrew. *Inventing the Louvre: Art, Politics, and the Origins of the Modern Museum in Eighteenth-Century Paris.* Berkeley and Los Angeles: University of California Press, 1994.
McCrone, David. *The Sociology of Nationalism: Tomorrow's Ancestors.* London: Routledge, 1998.
McHale, Maria. *A Singing People: English Vocal Music and Nationalist Debate, 1880–1920.* Ph.D. Diss., Royal Holloway, University of London, 2005.
McManners, John. *Church and State in France, 1870–1914.* London: S.P.C.K. for the Church Historical Society, and New York: Harper & Row, 1972.
McPhee, Peter. *A Social History of France 1780–1880.* London: Routledge, 1992.
Melamed, Daniel R. "Who Wrote Lassus's Most Famous Piece?" *Early Music,* 26 (1998), 6–26.
Messing, Scott. *Neoclassicism in Music: From the Genesis of the Concept through the Schoenberg/Stravinsky Polemic.* Ann Arbor: University of Michigan Press, 1988; reprint Rochester, N.Y.: University of Rochester Press, 1996.
Mongrédien, Jean. *French Music from the Enlightenment to Romanticism, 1789–1830.* Paris: Flammarion, 1985; trans. Sylvain Frémaux. Portland, Oregon: Amadeus Press, 1996.
Morris, Allan Scott. *The Wellsprings of Neo-Classicism in Music: The Nineteenth-Century Suite and Serenade.* Ph.D. diss., University of Toronto, 1998.
Mussat, Marie-Claire [Le Moigne-]. *Musique et société à Rennes au XVIIIe et XIXe siècles.* Geneva: Minkoff, 1988.
Mussat, Marie-Claire, Jean Mongrédien, and Jean-Michel Nectoux (Eds.) *Echos de France & d'Italie: liber amicorum Yves Gérard.* Paris: Buchet/Chastel, 1997.
Nectoux, Jean-Michel (Ed.) *Gabriel Fauré: His Life through His Letters,* trans. J. A. Underwood. London and New York: Marion Boyars, 1984.
Noël, L., and Réné Roussel. *M. l'abbé Nicolas Couturier. Organiste de la Cathédrale de Langres et directeur de l'Ecole musicale de la maîtrise, 1840–1911. Notes et souvenirs.* Langres: Lepitre-Jobard, 1911.
Nicolodi, Fiamma. "Risvolti nazionalistici nel mito dell'antico in Francia e in Italia,"

Musica senza aggettivi: studi per Fedele D'Amico, ed. Agostino Ziino. Florence: Olschki, 1991, 463–76.

Nora, Pierre (dir.). *Realms of Memory: The Construction of the French Past*. 3 vols., ed. Lawrence D. Kritzman, trans. Arthur Goldhammer. New York: Columbia University Press, 1996–98.

Nye, Robert A. *Masculinity and Male Codes of Honor in Modern France*. Berkeley and Los Angeles: University of California Press, 1998.

Owens, Jessie Ann. "Music Historiography and the Definition of 'Renaissance,'" *Notes*, 47 (1990), 305–30.

Pasler, Jann. "The *chanson populaire* as a Malleable Symbol in Turn-of-the-Century France," *Tradition and its Future in Music (Report of the SIMS 1990 Osaka)*. Osaka: Mita Press, 1991, 203–209.

Paul, Charles B. "Music and Ideology: Rameau, Rousseau, and 1789," *Journal of the History of Ideas*, 32, 3 (1971), 395–410.

———. "Rameau, D'Indy and French Nationalism," *Musical Quarterly*, 58 (1972), 46–56.

Perkins, Leeman L. "Published Editions and Anthologies of the 19th Century: Music of the Renaissance or Renaissance Music?" *La Renaissance et sa musique au XIXe siècle*, ed. Philippe Vendrix. Paris: Klincksieck, 2000, 95–132.

Peyrot, Madeleine. *Mon mari, Jean Peyrot (1887–1918)*. Unpublished typescript, Marseille, 1977.

Pierre, Constant. *Le Conservatoire national de musique et de déclamation*. Paris: Imprimerie nationale, 1900.

———. *Histoire du concert spirituel, 1725–1790*. Paris: Société Française de Musicologie, 1975.

Pistone, Danièle. "Rameau à Paris au XIXe siècle," *Jean-Philippe Rameau: colloque international organisé par la Société Rameau de Dijon, 21–24 septembre 1983*, ed. Jerôme La Gorce. Paris and Geneva: Champion-Slatkine, 1987, 131–40.

Prost, A. *Histoire de l'enseignement en France, 1800–1967*. Paris: Colin, 1968.

Rannaud, Jean-Philippe. *La maîtrise de la cathédrale de Moulins, 1860–1950*. Mémoire de Musicologie: Conservatoire National de Région de Clermont-Ferrand, 1984.

Ratner, Sabina Teller. "Camille Saint-Saëns: Fauré's Mentor," *Regarding Fauré*, ed. and trans. Tom Gordon. New York: Gordon & Breach, 1999, 119–44.

Ritterman, Janet. "Les concerts spirituels à Paris au début du XIXe siècle," *Revue internationale de la musique française*, 6 (1985), 79–84.

Rohan-Csermak, Henri de. "La *canonisation* de Palestrina et la mutation de la musique sacrée en France au XIXe siècle," *Ostinato rigore*, 4 (1994), 199–214.

Sadler, Graham. "Vincent d'Indy and the Rameau *Oeuvres complètes*: A Case of Forgery?" *Early Music*, 21 (1993), 415–21.

Sako, Ikuno. *The Importance of Louis Niedermeyer in the Early Music Revival in Nineteenth-Century France*. Ph.D. diss., University of Melbourne, forthcoming.

Samson, Jim. "The Practice of Early-Nineteenth-Century Pianism," in *The Musical Work: Reality or Invention?* ed. Michael Talbot. Liverpool: Liverpool University Press, 2000, 110–27.

———. *Virtuosity and the Musical Work*. Cambridge: Cambridge University Press, 2003.

Simms, Bryan R. *Alexandre Choron (1771–1834) as a Historian and Theorist of Music.* Ph.D. diss., Yale University, 1971.

———. "The Historical Editions of Alexandre-Etienne Choron," *Fontes artis musicae,* 27 (1980), 71–77.

Smith, Marian. "About the House," *Reading Critics Reading: Opera and Ballet Criticism from the Revolution to 1848,* ed. Roger Parker and Mary Ann Smart. Oxford: Oxford University Press, 2001, 215–36.

Smith, Rollin. "The Organ of the Trocadéro and its Players," *French Organ Music from the Revolution to Franck and Widor,* ed. Lawrence Archbold and William J. Peterson. Rochester, N.Y.: University of Rochester Press, 1995, 275–308.

Smither, Howard E., *A History of the Oratorio,* vol. 4: *The Oratorio in the Nineteenth and Twentieth Centuries.* Chapel Hill and London: University of North Carolina Press, 2000.

Strasser, Michael. "The Société Nationale and its Adversaries: The Musical Politics of *L'invasion germanique* in the 1870s." *Nineteenth Century Music,* 24, 3 (2000/2001), 225–51.

Swart, Koenraad W. *The Sense of Decadence in Nineteenth-Century France.* The Hague: Martinus Nijhoff, 1964.

Suschitzky, Anya. "Debussy's Rameau: French Music and Its Others," *Musical Quarterly,* 86 (2002) 398–448.

Sykes, Ingrid. *Female Piety and the Organ: Nineteenth-Century French Women Organists.* Ph.D. diss., City University, London, 2001.

Tallett, Frank, and Nicholas Atkin, (Eds.) *Religion, Society and Politics in France since 1789.* London: The Hambleden Press, 1991.

Tippett-Spirton, Sandy. *French Catholicism: Church, State and Society in a Changing Era.* Bastingstoke: Macmillan, 2000.

Tombs, Robert (Ed.) *Nationhood and Nationalism in France: From Boulangism to the Great War, 1889–1918.* London and New York: HarperCollins, 1991.

———. *France, 1814–1914.* London and New York: Longman, 1996.

Vallas, Léon. *Vincent d'Indy.* 2 vols. Paris: Albin Michel, 1946–49.

Vanhulst, Henri. "La musique du passé et la création du Conservatoire de Paris: sa présence dans les premières méthodes," *Revue belge de musicologie,* 26/7 (1972–73), 50–59.

Vauchez, André. "The Cathedral," in *Realms of Memory: The Construction of the French Past,* vol. 2: *Traditions,* dir. Pierre Nora, ed. Lawrence D. Kritzman, trans. Arthur Goldhammer. New York: Columbia University Press, 1997, 37–68.

Vauthier, Gabriel. "Un chorège moderne: Alexandre Choron d'après des documents inédits," *Revue musicale* [ed. Combarieu], 8/13–9/2 (1 July 1908–15 January 1909).

Vendrix, Philippe. " 'La musique montait, cette lune de l'art!': redécouvertes des musiques de la Renaissance à l'ère romantique," *La Renaissance et sa musique au XIXe siècle.* Paris: Klincksieck, 2000, 9–58.

Wallon, Simone. "Les acquisitions de la bibliothèque du Conservatoire de Paris à la vente de la collection Van Maldeghem," *Revue belge de musicologie,* 9 (1955), 36–46.

Wangermée, Robert. "Les premiers concerts historiques à Paris," *Mélanges Ernest Closson*. Brussels: Société Belge de Musicologie, 1948, 185–96.

Weber, William. *Music and the Middle Class: The Social Structure of Concert Life in London, Paris and Vienna*. London: Croom Helm, 1975.

———. "*La musique ancienne* in the Waning of the Ancien Régime," *Journal of Modern History*, 56 (1984), 58–88.

Wiley, Christopher. *Re-writing Composers' Lives: Critical Historiography and Musical Biography*. Ph.D. diss., Royal Holloway, University of London, forthcoming.

Williams, Adrian. *A Portrait of Franz Liszt by Himself and His Contemporaries*. Oxford: Oxford University Press, 1990.

Yon, Jean-Claude. *Jacques Offenbach*. Paris: Gallimard, 2000.

Index

Adam, Adolphe: and arrangement of "Dans ce doux asile," 16n44, 33, 76, 142; and biography of Rameau, 76–7, 131, 246; as critic of Moskova society, xvii, 32
Adam, Louis: 8, 14
Adam de la Halle: 33, 151, 153; and bifurcation of output, 165–7, 253; and the *chanson populaire*, 169; *Jeu de Robin et de Marion*, xiv, 112–13, 147, 164–73, 253; and modernity of style, 166–7; nationalist significance of, 167–9
advertizing: *see* publishing
Aichinger, Gregor: 107
Aix-en-Provence: early music in, 70, 74, 113
Alard, Delphin: 57–8, 89
Alizard, Adolphe: 50, 75n86
Alkan, Charles-Valentin: 40, 53, 55–6, 88
"Alla beata Trinita" (anon.), 35
Allegri, Gregorio: 27, 73, 97; *Miserere*, 9, 26, 35, 62, 105, 110
Ambros, August Wilhelm: 182, 186n30, 204
anthologies: *see* publishing
anticlericalism: 163n56, 194, 253; under Louis-Philippe, 6–7, 21, 37; and the Third Republic, 83, 97, 181, 199, 229–30; of Voltaire, 194, 254
Arbeau, Thoinot: *Orchésographie*, inc. "Belle qui tiens ma vie," 33–4, 164, 174
Arcadelt, Jacques: "Ave Maria" (attrib.), 13; "Il bianco e dolce cigno," 33
Ariosti, Attilio: xivn4
Arras: and the *Jeu de Robin et de Marion*, 112–13
Artusi, Giovanni Maria: 188
Association Musicale de l'Ouest (Beaulieu): 61
Auber, Daniel-François-Esprit: 79n98
Aubry, Pierre: 174
Augé, Lucien: 116, 159
Auguez, Numa: 86
Autun, cathedral of: 72–3, 108, 182

Bach, C. P. E.: 8, 14, 40
Bach, Johann Sebastian: 12, 38, 83, 105; in Alsace, 63, 101–2, 247; cult of, 102–5, 238–9; as dry, 54–5, 60, 102–4, 213; as expressive, 104–5, 236; and gendered critique, 54, 88, 216–17; and Handel compared, 87, 111, 211, 213–14, 217, 221,

286 INDEX

Bach, Johann Sebastian (continued): 234, 237–9; as inward, 213, 237–8; keyboard music of, 40, 51–5; as mystical, 236–7; organ music of, 55–6, 84–8, 97, 109; as over-learned: 58–9, 87, 102–3, 213; and Palestrina, 71, 73, 217, 236–7; as profound, 87, 237–9; as Protestant, 60, 111; resistance to recitative in, 61n43; as revered, 50–52, 98; rise of, 234–9, 249; as teaching/practice material: 8, 14–15, 54, 88; as universally Christian, 111, 236, 249; and virtuoso demands, 56, 58; and Wagner, 102–5, 234–7.

Bach, Johann Sebastian (works): *Art of Fugue*, 237; "Brandenburg" Concertos, 88–9n13, 90; Cantata "Ach Gott von Himmel," 100n45; Cantata "Also hat Gott die Welt geliebt" (inc. "Pentecost" aria), 100n45, 235; Cantata "Aus der Tiefen", 100n45; Cantata "Aus tiefer Not," 100n45; Cantata "Bleib bei uns," 63, 100n45, 110; Cantata "Du Hirte Israel, höre," 63; Cantata "Ein feste Burg," 98; Cantata "Geist und Seele wird verwirret" (Sinfonia), 87; Cantata "Gottes Zeit" (Actus tragicus), 98, 100n45, 101; Cantata "Ich geh und suche mit Verlangen" (Sinfonia), 87; Cantata "Ich hatte viel Bekümmeris," 100n45; Cantata "Ihr werdet weinen und heulen," 100n45; Cantata "Jesu der du meine Seele," 100n45, 239; Cantata "Phoebus and Pan," 98n41; Cantata "Schlage doch" (attrib.) BWV53, 105n67; Cantata "Wachet auf," 100n45; Christmas Oratorio, 98n41, 235; Chromatic Fantasia and Fugue, 53; Concerto in A minor for Violin, 15; Concerto in D minor for Keyboard, 53; Concerto in D minor for Three Keyboards, 53–4, 90, 102; Fantasia and Fugue in G minor for Organ, 56, 84–5; "Goldberg" Variations, 53, 90; "Italian" Concerto, 53, 90, 92; Magnificat, 98; Mass in B minor, 82, 92, 99–101, 103; Motet "Ich lasse dich nicht"/"Qui propter te crucem" (attrib./adapt.), 99–100; Motet "Jesu meine Freude" (inc. adaptation as "Tantum ergo"), 36, 99n42, 113; Motet "Komm, Jesu, komm," 99; Partita No. 2 in C minor for Keyboard, 90n17; Passacaglia and Fugue in C minor for Organ, 84; Prelude and Fugue in A minor for Organ (either BWV 543 or 551), 85; Prelude and Fugue in D major for Organ, 85; St John Passion, 100n45, 101; St Matthew Passion, xiv, 63, 68–9, 82, 92, 98, 101–3, 211; Sonata in B minor for Flute and Continuo, 86; Sonatas and Partitas for Unaccompanied Violin (inc. chaconne), 14, 57–8, 92, 245; Sonatas for Violin and Continuo, 90, 92–3; Suites for Unaccompanied Violoncello, 92; Suites/Overtures for Orchestra, 60; Toccata and Fugue in D minor for Organ, 84–5; Toccata in F for Organ, 56, 84, 86; "Wedge" fugue for Organ, 83; *Well-Tempered Clavier*: 8, 14–15, 52, 88, 90n17, 235

Baillot, Pierre: 8, 14–15, 57
Baini, Giuseppe: 32, 154, 161, 183
Baj, Tommaso: *Miserere*, 39, 74
Balbastre, Claude-Bénigne: 46n12
ballet: see dance
Bannelier, Charles: 86n7, 136
Barbedette, Hippolyte: 105n63, 238–9
Barbella, Emanuele: 14
Barbereau, Auguste: 44
Barthélemy, Charles: 124
Baudillon, Félix: 61
Bazin, François: 230
Beaujoyeulx, Balthazar de [ie. De Beaulieu & Salmon]: *Ballet comique de la reine*, 12, 23, 107, 128, 253
[Martin-]Beaulieu, Désiré: 44, 61–2, 63
Becker, Georges: 165
Bellaigue, Camille: 106n68, 107; and Bach/Wagner, 102–3; on Palestrina, 185–6, 192–3, 201–7, 254; political allegiances of, 202n100
Benoist, François: 28
Benoît, Camille: 107, 236
Berlioz, Louis-Hector: 17, 34; on Bach, 54;

and Choron, 26–7, 30; and
    Palestrina, 189, 191
Berry, duchesse de: 6, 6n14
Bertrand, Gustave: 122
Bizet, Georges: 15n43, 79
Blanchard, Henri: 54, 57, 59, 189, 248
Blaze, Henri: *see* Castil-Blaze
Blaze de Bury, Henri: 122
Blémont, Emile de: 112
Bleuzet, Louis: 93n23
Boëly, Alexandre-P.-F.: 14n36
Bohrer, Sophie: 40
Boisjoslin, G. de: xvn6, 107–10
Bordes, Charles: xiii–xv, 83, 105–11, 113;
    and Bach cantatas, 81–2, 93, 100,
    104, 106; beliefs of, 194; as editor,
    156; and Palestrinian music, 105,
    187, 200–1; at Saint-Gervais, 105–6,
    111, 192
Borel, Pierre: 244
Bory, A. de: and *orphéon* reform, 222, 226
Botte, Adolphe: 54, 58, 78–9
Bottée de Toulmon, Auguste: 12, 20–1,
    32, 165–7
Bourdeau, Emile: 74
Bourgault-Ducoudray, Louis-Albert: 44,
    87, 98n40; democratizing attempts
    of, 67, 69, 158, 201n97, 222–3; and
    Franco-Flemish school, 155; and
    French chanson, 157–9; and
    Handel/Bach revival, 211, 214, 216,
    218, 221–2; and politics, 247; and
    Schola Cantorum, 107, 111
Bourges, Maurice: 30
Boutarel, Amédée: 233
Brancour, René de: 162–3
Brenet, Michel [pseud. Marie Bobillier]:
    108–9, 174, 186n31
Bricqueville, Eugène de: 238n104
Brumel., Antoine: 20
Bruneau, Alfred: xiv, 242, 252–5; and
    anticlerical historiographies, 254–5
Burney, Charles: 88, 148, 183
Buxtehude, Dietrich: 106

Caccini, Giulio: 75n87; *Euridice*, 106; (and
    Peri), *Euridice*, 23
Cambert, Robert: 253; *Pomone*, 124
Campra, André: 70, 74, 175; "Domine me
    secundum," 113; *L'Europe galante*,
132; *Hésione* compared with Mozart,
    126
Candeille, Perre-Joseph: *Castor et Pollux*
    (incorporating Rameau extracts), 7,
    16, 75n86, 248
canonization: xxii; and conservatism,
    244–5; and narrowing of repertory,
    245–6
Canteloube, Joseph: 170
Caraguel, Clément: 137
Carissimi, Giacomo: 23, 70, 72, 82, 97;
    Jephte, xivn4, 106; *Miserere*, 113;
    Missa "L'homme armé" (attrib.), 20
Carlez, Jules: 191, 213
Carpentras, cathedral music at: 37–8, 74,
    114
Cart, William: 213, 225
Castera, René de: 108–9
Castil-Blaze [Henri Blaze, *dit*]: 27, 37,
    75n87, 154, 246
Catholicism (French), politics of: *see*
    clergy; *see also* Gallicanism,
    Ultramontanism
Cavalieri, Emilio de': 75n87; *Concerto
    passegiato* (attrib.), 14
Cavalli, Francesco: 75n87; *Xerse*, 23
Cecilianism: 31–2, 74, 83, 109
Chambonnières, Jacques Champion:
    46n12
Chambrun, comte de: 99, 134n50, 235
Chambrun, comtesse de: 98n40, 134n50,
    235
chanson (polyphonic): 34, 115–6, 147; and
    Frenchness, 157–60, 163, 175; *see also*
    Janequin, Lassus
chanson populaire: definitions of, 163–6;
    as "modern", 163; and regional/
    national character, 112, 162, 175–6,
    252; as used in sacred music, 115,
    153–5, 203–4
Chanteurs de Saint-Gervais: xiii, 81–3,
    100, 158, 162, 190; and Holy Week
    services, 105–7, 190, 192; and
    regional tours, 100, 108–10; *see also*
    Bordes
Charnacé, Guy de: on Handel, 218, 220
Charpentier, Gustave: 253; and street
    cries in *Louise*, 242
Charpentier, Marc-Antoine: 113, 120; *Le
    malade imaginaire*, 45, 135, 140

Chastelain de Couci, the: 12, 165
Chateaubriand, François-René: 180, 194–5
Chauvet, Charles-Alexis: 85
Chérion, abbé: 73–4, 109
Chopin, Fryderyk: and Bach, 15, 53
Choron, Alexandre-Etienne: 9, 116; and Berlioz commission, 26–7; choir schools of, 6, 25–7, 71, 108; and democratization, 29–30; and French early music, 17, 19–20, 37, 150; and Fétis, 22, 24–5, 148–9, 152–3, 180n4, 187; imitators of, 27; and Janequin chansons, 26–7, 156–7; and Palestrina, 182–3, 187, 190–91; program planning of, 27, 106; publications of, 7–8, 11–12, 48n17, 50; legacy of, 32, 39, 63, 82, 97
Chouquet, Gustave: 60n41, 124, 126n21, 165, 168
Clari, Giovanni Carlo Maria: 26, 97
clavecin music: 40, 56, 78; and Diémer, 89–92; as disparaged, 57, 78, as exquisite, 91, 93–5; and the picturesque, 56–7; *see also* harpsichord
Clément, Félix: as radical Ultramontane, 155, 195, 198–9
Clérambault, Louis-Nicolas: 87, 106
clergy, revivalist involvement of: 48, 63; and liturgical factions, 72, 181–2, 249; *see also* Gallicanism, Ultramontanism
Cohen, Henry: 79, 159; on French stage music, 127, 131, 135–6; on Handel decline, 232
Coligny, Charles: and the *orphéon*, 224, 227
Collasse, Pascal: 126, 175; *Les saisons*, 75n86
collected editions: *see* publishing
Colonne, Edouard: 87, 104; and Diémer, 90; and Ysaÿe/Pugno, 92–3
Comédie-Française: 45, 121, 135, 138–40
Concerts Populaires (Pasdeloup): 59–60
concerts spirituels: 7, 99; traditions of, 9–10, 27
Concordia: 98–9; and Bach revival, 82, 92, 98–9, 102–3; *see also* Fuchs, Henriette

Conservatoire, Paris: 48, 108; taught repertory, 8, 14, 109, 114n93; secular traditions of, 9, 199n86
Corelli, Arcangelo: 8, 14; *La follia*, 40, 57, 86, 245; Sonata for Violin and Continuo Op. 5/1, 58
Corneille, Pierre: 121, 145
couleur locale, and historical verisimilitude: 242
counterpoint, disparagement of, 34, 54, 102–3, 155; as anti-liturgical, 196–7
Couperin, Louis: 12, 124
Couperin, François:, 40, 46n12, 90n17; "Le carillon de Cythère," 91; and *clavecin* music, 11–12, 93; and Laurens, 38, 46; "Le moucheron," 57; "Les papillons," 91; "Le reveil-matin," 57, 91; "Soeur Monique," 56; "Les tours de passe-passe," 56; and sacred music: 48
Coussemaker, Edmond de: 150–51, 155, 165, 167
Couturier, Claude: 72, 188
Couturier, Nicolas-Mammès: 72, 188
Cressonnois, Jules: 214
Cristal, Maurice [pseud. Maurice Germa]: 12In9; on Handel, 219–20; on Palestrina, 190, 192

Danbé, Jules: 136–7, 158, 217
dance (*ancien régime*): 79, 83, 245; French properties of, 116, 141–3; gendered properties of, 143, 146, 252; praise for, 23, 34, 120; and Watteau's paintings, 94–5, 120–1, 146; *see also* Arbeau
Dandelot, Arthur: 104n58, 106n68
Dandrieu, Jean-François: "Le ramage des oiseaux," 91
Danjou, Félix: 12, 35, 72; as editor, 12, 184; and Laurens, 38; as radical Ultramontane, 32, 154, 196–8
Daquin, Louis-Claude: "Le coucou," 89, 91, 245
Darcours, Charles: 94n29
Dauriac, Lionel: 177
David, Félicien: 61, 211
Debussy, Claude: 142
Delaborde, Eugène: 46
Delaporte, Eugène: 66

Deldevez, Ernest: and Bach, 99; as editor, 46, 75–6, 144; and Lamoureux, 68–9, 232–3
Delécluze, Etienne: 32, 185, 189, 191
Delsart, Jules: 82, 89, 92–3
Delsarte, François: 47–50, 75, 78
Delsarte, Rosine: 47–9, 75
democratization (of music): 29–30, 59–60, 65–7, 86, 158; of *a cappella* sacred music, 110, 201; via Baroque choral music, 61–2, 212–13, 221–3, 239–40; and women, 230; see also *orphéon*
Denne-Baron, Dieudonné: xvii, 162
Deroye, Arthur: 69–70
Dessus, Antoine [*dit* Super]: 195, 198n82; attack on Palestrina, 200–1
Destouches, André-Cardinal: 175; *Callirhoé*, 126, 136; compared with Gounod and Wagner, 126; *Omphale*, 126, 132; (with Lalande) *Les éléments*, 132–3
Diémer, Louis: 53, 55n28, 98n40; and the Baroque miniature, 89, 90–6, 107, 144; as chamber pianist, 89–90; as editor, 90; as virtuoso, 88–9, 91; see also Société des Instruments Anciens
Dietsch, [Pierre-]Louis: 32, 35, 71, 74
Dijon, early music in: 69–70, 78
Doret, Gustave: 106n68–9
Dorieux, Gustave: 88n12
Dubois, Théodore: 87, 98n40, 109n75; and arrangement of Marcello, 47; and *maîtrise* inspections, 73–4
Dufay, Guillaume: 11–12, 20, 149
Dufort, Charles: 75
Dukas, Paul: 108n68–9, 114, 121n9
Dumont, Henri: *Messe royale* (unidentified), 113
Durand, Sextius: 216
Durante, Francesco: 97; *Litanies* in F, 8–10

Ecole de Musique Religieuse (Ecole Niedermeyer): and anticlericalism, 83; concert society of, 97–8; core repertories, 73; founding and organization of, 71, 96–8, 198; and propagandizing, 97, 109
economics of revival: xvi, 140, 232, 245

elitism: 59, 63–5, 94–6
Elwart, Antoine: 84–5
embellishment: ambivalence towards, 57–8, 60n41, 145, 214, 216
Emery-Desbrousses, F.: 94
Enfants de Lutèce, Les: 67, 201, 223; see also Bourgault-Ducoudray
Enfants de Paris, Les: 158, 201; see also Bordes, Bourgault-Ducoudray
England: 6, 220n41; choral culture of, 28, 44–5, 70, 222–4, 227, 230, 239; joint *orphéon* festival with, 66; and publishing culture, 61, 77, 128–9
Escudier, Léon: 32, 43, 230n77
Escudier, Marie: 32, 57
Expert, Henry: 108, 152, 251
Exposition Universelle: of 1867, 88; of 1878, 81, 97; of 1889, 89, 106, 233; of 1900: xiii–xv, 94, 252–4
Eymieu, Henry: 88n13, 235–6

fake pieces: xvii, 12–13, 22, 115–16
Falk, Annette: 56n30
Farrenc, Aristide: 47–9, 90
Farrenc, Louise: 47–9, 56
Fauré, Gabriel: 71, 79, 98n40, 111
Fayolle, François: 19–20, 180n4, 182
Ferchault, Guy: 13n32
Ferry, Jules: 119–20
Fétis, Edouard: 54, 150
Fétis, François-Joseph: 27, 38–9, 114; in comparison with Choron, 22, 24–5, 29; and *concerts historiques*, xiv, 5, 14, 22–5, 154, 156n30; and fake pieces, 12–13; on Franco-Flemish repertory, 24–5, 148–9, 152–4, 160–62, 197; on French early music, 17, 23, 34, 120; and the *Jeu de Robin et de Marion*, 164–5; on Goudimel and Palestrina, 183–5; on Palestrina, 179, 190; and theory of music history, 24–5, 73, 152, 168, 180, 188–9; reinterpretations of, 168, 188–9
Flandrin, Hippolyte: 190
folk song: see *chanson populaire*
Forkel, Johann Nikolaus: 149n8
Fournier, Edouard: 165, 167
France, changing borders of: 36, 101, 148–52
Franchomme, Auguste: 89

Franck, César: 56n30, 82, 105
Franco-Flemish polyphony (sacred): appropriations of, 24n70, 147–52, 160–62, 253; historiographical celebration of, 19–21, 152–3, 253; attempted rehabilitation of, 115, 170, 172–4; denigration of, 21, 24, 33, 153–6, 198; as repository of Frenchness, 115; *see also* chanson (polyphonic)
Francolin, Gustave: 226
Franco-Prussian War: and idea of cultural caesura, 45, 225n58; psychological legacy of, xviii, 119, 220, 225–6, societal legacy of, 215
Frenchness: xix, 157; in the chanson tradition, 34, 115–16, 158–60, 162–3, 174; in *clavecin* music, 93–6; defined against Wagner, 142; defining qualities of, 96, 142, 175, 252–3, 174, 176–7; in modern opera, xx, 7, 18, 122, 186, 251–2; in *la musique française*, 126, 142–3; threatened by cosmopolitanism, xx, 122, 250–1
Frescobaldi, Girolamo: 12, 87, 97, 106
Fréson, J.-G.: 237
Fuchs, Henriette: 98, 107; *see also* Concordia

Gabrieli, Andrea: 33, 152; "Angeli archangeli," 110
Gachet, Jacqueline: 13n32
Gagliano, Marco da: *La Dafne*, 106
Gallicanism: 21, 113, 181; musical traditions of, 19, 32, 41, 181–2, 246; and Palestrina, 182, 191; and regional liturgies, 37–8, 74, 246
Garcia, Manuel: 48
Garcin, Jules: 99
Garden, Greer: 13n34
Gasperini, Auguste de: 64
Gauthier, Théophile: 234
Gaviniès, Pierre: 57
Gebaüer, Ernest: 226, 228n71
Geminiani, Francesco: 8, 14
gender: and Bach, 54, 88, 216–17; and fear of feminization, 216, 226; and French chanson tradition, 158–9; and Handel, 146, 215–20, 228n72; and harpsichord music, 54, 56, 90–92; and *la musique française*, 143–6
Genet, Elzéar (Carpentras): *Lamentations*, 114; *Magnificat sexti toni*, 114; *Missa "A l'ombre dung buissonnet,"* 115
Geoffroy, Julien-Louis: 17–18, 128
Gerber, Ernst Ludwig: 88
Germa, Maurice: *see* Cristal
Germany (relation to): 128, 132–3, 181; in Alsace, 36, 101–02; emulation of choral culture of, 223, 231, 239; inferiority to, 18, 23, 38, 70, 76–7, 119, 215, 225, 250; as musical invader, 122–3; and publishing ventures, 128, 141
Gianturco, Carolyn: 13n32
Gibbons, Orlando: "The Silver Swan" ("Le croisé captif"), 107
Gigout, Eugène: 55, 56n30, 82, 97, 100, 107; at Trocadéro, 84–6
Gilles, Jean: 74
Gillet, F.: on the *orphéon*, 224–5, 228
Gillet, Georges: 82, 89–90
Ginguené, Pierre-Louis: 10, 17
Gladstone, William: 220n41
Gluck, Christoph Willibald: 17, 133, 140, 253
Gomart, Charles: 151
Goudimel, Claude: 39, 115, 152, 253; *Missa "Le bien que j'ay,"* 173; and Protestantism, 72–3, 183–5, 200; as supposed teacher of Palestrina, 19, 72, 183–4, 186n31
Gounod, Charles: 73, 79, 87, 101, 126; and Concordia, 98; *Méditation* on Bach: 47, 60; on Palestrina, 206
Gouzien, Armand: 46, 127n29
government (intervention of); in church music, xvi, 71–2, 199; in concert society funding, 232; in music education, 71, 83, 222; in folk song studies, 163; in publishing, 19–21, 48, 130, 134; *see also* Conservatoire, Paris; Ecole de Musique Religieuse
Grandval, vicomtesse Marie de: 134n50
Greffuhle, comtesse de: 111
Gregorian chant: *see* plainchant
Grillet, Laurent: 92
Gros, Adrien: 190
Grove, George: 129

Guédron, Pierre: 39, 97
Guéranger, Dom Prosper: 21, 180n4
Guibal du Rivage, Alexandre: 36–8
Guillot de Sainbris, Antoine: 82n2, 87, 134n50, 228; *see also* Société Chorale d'Amateurs
Guilmant, Alexandre: 55, 84–5, 96–7; and Schola Cantorum, 111; at Trocadéro, 79, 81–2, 85–8, 92, 104
Guiraud, Ernest: 137

Habeneck, François-Antoine: 15, 28, 53
Haberl, Franz Xaver: 172
Hallays, André: 108
Handel, Georg Frideric: 45, 59–61, 247; as accessible, 60, 86–7, 111, 213, 218, 221; compared with Bach, 87, 111, 211, 213–14, 217, 221, 234, 237–9; and confidence-inspiring style, 218–20; contrafacta, 12; as crowd-pleaser, 221, 238; decline of interest in, 211, 231–4, 247; as Latin, 214–15; legacy for French choral music, 211; and monumental grandeur, 28, 146, 214, 222, 227–8; oratorios as secular, 214; as popular, 86, 111, 120; as "Republican," 111, 233, 247; as too militaristic, 233; as virile, 146, 217–19; as warlike, 217, 219–20, 228n72
Handel, Georg Frideric (works): *Acis and Galatea*, 8, 67, 69, 214, 218, 222; *Alcina*, 60; *Alexander's Feast*, 8, 26, 28, 39, 62, 67, 69, 214; *Athalia*, 26; *Brockes-Passion*, 60; Concertos for Organ, 84–5, 87, 96–7; *Israel in Egypt*, 82, 111, 233; *Jephtha*, 39; *Judas Maccabaeus* (inc. victory chorus), 8, 26–7, 35, 60, 65, 69–70, 157, 211, 216, 246; *Messiah* (inc. Hallelujah chorus): xv, 26–8, 36, 38, 46, 60, 68–9, 101, 211, 213, 232–3, 246; *Ode for Saint Cecilia's Day*, 63, 68, 211; *Rinaldo*: 47; Sonatas for Violin and Continuo, 86; *Samson*, 26, 47, 72, 157; *Solomon*, 60; *Saül* (pasticcio), 8; Suites for Keyboard (inc. G minor passacaglia): 8, 40, 56, 89–90, 93, 245; *Xerxes*, 93
Handl, Jacob: "Ecce concipies," 106n67

Haraucourt, Ed. d': 235
Harcourt, Eugène d': xv–xvi, 87, 90, 93n23, 99, 106n69
Harold, Michel: 121n9, 127
harpsichord, use in performance: 40, 89, 93n26, 98n38; *see also clavecin* music
Hasse, Johann Adolf: 8
Hawkins, John: 183
Herder, Johann Gottfried von: xix
heritage: construction of, 93–6, 123–5, 127–8, 130, 134, 142–3, 147, 164–5, 175–7; heritage industry, xv, 241; *see also* Frenchness, museum spirit, nationalism, national pride, Renan
Heugel, Henri: *see* Moreno [*pseud.* Heugel]
Heulhard, Arthur: 46, 122n14; and *La chronique musicale*, 123–25, 134
Heyberger, Joseph: 99
Hillemacher, Paul & Lucien: and Wagnerian adaptation of Bach, 235–6
Hiller, Ferdinand: 14, 53
Hoffmann, E. T. A.: 179
Holman, Peter: 13n32
Houssaye, Arsène: 139
Huebner, Steven: 79n98
Hugo, Victor: 26, 175, 195

identity: *see* Frenchness
ideology: and revivalist factions, 111, 113–4, 121n6, 122n14, 135–6, 170, 193–201, 246–9; *see also* Gallicanism, Republicanism, Ultramontanism
Imbert, Hugues: 106n68
Indy, Vincent d': 111; and chanson-based masses, 174; and early French opera, 132–3, 141; and Palestrinian music, 105, 204–5; as propagandist, xv, 107–8; and response to Bruneau, 253–5; and Wagner, 105, 122n14, 132
inferiority (French musical): *see* Italy, Germany, nationalism, national pride, regeneration
Ingegneri, Marc'Antonio: Responsories (attrib. Palestrina), 35, 182
Italy, musical relations with: 4, 7, 16, 19, 23, 41, 128, 250–1; inferiority to, 38, 76–7, 116, 250; superiority to, 147

Jaëll, Alfred: 54
Janequin, Clément: 26, 32, 97, 107; appreciations of, 156–60, 162; *La bataille de Marignan*: xivn4, 19, 33, 35, 65, 67, 72, 101, 110, 115, 157–60, 217, 246; *Le chant des oiseaux*, 156, 162; and Charpentier (Gustave), 242, 253; *Les cris de Paris*, 19, 39, 157; Missa "La bataille de Marignan," 156
Janin, Jules: 135
Jommelli, Nicolò: 48; "Confirma hoc, Deus", 8; *Miserere* in G minor (attrib.), 11–12; *Requiem* in E flat, 8, 11, 72
Jonciéres, Victorin: 134n50
Josquin Desprez: 20, 105, 115, 253; appropriations of, 149; *Déploration sur la mort de Jehan Ockeghem*, 19; liturgical use of chansons as subversive, 254; Missa "D'ung autre amour", 154–5; Missa "L'homme armé" (unidentified), 24; *Stabat mater*, 11–12, 39–41
Jullien, Adolphe: 94n29, 108, 122n14, 130; on Rameau, 132, 143–4

Keiser, Reinhard: *Der königliche Schäfer oder Basilius in Arcadien*, 23
Kerle, Jacobus de: 20; Missa "Regina coeli," 110
Kerney, L.: 232
Ketten, Henri: 53
Kiesewetter, Raphael Georg: 182
Kreutzer, Léon: 63n50, 165
Kunc, Aloys: 74, 107

Labat, J.-B.: 158
Lacombe, Louis: 66
Lacome, Paul: 167, 192–3; on *la musique française*, 122n14, 125–7, 132–4, 136
Lacoste, Louis de: 95
Lafage, Adrien de: 32, 66, 187; edition of Palestrina, 11, 74; on Goudimel and Palestrina, 183–4; on Josquin, 154–5
Lajarte, Théodore de: 124, 222; as editor, 127, 130–2, 145
Lalande, Michel-Richard de: 33n97, 181, 247; "Dixit dominus," 37–8; "O dulcis amor," 74; and regional liturgies, 37–8, 74, 113; " Te Deum," 37; "Tota pulchra es," 74; (with Destouches) *Les éléments*, 132–3
Lambert, Michel: 39, 41
Lamennais, abbé Félicité de: 26, 194, 198n82, 200–1
Lamoureux, Charles: xvi, 82, 90, 92; and Baroque oratorio, 68, 98, 232; *see also* Handel (works), Société de l'Harmonie Sacrée
Landini, Francesco: 12
Landowska, Wanda: 56
Langres, cathedral of: 72–3, 108–9, 182, 188n41, 199–200
La Rue, Pierre de: 115
Lassus, Louis de: 142, 214, 222
Lassus, Orlande de: 32, 48, 82–3, 105, 107; as French, 152, 160–3; "Fuyons tous d'amour le jeu," 35, 65, 156, 162; "Margot labouréz les vignes," 35, 156; Missa "Douce mémoire," 156, 170, 173–4; "Mon coeur se recommande à vous" (attrib.), 13, 115–16; *Penitential Psalms*, 35, 162, 196; "Quand mon mary vient de dehors," xivn4; and style, 115–6, 155–7, 189–90
Launer, Marie-Pierre: 11, 45
Laurens, Jean-Joseph-Bonaventure: 11, 37–8, 114, 246
Lauziéres-Thémines, Achille de: 134n50
Lavoix *fils*, Henri: 127, 130, 132, 138n65, 159
Leclair, Jean-Marie: 8, 57, 124; Sonata in C minor for Violin "Le tombeau" (III/6), 58; Sonata in D for Violin (IV/3), 58
Lecocq, Charles: 143n86
Le Couppey, Félix: 57
Lefébure-Wély, Alfred: 55
Lefèvre, Gustave: and Société des Concerts de l'Ecole de Musique Religieuse, 97–8, 187
Legouvé, Ernest: 193
Leisring, Volckmar: "O filii, o filiae," 35
Le Maistre, Matthaeus: 97
Lemmens, Jaak Nikolaas: 53, 55–6, 82, 85, 88
Lenoir, Alexandre: 5
Leo, Leonardo: *Miserere*, 8, 11
Léon, Hermann: 75n86

Leonardo da Vinci: reputation of, 206
Lévêque, Charles: 168
Liberati, Antimo: 183
Liszt, Franz: 84, 89, 193, 200
Locatelli, Pietro Antonio: 8, 14
Loeillet, Jean Baptiste: 89
Loret, Clément: 96–7
Lotti, Antonio: 97, 105, 107; *Crucifixus*, 109n75
Lully, Jean-Baptiste: 33, 48, 107, 175, 253; conflicting meanings in, 143, 145; and dance, 96, 131, 145; and lack of champions, 136; measured against Molière, 138, 140; "nationality" of, 126, 131, 143; and royalist prologues, 131; vicarious revival of, 140
Lully, Jean-Baptiste (works): *Acis et Galatée*, 75; *Alceste*, 75; *Armide*, 23, 39, 41, 143; *Atys*, 75n86; *Bellérophon*, 130n38; *Le bourgeois gentilhomme*, 45, 79, 96, 135, 137–40; *Le mariage forcé*, 143; *Monsieur de Pourceaugnac*, 137–8; *Persée*, 23, 130n38; *Phaëton*, 130n38; *Proserpine*, 130n38; *Psyché*, 45, 138–9; *Thésée*, 127, 130n38
Lyon: and early choral music, 101

Machaut, Guillaume de: 12, 32
Magnard, Albéric: 141
Mainzer, Joseph: 30
maîtrises: 69–70, 72–4, 83–4; *see also* anticlericalism, Autun, Langres, Moulins, Rouen
Malherbe, Charles: 114n92, 133n48, 141
Mallarmé, Stéphane: 87
Malleville, Charlotte [Tardieu] de: 40, 53, 55–7, 59, 90, 98n38
Marcello, Benedetto: 46n12, 108n73; decline of interest in, 61, 83, 210; "I cieli immensi narrano," 28, 36, 39, 46–7, 65–6, 72, 245; *Salmi* [*Estro poetico-armonico*], 11, 26
Marenna, De: 138n65
Marmontel, Antoine: 15, 90n17; pupils of, 15n43, 105
Martine, Jacques-Daniel: 17
Martini, padre Giovanni Battista: 85
Marty, Georges: 109, 114n93
Massart, Aglaé: 53, 55n28
Massenet, Jules: 79, 87, 242

Mathieu de Monter, Emile: 66, 212–13
Mattmann, Louise: 53
medieval period: and collectivism, 188; conflicting interpretations of, 194–5; and nationalism, 195; *see also* Palestrinian music, Renaissance
Mel, Rinaldo del: 150, 183
Ménil, Félicien de: 106n68, 149, 151
Mercadier, Auguste: 103
Méreaux, Amédée: 32, 64, 66; *concerts historiques*, 39–41; as editor, 47–8, 49–52, 90; as pianist, 53, 56; tastes contrasted with Choron and Fétis, 40; *see also* Rouen
Meyerbeer, Giacomo: 66, 122, 125; and *couleur locale*, 242
Michaëlis, Théodore: 77, 87, 123, 127–34, 141, 251
Michelet, Jules: 195
Milanollo, Teresa: 87
Mocquereau, dom André: 107
Molière, [pseud. Jean-Baptiste Poquelin]: 120–1, 137–40, 145
Mongin, Marie: 49, 53–4, 56, 90
Monteverdi, Claudio: 75n87; and Fétisian historiography, 73, 152, 188; *Orfeo*, 23, 106
Morales, Cristóbal de: 20, 115
Moreau, Gustave (*Athalie* and *Esther*): 113–14
Moreau, Henri: 96
Morelot, abbé Stéphen: 32, 72
Moreno, Henry [pseud. Henri Heugel]: 135
Moscheles, Ignaz: 40
Moskova, prince de la [Joseph-Napoléon Ney]: 49; and the Ecole Niedermeyer, 71, 97; and Janequin chansons, 156–8; and Palestrinan revival, 63–4, 187; and the Société des Concerts de Musique Vocale Religieuse et Classique, 31–6, 107n70, 156–8, 167
Moulins, cathedral of: 72–3, 108–9
Mouton, Jean: 39
Mozart, Wolfgang Amadé: 26, 48, 66, 140, 168
Munch, Ernest: 102
Musard, Philippe: 28
museum spirit: xiv, 4–7, 10, 21, 23, 121; of Choron, 25–7; and cynicism, 43–4;

museum spirit (continued):
  and education: 5; and French drama, 138; and the politics of funding: 5–6; and secularization: 5, 115, 173–4, 199
music education: history of general, 119–20; and *clavecin* music, 123; and Italian Baroque repertory, 9–10, 14; and the *orphéon*, 224–6; *see also* Conservatoire, Paris; Ecole de Musique Religieuse; Schola Cantorum
musique française, la: *see* stage music

Nadaud, Edouard: 90
Nanino, Giovanni Maria: 97, 107
Napoléon I: and Italianism, 7n18, 19
Napoléon III: and clericalism, 71, 197
nationalism: and competitiveness, 149–50, 168, 210, 231; definitions of: xviii–xx; and elitism, 94–6; and Janequin, 33, 157–9, 246, 253; *see also* England, Germany, Italy, national pride
national pride: xix, 250–2; appeals to, 18–20, 120, 122, 128–30, 141; fragility of, xix–xx, 20, 122, 125, 231
neo-classicism: and pastiche, 79, 141, 242–3
Ney, Joseph-Napoléon, *dit* prince de la Moskova: *see* Moskova
Niedermeyer, Louis: 12–13, 31–2, 35, 71, 187; and *Stradella*, 242
Nilsson, Christine: 215
Nisard, Théodore: 63n50, 165, 167–8
Noiseux, Jean-Pierre: 170n85

Obin, Louis-Henri: 75n86
Ockeghem: 41, 148
Offenbach, Jacques: 137, 139
Orphéon de Paris: 65, 224n55
orphéon movement: 11, 65–7; and debates as to proper function, 224–6; decadence of, 222, 224–6; and democratization of music, 30, 59, 69–70; and early music performance, 65–7, 99n42, 110, 158, 222n50 and *embourgeoisement*, 229; history and traditions of, 223–4; and military symbolism, 224, 226; reformist challenges to, 222–3, 226–7, 232; and women, 64–5, 228–30; traditional repertory of, 65
Ortigue, Joseph d': 26, 35, 71, 195–6, 244

Palestrina, Giovanni Pierluigi da: 20, 83, 107, 249; and Bach, 71, 73, 217, 236–7; and liturgical politics, 179–81, 193–207; and liturgical reform, 72–4, 108, 179–80; and nationalist myth, 179–80, 186; performance trends in, 180, 187, 191, 206; as Renaissance man: 195; Romantic interpretations of, 180, 191–3; as savior of church music, 72, 153, 179, 185; teacher(s) of, 19, 150, 179, 182–4
Palestrina, Giovanni Pierluigi da (works): "Adoramus te" (attrib.): 12–13, 65, 116, 182, 184; "Ave Maria" (unidentified), xivn4; "Alla riva del Tebro," 28, 39; "Dies significatus," 106n67; *Improperia*, 9; *Lamentations*, 114; Magnificat (unidentified), 106n67; "L'homme armé" masses, 155, 172–3, 182–3n14, 203–4; *Missa Ad fugam*, 11–12, 35; *Missa brevis*, 106n67; Pope Marcellus Mass, 35, 101, 105n67, 185, 189, 198; "Rex virtutis," 109n75; "Sicut cervus," 72; *Stabat mater*, 9, 11, 66, 105, 188, 191, 192n58
"Palestrinian style": as accessible, 110–11, 201; and collectivism, 201–3; as comforting, 189; and counterpoint, 182, 196–7, 201, 205; as egotistical, 200; as exclusive, 30, 64–5, 67, 196–8; as expressive, 188; as harmonic, 155, 182, 184, 186, 190–91, 196, 198; as incorporeal, 190, 192–3; as inward, 186; as irreligious, 196–7, 199–201; as a *juste milieu*, 187–9, 198–9, 207; as learned, 160; as medieval, 180–81, 191, 201, 203; as mystical, 192; as nearly Protestant, 184; as polyphonic, 196–7; as pure, 168, 189–90; as repressive, 254; as sensual, 189
Panofka, Heinrich: 31

Parent, Armand: 89n14
Pasdeloup, Jules: 59–60, 92; and Baroque oratorio, 68–9, 211, 232
patriotism (cultural): xviii–xx, 134, 176–7; and Fétis, 24, 148, 153; and Ultramontanism, 181
pedal piano (and Bach): 55–6, 88, 90, 101
Pellegrin, Claude: 74
Pergolesi, Giovanni Battista: 14, 36, 46n12, 97; decline of interest in, 210; in the liturgy, 73, 108; *La serva padrona*, 23, 45; *Stabat mater*, 7, 9, 39, 113, 191
Peri, Jacopo: 75n87; (and Caccini), *Euridice*, 23
Perne, François-Louis: 19n59, 149
Perrin, Emile: 140
Perruchot, abbé: 105
Persuis, Louis-Luc Loiseau de: 29–30n88
Peyrot, Jean: 112n86
Piccinni, Niccolò: 17
picturesque, the: as disparaged, 145; as applauded, 157–8
Pirro, André: 107
Plainchant: xxi, 71, 174n91, 195–6; as democratic, 200; and the *Motu proprio*, 179–80; as obstacle to music education, 225; and Ultramontane debates, 111, 195–7
Poisot, Charles: 48n17, 69–70; and Rameau, 76–9, 114n92
Polignac, prince Edmond de: 107
Polignac, princesse de (Winnaretta Singer): 53, 83, 242
Porel, Paul: 139
Porro, Pierre: xvi, 7, 10–11, 27
Pothier, dom Joseph: 107
Pougin, Arthur: 91, 122n14; and Adam de la Halle, 165, 167; and French Baroque music, 94, 121n9, 124, 126n21, 130–1, 136; on oratorio, 210, 218, 221
Proske, Carl: 196
Protestantism: and music education, 225–6; and Palestrina, 184, 200; *see also* Renaissance
Proudhon, Pierre-Joseph: 198
publishing: 11–13, 45–50; and advertizing, 46, 49, 128–9, 251; and cheap editions, 61, 65, 212; and editorial rivalry, 49–50; and fake pieces, 12–13, 46–7; and monuments, 5, 114, 127–34, 141; of teaching materials, 9–10; and subscribers, 11, 47–8, 133–4; role of music supplements in, 46, 123–4, 159
Pugnani, Gaetano: 8
Pugno, Raoul: 53, 82, 92–3
Purcell, Henry: 38; *King Arthur*, 106

Quinet, Edgar: 195, 200

Racine, Jean: 113, 121, 145
Raguenet, François: 136
Ralliement: 170, 181n11, 194
Rameau, Jean-Philippe: 12, 40, 46n12, 253; and *chanson populaire*, 175–6; church music of, 113, 181; and dance, 76, 131, 141, 144, 176; as dramatic composer, 131–2; editions of, 77, 83, 114, 134, 141; Fétis on, 23–4; gendered critiques of, 144; and grandeur, 76, 144; impossibility of staging works, 140; legacy of, 132; originality of, 143, 145; reception in Dijon, 77–8; and stylistic extremes, 143–5
Rameau, Jean-Philippe (works): *Castor et Pollux* (inc. "Dans ce doux asile"), 7, 16n44, 33, 76, 131, 142, 144; "Les Cyclopes," 91; *Dardanus*, 12, 65, 83, 91, 144, 242; *Les festes d'Hébé*, 130n38, 135, 144–5; *Hippolyte et Aricie*, 65, 75–6, 141, 144, 217; *Les Indes galantes*, 77; "Laboravi," 114; "Les niais de Sologne," 56; *Pièces en concert*, 90; "Quam dilecta," 114; "Le rappel des oiseaux," 56, 91; *Samson*, 124; "Les tendres plaintes," 56; *Le temple de la gloire*, 12; *Zoroastre*, 131n40, 144
Ranke, Leopold von: xix
Récy, René de [pseud. J. Trezel]: 213, 237
regeneration: xvi, xviii, 59; of French musical culture, 29, 52, 123–4, 130; of Catholic sacred music, 63, 71–4, 189; via Baroque choral music, 212–13; *see also* Schola Cantorum
regionalism: xxi, 36, 38, 62–3, 112–13; in church music, 37–8, 74, 246; and

296 INDEX

regionalism (continued):
    lack of Parisian recognition, 63;
    across national borders, 150
Régnier, Joseph: 187, 197
Remaury, Caroline: 56
Remy, Guillaume: 89n14, 93
Renaissance, the: 180–81, 194–5;
    conflicting periodizations of, 181,
    195, 203–5; and cultural
    emancipation, 194; and
    individualism, 174, 181; and
    insincerity, 195, 201; and
    Reformation, 181, 195; and
    secularization, 181; see also
    Protestantism
Renan, Ernest: and "collective
    memory/forgetfulness," xx, 120, 130,
    147, 176–7
Republicanism: and Catholic music,
    107, 170, 181–2, 199; and Handel,
    111, 227–8, 231, 233, 247; and
    "monarchical" culture, 121, 248;
    radical, 163; and unifying instinct,
    175, 228
Réty, Hippolyte: 189
Reyer, Ernest [pseud. Rey]: 98n40, 121,
    133n46, 237; on oratorio, 216–17,
    221
Rillé, Laurent de: 65–6, 134n50
Robert, Gustave: 93, 104
Rochlitz, Friedrich: 13
Rodrigues, Edouard: 28, 31, 47, 50,
    60n42
Roger, Gustave-Hippolyte: 75n86
Roger, Louis: 164, 190–91, 213; on
    orphéon culture, 222–3, 227, 228n71
Rolland, Romain: 205n109
Romain, Louis de: 230
Romanesca, La (anon.): 14–15, 39–40, 57,
    245
Ronsard, Pierre de: 175
Ropartz, Guy: 110
Roquefort-Flaméricourt, J.-B.-B. de: 165,
    253
Roqueplan, Nestor: 139
Rouen: early music at, 38–41, 64–5; and
    cathedral music, 72, 182
Rousseau, Jean-Jacques: 34, 125–7, 136; Le
    devin du village, 7–9, 16–17, 38, 251
Roussel, François: 13

Saar, Louis: 102
Saint-Etienne, Sylvain: 61, 63, 212
Saint-Saëns, Camille: 63, 98n40, 239,
    253; as pianist, xiv, 53, 55–6, 86, 90;
    as Ramiste, 18, 114, 141
Saint-Yves, D.A.D [Déaddé]: 135
Sarcey, Francisque: 138
Sarasate, Pablo de: 82
Sarrette, Bernard: 4
Scarlatti, Alessandro: Laodicea e Berenice,
    23
Scarlatti, Domenico: 8, 40, 46n12,
Schlesinger, Léon: 91, 116
Schmitt, Georges: 63, 71
Schoelcher, Victor: 76, 87, 247; on
    Handel, 209, 211, 220; and Handel
    collection, 233–4
Schola Cantorum: xiv, 113, 176; as anti-
    Gallican, 113, 115; as anti-Handelian,
    111, 247; attacked by Bruneau, 253–5;
    Palestrinian orthodoxy of, 204–5;
    propagandizing of, 107–11; and
    Rameau stagings, 242
Schumann, Clara: 54
Schuré, Edouard: 237
Schütz, Heinrich: 82; St Matthew
    Passion: xivn4; Symphoniae sacrae,
    106
Scudo, Paul: 32, 55, 56n30, 106n68; on
    Janequin chansons, 158, 162; on
    Palestrina, 189
Seghers, François: 44
Senfl, Ludwig: 20
Servières, Georges: 107
Sighicelli, Vincenzo: 86
Simon, H.: 230
Société Académique de Musique Sacrée
    (Vervoitte): xvii, 44, 46, 63–4, 72, 162
Société Académique des Enfants
    d'Apollon: 8, 31
Société Bouieldieu (Rouen): 64
Société Bourgault-Ducoudray: see
    Bourgault-Ducoudray
Société Chorale d'Agen: 66
Société Chorale de Dijon: 69–70
Société Chorale des Amateurs (Guillot de
    Sainbris): 82n2, 228–9
Société Chorale Le Louvre: 67, 158
Société de Chant Sacré (Strasbourg): 63,
    101

Société de l'Athénée: 68
Société de l'Harmonie Sacrée
    (Lamoureux): xvi, 44–5, 68–9, 211
Société des Concerts de Chant Classique
    (Fondation Beaulieu): 44, 62, 98
Société des Concerts de l'Ecole de
    Musique Religieuse: see Lefèvre;
    Ecole de Musique Religieuse
Société des Concerts de Musique Vocale
    Religieuse et Classique: see Moskova
Société des Concerts du Conservatoire:
    29, 59, 121; and Baroque oratorio,
    68–9, 99, 103, 211, 231–2; and choral
    inadequacy, 28, 99; and
    conservatism, 5–6, 109, 232–3;
    repertory of, in piano reduction, 47
Société des Dames (Dijon): 69–70
Société des Grandes Auditions de France:
    and Handel, 111, 233
Société des Instruments Anciens (Van
    Waefelghem, Diémer): 89, 92–6,
    146, 176
Société des Instruments à Vent (Taffanel):
    89
Société des Oratorios (Pasdeloup): 68,
    212–3
Société du Grand-Concert (David): 61–2,
    211
Société La J.-S. Bach (Lyon): 101
Société L'Euterpe: 82, 99
Société Sainte-Cécile (1850–55): see Seghers
Société Sainte-Cécile (from 1865): see
    Weckerlin
Société Sainte-Cécile (Toul): 109
Solesmes, abbey of: 107, 194
Soullier, Charles: 61
Staël, Mme de: 237
stage music (la musique française): attacks
    on, 16–19, 58, 127n29, 135; attempts
    to rehabilitate, 40–41, 75–9, 113–14,
    116, 125–34, 252; compared with
    classical drama, 121–2, 145–6; dance
    music of, 120, 131, 142–3, 146; and
    problems regarding declamation,
    16, 76, 121, 127, 144, 146; and
    publishing projects, 123–34; and
    remplissage, 135–6, 138; staged
    performances of, 135–40
Stamaty, Camille: 47, 55
Stendhal [pseud. Henri Beyle]: 17

Stockhausen, Franz: 101
Stradella, Alessandro: Aria di chiesa,
    "Pietà, Signore" (attrib.), 12–13, 36,
    47, 60, 116
Strasbourg: and Bach/Handel choral
    music, 63, 101–2, 247; and Baj, 39
Szarvády, Wilhelmine: 46, 53–4, 56, 59, 90

Taffanel, Paul: 82, 86, 89–90, 92
Tartini, Giuseppe: 8, 14
Taskin, Pascal[-Joseph]: see harpsichord
Tellefsen, Thomas: 48, 53
Thémines, Mark de, see De Lauzières-
    Thémines, Achille
Thibaut, Anton Friedrich Justus: 114
Thoinan, Ernest: 143
Thomas, Ambroise: 134n50
Tiersot, Julien: xiv, 105, 107, 152; and
    Adam de la Halle, 112, 167, 169; on
    Bach, 235, 237–8; on the chanson
    populaire, 163–4, 169, 254; edition of
    Adam de la Halle compared with
    Weckerlin, 169–73; on the Franco-
    Flemish school, 170, 172–4, 203; on
    Handel, 233; as historian, 174–7
Tinctoris, Johannes: 19–20, 150–51
Torchet, Julien: 103

Ultramontanism: 21, 31, 83, 185, 193; and
    collectivity, 191, 195–7; and problem
    of overt patriotism, 181, 251; and
    liturgical music (moderates), 71–2,
    107–8; and liturgical music
    (radicals), 111, 180, 194–201

Vaucorbeil, Auguste-Emmanuel: 98n40,
    121, 134n50
Vervoitte, Charles: 63–5, 67, 72, 114n92,
    116, 162; as inspector of maîtrises, 73;
    and Palestrinian music, 187; and the
    Vatican, 64n52; see also Société
    Académique de Musique Sacrée
Viadana, Lodovico: 110
Viardot, Paul: 82, 86
Viardot, Pauline: 48, 56n30, 60n41,
    75n86, 134n50
Victoria, Tomás Luis de: 72–4, 105, 107,
    115, 189–90; Missa "O quam
    gloriosum," 106n67; "O Jesu dulcis"
    (attrib.), 35; "O vos omnes," 35

Vierne, Louis: 82
Vieux Paris, le: xiii-xiv
Vitali, Giovanni Battista: 245
Vitet, Ludovic: 155
Vizentini, Albert: 137–8
Voltaire [pseud. François-Marie Arouet]: 124, 140, 194–5
Vos, Camille de: 65, 227–8
Vos, Hippolyte de: 104n59

Waefelghem, Louis van: xiin4, 82, 93
Waelraut, Hubert: 97
Wagner, Richard: 59, 69, 78, 126; and Bach, 102–5, 234–7; and *la musique française*, 133; and Wagnerian early-music enthusiasts, 92, 122n14, 234–5, 244–5
Wartel, Thérèse: 40, 53
Watteau, Jean-Antoine: 95–6; *see also* dance
Weber, Johannes: 98n40, 215–16; and disparagement of *la musique française*, 127; and support for *la musique française*, 130, 133–6, 138n65, 248

Weckerlin, Jean-Baptiste: 13, 32, 98n40, 116, 150; and Adam de la Halle, 167, 169; and the *chanson populaire*, 163–4, 175, 254; edition of Adam de la Halle compared with Tiersot, 169–73; as editor, 135, 137, 165, 167; and Franco-Flemish polyphony, 155, 163; and the Schoelcher Handel collection, 234n89; and Société Sainte-Cécile, 44, 53, 68, 211
Widor, Charles-Marie: 82, 98
Wilder, Victor: 130, 217
Wilhem, (Guillaume-Louis-)Bocquillon: 30, 223; *see also* orphéon
Willaert, Adrien: 152
Witt, Franz Xaver: 156n30
Wolff, Auguste: 53
women: and early keyboard music, 40, 53–4, 56; and education, 229–30; and elite amateur choirs, 31, 64 and feminist demands, 215; and mixing of sexes in choirs, 65, 228–30

Ysaÿe, Eugène: 82, 92–3